Nenia Britannica

NENIA BRITANNICA:

OR,

A SEPULCHRAL HISTORY

OF

GREAT BRITAIN;

FROM THE EARLIEST PERIOD TO ITS GENERAL CONVERSION TO CHRISTIANITY

BY THE REV JAMES DOUGLAS, F.A.S.

CHAPLAIN IN ORDINARY TO HIS ROYAL HIGHNESS THE PRINCE OF WALES

"QUIS AUTEM EST, QUEM NON MOVEAT CLARISSIMIS MONUMENTIS [illegible] CONSIG[illegible]"

CIC [illegible]

LONDON:
PRINTED BY JOHN NICHOLS,
FOR GEORGE NICOL, IN PALL MALL BOOKSELLER TO HIS MAJESTY
MDCCXCIII

NENIA BRITANNICA:

O R,

A SEPULCHRAL HISTORY

O F

GREAT BRITAIN;

FROM THE EARLIEST PERIOD TO ITS GENERAL CONVERSION TO CHRISTIANITY

INCLUDING

A COMPLETE SERIES OF THE BRITISH, ROMAN, AND SAXON SEPULCHRAL RITES AND CEREMONIES, WITH THE CONTENTS OF SEVERAL HUNDRED BURIAL PLACES,

Opened under a careful Inſpection of the AUTHO

THE BARROWS CONTAINING

URNS, SWORDS, SPEAR-HEADS, DAGGERS, KNIVES, BATTLE-AXES, SHIELDS, and ARMILLÆ —Decorations of Women, conſiſting of GEMS, PENSILE ORNAMENTS, BRACELETS, BEADS, GOLD and SILVER BUCKLES, BROACHES ornamented with Precious Stones, ſeveral MAGICAL INSTRUMENTS, ſome very ſcarce and unpubliſhed Coins; and a Variety of other curious Relics depoſited with the Dead

TENDING TO ILLUSTRATE THE EARLY PART OF

And to fix on a more unqueſtionable CRITERION for the STUDY of ANTIQUITY

TO WHICH ARE ADDED,

OBSERVATIONS on the *CELTIC, BRITISH, ROMAN,* and *DANISH* BARROWS, diſcovered in *BRITAIN.*

BY THE REV JAMES DOUGLAS, F.A.S.

CHAPLAIN IN ORDINARY TO HIS ROYAL HIGHNESS THE PRINCE OF WALES

Quis autem eſt, quem non moveat clariſſimis monumentis teſtata conſignataque Antiquitas?

Cic. de Div. lib. 1

LONDON

PRINTED BY JOHN NICHOLS,

FOR BENJAMIN AND JOHN WHITE

MDCCXCIII

TO HIS ROYAL HIGHNESS

GEORGE AUGUSTUS FREDERICK,

PRINCE of WALES,

Earl of CHESTER, &c. &c. &c.

THESE pages, which have preſerved, for the uſe of Britiſh Hiſtory, the intereſting ſepulchral relics of an antient people, the inhabitants of a kingdom, over whom HIS ROYAL HIGHNESS is deſtined by Providence to reign at a period the author is certain Filial Piety wiſhes far diſtant, are reſpectfully inſcribed by

HIS ROYAL HIGHNESS's

Moſt obedient humble ſervant,

JAMES DOUGLAS.

P R E F A C E.

F the ſtudy of Antiquity be undertaken in the cauſe of Hiſtory, it will reſcue itſelf from a reproach indiſcriminately and faſtidiouſly beſtowed on works which have been deemed frivolous. In proportion as this ſtudy has been neglected by antient or modern hiſtorians, authority will be found to deviate from conjecture, and the eye of reaſon more or leſs taught to diſcern the fable which the pomp of hiſtory has decorated; it ſhould therefore, inſtead of being accounted the dreg, be ſtyled the alembic, from which is drawn the purity or perfection of literature.

The inſcription or the medal are the only facts which can obviate error, and produce the ſubſtitutes for deficiency of antient records: when theſe are wanting, in vain will the human mind be gratified by the moſt acute inveſtigation; incredulity will ariſe in proportion as the judgement is matured.

By contemplating the relics diſcovered in our antient ſepultures, the hiſtorian may have an opportunity of comparing them with ſimilar relics found in different places, and on which arguments have been grounded by authors who have written on the antient inhabitants of Britain. If a medal or inſcription be found in a ſepulchre among other relics, the undoubted characteriſtic of the cuſtoms of a people at the time of the depoſit, and the ſuperſcription on the medal or the inſcription evincing a low period, it will be a ſelf-evident poſition, that ſimiliar relics under ſimilar forms of ſepulture, diſcovered in other parts of the iſland, cannot apply to a period more remote; hence the moſt trifling fact will invalidate many received opinions, and hiſtory be reduced to a more critical analyſis.

To explore this country in all directions, to violate the ſacred aſhes of the dead, and which human nature muſt feel reluctant to undertake, to drag to light the concealed treaſures of old times, were a labour beyond the capacity of one man; and as a ſenſe of duty to his profeſſional ſtudies has confined the Author to certain limits, much of this intereſting purſuit has been left to other Antiquaries, whoſe labours will doubtleſs produce a ſucceſſion of diſcoveries, which, by degrees, will convey a great acceſſion of light to the dark pages of hiſtory. He is, however, amply gratified, if what has been hitherto accompliſhed will be deemed ſufficient to acquit him of thoſe obligations by which he ſtands pledged to the Public.

No poſition in the work has been aſſumed on mere conjecture; and when deductions have been made, they have been founded on a ſcrupulous compariſon of facts; but, free to form his own opinion, the work has been arranged under ſuch heads, that the reader may frame his own concluſions, without any apprehenſion of being involved in the confuſion of ſelf-opinionated theory.

All nations deriving their origin apparently from one common ſtock, have uſed, in many reſpects, the ſame funereal cuſtoms; but the progreſs of ſociety having evidently produced many ſpecific diſtinctions, they may be methodically arranged, and the identity of a people recognized.

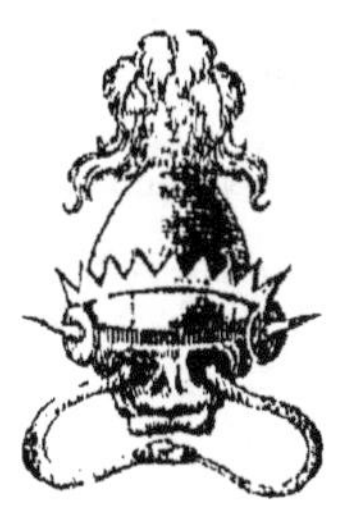

NENIA BRITANNICA.

THE sepulchral remains of the antient inhabitants of Britain will convey little information to the Historian, unless, enabled by the discovery of facts, he can ascertain some fixed *data* for the principles of argument. I shall therefore begin this work with a description of the SMALL CONIC TUMULI that are frequently discovered in this island, and which are productive, when neatly and correctly explored, of many curious and valuable relics, the test of these *data*.

These *tumuli** are generally found on barren ground, on commons, moors, sometimes on parochial grounds near villages, of no great name or importance in history. When discovered on cultivated land, their cones or congeries have been levelled by tillage; and it is only by a casual discovery with the plow, or the accidental use of the spade and pick-axe, that the contents of these interments have been found. They seldom exceed *thirty-three feet* in diameter, the smallest *thirteen*, the medium *twenty-three*, and the largest *thirty-three*. They are raised of earth, sometimes excavated from a spot of ground near the range, and sometimes very neatly fashioned, with the circumjacent sod raised from the plain: their height was originally proportioned to their circumference; but time has compressed their cones, and in many places

* They are mentioned by Richard of Cirencester as the graves of the Britons, *Sepulchrum tumulus ex cespitibus erigit*. Cap. III. p. 8. Sect. 23. which the sequel will prove them to be, and raised about the fifth century.

In

laid them almoſt level to the ſurface of the ground. They are generally ſurrounded with a narrow trench, which ſeems to have been faſhioned from a funereal ſuperſtitious cuſtom, and not applied to the common or ordinary intent of ſepulchral decoration.

The ciſt in which the body was depoſited is not always of the ſame depth; ſometimes it does not penetrate the native ſoil more than half a foot; but when the body has been ſumptuouſly buried, it will exceed ten feet *.

* For a more intimate and ample diſcourſe on theſe ſepulchres, I ſhall beg leave to refer the reader to OBSERVATIONS, ARGUMENT, HISTORIC RELATION, and GENERAL CONCLUSION, in the bulk of the letter preſs, after the deſcription of the plates: this will hinder a tedious reference to notes, which often obſtructs the reader in a comprehenſive ſurvey of the ſubject, and but too often bewilders him in a tedious detail of matter.

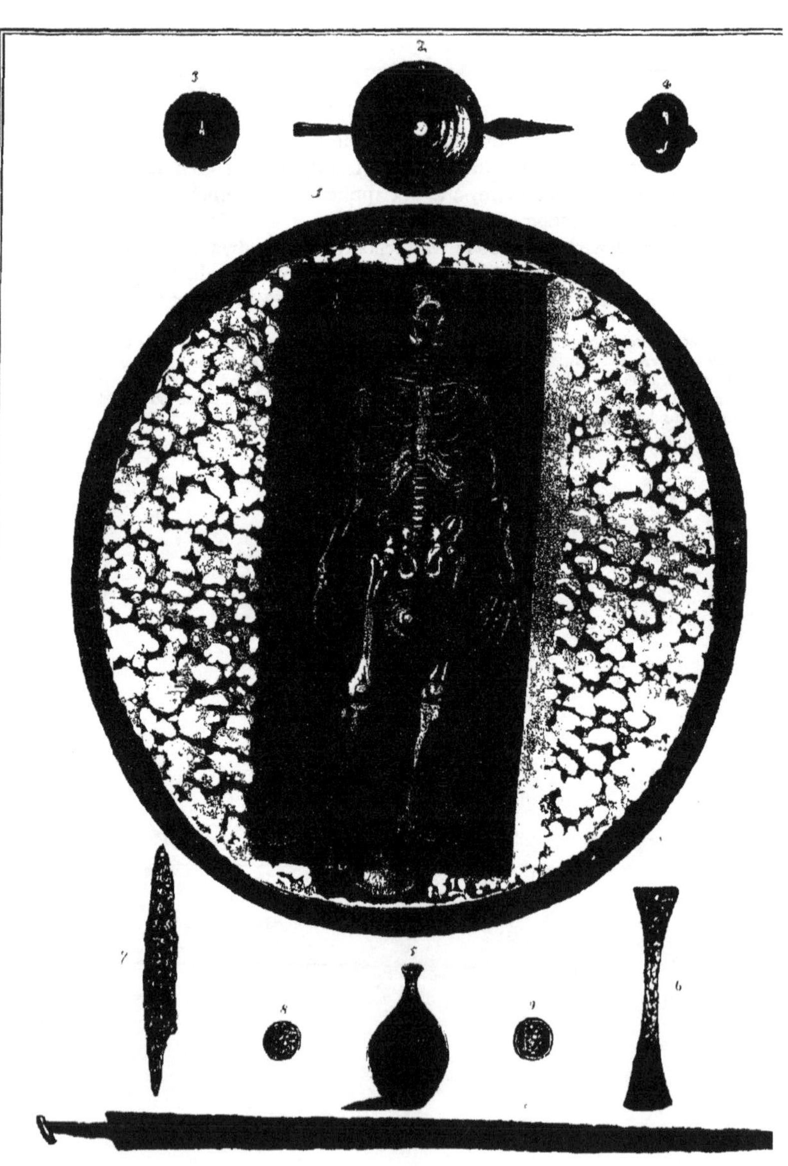

TUMULUS I.

FIG 1 repreſents an horizontal ſection of a tumulus opened on Chatham Lines*, the ciſt in which the body was depoſited, the arms, &c the looſe excavated chalk and the vallum round the tumulus, in its original ſtate before the mound was levelled

The ciſt was near eight feet in length, three feet in breadth, and four feet below the level of the native ſoil, when the upper coating was thrown up, the latter about half a foot in thickneſs

The body in the meridian; head to the ſouth. The bones of a male adult, obvious by their ſize and texture. The length and thickneſs of the fiſtulæ bones were ſuch, as to admit of the aſſertion, without occurring to other marks of the diſtinction of the ſexes, or to the arms depoſited by the ſide of the ſkeleton.

The bones much conſumed by age, but, on repeated experiments, they were found to contain a great portion of volatile alcali

No appearance of a coffin

* In September, 1779, when the lines or military works were repairing, under the command of Colonel Debbieg, to whoſe liberal taſte in literary purſuits I am indebted for the civilities with which he facilitated my diſcoveries at Chatham, the labourers and ſoldiers with the pick-axe and ſpade, in [illegible] a range of theſe ſmall *tumuli*, threw up ſome ſpear heads, umbos of ſhields, and a few other fragments of arms

Theſe tumuli were ſituated on the weſtern ſlope of the ſteep hill which faces the town of Rocheſter and which deſcends to the barrack gate they are bounded by a conſiderable [illegible] the road [illegible] to the ſoldiers barracks, and on the other, to the eaſt, by the [illegible] of the works, which incloſes a magazine and a [illegible] over it The barrack wall is the extremity on one ſide, and the [illegible] parapet and ditch of the fortification on the other

The ſoil is chalky, has been ploughed over, gardens were upon it, and before it was purchaſed for the king's ſervice, there was a rope-walk preciſely on the ſite of the *tumuli*

In the year 1756, when the lines were firſt thrown up, under Colonel Demeretz ſome of theſe graves were accidentally uncovered and the tents of the Hanoverian encampment was fixed on them The remains of the ſoldiers' kitchen were to be ſeen on the [illegible] of the burial ground, and doubtleſs, when they were raiſed, many *graves* were broken into, and their relics wantonly diſperſed

Fig 2 An iron ſpear-head and *umbo* of a ſhield. The ſpear-head fifteen inches long, and the *umbo* four inches in diameter

The ſpear-head on the right ſhoulder; the point in a line with the head, the haft containing decayed wood, which, by the texture of ſeveral ſimilar ſpecimens in my poſſeſſion, appears to be of aſh. The metal is reduced to a calx, and which by the ſmalleſt preſſure is liable to be diſunited

The umbo or boſs of the ſhield was found on the center of the thigh-bone

Fig 3. An iron ſtud with a pin in the center: uncertain in what poſition this laid near the body; but by the impreſſion of decayed wood upon it, it appears either to have been driven into the end of the ſpear at the handle, or into the ſhield

Fig 4 A braſs buckle; near the laſt bone of the *vertebræ*, or cloſe to the *os ſacrum*

Fig 5 A bottle of red earth at the feet of the ſkeleton; twelve inches in height, and five inches in its largeſt diameter

Fig 6 A thin plate of iron exactly in the center and under the umbo; four inches and an half in length, two rivets at the end, and ſeems to have received the end of the rivets of the umbo through the wood, as its bracer or ſtay.

Fig 7 A knife on the right ſide, with impreſſions of decayed wood, and very diſcernible impreſſions of cloth upon it The wood appears to have been its caſe, particularly as the end is fitted for an handle of this material, and which contains a great portion of the ſame adhering to it.

Fig 8 and 9. The face and reverſe of an iron ſtud, four of which were found near the umbo of the ſhield, ſimilar ſtuds are often ſeen on the Scotch orbicular ſhields, the ſtuds of which are generally of braſs, the ſame as the umbo

Fig. 10 An iron ſword, on the left ſide; thirty-five inches and a quarter the whole length, the blade from the handle thirty inches, two inches broad; flat, double edged, and ſharp pointed; a great portion of wood covering the blade, which indicates that it was buried in a ſcabbard, the external covering being of leather, and the internal of wood

For a further deſcription of this tumulus, ſee OBSERVATIONS

TUMULI

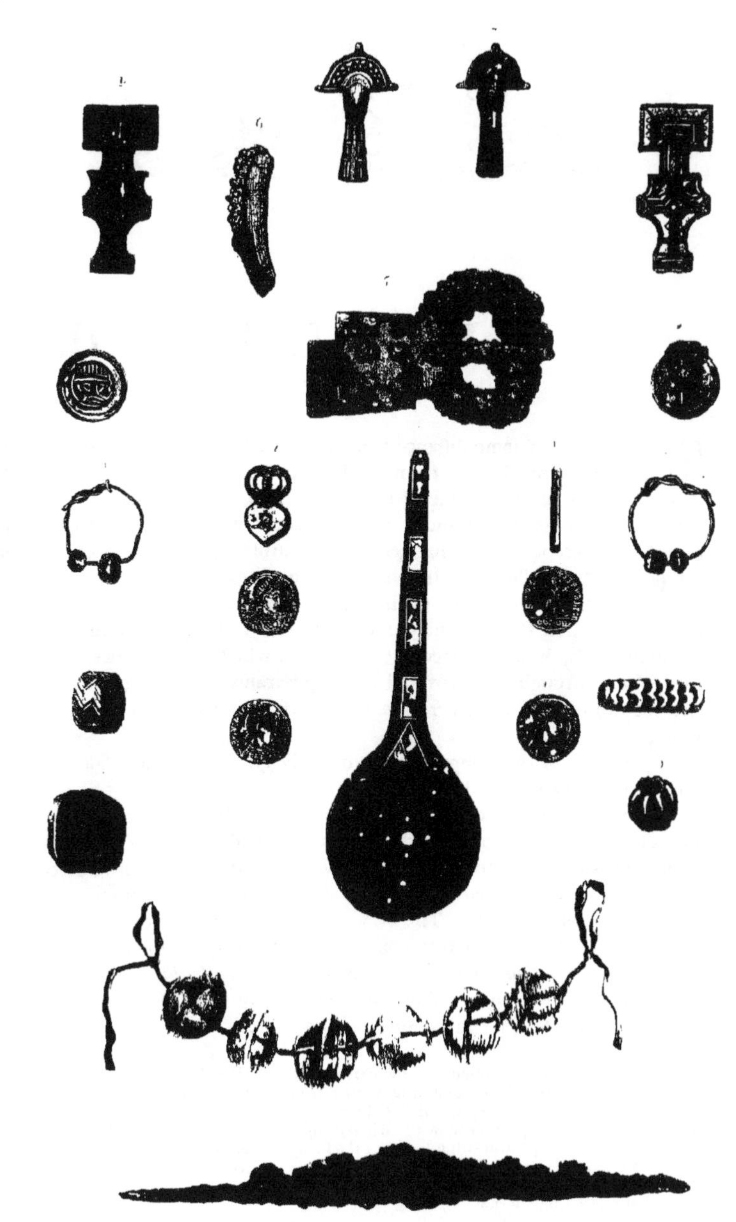

TUMULUS II.

SITUATED at ſome diſtance from tumulus I. in the ſame range of *tumuli*. The ciſt about five feet from the level of the upper ſoil. The head of the ſkeleton to the South. Some of the bones entire, and ſtill containing their animal matter, ſome were reduced to an impalpable earth *, which inſtantly diſunited on the touch, the ſmallneſs of the fiſtular bones, the apparent ſize of the pelvis, their diſſolution in conſequence of their ſmallneſs, or perhaps delicacy of texture, much more ſo than thoſe of tumulus I. and the nature of the relics, prove that the body here interred was that of a young female. A dark coloured earth, which ſheeted the body, and which on the ſides of the grave, in a ſection through it, diſcovered ſome appearance of a decayed ſubſtance, and the breadth of it, gave me reaſon to ſuppoſe the body had been encloſed in wood.

Fig. 1. One of two copper claſps, ſtrongly gilt, on the left ſide of the ſkeleton, near the loweſt vertebre.

Fig. 2. The reverſe of fig. 1. The *acus*, which perforated the garment, is of iron or ſteel, and is received into a curvated piece of copper as its ſtay. The wire which formed the *acus* moved vertically, and when received into the veſtment was compreſſed into the claſp, in the ſame manner as the *fibula ſubnectens* of the Romans. The calx of the iron has preſerved ſome filament of the robe, which, by a very common analytical experiment with fire, proves the part of the robe next to it to have been of *linen*, the texture of which was tolerably fine. The ornaments on the claſp are engraved, and they ſeem to have been very much uſed by the wearer.

* In a diſſertation on the Antiquity of the Earth, read at the Royal Society 12 May, 1785, and ſince publiſhed with additions, I had occaſion to mention the bones found in this *tumulus*, which I ſaid *were entire*. I here beg leave to explain, that I meant the bones that were preſerved; for it frequently happens, that bones may be found in a friable ſtate apparently entire, but when handled immediately fall into duſt. The argument will ſtill acquire the ſtrongeſt validity, as we find the bones in tumulus I. were perfect, the texture palpably ſolid, and the body interred at the ſame date, which the ſequel will inconteſtably prove. The ſcull of the ſkeleton is now preſerved in my collection, with the under jaw and the two femur bones.

Fig. 3 One of two copper clasps strongly plated with gold The workmanship is in part stamped, and performed with milling, which is very observable on the chain described in the centre line, and on the edges of the clasp. The ornament in its rough state seems to have been cast, and afterwards tooled upon Found on the left side, rather lower down than fig 1

Fig. 4. The reverse of fig 3 The *acus* of the same metal, as the one of fig 2. and fitted in the same manner to the ornament These clasps have not been so much used as fig 1 The ornament is sharper, and the gold in a perfect state

Fig 5. An iron buckle, with a tail, to receive a girdle or belt the position on the left side, close to the clasps, fig 1 The tail which received the girdle, or belt, is of a mixed metal, perhaps the *Aurichalcum* of Pliny, and washed with silver On the smooth surface on the metal, as well as on the iron buckle, are very accurate impressions of fine cloth, some of which I picked off, but found, on analysing, that the calx of iron had permeated the cloth to that degree as left no room to ascertain whether it was silk, linen, or woollen, but, from other specimens, I suspect it was linen

Fig 6 A fragment of an IVORY ARMILLA *, and which still contains its volatile alcali On the right side, close to fig 7

Fig. 7 One of two circular clasps of copper, plated with gold. The stamp, or cast, of the ornament, is not unlike a Gothic representation of the human face The face of the clasp has a high rim projecting from it, the breadth of the interior circle On the breast, near the collar bone.

Fig 8. The reverse of fig. 6. The *Acus*, similar to those of fig. 2 and fig 4 The iron which composed it accreted to the metal of the clasp, and in its calcareous state enclosing the filaments of cloth, which, on an accurate experiment, appears to be of linen, the same as preserved on fig. 2.

Fig 9 A SILVER SPOON, ornamented with garnets †; the bowl perforated and washed with gold, which is in some places much worn off. The garnets are

* This Ivory Armilla should have been represented in a plate prefixed to the Dissertation, which I mentioned in the foregoing note, but the relics not having been at that time arranged from my note-book as they now are, this fragment was blended with other fragments of an Ivory Armilla, found in a tumulus near it, and which, through mistake, I engraved the fact is equally established, though the arrangement was not so critical as it should have been

† This perforated spoon appears to have been a magical implement, and to have answered the use of the sieve and sheers described in the Third Idyllium of Theocritus

> Εἶπε καὶ Ἀγροιὼ τἀλαθέα, ΚΟΣΚΙΝΟΜΑΝΤΙΣ
> Ἁ πρᾶν ποιολογεῦσα, παραιβάτις, οὕνεκ' ἐγὼ μὲν
> Τὶν ὅλος ἔγκειμαι, τὺ δέ μευ λόγον οὐδένα ποιῇ

It was suspended by a string, which perforated the hole at the handle, and seems to have been thus used Idem admissum cribro forcipi imposito et forcipe binis tantum apprehenso utrique elevato digitis, eidemque, praefatis precibus et recitatis nominibus suspectorum quorumque, appellato cribrum, vel tremat, vel nutat, vel convertitur, eum imputant reum furti, de cujus authore quaestio instituitur Joannes Georgius Godelmannus, lib I cap V p 45 Subsequent discoveries in these kind of *tumuli* will shew the *sheers*, another specimen of the sieve of a different form, and various other implements, descriptive of various orders of magic in use among the antients from the earliest period of time, and transmitted to the modern ages from the Eastern nations, from whence, in the course of this work, we shall find these *tumuli* relics to have been introduced into this island

In the luxurious reign of Charles II which, with the extirpation of fanaticism, also eradicated all superstitious belief in these customs, we find Butler mentions the magical virtue of the *sieve* and *sheers*.

In

are enchaſed in a projecting ſocket of ſilver, as deſcribed in the drawing. They are ſet on a gold foil, which foil, from ſimilar ſpecimens in my collection, ſeems emboſſed in chequers, by a ſtamp or milling inſtrument, to add luſtre to the ſtone. On the edges of the handle is a delicate beading, and in the interval of the ſetting are ſmall circular marks, ſo often found on ornaments of the lower empire, and which, in my opinion, are the ſure criterion to diſcriminate ſuch ornaments. The reverſe of the ſpoon has a neat brace faſtened with ſix rivets, to mend a fracture near the handle, on the edge of which is impreſſed a chain of the above circular marks. The ſilver of the bowl is as thin as the ſilver pence of ſome of our early Saxon kings. The back of the handle is worn very ſmooth, particularly the edge, which circumſtance, with the perforation at the top, ſhews it to have been pendant to ſome part of the dreſs. The handle and bowl has been hammered out of one piece of ſilver, and the ſockets of the ſtones are faſtened with rivets, which penetrate the handle. When taken out of the grave the ſilver parts where the gold was worn off were much corroded with a black *patina*. A little below the *os ſacrum*, between the femur bones.

Fig. 10 & 10. Two ſpecimens of *ten ſilver wire rings*, with beads pendant to them *. The wire when the ring or circle was formed, was faſtened with a ſimple twiſt. The beads conſiſt of glaſs, amber and red vitrified earth. Some rings have only one bead pendant to them. The ring under fig. 7. contains a light green opake bead, to imitate a tourquoiſe ſtone; and the other, the ſmalleſt, of a crimſon coloured glaſs, in imitation of a garnet or hyacinth. The other ring perforates two beads, of a vitrified red earth, in imitation of the blood ſtone. The other beads conſiſt of two of amber, very neatly turned; two of a carnation colour, one of a deep carnation, and the other of amber: one of a darkiſh tourquoiſe; one of a light bright verditer green †: three of red

In magic he was deeply read,
As he that made the brazen head,
Profoundly ſkill'd in the black art,
As Engliſh Merlin for his heart,
But far more ſkilful in the ſpheres,
Than he was at the *ſieve* and *ſheers*. — Hud. Cant II.

Again we have,

Than th' oracle of *ſieve* and *ſheers*
That turns as certain as the ſpheres. — Cant III.

A pretended divination, at this day, is made with theſe inſtruments in ſeveral places; and ſomewhat in the manner deſcribed by Godelmannus.

* As theſe rings lay near the *armilla*, I am inclined to think they made part of the ornament. Such ſpecimens may be noticed in Count Caylus, one of which with ſeven rings to the armilla or bracelet, T. I. pl. xxxi. he conceives to be the *trochus*, a muſical inſtrument of the Greeks and Romans, and which abſurd idea he ſeems to have taken from Mercurialis, lib. III. p. 219. where a muſical circular inſtrument is engraved; but which cannot poſſibly have any relation to the one the Count has publiſhed. In December, 1785, an engraving of a ſimilar bracelet was preſented to the Society of Antiquaries. The rings, fig. 10 and 10, ſeem to be too ſlight to have been worn on the fingers. The pendant ſtones were ſuppoſed to contain magical virtues. See Pliny, lib. xxxvii. cap. 8. ſpeaking of the green ſtone, which he calls Molochites, here imitated in glaſs, he ſays it had a virtue or charm to preſerve infants from harm—et infantium cuſtodiæ quadam innato contra pericula ipſorum medicamine. In the ſame chapter he mentions the glaſs beads to the rings, as counterfeits of precious ſtones, *e vitro adulterinæ*, &c. Chap. 9. contains various deſcriptions of gems, moſt of which have magical powers attributed to them, and which ſubſequent diſcoveries in theſe *tumuli* will ſhew were uſed for theſe purpoſes as well as ornaments of dreſs.

† Pliny ſays, in the ſame chap. neque eſt imitabilior alia mendacio vitri. There is no precious ſtone ſo eaſily to be counterfeited with glaſs as the Tourquoiſe, and this is well exemplified in the glaſs ſpecimens here deſcribed. Being of an opaque glaſs, there is hence a poſſibility of diſcerning the difference between the real and counterfeit. The green ſtones of a deep colour he calls *molochites*,

those

red earth; one of a pearl-colour glaſs; one of a darkiſh blue; one of a light blue; one of an opaque dark brown colour, which cuts eaſily with a knife, and is compoſed of an aſphaltic earth, or of ſome aromatic not unlike the former in ſmell. This bead is faſhioned with greater pains than the other, of a ſquare ſhape, with the angles cut in a diamond faſhion and ſomewhat larger, and doubtleſs tranſported into this iſland from the Eaſt In all, eighteen in number. Some parts of the rings are decompoſed with laying in the earth Found near the *pelvis*

Fig 11. A fluted piece of braſs, like the tag of a lace; and which appears to have been uſed for this purpoſe on ſome parts of the dreſs: found near fig. 1.

Fig 12 A ſmall buckle of the ſame metal, as the tail of fig. 5 The reverſe has a rivet · an evident mark that it ſerved for a ſmall leather belt. The tongue of iron, found near fig 11.

Fig 13 A ſilver perforated coin ‡, as thin as a ſilver penny of our early Saxon Kings The inſcription round the head, DN. ANTHEMIVS PP. AVG.

Fig 14 The reverſe a figure ſeated in a crural chair, reſting on the rudder of a galley The inſcription SLVS REI PVBLICE *ſlvs* a miſtake of the mint maſter for SALVS no uncommon thing among the coins of the lower empire. On the exergue CONOB or, as I read it, *Conſtantinopoli Officina Secunda.* B the Greek numeral *ſecunda*, the Romans frequently uſing the Greek numerals on their coins; particularly in the Byzantine empire, on the declenſion of the republic.

The figure on the reverſe is not well made out in the plate, being too imperfect on the coin to hazard a repreſentation

Fig 15. Of thin ſilver perforated the inſcription too much defaced to make any thing certain of . . ANVS was conſpicuous, and it may read, *Gratianus. Valerianus Martianus Majorianus*, or *Valentinianus* I think the latter emperor. The reverſe GLORIA ROMANORVM The figure too much defaced to deſcribe with accuracy

Fig 16 Of thin ſilver, perforated, the inſcription DN. VALENTINIANVS PF. AVG. The reverſe VIRTVS ROMANORVM. Theſe coins were found with fig. 10. on the right ſide of the ſkeleton, ſo much corroded, that having carefully ſent them to a friend for his inſpection, on their return by letter, they were broken into ſeveral pieces The one of *Anthemius* was the leaſt injured, and is now in a tolerable ſtate of preſervation

N B. There was a braſs perforated coin, the impreſſion quite defaced, found with them

thoſe of a ſea green *chryſoprasius* There is a ſtone, which he calls Eumetres, of a pale green, which the Aſſyrians call the gem of Belus, the moſt ſacred of their gods it is applied very frequently to ſuperſtitious invocations, exorciſms, and moſt magical uſes See lib xxxvii cap 10

‡ The coin of Anthemius is valued by M Beauvais in our Engliſh money, at about five guineas They ſeem to have been worn as pendants, either as ornaments or ſome kind of amulets. Abbé Fortis, in his Travels into Dalmatia, p 66 ſays, the Morlack women wear ſtrings *of ſilver coins to their caps* among which are often found ſome antient and valuable This circumſtance has frequently been obſerved by modern travellers, and in particular in Sicily, where the peaſant women have been decorated with ſome very rare and well preſerved Syracuſian coins In Mr Duane's ſale was ſold an Onyx ſet in gold, that accompanied a gold coin of the Emperor AVITVS, ſet in a rim and a gold loop, to hang it as a pendant They were found in May, 1758, in a barrow on Blood Moore Hill, near Pakefield and Leyſtoff, in Suffolk, with a necklace of rough garnets, to which they were *pendant* The necklace is in my poſſeſſion The Onyx, with an intaglio of tolerable workmanſhip, repreſented Caſtor and Pollux This penſile ornament was bought, at no ſmall ſum, for a Roman *bulla*

Fig.

Fig. 17 A bead of red opake glass waved with yellow streaks.

Fig. 18 A bead of glass composition streaked with various colours.

Fig. 19. A bead of black glass.

Fig. 20 A bead of fine clear high-coloured amber *.

N. B. These beads were found together with the coins.

Fig. 21 Six beads of rock crystal †: near the *radius* and *ulna* of the arm.

Fig. 22 An iron knife, on the left side, close to fig. 1. The metal entirely decomposed,

* Amber was in great esteem among the antients. The Romans, after the custom of the Greeks, who attributed great virtue to it, established a traffic for it with the Germans, who brought it into Pannonia, Istria, and thus to the Roman provinces. See Pliny, lib. xxxvii. cap. 3. The women of Lombardy, according to this old historian, wore collars of it, as much for a charm against wens, in the neck, which those women are subject to, as for ornament; he also observes, that women only set the most store by it. Amber beads, he says, worn about the necks of children as amulets, are charms against poison and witchcraft. Callistratus says, they are good for all ages, and to preserve the wearers from frights, by which their senses may be disordered; and, whether worn as a necklace or taken inwardly, creates a free urinary discharge. Pliny ascribes great medical properties to it. It was known as a fossil by the antients, as appears by this passage: *Philemon fossile esse, et in Scythia erui duobus locis.* See Pliny, lib. xxxvii. cap. 11. Nero adorned his theatres with it, and hence it seems to have been universally known at Rome. In a sonnet to the Empress Poppæa, he compared her hair to amber, and from that time the Roman ladies esteemed that colour for their hair, and also used it much as an ornament for their apparel.

The bright *red coloured amber* was the most prized. It had various names among the antients; that of a white colour was called Electrum, that of a red Snalternicum; the Germans called it Glessum, because it was clear like glass. See more of this relating to the amber found in Britain, Diodorus, p. 348, and Strabo, 309. Amber-beads, throughout all ages, seem to have been the ornaments of the women. In Scotland, where the custom was retained within these two centuries, and, as I suspect from the Lower Britons, the women ornamented themselves with amber. Leslei, p. 29.

† See a singular coincidence of facts respecting these six *Crystal beads*, in Brown's *Hydriotaphia*, Urn Burial, p. 23. where a Roman urn is described, preserved by Cardinal Farnese, which contained *ornaments of amber*, a *Crystal Ball*, three *Glasses*, two *Spoons*, and six nuts of Crystal.

There is reason to suppose that these beads were appropriated to some mystic hymeneal purpose, especially as they appear to have been worn round the wrist of a female, and found near to the ivory armilla. The antient Cabalists used this number in a procreative sense, by multiplying the MASCULINE THREE, into the FEMININE *number two*, the produce being *Six*; and so *six into six* is *thirty six*. Thus in one sense it related to the *male* and *female*, and in the other to procreation, and therefore it was in a physical cabalistical sense prefixed to animal nature. See Philo in lib. de Mund. Opif. Ἄρρεν τε καὶ θῆλυς [illegible] ἐκ [illegible] δυνάμεως [illegible], &c. The Mosaic Cosmology was also by the antient Jewish fathers explained in the Cabalistical number Six—the number of days, in which creation was operated, and which they always applied to vivified nature.

It was also called Φίλιος, Beloved, and Φιλο[illegible], Copulation, because animals of the same species have a reciprocal attachment for each other. See *Harriot's Georgia*, p. 64. Also Ζυγία and Ζυγῖτις, because they are yoked or coupled together. This mystic number Six was also called Ἀφροδίτη, Venus, and Ἄκμων, an anvil, but I should rather suppose Ἀκμής, *unwearied*, applied to venereal copulation, to the unerring, constant, and endless nature of propagation. See *Nicomachi Gerasi. Arithmet. Theolog.* lib. 1. See also Meursi Denar. Pythag. where many other names are prefixed to this number.

The armilla, with *ten* pendant rings, is also an hymeneal appendage, and which is of the same mystic import, as the *number four* was held in the greatest possible veneration by the Antients. See the Golden Verses of Pythagoras, 47.

> Ναι μα τον ἁμετερα ψυχα παραδοντα ΤΕΤΡΑΚΤΥΝ
> Π[illegible] φυσεως, αλλ [illegible]
> Thee by his name I swear, whose sacred Lore
> First to mankind explain'd the mystic *Four*,
> Source of Eternal Nature and Almighty Power. Rowe's Translation.

We therefore find the power of the *Decad* to be *four*, for before we can arrive at a perfect *Decad* we discover all the virtues and perfection of the *ten* in *four*. For example, in assembling all the numbers from one to four inclusively the whole composition makes ten.

1
2
3
4

10

decomposed, or changed to a calcareous state. The end, which was inserted into the handle, has impressions of wood upon it, which shews the handle to have been made of that substance

In this grave I observed several *shards* and *pebbles*, which are by no means natives of the chalk, and which I have reason to think had been intentionally thrown in with the body *

For further remarks, see OBSERVATION.

Thus the *four* holding the middle place between the increased unit, and the virgin *seven* (see *seven* rings to the Armilla or bracelet of Count Caylus), so called by the Pythagoreans, who compared it to Minerva, has alone received the virtues and powers of *the numbers producing* and *produced*, which are contained in the Decad Thus there is a divine and religious signification prefixed to the number *Ten* or *Four*, and an animal figurative sense prefixed to the number *Six* produced from a different and less comprehensive arithmetical root See a more full and particular investigation of these mystic numbers very learnedly explained by M. Dacier, in his Annotations on the Commentaries of Hierocles on the Golden Verses of Pythagoras A treatise on this subject would be endless, but I trust it will be sufficient to prove, that from hence we may deduce the origin of the *marriage ring*, and shew that there was a very comprehensive meaning prefixed to this custom for a more satisfactory disquisition, I shall refer the learned reader to Johannis Kirchmanni de Annulis, cap xviii where he may collect a profusion of matter relating to this antient conjugal custom of wearing rings or Armillæ But from what has here been briefly said on the subject, little doubt must remain as to the real meaning of the deposit of the *ten silver rings*, the *armilla*, and the *Six Beads of Crystal*, which number were also found in the *Farnesian urn*, above quoted, and doubtless the inhumated relics of some wedded female

* I have had occasion frequently to make this observation in these kind of *Tumuli* It is not improbable, that this custom furnished Shakespeare with this line in Hamlet.

Shards, flints, and *pebbles* should be thrown on her.

Those persons who committed suicide, being deprived the Christian rites of burial, were perhaps interred after this manner peculiar to the Pagans.

TUMULUS

T U M U L U S III.

THIS Tumulus was opened on Chatham Lines, in the same range with Tumulus I and II

Fig I. An iron Spear Head fifteen inches long, which, to give a more perfect idea of the nature of these relics, I have represented in the state when taken out of the earth I have also selected the contents of this grave, for a more correct and natural description of them, and to ascertain their analogy with the arms in general that are discovered in these small kind of tumuli *. The spear was

* In the Gentleman's Magazine for March, 1766, there is a letter from the late Dr Stukeley to Mr. Peter Collinson, F R S giving an account of several British Antiquities found near Chatteris in the isle of Ely, accompanied with a plate of a sword, the umbo of a shield, a spear head, a glass vase, and an earthen urn The dimensions of the sword correspond with the one I found in Tumulus I. The spear is of the same nature, only smaller, than the one described in the above Tumulus The umbo is exactly similar With the greatest energy and critical definition the Doctor describes these remains to be 3000 years old, and to have belonged to one of the first inhabitants of this island He thinks the sword was of the fabric of Damascus, and to have been brought hither by the Midianite Merchants who came to Britain with the Tyrian Hercules, to seek for tin Strange are the meanderings of Antiquaries when they have no grounds for conjecture! We shall have, in the course of this work, the strongest testimonies to prove the contents of this Tumulus found in the Isle of Ely to have been the remains of the latter Britons, instead of the old and first colonizers Dr Stukeley having taken his report, as to the critical position of these remains, from the description of a Lord of the manor, a Mr Fawcet, of that isle, who doubtless had them brought to him by some labourers, shews that very little confidence can be placed in his narrative It is only by the local deposit of the relics, when accurately surveyed that a perfect knowledge can be acquired of their respective owners This we shall find to be the case of the glass vessel, which was not found in the same grave, and the place of its deposit not ascertained In his paper to Mr Collinson he mentions the account which Mr Jacob of Faversham transmitted to the Society of Antiquaries on the 22d of February, 1759, of a body being found on Barham Downs, which the Doctor says was of an old Briton, glass beads being round the neck of it This he concludes to be the case, because he observed beads to have encircled the necks of the British kings on their coins The contents of the graves opened at that period are now in my possession, and [illegible] correspondence with Mr Jacob, whose kind services to facilitate my *[illegible]* enquiries I am here happy to acknowledge with a high sense of obligation, I am clearly of opinion that the beads were not found in the same grave with the arms described in Mr Jacob's paper The late Rev Bryant Faussett of Heppington near Canterbury, critically opened the remainder of these *tumuli* on Barham Downs; and, on a survey of his discoveries, I do not find (for numerous have been his discoveries in various other sepulchral ranges of Barrows) any grave that contained beads with arms and this has also been fully substantiated by the many ranges of tumuli that I have ransacked The arms are found in distinct graves, shewing the same to be appropriated to the men, and the beads to the women This glass vessel also, on which Dr Stukeley has given an elaborate treatise (see his Paper to the Society of Antiquaries, Mar 15, 1764, to prove that this island was originally peopled from Tyre) was part of the contents of a woman's interment, to ascertain which, the strongest proofs will, in a future part of this work, be advanced

deposited on the right shoulder, in a parallel horizontal direction with the body From a multitude of similar specimens of these weapons, with impressions of a coarse linen cloth, it is probable they were enclosed in the coffin, or placed near the funeral vestment. The socket into which the handle or shaft was introduced contains the impression of decayed wood adhering to the rust, and, on observing a line of discoloured chalk in the direction of the body, I am inclined to think the spear was buried entire, which, from the length of the cist that contained the body, could not exceed six feet and an half in length The metal is reduced to a calx, and will break asunder on the smallest pressure

Fig 2 Iron boss, or umbo of the shield, five inches in diameter, and about the same in height, two feet from the end of the grave, and laid between the bones of the leg.

Fig 3. The umbo in profile

Fig 4 An iron knife, six inches long, with very perfect impressions of coarse linen cloth about the middle of the blade, which, by the impression of wood on it, appears to have been deposited in a case of this material. The handle was also composed of wood. On the left side near the middle of the body

Fig. 5 Fragment of an iron buckle, near the knife, indicating the same to have served a belt, and which, with the evident appearance of accreted cloth upon it, proves the body to have been inhumated in its accustomary apparel.

Fig 6 The *femur* bone delineated, to shew its texture, and to prove the body to have been that of a male adult.

Pl. 4

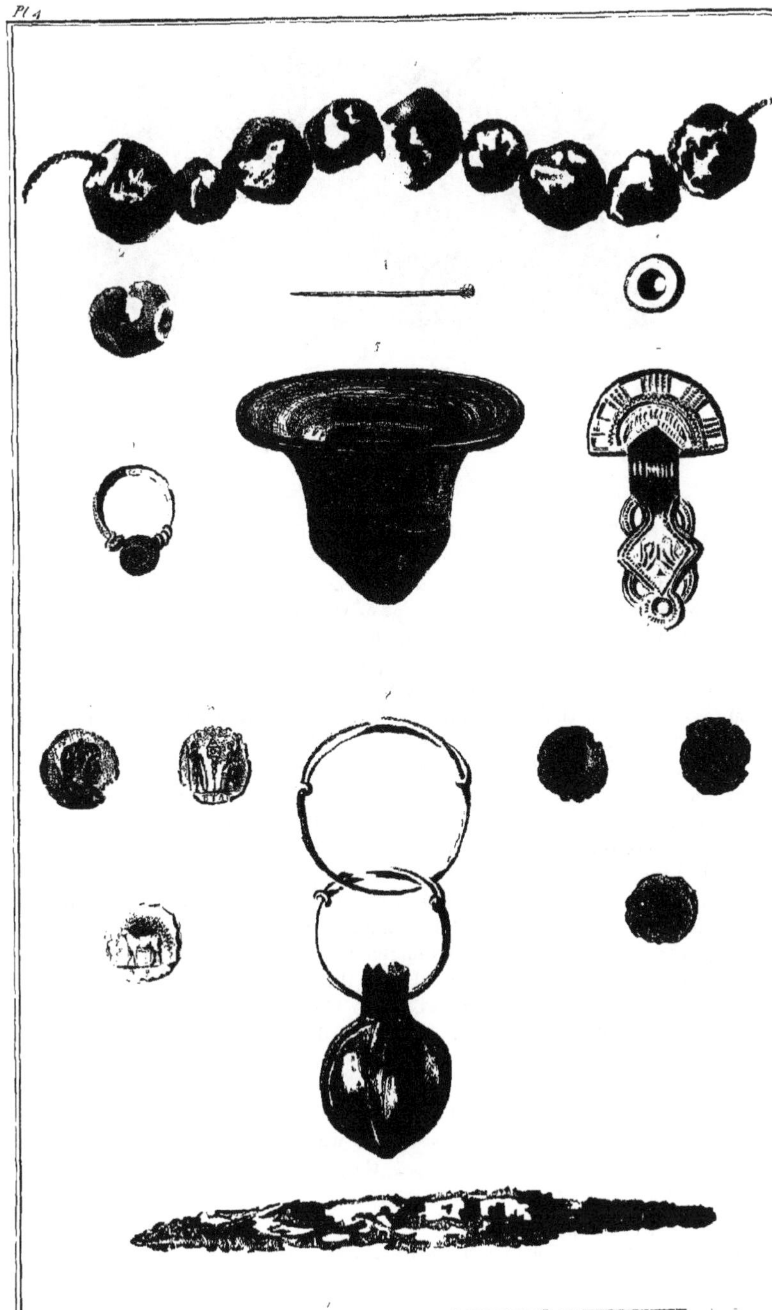

TUMULUS IV.

OPENED the 10th of August, 1782, being the 86th in my Note-Book. It formed one of the groupe with Tumulus I. II. and III. and was situated at the distance of 33 yards from them, near the scarp of the hill which faces Chatham church, and within the gorge of the sloping bastion of the King's lines.

The cist which contained the body did not exceed a foot and half from the sod, and not more than four feet in depth.

The teeth were perfect, especially the enamel, which I have remarked to be always recent in chalk to almost any length of time, when the other parts of the skeleton have been entirely disunited.

Some parts of the skull were preserved, particularly the lower jaw, and some of the fistular bones were conspicuous; their delicate texture, joined with the smallness and good preservation of the teeth in their natural state, inclined me to pronounce this interment to have been that of a young female subject. The head in the north direction.

IV Fig. 1. Pl. IV. Nine AMBER BEADS of a bright and deep orange colour, of the size represented in the plate. The complete number found were THIRTY-SIX, and, when strung afresh, formed a double row; the circle of which being nearly four inches in diameter, and found near the neck, without a doubt, shews the same to have been used as a NECKLACE. They are not worked into any regular form, and appear to have been selected from native lumps, and chipped into the shapes represented in the plate. As glass by laying in the earth acquires an opaque thin coating, which some call *armatura*, or *electrum*, so the amber has acquired a cloudy substance seemingly tinctured with the chalk.

Fig. 2. A BLUE GLASS BEAD embossed with three circular pieces of varied coloured glass, of white and orange; the fractured part is where a piece is broken out.*

* This bead is something similar to the smallest rayed amulet which Mr. Pennant has engraved in his Brit. Zool. 8vo Ed. 2. vol. III. p. 33. under the article Snake.

Fig 3. A BROWN RED BEAD of vitrified earth These beads were found near the ſide of the ſkeleton

Fig 4. A METAL PIN. The workmanſhip in every reſpect ſimilar to our large modern pins of braſs. Found near the left ſide.

Fig 5. A GLASS CUP *, of a deep green colour The drawing is the exact ſize Three and $\frac{4}{10}$ inches diameter over the rim, two inches deep, and $\frac{2}{10}$ of an inch in thickneſs at the rim. Found inverted near the left ſide about the center of the body.

Fig 6 A SILVER RING, twiſted in a convoluted form near the bones of the hand

Fig 7. A SILVER BROACH three inches in length, delicately worked with a beading, inlaid in a remarkable curious manner with the ſame metal, gilt and ornamented at the tail with a deep coloured hyacinth ſtone. The reverſe contains a claſp and an iron tongue ſimilar to Fig 4 Pl. II The calx of the iron tongue has a very perfect impreſſion of linen cloth †, and on the ſilver part is accreted a diſtinct filament or thread

Fig 8 A CRYSTAL BALL ‡, *encloſed in a lap of ſilver*, pendant to two ſilver rings The cryſtal appears to be in its native ſtate unpoliſhed by art Found on the left ſide cloſe to the cup.

Fig 9.

* Theſe glaſs ſepulchral veſſels have been frequently found in theſe kind of *tumuli* They are always faſhioned without a baſe to ſtand on, and, like the Roman *lacrymatories*, or tear-bottles, they ſeem to be appropriated only to funereal rites See Pl V N° I Fig 7 As they generally occur with inſtruments of magic, it is very probable they contained the *aqua magica* See Prop lib IV. Eleg I.

Aut ſi quis motas cornicis ſenſerit alas,
Umbra neque, *hæc magicis mortua prodit aquis*

Anno 1767 was opened at the ſouth end of Stowbridge, in the road to Grange, a barrow called King Barrow, 100 feet diameter, its perpendicular height 12 feet, out of which was taken a decayed oaken cup, *three inches* over the mouth *two* at the bottom, its depth two, and its thickneſs $\frac{2}{10}$ of an inch *See the drawing in Hutchins's Hiſtory of Dorſet* The bottom is rounded See Chifletius of the Tomb of Maria wife to the Emperor Honorius, p 55, on Childeric's Tomb, ſee alſo Brown's Hydriotaphia, p 28 where theſe relics occur in tombs.

† Whenever the quality of cloth is mentioned, the reader may be aſſured the ſame has undergone an *analytical* experiment The apparent wonderful preſervation of cloth during ſuch a length of time, ſince theſe remains have been interred, is critically accounted for by the *patina* and *ruſt* of metals incorporating themſelves with it

‡ It was my intention to have referred the reader, for the diſcuſſion of this very remarkable and curious relic, to OBSERVATIONS on Tum IV, but, as much matter is at hand, and as the ſentiments of learned men may poſſibly tranſpire before my work is completed, I have been induced to ſubjoin the following remarks, that a more full and elaborate diſſertation may be accompanied with the materials which I have already framed for the purpoſe If thoſe gentlemen will contribute to my reſearches on this ſubject, and who may have ſome ſimilar ſpecimens in their poſſeſſion, their communications will be properly regarded

Montfaucon ſays, 20 of theſe *cryſtal-balls* were found at Rome towards the latter end of the ſixth century in an alabaſter urn, by the canons of St John of Lateran The urn alſo contained a *gold ring*, enchaſed with a ſtone, a *needle*, an *ivory comb*, and *ſome ſprigs of gold* This author ſays, they have been rarely found in tombs See *Tom* I p 15 When the tomb of King Childeric, who was interred anno 436, was opened at Tournay anno 1653, with a profuſion of magnificent ornaments, was found a *cryſtall-ball* See the drawing and deſcription, p 243, in *Chifletius*, who has written a learned and very elaborate account of the diſcovery of this tomb See alſo p 13, in Browne's *Hydriotaphia Urne burial*, a *cryſtal ball* found in the Funchal-urn, the particulars of which have been already cited in p 9 of this work

In the British Muſeum there is a very fine *cryſtal ball*, but no hiſtory apparently attached to it

Godfrey Fauſſett, Eſq, of Heppington, near Canterbury, has a *cryſtal-ball* in his cabinet, which was taken out of a tumulus on Barham Downs, with a *glaſs* veſſel Another *cryſtal ball* was found at Aſh in Kent, in a tumulus with a *glaſs cup*, as I have ſome reaſon to think, and a *gold fibula*, which are in my poſſeſſion Several ſpecimens of cryſtal, ſome cut, ſome in their natural ſtate, taken out of ſepulchres, are alſo in my cabinet Sir William Fagg, of Myſtole, near Chartham Downs in Kent has a cabinet of *tumuli* relics, amongſt which is a *cryſtal ball*, found with a *circular gold plated fibula* a

Fig 9 A ROMAN COIN of the small Brass Round the head FL IVL CON STANTIVS NOB C

Fig 10

glass vessel, and other relics in a [illegible] of *tumuli*, on Chartham Downs A copy of a manuscript of a Dr Mortimer, on the subject of these barrows, is now in my possession See Pl V N [illegible] where these relics are engraved This true English hearted Baronet, with an hospitality that I am [illegible] happy to record, permitted me to make what use I thought proper of his cabinet, which, joined with the repeated civilities I have received from his relation, H Godfrey Faussett, Esq, of [illegible], has enabled me to establish, by analogy, some interesting facts, that respect the nature and history of these sepulchral remains The particulars of this gentleman's favours I shall postpone to a future passage of this work

It is well known, the antients, in respect to divination, reposed the greatest confidence in gems and other stones Zoroaster used the *astroite* in magical rites [illegible] *astroites* [illegible] laudes ejus in magicis artibus Zoroastrem cecinisse Quidam diligentius de [illegible] produnt See Plin lib xxxvii c ix Democritus [illegible], the [illegible], called *[illegible]*, by some called *[illegible]*, or *[illegible]*, and which he has much celebrated, is used in various ways for prophesying, or fortune telling *Zachalias* the Babylonian, in his books dedicated to king Mithridates, thinks the fate of man may be predicted from gems Humanis gemmis attribuit [illegible] Plin ib The *[illegible]*, or blood stone, the above Babylonian *[illegible]*, is efficacious in petitions to great men, and in the [illegible] of battle procureth victory I have in my collection a circular stone of this kind, ornamented with silver and a silver ring to suspend it by Though Pliny very elaborately has recorded the opinion of magicians in respect to the divination which they pretend to obtain from stones, he nevertheless, speaking of the magical stone, *[illegible]* [illegible], thinks no great confidence should be placed in magicians *Magorum [illegible]* [illegible] his words

From the sultry climes of the East, magic seems first to have originated through all changes of government, empire, and religion, it appears to have assumed a wonderful controul over the actions of men, over the vulgar as well as over the more enlightened parts of society, [illegible] of the Pagan relics discovered in our sepulchres, particularly the magical instruments, will be found to have derived their origin from those climes Some proofs towards the *establishment* of this interesting truth will be advanced in the course of this work

If the reader will refer to Colonel Vallancey's fourth volume of his *Coll Tanea de Rebus Hibernicæ*, he will find an engraving, and a learned description, of the [illegible] It is a *Druidical Speculum*, which the Druids pretended would draw down the [illegible], the essence or spiritual fire and presence of Aesar (God) whenever they consulted the Oracle [illegible], is the magical stone of speculation, and which we shall find to have prevailed from the remotest period of time throughout all the British Isles to the present day

The use of this stone was strictly forbidden to the Jews by Moses in the xxvith chapter of Leviticus "Ye shall make you no idols nor graven image, neither rear you up a standing image, neither shall ye suffer the stone, משכית [illegible], to be within your dominions" The Vulgate English have mistaken the sense, but the LXX, who translate it *[illegible]*, [illegible], are perfectly correct, and backed by the opinion of Spencer de Legibus, vol I we shall have the full meaning of this magical instrument as used by the antients He says, [illegible], derived from [illegible], [illegible] contemplor, consulto Skopon, non speculum tantum sed etiam [illegible] [illegible] [illegible], speculor, contemplor, intueor, observo animo agito [illegible], divinatio in [illegible]

This stone is again forbidden in Numbers xxxiii v 52 "Then ye shall —— destroy all their משכיתם Mischiothim, translated *[illegible]* by the Septuagint, and [illegible], *pictures* in the English version See p 10 of the Coll de Reb Hib

The Hebrew *Maschith*, according to Spencer, has been variously translated, and accommodated to the phrases of writers, [illegible], *lapidem [illegible]*, [illegible] *[illegible]* [illegible] [illegible] occurs also, [illegible] *custodem*, *[illegible] speculatorem* In the Greek version this is frequently the case, [illegible] *speculator* [illegible] See Ezek xxxiii [illegible], also Kings ix [illegible] After having enumerated various [illegible] given to the word *Maschith*, Spencer concludes thus, "[illegible] *Maschith* [illegible] et [illegible] [illegible]"

Delrius, in his Disquisit Magic [illegible] cap 2 p [illegible], says, [illegible] [illegible] [illegible] Levit xxvi [illegible] *lapidem [illegible]*, [illegible] *lapidem [illegible]*, vel, [illegible] *prospectus*, and, this is what Dr [illegible] seems to refer to See his Note [illegible] D [illegible] [illegible] divinationi [illegible] [illegible]

From what Spencer has said, no decisive information can be acquired on the import of the word *Maschith*, but, by comparing the subsequent uses to which the *crystal* [illegible] has been applied to the import or meaning of the word, little doubt will, I think, remain but that the *crystal ball*, Fig [illegible] is the real *Maschith* to which the Hebrew text alludes

I shall waive, in this note, a critical enquiry into the use of this CRYSTAL BALL, and refer the reader to *Observations on Tum IV* where a more elaborate discourse will be given on it [illegible] The enquiry would naturally lead me to the long controversy on the Urim and Thummim mentioned in Scripture, on which so much has been said by the learned Spencer and Dr Prideaux [illegible] De Urim & Thummim [illegible] [illegible] I shall, however, in this place remark, that antient as well as modern pretenders to [illegible] have [illegible] to imitate this instrument of divine revelation, called Urim and Thummim [illegible] [illegible] visions and apparitions,

Fig. 10. The reverse, GLORIAE EXERCITVS. The letters on the *exergue* are not distinct. [illegible] are only legible.

Fig. 11.

nitions, the Ruach Hecodesh, the inspiration of the the Holy Ghost, and the Beth Kol, the daughter of a voice, or an echo. The false prophet pretended, that their presiding genius, their *light* or spirit, conveyed their wills to them by the same method which Jehovah conveyed his will, or the knowledge of things past or to come, to the true prophets, by oracle, by dreams, visions, speech, &c. and imitated, as far as they could, the true prophets in their actions: hence the Oracular Groves of Dodona, the Delphic Oracle, the Roman Soothsayings, &c.

Hence, in our more modern times, we hear of the CRYSTAL of Paracelsus, in which are seen things past, present, and to come. Paracelsus, as may be seen in his life by Boerhaave, had travelled to the East, and from thence probably he brought this magical secret. Joachim Camerarius mentions a round *crystalline gem*, inspected by a chaste youth, wherein the youth, discerning an apparition, could receive intelligence of any thing he required. See Martin of the Western Isles, p. 167; see also Godelminus, lib. [illegible] p. 42, who relates the same story.

In the life of Lilly there is a profusion of predictions related by the CRYSTAL BALL, particularly the celebrated visions and mysterious operations of Dr Dee and Mr Kelly. His stone is expressly described as round, pretty big, and of CRYSTAL, which [illegible] the shew stone and HOLY STONE. In his book of Conjuration, he describes the mode of invocation, and the appearances of the spirits.

There is little doubt, from the foregoing remarks, but what Dr Dee, as he was known to have been a good scholar, had studied the Rabbinical SHECHINAH, which may be gathered from this expression of Lilly, "I have read over," says he, "his book of conference with spirits, and thereby "perceive many weaknesses in the manage of that way of *Mosaical learning*." However, Lilly does not deny but the angels will, when properly invoked, appear, and reveal the things required of them.

In the life of Lilly, there is also a strange prophecy mentioned of the restoration of Charles II which was predicted by the inspection of the CRYSTAL.

There is also mention made of one John a Windor, a scrivener, whom he calls a speculator, a name which I apprehend to be given him from his pretended art in the use of the crystal. Lilly says, on this man's examination before Sir Henry Wallop, he said, that, on a visit to Dr. Dee at Mortlake, he copied out of his book, in secret, an invocation to raise spirits, which it seems the Doctor had used for that purpose. The invocation was in part thus:

"Per virtutem illorum qui invocant nomen tuum

"Hermeli——mitte nobis tres angelos," &c.

These two prophecies were not given vocally by the angels, but by inspection of the crystal in types and figures, or by apparition the *circular way*, where, at some distance, the angels appear, representing, by forms, shapes, and creatures, what is demanded.

According to Lilly, Dr Dee was wholly devoted to the study of magic, and seems to have travelled for information. He was very learned in Greek and Latin, he was an excellent astronomer of his time, and well skilled in general knowledge. Dr Dee had a servant, whose name was Kelly, who also acquired the art of speculating with the crystal. See the use of the crystal ball in Dr Dee's book of Conjuration.

There is a passage in Lilly's life, which seems to favour an opinion that this art of speculating was only peculiar to certain persons, and that the crystal was common in many families, who pretended to, or who had a confidence in, these mysterious operations. He says, he was well acquainted with one Sarah Skelhorn, who had been speculatrix to one Arthur Gauntlet, probably a conjurer, in Lilly's words, a professor of physic and a very lewd fellow. *This Sarah*, says he, *had a perfect sight, and indeed the best eyes for that purpose he ever did see*. On the death of Gauntlet, she lived with one Mr Stockman in the Isle of Purbeck: her mistress being desirous to accompany her mother the Lady Beaconsfield unto London, who lived twelve miles from her habitation, she caused Sarah to inspect her CRYSTAL, to see if her mother was gone. The angels appeared, and showed her mother opening a trunk, and taking a red waistcoat out of it.

This Sarah Skelhorn's invocation to the crystal began,

Oh, ye good angels, only and only, &c.

There was one Ellen Evans, daughter to Evans, who was Lilly's tutor, who had likewise the gift of speculating the crystal, and her invocation began with,

O Micol, O tu Micol, regina pigmeorum veni, &c.

This kind of magical apparatus, by the testimony of Lilly, appears to have been practised in many families of note. Sir Robert Holborn conducted one Gladwell of Suffolk to Lilly, to whom a Mr Gilbert Wakering gave his beril when he died. This stone was of the [illegible] of a large orange, set in silver, with a cross on the top, and another on the handle, and round about engraved the names of the angels RAPHAEL, GABRIEL, URIEL. This Gladwell had once [illegible] and conference with two of the Angels, URIEL and RAPHAEL, but lost them by his carelessness, and, as Lilly says, he was offered, by this Gladwell, two hundred pounds to have assisted him in the recovery of them: but Lilly being, for what cause he does not assert, hurt at this proposal, though it should seem perfectly [illegible] to restore this Gladwell to favour with the angels, rejected the offer. [illegible] times, if well considered and well observed, do [illegible] the matter any thing he defines, but he [illegible] very wisely, for such a blockhead, *Amant secreta, fugiunt aperta*.

Fig. II. A ROMAN COIN of the small brass. The inscription defaced. The contour of the head shows it to be of the II. VALENTINIAN.

Fig

There was one Mortlack, an impostor, in Lilly's time, who pretended to speculations, and had a *crystal*, a call of Queen Mab, by which he deceived many persons; but, when brought into Lilly's company, and making his invocation, nothing appeared, confessing he could do nothing while his competitor was present.

This passage in Lilly shews that the art of speculating the crystal was very prevalent in this æra. "All the antient astrologers of England," says he, "were much astonished at my manner of writing; "especially one old Mr. William Hodges, who lived near Wolverhampton, and many others, who "understood astrology competently well, as they thought. Hodges swore I did more by astrology "than he *could by the* CRYSTAL and use thereof, which he understood as perfectly as any one in Eng-"land. He resolved questions astrologically; nativities he meddled not with; in things of other "nature, which required more curiosity, he repaired to the CRYSTAL, and invoked for his angels, "RAPHAEL, GABRIEL, and URIEL." Here follows a story of the CRYSTAL. One John Scott, travelling into Staffordshire, resided with Hodges a month or six weeks. On his return to London, he desired Hodges to show him the person and features of the woman he should marry. Hodges carried him into a field not far from his house, and, pulling out his CRYSTAL, bid Scott set his foot to his, and soon after made him inspect, when, asking him what he saw, he replied, "I see a ruddy com-"plexioned wench in a red waistcoat drawing a can of beer." "She must be your wife," said Hodges. As Scott was under promise of marriage to another woman, he denied the possibility of this. But two years afterwards, on a journey to Dover, on his return, he put up at an inn at Canterbury, but, mistaking the pantry for the setting room, he saw the identical girl which was shown to him by Hodges in his CRYSTAL drawing of beer. An attachment soon taking place, he was married to her, and thus the vision of the CRYSTAL was perfectly accomplished.

After this follows a story of a gentleman, who applied to Hodges for the recovery of his horse that was lost, and it might not be improbable that he applied to the crystal for this purpose.

In Lilly's time they talked of being called to the CRYSTAL, as Methodists when they say they have had a call to the *Grace*.

In an unpublished manuscript in the British Museum, N° 3849, is related the manner of proceeding to discover any thing in a CRYSTAL.

2d Part. *Forms of Conjuration.*

3d. Experiments for finding out theft, treasure, &c by the CRYSTAL.

I have here subjoined an extract from the manuscript, which appears to have been written in the time of Elizabeth or James the First.

"Here followeth an experiment, approved and unknowne, of Ascaryell, to see most excellent and "certainlye in a CHRISTALL STONNE what secreet thou wilt.

"First, take a CHRISTALL STONE, or a glasse, the greater the better, so that it be fayre and cleane, "without any ragges, cracke, or holes broken within; and thou must have *a thonge of harte skinn*, to "wrappe thy stone in, so that thy stone may be well seene in the middest of the bindinge; and ever, "when thou dost wrappe the stone about with the thonge, say thus: *In nomine sanctæ trinitatis et dei-"tatis hanc gemmam recondo.* Then holde the crystall stone, which is so dight in thy right hande, against "the sun, which must be done in the heate of the sun at noone, when the sun is in the highest and "hottest, and soe call him in such likeness as thou wilt by the conjuration followinge, and he will "come and shew thee whatsoever thou wilt in all countryes, of all things, whatsoever thou wilt ask "him, and thou shall command him to bringe his followers with him, and he will bringe one "Mathayas with him, and another also will come with him."

Sequitur conjuratio.

Conjuro vos Centony Caton, messitone messiton, messycon vel myrteron, qui habitatis in Bosco, ego vos conjuro et precipio vobis cum sociis vestris ut sitis parati obedienter mihi, et ad omnia præcepta mea adimplendo. Conjuro te Askaryel Abylon vel Boat, per patrem et filium et spiritum sanctum, qui est Alpha et Omega, principium et finis, per tremendum diem Judicii, et per virtutem Dei viventis, et per omnia nomina ejus effabilia et ineffabilia. Quatenus tu Askaryell IN ISTAM GEMMAM CRISTALLINAM *sine mora citissime venias, in propria persona tua et in pulchra hominis forma et sertum in tuo capite et mihi visibiliter te ipsum demonstres, et omnibus circumstantibus ibi appareas et socios tuos tecum adducas ut te et illos aptissime videre possimus, per desiderium meum et meas conjurationes et per omnia quæ tibi jussero. Et si hoc non feceris in virtute et per virtutem Dei, et per potestatem magnam quam Deus habet super te, ego condemno te Askaryel in infernum et ignem inextinguibilem usque ad ultimum Diem judicii. Fiat fiat.*

Nisi citius appareas, et ad omnia interrogata veraciter respondeas, et statim et sine mora cum te vocavero ad instantem meam venias omnibus horis.

Conjuro te Askariell, per Deum patrem omnipotentem et per Jesum Christum ejus et per Sanctum Spiritum trinitatem personam per quæ tu es substantiæ ejus, per providentiam sanctam qua Deus in monte suo fecit, [illegible] sapientiam per quam cælos suspexit, et terram decorum fundavit, per [illegible] terræ et maris et omnia quæ [illegible] sunt per [illegible] abyssi, per quatuor elementa, et per virtutem quam in elemento [illegible], et per [illegible] et per potestates Dei [illegible], et [illegible] ordinavit, per angelos et archangelos, per [illegible] dominationes, potestates [illegible] virtutes [illegible], et per [illegible] officia, et per [illegible] conjurationes, et [illegible] alias, et per eas quæ [illegible], et per [illegible] quæ [illegible] firmamento et in firmamento sunt, per omnes cælos, et omnes virtutes [illegible], et per omnia quæ [illegible] Deus ad laudem et [illegible] nominis sui majestatis, conjuro te Askaryell, per duodecim patriarchas, per duodecim [illegible], per duodecim apostolos Domini nostri Jesu Christi, per sanctam Mariam, matrem Domini nostri Jesu Christi, [illegible], per quatuor angelistas Jesu Christi et per sanctum evangelium Christi, per [illegible] Deus Sabaoth, et per [illegible] majestatis [illegible], et per [illegible] instantem,

per

Fig. 12. The reverse of Fig. 11. No intelligible inscription. The figure of a VICTORY.

Fig.

per quatuor cælestia aurea candelabra, per sedem magistatis, per thronum Dei, per altare aureum quod est ante conspectum Dei, per fulgura, tonitrus, et voces, quod egrediuntur de throno, per merita omnium confessorum, et per reliquias omnium sanctorum, et per omnes sanctos et sanctas virgines et cælo, et per omnes sanctos quæ Deum semper laudent et adorent Quatenus tu Ascaryell statim et sine mora venias, et in ISTUM SILLU... ... ... intres, in propria persona tua, et in pulchra forma humana, et sertum in tua capite, et ... sibes ... mihi, et omnibus circumstantibus citissime appareas, et socios tuos tecum adducens ut te et illos aptissime videre possimus, per desiderium meum, et per meas conjurationes et per omnia quæ tibi jussero, at si hoc non feceris in virtute et per virtutem Dei et per potestatem quam Deus habet super te, ego condemno te Askariell in infernum, et in ignem inextinguibilem usque ad diem Judicii, nisi citius hic appareas, et ad omnia interrogata mea veraciter respondeas, et statim et sine mora cum te vocavero, ad meam instantiam venias omnibus horis

Adhuc conjuro te Askariell, per eum qui est Alpha et Omega, et per ista sancta nomina Dei quæ sunt hic, Eoel, Abiel, Ananiael, Amay, Hagyos, O Theos, Deus omnium potentias, Hiectita, Grammaton, Onythbeon, Almaron, Stimulamaton, Isboran, Elyphares, Ensflon, Hysterion, Adonay, Rufus, ...avaron, Cryon, Jehovah, Esbra, Eloym, Saton, Leceoni, Messias, Leyste, Lustion, Almarias, Archima, Rabur, Oneia, Elbrac, Flos, Egepate, Regum, Abraca, Rota, Igeta, Amazim, Censius, Saday, Candor, Decor, Candos, Elfel, Nazarenus, Helenon, Abecor, ...yeya, El, Elion, Saray, yma..., Anabona, Emanuel, Quatenus, tu Askariell, sine mora et statim venias, & ut supra

Adhuc conjuro te Askariell, per alia sancta nomina Dei secreta, quæ sunt hic, Ersfel, Deus, Apies, Eloy, Ursta, gloriosu..., lenus, or, unigenitus, ..., vita, ...ams, homo, sapientia, virtus, principium et finis, fons et origo, paracletus mediator, agnus, ovis, ...tulis, Aries, verbum, splendor, Sol, gloria, lux, et Imago, panis, flos, ...tis, mons pons, Janua, petra, lapisque Angularis, pastor, propheta, sacerdos, athanatos, Kyros, Theos, parton, craton, ysus, igerion, Araphineton, albinago, Ebrutone, talpa, Sameio, Agla, Ihesus Christus, Tetragrammaton, Sabaoth, Quatenus tu Askarieli, & ut supra

Conjuro te Askariell, per bonitatem domini nostri Jesu Christi, et per incarnationem, nativitatem, et circumcisionem ejus, et per baptismum ejus, et per jejunium ejus, et per humilitatem, qua pedes discipulorum ejus lavit, per crucem et passionem ejus, et per omnes ejus pœnas quas in cruce sustinuit, pro redemptione humani generis totius, per coronam spineam quam in capite suo portavit, et per clavos quibus manus et pedes ejus confixi fuerunt, et per lanceam quæ latus ejus aperuit, et per aquam et sanguinem, qui de latere ejus fluxerunt, per precationem solatam, quam patrem suum invocavit, et per animum ejus quam in manus patris ejus commendavit, et per virtutem qua velamen templi discissum fuit, Sol obscuratus fuit, et tenebræ factæ fuerunt super universam terram, et sepulcra aperta sunt, et multa corpora sanctorum qui dormierant surrexerunt, per hæc, et omnia alia prædicta, conjuro te Askariell, et præcipio tibi, Quatenus statim et sine mora venias, et in istam gemmam christallinam citissime intres, in propria persona tua, et in pulchra forma humana, et sertum in tuo capite, et mihi vel ... omnibus his circumstantibus cito appareas, et socios tuos tecum adducens, ut te et illos aptissime videre possimus, et sine timore, terrore, vel nocumento mei corporis mei animæ vel cujuscunque creaturæ Dei, et ad omnia interrogata mea veraciter respondeas sine fraude vel mendacio, ... quacunque, per desiderium meum, et meas conjurationes et per omnia quæ tibi jussero, et si hoc non feceris in virtute et per virtutem Dei, et per potestatem quam habet super te, condemno te Askaryell in infernum, et in ignem inextinguibilem, usque ad ultimum diem Judicii, fiat fiat fiat. Amen

Nisi citius hic appareas, et ad omnia interrogata mea veraciter respondeas, et statim et sine mora cum te vocavero ad instantiam meam et per præcepta mea vir ... omnibus horis

" And yf he come not at the third call, condempe him saying thus

Ego condemno et condemnato te Askariell in ignem eternum, et inextinguibilem, in virtute et per virtutem Dei ..., et per potestatem quam habet super te Deus, in locum igni, et sulphuris, et in pœna ater ... sustineas habet, et omnia alia maledicta donec pr... appare... ..., et totam voluntatem meam adimplas

" And yf he come not the first day, call him the second, and if not the second, call him the third, " until he come, then bind him to you, *ut in aliis experimentis*," &c.

It is not difficult to observe, that this is a jumble of much absurd nonsense, but as the matter is curious, so far as it relates to this magical relic as found in a very antient sepulchre, I have thought proper to rake it up

I trust little doubt will now remain, but the CRYSTAL-BALL, fig 8 was a magical instrument, and used perhaps in a similar way to the one described in this manuscript These CRYSTAL-STONES seem to have been suspended WITH LAPS OF LEATHER, or *thonge of harte-skin*, meaning *deer skin* The CRYSTAL in the *plate* shows exactly the method of suspending it with the difference of its being enclosed in *silver* instead of *leather*.

MICHAEL, RAPHAEL, GABRIEL, and URIEL were also, it seems, the attendant spirits on the speculators of the *crystal*, and who were generally obedient to immaculate, religious, and well disposed persons As there is a remarkable coincidence of facts, in this instance, with the particulars found in the grave of MARIA, eldest daughter of Stilicho, who was married to the Emperor Honorius, and supposed to have died anno 404, before the marriage rites were consummated, in the same century that my CRYSTAL-BALL was interred, I shall, as the subject is uncommonly curious, take the liberty to intrude the description of this lady's funeral magnificence verbatim from Chiffletius, p. .5, which may also possibly throw some lights on the relics of Tum. IV. " *Laurentius Surius in Commentario Rerum in Orbe gestarum sub initium anni* 1544, mense *inquit* Februario Romæ in Vaticano, haud procul a Basilica S. Petri fundamenta foderentur, inventa est marmorea arca longitudine pedum octo et semis, latitudine quinque, et sex altitudine, in qua condita fuit MARIA, HONORII Imp. conjux, quæ *virgo* obiit, morte abrepta ante nuptias In ea arca corpore absumpto, aliquot tantum DENTES superfuerunt, Capillique, ac *librarum* ossa duo præterea *vestis* et *pallium*, quibus tantum *auri* fuit intextum, ut ex his combustis auri pondo XXXVI collecta fuit Erat insuper *capsula argentea* longa pedem unum et semissem, latitudine digitorum XII in qua *vascula multa* ex *crystallo* nonnulla quæ ex *achate* perpulchre elaborata Item, *Annuli aurei* XL variis pretiosis ornati Erat et Smaragdus auro inclusus, in eoque sculptum caput, quod creditum est ipsum HONORIUM referre Præterea in auro, MONILIA ATQUE muliebria ornamenta, in quibus una crux, quam hodie *Agnus Dei* vocant, per cujus ambitum inscriptum erat MARIA NOSTRA FLORENTISSIMA Lunulaque ex auro, et in ea hæc nomina MICHAEL, GABRIEL, RAPHAEL, *Græcis literis* Item velut racemus ex smaragdis aliisque gemmis contextus, et aliud monile longitudine XI digitorum, inscriptum hoc DOMINO, NOSTRO

5

HONORIO

Fig 13 A ſmall baſe SILVER ROMAN COIN of the lower empire The head-ſide too much corroded to make out an inſcription. The reverſe, an animal apparently a ſheep

Fig 14 A corroded ſmall BRASS COIN.

The above coins were found near the CRYSTAL-BALL, GLASS VESSEL, RING, and FIBULA

Fig 15 A KNIFE The metal corroded, having entirely loſt its magnetic property Near the left ſide

For a further deſcription of this Tumulus, ſee OBSERVATIONS on TUM. IV

HONORIO *hinc* DOMINA NOSTRA MARIA Ad hæc inerat forex ex CHELIDONIA LAPILLO, COCHLEAQUE et PATERA EX CHRYSTALLO Item PILA, ex auro, ſed quæ in duas partes dividi potuit. Innumeræ pene *ch* inerant *gemmæ*, quarum et ſi pluimæ vetuſtate corruptæ, nonnullæ tamen recentem admirandamque pulchritudinem retinebant Et hæc omnia Stilico filiæ dedit pro dote"

The inferences which may be drawn from the contents of this ſepulchre, and compared with Tum IV cannot fail to ſtrike the moſt unnquiſitive mind It is remarkable, that the *pila ex auro* ſhould ſo ſtrictly accord with the explanation of the word Aeromantia by Spencer, *divinatio in inſpectione aeris* for doubtleſs this golden ball was uſed as a magical ſpeculum as the names of the angels MICHAEL, GABRIEL, and RAPHAEL, found with it, ſeem to affirm, and the ſame names are invoked with the CRYSTAL BALL in the time of Lilly But as a further detail would ſwell this note to an undue and tireſome compaſs, I muſt beg leave to refer the curious reader to OBSERVATIONS on the ſame What has already been ſaid is ſufficient to ſhow that much confidence was placed in the magical virtues of the CRYSTAL, and matter enough advanced to render a *modern conjurer* ſufficiently expert in the uſe of it If he wiſhes to enquire more profoundly into the myſteries of magic, I beg he may conſult Joannis Wierii, De Præſtigeis, 1568, *Magica ſeu mirabilium hiſtoriarum de ſpectris et apparitionibus* The works of a Jeſuit, Pet Thyræus, *Dæmoniaci hoc eſt De Obſeſſis a Spiritibus Dæmoniarum Hominibus*, and my worthy friend Joannes Georgius Godelmannus, who is very confident of the high magical efficacy of the CRYSTAL But his prophets does not conſult the good angels above cited. *Aliqui* ſunt qui dicunt, et in CRYSTALLO ſpeculo, vel VITRO PLANO *Diabolum* conſuluit Anno 1530, Sacerdote in CRYSTALLO theſauros Noriberge oſtenderat *Dæmon*

If my CRYSTAL BALL be productive of theſe wonderful virtues, ſurely my laborious reſearches among the ſepulchres of the antients are ſufficiently rewarded by this valuable diſcovery, but as I am afraid of tampering with the devil, and perfectly ſatisfied with holding conferences with my good friends of earthly condition, ſo I refer the more inquiſitive genius to a conference with MICHAEL, GABRIEL, RAPHAEL, URIEL, and the reſt of them, and for which purpoſe he is highly welcome to make uſe of my CRYSTAL and the curious INVOCATION which I have here cited.

TUMULUS V.

AS the contents of this *Tumulus* are fimilar to *Tumulus* IV. I have placed them together for a more natural and clofe comparifon. It forms one of a groupe *, fituated on Chartham Downs, four miles from Canterbury, on the eftate of Sir William Fagg, of Myftole, and was opened under the direction of Charles Fagg, Efq, in the prefence of a Dr Mortimer, in the year 1730.

The account of this Tumulus in Dr. Mortimer's manufcript is too imperfect to hazard a critical defcription; I fhall therefore only fet down † the particulars as they occur from my own *ocular* infpection.

The bones were almoft mouldered away, no remains of a coffin; and the cift about the fame depth as that of Tum. II.

Fig. 1. A CIRCULAR FIBULA ‡, compofed of a thin fillagree plate of gold on a plate of filver, $1\frac{7}{10}$ inches diameter; and $\frac{1}{10}$ of an inch in thicknefs is the whole *fibula*; but the gold plate does not extend beyond the four fmall hemifpheres. The workmanfhip of the two exterior circles is precifely fimilar to the angular chain on the fecond rim of the long fibula, Fig. 7. Pl. IV. and is evidently wrought with a milling inftrument, and inlaid with filver. In the centre is an hemifphere of ivory, $\frac{1}{2}$ an inch diameter, in which was probably the ftone, fig. 4. found in the barrow: the next circle and four right angular rays are thin plates of gold fet with garnets, having a triangular piece of lapis lazuli at the extremity, and a femicircular fetting of the fame ftone at the bafis of every ray clofe to the center ivory hemifphere. Between each ray is a gold enchafing, which contains a fmall ivory hemifphere of $\frac{1}{4}$ of an inch dia-

* See the plan of *Chartham Downs Tumuli*. This tumulus is marked A, and one of the largeft in the groupe. They are fuppofed to be Roman fepulchres by Dr Mortimer, and by Mr Lewis of Margate in Kent, whofe manufcripts are in my poffeffion. They are called *Dane Burrows* or *Dane Banks*, a name which the country people, in feveral parts of England, generally prefix to moft of our antient remains. The Danes being the laft barbarous invaders who, with devaftation and blood, over run this ifland, impreffed the inhabitants with fuch a remembrance of their horrid cruelties, that our antient memorials are almoft univerfally funk into their name.

† In December, 1782, on a tour into Kent, to open a range of thefe fmall tumuli on the coaft, at a place called St. Margaret's at Cliff, fituated between Deal and Dover, and mentioned by Dr Stukeley in his Itinerarium Curiof. p. 120. I vifited the collection of Sir William Fagg, to whofe civilities I am indebted for a copy of Dr Mortimer's manufcript, and for the permiffion of making drawings from the above relics.

‡ I have *thirteen* great and fmall *fibulæ* of this kind taken out of *tumuli*, all differently enchafed, particularly one of gold, and extremely beautiful in tafte and workmanfhip. They are extremely rare, and feldom feen in cabinets.

meter,

Pl 5
N° 1

meter, in the middle of which is a ſocket, in one whereof is remaining a round garnet, and in another the chequered gold foil under a garnet that is loſt

The reverſe of this *fibula* is ſimilar to the reverſe of the *fibulæ* deſcribed in Pl II and fig 7 of Pl IV.

Fig 2. A Gold pensile Ornament, $\frac{6}{7}$ of an inch diameter, ornamented with four gold circular corded wires, and a croſs of the ſame corded wire in the center.

Fig 3 A ſpherical Crystal-ball, $1\frac{1}{2}$ inch diameter.

Fig. 4 A ſmall round Tourquoise Stone

Fig 5. A Gold Pin and Chain, an inch long, faſtened to the gold pendant, fig 2

Fig 6. One of two Gold enchased Pendants, $\frac{5}{8}$ inches long, and $\frac{1}{2}$ broad, with a *garnet ſtone*; one of the ſtones being out, diſcovered a gold chequered foil, ſimilar ſpecimens have been heretofore deſcribed, and which always accompany the ſetting of theſe kind of ſepulchral relics.

Fig 7 One of two Glass-vessels, the ſize of the drawing, of a yellowiſh green colour, $2\frac{1}{2}$ at the orifice, $3\frac{1}{2}$ at the belly, and $2\frac{1}{2}$ at bottom, which is rounded, from the brim a ſpiral cord in the glaſs convolutes to the bottom, where it traverſes four times in a figure 8. and terminates in the center *.

Theſe veſſels were cloſe to the relics, fig 2 4 5 and 6; and doubtleſs the others would, had they been elaborately explored, have been found near them

In this *tumulus* was alſo found a fragment of a *braſs veſſel*, extremely thin, with the remains of an handle on the rim, $6\frac{1}{2}$ inches in diameter, and $1\frac{3}{4}$ inches deep This Dr Mortimer tranſlated into a helmet, and believed the handle to have been an hinge, and, by his deſcription, ſeems to have contained impreſſions of linen or woollen cloth The contents of ſucceeding tumuli will ſhow ſome ſpecimens of theſe veſſels of a mixed metal, and ſome of them ſtrongly gilt.

For further particulars ſee Observations on No. 1 of *Tum* V.

N° 2 PLATE V.

Fig 1 2 and 3 Specimens of *ſheers* †, from the tumuli on Chartham Downs: they were found with ornaments of women; but, as I cannot diſcriminate with any accuracy the relics which accompanied them, I have declined to enumerate other particulars which are not diſtinctly marked in Dr. Mortimer's manuſcript This gentleman ſeems only to have regarded the trinkets of value, ſuch as bits of gold and ſilver, and which he deſcribes minutely, without attending to the iron relics Many things in Sir William Fagg's cabinet are promiſcuouſly blended, without a poſſibility of knowing to what *tumulus* they can

* The manuſcript of Dr Mortimer ſays, this veſſel, which he calls an *urn*, contained an aromatic ſmell

† That ſuperficial dazzling writer Le Sieur Voltaire, ſays, the invention of ſciſſars, or ſheers, is not certainly of remote antiquity See his Dictionnaire, Philos Chap on Luxury

The above ſpecimens have loſt their magnetic quality by age, and by *coins* and other relics found in the ſame kind of *tumuli*, appear to have been depoſited in the fifth century See Observations, &c.

be referred I am, however, fatisfied that the *fheers* were found with womens trinkets, having had a more correct account * of the particulars.

I faid in the notes to *Tum* II that fpecimens of fheers would be given in a future plate, to fubftantiate the conjectures on the ufe of the *fieve and fheers* in magical rites, and as relics depofited with the dead. As I am not enabled to give a fpecimen of thefe implements difcovered in the fame tumulus with the former magical inftrument, I muft beg leave to fubmit them as they occur to the reader's confideration, without a pofitive determination in this place on their ufe Doubtlefs, as in thefe days, they were applied by the ladies for two-fold purpofes; in domeftic ufes for the arrangement of their attire, as well as for the good or unfortunate prediction of their tender attachments to the myfteries of love. "Illum adminiftrant CRIBRO FORCIPI "impofito et forcipe binis tantum apprehenfo, atque elevato digitis itidemque, "præfatis precibus et recitatis nominibus fufpectorum, quorumque appellato, "*cribrum* vel tremit vel nutat, vel convertitur, cum arguunt reum fceleris, de "cujus authore quæftio inftituitur," which I have before cited from Godelmanus.

For further particulars fee OBSERVATIONS on N° 2. of Tum. V

* Mr Fauffett of Heppington was with me, whofe father was prefent at the opening of thefe barrows, and who had opened fome himfelf on the fame Downs The experience of his fon, who has great knowledge and tafte in the cabinet of *tumuli* treafures, which he poffeffes from his father, has confirmed me in the affertion of thefe relics being found in the graves of the women.

TUMULUS

Pl. 6

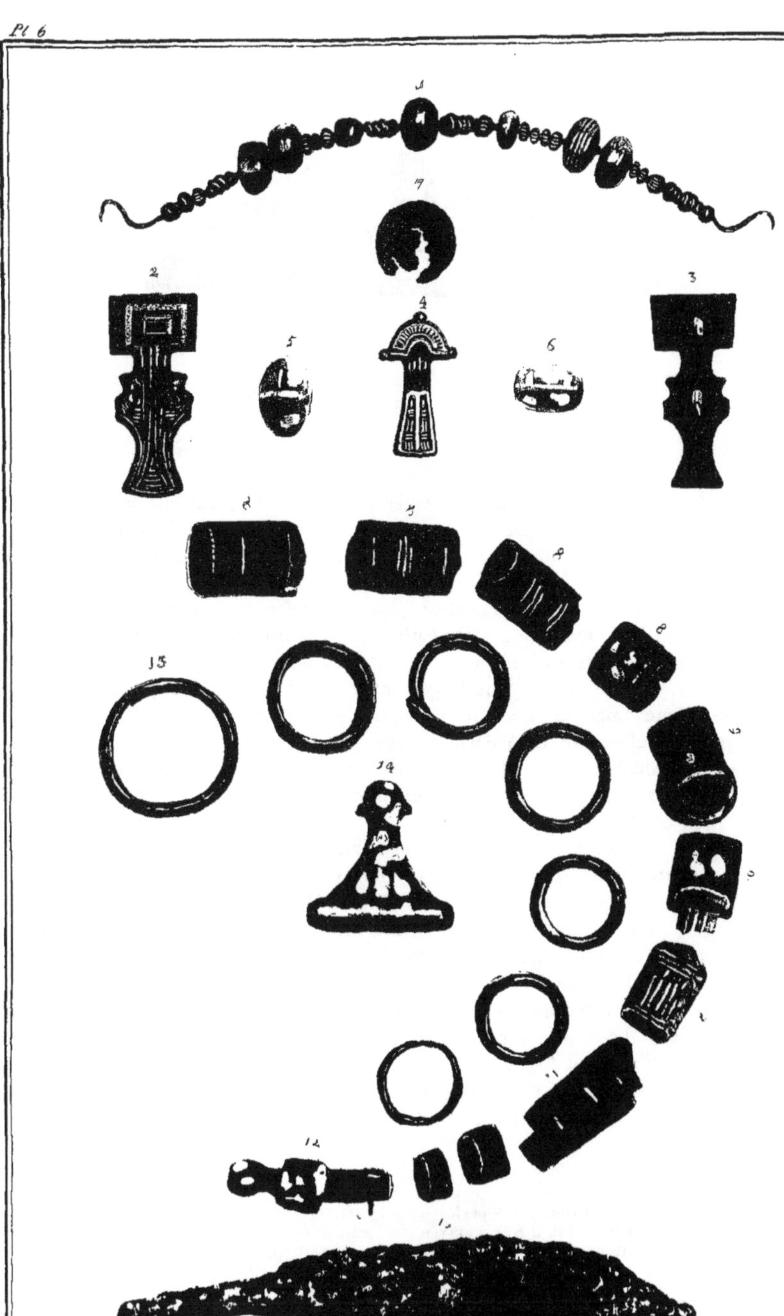

TUMULUS VI.

CHATHAM Lines, about the center of the clufter, the cift only one foot under the fod, and not a foot in depth. The bones almoft perifhed; yet what remained of them fufficiently difcernible to afcertain the pofition of the relics. The head to the north.

Fig. 1. Various coloured BEADS of *glafs* and *amber* flat and round, fome in fhape of *pullies* *, fome to imitate pearls of a beautiful and delicate texture, and in their prefent ftate difficult to be difcerned from them. They are expreffed in the drawing by rays. The larger beads are of black and apple-green glafs. Some of the fmall ones are of a bright light verditer green. Thofe in the fhape of pullies are of a dark opaque brown colour, and here and there one of a reddifh brown. The two medium fize beads on the fide of the center bead are of amber. The compleat number are *forty-three*, and found near the neck of the fkeleton.

Fig. 2. One of two GOLD ENCHASED PLATED COPPER FIBULÆ, or clafps, with a garnet-ftone in the center, of the fame kind of workmanfhip as thofe defcribed in Pl. II. fig. 3. Found near the middle of the right fide of the body.

Fig. 3. The REVERSE of fig. 2. which fhews the projecting pieces of metal to receive the tongue, and fimilar to the reverfes of the circular and oblong *fibulæ* before defcribed.

Fig. 4. A STRONG GOLD PLATED FIBULA, the reverfe, fimilar to fig. 3. The femi-circular head is not unlike the architecture of the Saxon and Norman arches. Found near Fig. 2.

Fig. 5. and 6. TWO CRYSTAL perforated BEADS found near the *fibulæ*.

Fig. 7. A very thin circular fragment of filver, found under the *cryftal bead*, fig. 5.

Fig

* See Stukeley's Defcription of Stonehenge, a barrow opened on Salifbury-Plain, in which beads like *pullies* were found. I fhall here tranfcribe the particulars which concern the beads. "Beads of "all forts, in great numbers, of glafs of divers colours, moft yellow, one black, many fingle, many "in long pieces, notched between, fo as to *refemble a ftring of beads*, and thefe were generally of a "blue colour. There were many of *amber*, of all fhapes and fizes, *flat fquares*, long fquares, *round*, "oblong, little and great. Likewife many of earth, of different fhapes, magnitude, and colour, "fome *little* and *white*, many large and flattifh like a button, others like a *pully*."

I

There

Fig 8 Detached fluted appendage of a BRASS GIRDLE

Fig 9 Repreſents a *fluted piece* adhering to a BRASS RING as taken out of the grave

Fig 10 A fluted piece which contains a piece of leather †

Fig 11 A fluted piece in three detached *laminæ*.

Fig 12 A LOOP of BRASS, and a thin plate of braſs with a pin, with which it is perforated, and apparently to ſecure it to a cap of leather, to which the whole apparatus ſeems to have adhered

Fig 13. BRASS RINGS, which ſeem to have been connected with the girdle

Fig 14. A fluted BRASS PENDANT, which appears to have been faſtened to the *loop* of fig 12

This appendage was in part under the laſt bone of the *vertebræ*, and went to the pelvis, which is now tinged with verdigreaſe, and which I preserved The poſition will therefore admit of the propriety of aſcribing it to a *girdle*, with which the deceaſed, being a female, ſeems to have worn, and to have been interred with.

Some of the *fluted* pieces have longitudinar raiſed lines upon them, the cavities of which contained thin *laminæ* of ſilver, ſomething ſimilar to that of fig 7, and which contained a white impalpable duſt, ſerving, as I have reaſon to ſuppoſe, the uſes of an amulet, to which the whole of the relic was adapted.

Fig 15. An IRON KNIFE, which retains its magnetic property, but which is almoſt converted into a calx Found near the *fibulæ*

For further particulars, ſee Obſervations on TUMULUS VI.

There is the greateſt poſſible analogy between theſe beads deſcribed by Stukeley, and thoſe which I found in the above *Tumulus* Thoſe which he found were contained in an urn with burnt bones, and, as he ſays, had undergone the fire In this the Doctor appears to have been deceived, at leaſt they could never have undergone the heat of the ſame fire which conſumed the body, which doubtleſs muſt have melted the glaſs, and quite conſumed the amber

Some of theſe beads, which were diſperſed when at Dr Stukeley's deceaſe his collection was broken up, are in my poſſeſſion, and do not ſeem to have undergone the leaſt degree of fire, which glaſs will ſoon diſcover when expoſed to it

* Theſe *girdles* are mentioned by Oſſian, ſee vol I p 115 An *hundred* of them are promiſed by a chief as uſeful to "high boſomed women, and as the friends of the birth of heroes" Mr Whitaker from Oſſian, ſee his *Hiſtory of Mancheſter*, ſays, they have been preſerved in many families of *Highlanders nearly to the preſent period*

The cuſtom of uſing theſe amulets ſeems alſo to have been handed down to the year 1537, when the Catholics adopted them for their ſuperſtitious ceremonies See Dr R Layton's letter to Lord Cromwell, preſerved among Mr Dodſworth's MS collection in the Bodleian library "I ſend you "alſo our LADY'S GIRDLE of Bruton, red ſilke, a ſolemn relick, ſent to women in travail, Mary "Magdalen's *girdle*, which Matilda, the Empreſs, founder of Farley, gave with them, as ſayeth the "holy father of Farley"

† It is not uncommon to find leather preſerved in *tumuli*, eſpecially where it has laid near copper and other metals, but particularly the former The quality of the copperas which that metal emits by lying in the earth, will preſerve animal ſubſtances for ages Inſtances of this are frequently met with The Collection at Leiceſter houſe exhibits the hand of a man which gripes the *braſs* handle of a ſword, found in Chatham church yard, and the only part of the body preſerved See alſo Mr Whitehurſt's Antiquity of the Earth, where there is an account of a human body found in a copperas mine the man by accident fell into the pit, and, ſeventy years afterwards, the features of his face were very diſcernible, and the body in a perfect ſtate of preſervation

TUMULUS

Ld fc. in Aqua Tinta

TUMULUS VII. and VIII.*

THESE TUMULI have been diſcovered at remote diſtances from each other in this iſland, and which, by their analogy with Tumulus III. muſt produce ſome facts as to the date of their interment.

Fig

* It was my intention to have confined myſelf entirely to the deſcription of facts on the periodical publication of theſe ſheets, and to have couched my notes and other remarks under a methodical arrangement of obſervations, &c. in the bulk of the letter-preſs, which arrangement I mean ſtill to obſerve. Conſidering that time might elapſe before the publication would be finiſhed, I have thought proper to hazard ſome remarks, in hopes that freſh matter may ariſe to ſtrengthen my argument, and to encourage my antiquarian correſpondents to communicate their materials. I know, from ſad experience of the verſatility of human nature, how vehement men are, and have been, in crying out for matter of fact, as a ground work for their ſyſtems, as a ſtimulus to promote their enquiries. I have known, when they have acquired this long-ſought for treaſure, that poſſeſſion has ſuppreſſed their future labours, and the moſt valuable materials have been conſigned to the moſt wretched of all inheritance, ignorance and oblivion. From theſe ſentiments I have been induced to hazard my own thoughts, and to ſuffer my literary combinations on the ſubject to circulate as I advance in my work. This will alſo leſſen my future labour, and may poſſibly gratify the reader who is not diſguſted at the anticipation of his own conjectures: but, above all, the gloomy apprehenſion of the ſhortneſs of life, the recollection how few things within the natural ſcope of man's exiſtence can be collected on any given ſtudy, digeſted and aſſorted in ſuch a manner as may flatter the critical labours of an author, have impelled me to take advantage of a period of life beſt adapted for diligence, and a condition in human affairs perhaps not altogether ill calculated for the neceſſary aſſiduity

H

to

Fig. 1 *Iron umbo of a ſhield*, found at a ſand-pit near Aſh in Kent *, anno 1771 I received it from my much eſteemed friend, Mr Jacob, of Faverſham, with other tumuli relicks from the ſame place I believe it was not deterred with an eye to its poſition in the grave, but was accidentally thrown up by labourers in digging of ſand from the pit, which had ſerved the ſaid purpoſe ſeveral years; in the courſe of which, innumerable remains of ſepulchral relics were diſcovered; many of them have been preſerved by the activity of two or three neighbouring gentlemen †, but I lament that the far greater part, eſpecially thoſe of any value, and by which curious information might have been collected, ſuch as coins of gold and ſilver, and ornaments of dreſs of the ſame metal, have been conveyed to the melting-pot

The diameter of the UMBO rather exceeds ſix inches Its weight is 3[illegible] It is ornamented at the top with a *thin plate of ſilver*, on a ground of a mixed metal, compoſed of copper and calamine, riveted to the iron point Round the rim are five ſtuds of the ſame mixed metal, the heads thinly plated with ſilver, and which, penetrating the rim, ſerve as rivets into the wood to faſten it. Remains of wood are ſtill adhering to the ruſt, and by the grain they ſeem

to complete theſe kind of undertakings Theſe were the principal conſiderations which inclined me to circulate the materials of this work as they here make their appearance, detached, and in ſome reſpects fragmented Be it then my ſolicitude, when I have amaſſed the fragments, to methodize them, arrange the fitteſt of them for the literary ſtructure, and exhibit them, towards the concluſion of the work, under ſuch an aſpect as may invite the reader, pleaſed with theſe kind of ſtudies, to comprehend and regard the utility as well as the appearance of the edifice

* This ſpot has been conſidered as the burial place of the ſtation of Richborough, which lies at a few miles diſtance, the profuſion of relics, Roman coins, and other apparent remains of theſe people, found there, ſerved to confirm this belief in the minds of ſeveral well informed Antiquaries in that neighbourhood It was a natural conjecture, eſpecially as the ſtation of Richborough was a place of ſo much note in the Lower Empire, to which æra moſt of theſe relics ſeemed to apply But, without conſidering the unreaſonable diſtance for a place of interment, it being known the Romans buried the dead without the walls at a ſmall diſtance from them, it is to be obſerved, that a coin of the fine gold of Conſtantinople, of the Emperor Juſtinian, was found in a grave there, anno 1760, and now in the poſſeſſion of G Fauſſett, Eſq, of Heppington Juſtinian lived in the ſixth century, anno 530, and at this period the Saxons were in poſſeſſion of that part of the coaſt, and there remains little doubt but the walls of the ſtation were at that time dilapidated by them See Stukeley's thoughts on this ſubject, p 118 of his Itin Curioſ This is alſo confirmed by Gildas, who ſays, the cities or towns, from the weſtern to eaſtern coaſt of Britain, were burnt and laid waſte by the Saxons Be it alſo conſidered, at this period the Romans, that is, the legionary eſtabliſhment of them, which would have been ſtationed at Richborough, were effectually withdrawn from the iſland Were I to hazard my conjectures on the dilapidation of Richborough, I ſhould ſay, as there is no ſign whatever of any repair prior or ſubſequent to the firſt ruin of the walls, ſo the Saxons could not have conſidered it as a place of military or civil uſe, who muſt, on their ſubduction of the iſland, have been ſenſible of the value of mural faſtneſſes to defend themſelves in return againſt invaſions it therefore appears, that as Richborough, being one of the caſtles built by the Emperor Theodoſius, on the *Littus Saxonicum*, to defend the ſea coaſt from Saxon pirates, ſo the Saxons, to commit their depredations more freely, threw down the walls, which ſince that period appear to have been entirely deſerted, conſequently, we cannot reaſonably ſuppoſe, as no military or civil eſtabliſhment was then exiſting at Richborough, ſo, abſtracted from the diſtance, the burial place at Aſh could not have belonged to the ruined ſtation

† William Boys, Eſq, of Sandwich, a gentleman fond of theſe purſuits, and whoſe politeneſs very much contributed to my barrow reſearches in that neighbourhood, with the liberal ſpirit of a ſenſible Antiquary, collected aſſiduouſly many rare relics from Aſh, which would otherwiſe have been carried to the ſilver ſmith's furnace, and others of leſs value diſperſed It is from him I was favoured with the drawing of the ſpear, and a correct account of ſome other remains from that burial-place, and others in the neighbourhood, which will appear in a future paſſage of this work

The late Rev Bryant Fauſſett, of Heppington, collected many relics from Aſh, ſeveral fell into the hands of my friend Edward Jacob, Eſq, of Faverſham, and are now in my cabinet.

Towards the year 1773, in paſſing through Aſh, I obſerved ſome children looking with much eagerneſs among the ſand in the pit on enquiry, they told me they were picking up glaſs beads, ſeveral of which I received from them, and, by their direction, I found in the miller's houſe, ſituated cloſe to the pit, many remains of iron arms taken from thence, which, I find, were ſince procured from the mill by the Rev Mr Fauſſet About that period I remember preſenting Sir Aſhton Lever with the beads, and they are now in his late unfortunate Muſeum

to be of ash. The concavity is continued to the point, and does not exceed $\frac{1}{10}$ of an inch in thickness. When in its perfect state it must have exhibited a great accuracy and elegancy of workmanship Apparently it was hammered on a mould, afterwards polished to great lustre *, and used by the warrior more perhaps for ornament than actual use, unless it served, as the Erse poet has related, for the din of martial prowess before the troops engaged, when the warrior sounded his shield with the stroke of his arms †

Fig 2 and 3 HEADS OF IRON SPEARS ‡; the drawings the exact size. Fig. 3 found in the same pit at Ash, and at the same period as the *umbo*, and might possibly have been the companion to the umbo in the same grave

Fig 2. and 4 Found at Baggrave, in Leicestershire, on the estate of Dr. Burnaby, who did me the honour to place them in my collection, with various other fragments of arms, and some other sepulchral relics from the said place

* His *shining shield* is on his side like a flame on the heath at night, when the world is silent and dark Ossian, Book II

† He went and struck the *bossy shield* The hills and their rocks replied

Again,

Swaran struck his *bossy shield*, and called the son of Arno

And again,

The hero struck the *shield* of his alarms Ossian, Book I

Far be it from my thoughts to enter the lists of Mr Macpherson's friends or opponents, and to use my materials in this work as an apology for supporting either party I wish to be clear of any literary controversy, knowing too well how small and subtle is the pivot which turns the sincerity of mens' views, and the impartiality of their intentions, against their private comforts I shall, however, ingenuously assert, that, on repeated perusal of his poems, I have found a strong analogy in the descriptions of the funereal customs of the people whom the poems celebrate, with the actual discovery of antient remains taken from *tumuli*, as well as an infinite number of other facts that relate to the same, which convinces me that either Mr Macpherson must have been profound and curious in the history of the Celtic customs, or there can be no room left to doubt his having some materials to vouch for the authenticity of the poems in question

The sequel of this work will shew beyond a doubt that the small barrows found in clusters are to be attributed to the descendants of the Celtæ, whom Cæsar and Tacitus say first peopled Britain See lib v of the former, and lib 1 c 2 of the latter I shall only here remark, that the people who were buried under the small grassy tumuli found in clusters were evidently a lower people in comparison to the antient Britons, that their arms, the structure of their sepulchres, are similar in many respects to those described in Ossian that they are oftentimes concentered to antient Celtic interments, is as apparent in one small range I in part opened at St Margaret's, on the Cliff between Dover and Deal, where I found nearly in the center of the cluster a large antient Celtic barrow, which contained burnt bones, and to which the smaller ones were concentered On Salisbury-plain, near antient Celtic monuments, some few clusters have been found, particularly the groupe which Dr Stukeley mentions, one of which contained beads and other similar relics to those I have described, with this difference, the barrow contained an urn with burnt bones, an indication only that it exceeded a few years the date of those with the body inhumated As Christianity became more general, so burning the dead was disused or indeed, about this period, as I suspect, the Pagans were also, in common with the Christians, interdicted the use of burning the bodies of the dead

‡ Tacitus says (see his Vit Agric) the Britons were armed with *large and blunt swords* and *small bucklers* This doubtless precisely agrees with the swords and bucklers found in these *tumuli*, the arms of their descendants, three hundred years and upwards after his history was written But are not Barbarians chiefly armed after this manner? Procopius de Bell Goth in various places describes the Goths, and the swarm of the Northern nations, that made inroads into Spain, Italy, Africa, and indeed over almost the then discovered world, to be thus armed When Gildas mentions the targets, swords, and spears, which the Romans desired the Britons to arm themselves with, against the Picts and Scots, they were doubtless of the same kind as those I have described

The Romans who fought in a compact body after the Grecian system of tactics, applied the short mucronated sword to their military tactics, which favoured their close encounter The Barbarians, on the other hand, approached the enemy in a loose order, and trusted to the random cut of their front line, while the javelins or spears were often urged against the enemy in the second line, which kept the enemy at a distance Agricola encouraged the three Batavian and two Tungrian cohorts to close with the enemy who kept off the Romans by this kind of fighting Compare therefore, the sword, shield, and spear in [illegible] to this description of Tacitus, and the frequent allusions of Ossian to the same kind of arms, the people to whom they must be consequently assigned will most probably be established, and the period will naturally follow from the discovery of the coins

The

They are apparently the contents of the same *tumulus* The umbo, *fig* 4 has five rivets, which perforate the rim as in *fig* 1 The iron is of the same thickness decayed wood is also adhering to the interior part of the rim, the metal is not entirely corroded, as is the case with the umbo found at Ash, which I apprehend to arise from the difference of the soil The interment at Baggrave seems to have been made in a stiff marley soil, and the one at Ash in a loose dry sand. The latter, I have found by experience, will not preserve metal and other substances so long as the former The remains of human bones, and the relics buried with them, I have particularly noted at the Ash burial-place, have been nearly consumed, excepting now and then some of the teeth are discernable, the other parts of the body being entirely decomposed: whereas Dr Burnaby presented me with the under jaw of a young subject from Baggrave, which is in a perfect state of preservation

I have a perforated circular *bone ornament*, which served to receive the latchet of the dress, to compress the same to the body, from these tumuli, in the most perfect state The spear is also very little corroded in comparison to the iron arms found at Ash

I have mentioned these particulars, to shew that no deduction in point of age can be drawn from the recent qualities of the metal found in these sepulchres; seeing that the difference of soil operates a dissimilar state of preservation.

In the course of this work many ranges of *tumuli* will be produced, which contained arms precisely similar to those which I have described, and many that have been accidentally discovered in cultivated land The assemblage of these facts can be the only means of producing comparisons which render an argument of force, and conduce to the historical truths which depend on such discoveries. For further particulars see OBSERVATIONS, &c.

* See a corroboration of this circumstance, Pl. IX. which describes a *Tumulus* opened at Ash

TUMULUS

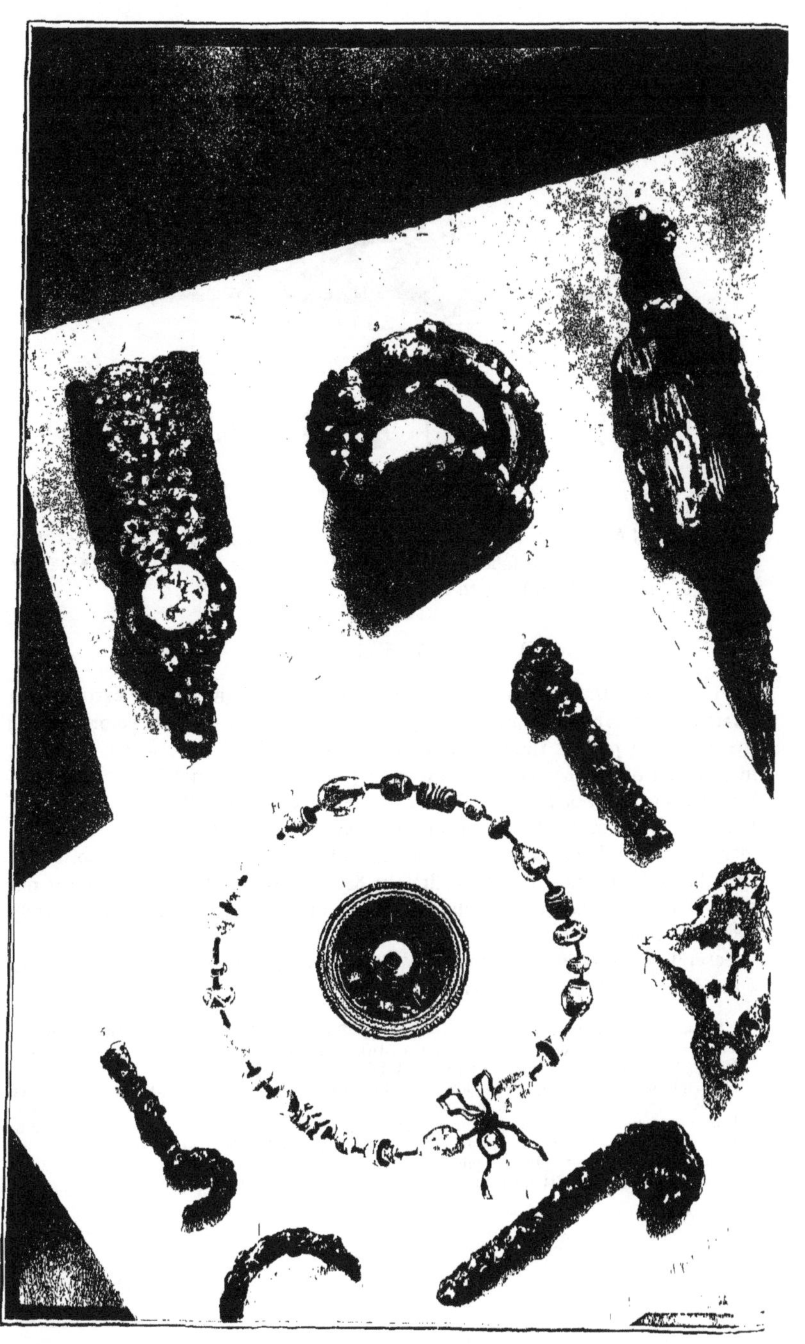

TUMULUS IX.

CHATHAM lines opened the 10th of August, 1782. The bones very large, the texture solid and well preserved. The cist less than three feet from the surface. The head to the North.

PLATE VIII. N° I.

Fig. 1. The fragment of an IRON BOW BRACE *. Towards the extremity, a BRASS circular cap of a pin, which perforates the iron; at the point a rivet; the projecting part of the pin shows the thickness of the bow, which could not in that part of the center have exceeded $\frac{3}{4}$ of an inch; unless the rivet had been let into the wood. The sides of the brace collapse to the thickness of the bow, and in the cavity the remains of the bow are very conspicuous. The fragment seems to have been about one half of the brace, and by its horizontal state shows the bow to have been straight before it was strung. The iron is not more than $\frac{1}{10}$ of an inch in thickness. Found on the left side of the body about the center.

Several arrow heads were found in these tumuli, which will be described in a future place. See OBSERVATIONS.

* "Raise, Oscar, rather raise my tomb ——————But, remember, my son, to place this sword, "*this bow*, and the horn of my deer, within that dark and narrow house, whose mark is one gray "stone." See Ossian, the poem of Fingal, Book IV.

The Laplanders, to this day, inter with the dead *their bow* and arrows, hatchets, swords, &c. which they conceive will be useful to them in a future state. See Keysler, p. 173, his Antiq. Sept. et Celtic.

This appears to have been the custom of most of the Northern nations from the earliest period of time. See the *[illegible]* c. v. Saxo lib. 8. where the antient Northern people threw money and other things of value into the funeral pile, as a certain means of conducting the dead to the sacred Valhalla, or the hall of the slain, where they believed their great deity Odin presided.

TUMULUS X.

CHATHAM Lines, Auguſt, 1782. The bones much conſumed; thoſe that remained ſhow the ſubject to have been an adult. The ciſt exceeded four feet in depth *.

No. I. Fig. 2. An IRON BOW BRACE †. The drawing of the exact ſize, and ſhews the concave part. When entire, to judge by the proportion, it muſt have exceeded 10 inches in length. The wood of the bow is ſtill preſerved in the inner part by the accreting quality of the ruſt; the grain ſeems extremely fine, the *brace* is perfectly horizontal. It ſhould ſeem the bow when unſtrung muſt have

* Experience in theſe purſuits has ſhewn, that the deeper the body has been interred, the more the bones have been periſhed.

† About the æra in which the remains of theſe people were interred, archery prevailed univerſally over Europe. The Alans, Vandals, Gepides, Huns, Burgundians, Herulians, Saxons, Angles, and Franks, all the Northern nations, whom the Romans called Barbarians, ſeem to have uſed the bow with the greateſt poſſible execution in war. This arm has ever been a natural defence for an uncivilized people againſt the diſciplined troops they have encountered. When the Roman legions, on the declenſion of the republic, loſt that order which they obſerved in their former wars, the bow ſeems to have been a weapon which they very much adopted in their arms. See Procopius de Bell. Goth. lib. ii. cap. i. deſcribing the bravery of Chorſomantus, who was by birth an Hun, and one of the moſt expert archers under Beliſarius. Againſt the Perſians, whoſe troops were chiefly compoſed of archers, with ſlender bows but little bent, Beliſarius alſo oppoſed archers whoſe bows were ſo ſtiffly ſtrung, that their arrows pierced the mail of the enemy, while the Perſian arrows recoiled from the Roman corſelets and helmets. See lib. i. cap. xiv. Many ſubſequent paſſages in this author concur to prove that the Roman army was recruited, or incorporated with the Barbarian tribes that had plunged into Italy, and that the legions admitted the arms with which their allies were beſt acquainted, eſpecially when the battles at this æra were chiefly of an excurſionary nature, the arms muſt have been ſuited to that mode of fighting. The legions had doubtleſs ſome remains of their old tactics left, with which they had ſhaken the moſt formidable empires of the world, but their diſcipline being impaired by the rapid changes in their government, their princes, their territories, the alarming inroads and conqueſts of their Northern enemies, left them no time for diſcipline. While the Eaſtern empire was ſecure, and perhaps well defended by veteran legions trained in their old ſchool of tactics, the Weſtern being ſhaken on all ſides, divided with internal domeſtic commotions, as well as external

have been ſtraight *. At the end of the *brace*, where ſome part of it is broke, there is an iron pin which penetrated into the wood as a rivet at the ſame diſtance from the center, there is a perforation which ſerved the ſame purpoſe, the pin being loſt Found towards the center of the ſkeleton, and in this, as in TUMULUS IX there was no appearance of any other iron whatever. See OBSERVATIONS.

external hoſtilities, their general was compelled to adopt the fitteſt and readieſt expedient againſt the enemy, and whatever allies from the Barbarian tribes he admitted among his troops, being more ſtubborn and leſs ſubject to a republican controul, they were, in times of ſuch imminent danger, permitted to uſe their own arms in war, and, doubtleſs, thoſe arms were oppoſed in the ſame order againſt their kindred clans, with whoſe ſkill in the offenſive and defenſive arts of fighting they were beſt acquainted Hence we find Beliſarius truſted the allies in the irregular excurſions of the field, while his better diſciplined legions waited the attack, which enſured them victory by their cloſe order, and their cloſe encounter Mr Gibbon, ſpeaking of the Roman auxiliaries, remarks, "that the far greater part "retained their arms, to which the nature of their country, or their early habits of life, more par-"ticularly adapted them By this inſtitution, each legion, to whom a certain proportion of auxiliaries "was allotted, contained within itſelf every ſpecies of lighter troops and of miſſile weapons" Though this paſſage evidently applies to the legions of the flouriſhing æra of the republic, it will ſerve to corroborate my teſtimony in the above inſtance Vegetius ſays, "That the Roman ſoldiers en-"countering the Goths, having no armour on their heads or bodies, were frequently entirely defeated "and ſlain by the great flight of their arrows" The argument, ſhowing the Romans to have adopted in the lower ages the uſe of bows and arrows, is fully confirmed by the emperor Leo, who, in his Military Inſtitutions, (ſee cap 6 ſect 5) commands all the Roman youth, till they arrive at forty years of age, to carry *bows and quivers of arrows* See alſo cap 11 ſect 49 where he enjoins the Romans, who are not called out to war, to *keep bows and arrows* in their houſes for careleſsneſs herein, he ſays, had occaſioned diſaſters to have befallen the Roman ſtate.

* Procopius, de Bell. Gothic lib 1 cap. XIV ſays, *the bows of the Romans were much bent, ſtiff and hard.*

TUMULUS

T U M U L U S   XI.

CHATHAM Lines, Auguſt, 1782. The bones large and well preſerved. The ciſt about three feet in depth.

Plate VIII Fig 3 Two of ſeveral detached *Iron rings* adhering to each other by the accretion of ruſt, and no appearance of their having been united in links like a chain Found near the center of the body in the center of the ciſt, and appear to have been buried with it, ſerving as relics, perhaps, adapted to a funereal cuſtom *, or worn perhaps on ſome part of the dreſs by the perſon when living; but which, as being found in a cluſter, could by no means have ſerved the uſes of iron rings to a coffin, cheſt, or any wooden apparatus depoſited with the body eſpecially as no wood was found accreted to the iron, which is obſerved to be generally the caſe where iron and wood have been buried near each other.

See OBSERVATIONS.

* Tacitus ſays, *De Moribus Germanorum*, Fortiſſimus quiſque *ferreum annulum*, ignominioſum id genti, velut vinculum geſtabat, donec ſe cæde hoſtis abſolveret

In the graves which contain the female ornaments ſmaller rings of iron very frequently occur See N° II fig 7

TUMULUS XII.

N° II.

ON Chatham Lines, opened September, 1779. The cist in which the body was deposited upwards of four feet in depth. The bones of a fine texture, and much perished. The head in a North direction.

Pl. VIII. fig. 1. A CIRCULAR ENCHASED FIBULA of silver gilt*, one and ¾ of inch in diameter, and $\frac{1}{7}$ of an inch in thickness. The center small stone is a garnet on a small chequered gold foil, surrounded with a silver chain, and enchased in a pearl, or a hard shining shell of a similar nature, which is also set with a silver corded chain; by handling, it appears to be detached from the pearl, and originally fastened with a metallic cement. Uniting to the center circle, which contains the pearl and the garnet, are three garnet stones, and in their intervals three others, all of which are enchased in a silver socket, on a chequered gold foil, projecting from the ground of the *fibula*, and described in the drawing by a darkish tint. The angular chain is similar to those described in Tumulus V. fig. 1. on the circular fibula, and on the long *fibula*, fig. 7. Pl. IV. It is wrought with considerable more uniformity and delicacy, than can be described in the engraving. It laid near the breast of the skeleton, and, before it was rubbed, the reverse near the iron acus, which received the robe, contained the accreted filaments with which the robe was composed. The silver is very pure, and the ornament seems to have been but little worn. The reverse contained an *iron vertical acus*.

* Pancirolus, in his *Notitia Dignitatum*, p. 36. under the head of *Notitia Insignium Viri Illustris Magistri* [illegible] describes the painted emblems or allegorical figures of the provinces, to be something similar to the above fibula, fig. 1. I have here extracted two of the figures with the description. See p. 36 and 37.

PRIMA FLAVIA GEMINA. Rubeum circum, rubeum [illegible] habuit, albo capite [illegible] [illegible] globum, duobus [illegible] circulis [illegible] cinctum.

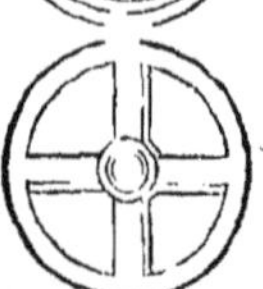

SECUNDA FLAVIA GEMINA. In primis luteum [illegible] umbilicum, duobus circulis, viridi luteoque cinctum habet, quem sæpe in viridis aggeres [illegible].

These [illegible] seem to have been adopted by Constantine in the East, who, flattering his ostentation of pomp, imitated the affected state of the Asiatic princes. Every order of the state was marked with the most scrupulous exactness (see Gibbon, p. [illegible]), and its dignity displayed in a variety of trifling and solemn ceremonies. The codicils or patents of the principal officers of the empire were curiously emblazoned with emblems adapted to explain the nature and high dignity of their office; the images or portraits of the reigning emperors, a triumphal car, the book of mandates placed on a

Fig 2 TWENTY FIVE BEADS *. The oval beads are pale and clear native amathysts †. Those in the form of a barrel are of a red vitrified earth the longitudinal are of rayed opaque red and white glafs with a lucid ray, which, by laying in the earth, has acquired the armatura to fo beautiful a degree, as to produce a variety of burnifhed gold tints, varying as often as the beads are moved, the fmaller are of amber, the three beads with convoluted ftripes are of red opaque glafs, and the ftripes yellow Found near the head of the fkeleton.

Fig. 3 A fmall GOLD PENSILE ornament ‡, enchafed with a very clear native hyacinth The loop fimilar to the loop of the penfile ornaments, Pl V N° I fig 2 and 6. and to the one that was fold in Mr Duane's fale, found in a barrow The gold is pale and feems adulterated Found with the beads

Fig 4 One of two BRASS perforated trinkets: the metal extremely thin; they feem to have been part of the bead attire

Fig 5 and 5. FRAGMENTS OF IRON; feveral of which in the fhape of hooks, and a great quantity of other fragments of the fame metal of the fame fize, lay near the center of the grave fome were interlaced with fmall rings, others adhering together in fmall laminæ, but in fuch order as to hinder the admiffion of any tolerable conjecture on their ufe

Fig 6 IRON fragment of the above appendage.

Fig 7 Fragment of an IRON RING

Fig 8 PART OF THE UPPER JAW, which exhibits a tooth not grown out of the focket; and which was here delineated to prove the remains of the body to have been of a young fubject.

Several fhards or pebbles, by no means the produce of the chalk in which thefe bones were interred, appeared in feveral places of the cift

For further particulars, see OBSERVATIONS

* Female ornaments of this nature have been worn from the earlieft antiquity by the moft favage as well as the moft polifhed people The favages of the uncivilized continent wear them to this day, and we want no vouchers to prove that the moderns are equally pleafed with fuch decorations. The marbles, medals, and other remains of the GREEKS, exhibit their ladies adorned with them Their writings are alfo fcattered with relations of this cuftom

Καὶ ταινίη δ' μαζῶ,
Καὶ μαργάρῳ τραχήλων.

ANAKP ᾠδ [illegible]

The Romans, who imitated thefe fublime and ingenious people in their virtues as well as their foibles, feem equally attached to thefe ornaments Pliny, lib 35 c 3 fpeaks of the magnificence of the ladies in this refpect Plautus, in the first fcene of Truculentus, hints at this kind of attire See alfo Horace, 1 Ep xvii 55

Nota refert meretricis acumina, fæpe catellam,
Sæpe periscelidem raptam fibi flentis ———

Ovid is particularly explicit on gems with which the Roman ladies were decorated, as alfo moft of the Latin poets but it is to the writers of the lower ages we muft defcend for a comparative defcription of thefe riches, then in which they were interred with the dead

The ancient fathers of the church inveighed moft bitterly againft the extravagant ufe of thefe ornaments in their days Tertullian de Cult Fam lib. 1 c 6 p 153, fays, many thoufand pounds, *decies feftercium*, were expended on a ftring of pearls: and is very fevere with the [illegible] for indulging this luxury Clemens Alexandrinus, Pedag lib iii c 2 p 219, pours down a heavy denunciation on this fafhion he fays, women are fo extravagant in thefe purfuits, that Syrian, Indian, or Ethiopian treafures, or the golden ftreams of Pactolus, cannot fatisfy their vanity St Cyprian, de Difcipl et Habit Virgin p 161 fays, it is a great crime for virgins to adorn themfelves with gold and gems; but fays, that fire, crofs, fwords, or wild beafts, are the precious jewels of the flefh, and better ornaments of the body, and which are to be preferred to thofe which attract the eyes of young men, and inflame their paffion St Peter fays (vid Conftit Apoft lib 1 c 3 p 804), that a virgin excites by this kind of wanton and lafcivious drefs unchafte defires in the other fex Tert de Cultu Fœminarum, lib 2 c 4 fays, proftitutes were chiefly adorned with precious ftones, pearls, and golden ornaments Clemens Alexandrinus, in his Pedag lib iii c 11 p 245 inveighing againft this female luxury of wearing gold, filver, amber, and jewels, as ornaments, gives us to underftand that *[illegible]* or *[illegible]* chiefly produced them St Gregory Nazianzen, in Laud Gorgoniæ, Or [illegible] p 181 extols his fifter to the higheft degree for her fimplicity "fhe ufed," he exclaims, "no *gold* to adorn herfelf, no "*yellow hair*, tied in knots and arranged with curls, no tranfparent garments, *brilliant ftones, or jewels*," &c

† See Pliny's Nat Hift lib xxxvii cap ix where they are called the *gems of Venus* He fays, they are found in India in the part of Arabia, which lies near Syria, in the leffer Armenia, Egypt, and in Gaul The ancients pretended they had the power of preventing the ill effects of wine

‡ See Pliny ib who accurately defcribe this gem when they are clean, he fays, they are ufually fet in a loop of gold, which adds to their luftre

TUMULUS

1
2
3
4
5
6

TUMULUS XIII.

ASH, the 7th of May, 1783. The tumuli at this place, as I have before remarked, are ſituated on a ſandy ſoil. The range has been broken into for many years in digging of ſand, and which now preſents the appearance as deſcribed in the *vignette*.

A. The *level of the ground*, which is now a ploughed field.

B. *The depth which the interments are generally diſcovered*, and where I diſcovered ſeveral about four feet from the upper coating of the ſoil: they ſometimes are found at a leſs, and ſometimes at a greater depth †.

C. The *lower mill*, which ſtands on the level A. and to the right of which Tum. XIII. was opened ‡.

D. The *higher mill*, which is ſituated on the fore ground, and which ſtands on an eminence ‖.

E. The arena of the ſand-pit, which has been excavated.

F. The entrance of the ſand-pit.

This Tumulus was ſituated between the lower Mill C, and the higher mill D. The bones were in ſome reſpects perceptible, but crumbled away on the touch.

Pl. IX. Fig. 1. *Seventeen* of THIRTY THREE beads, towards the weſt end of the grave near the head. *Eleven amethyſts*, expreſſed in the drawing in an oval ſhape of the ſame ſize, and of a deep purple tint; *nine* of an orange-coloured vitrified earth, expreſſed in the drawing in the ſhape of a barrel; *four* of white glaſs, and in the ſhape of a barrel; *one* of a reddiſh brown opaque glaſs; *two* of a verditer tranſparent glaſs, approaching to a blue colour, in the ſhape of a barrel; *one* of an *opaque yellow glaſs*, ſmall and round; *one* of an *opaque grey glaſs*, ſmall

* See the note to Tum.

† I have often obſerved in the native ſand a blackiſh ſtratum of ſoil about a line in breadth, at the depth above deſcribed, and this has been always the ſure indication of an interment.

‡ At a ſmall diſtance from this mill, near the ſand pit, I opened a trench, and, diſcovering marks of a factitious earth in the native ſand, was fortunate enough to open a grave with much care and order. It produced the boſs of *a ſhield, ſpear head, knife*, and a *veſſel* of grey earth, in ſhape ſimilar to Fig. 5. of Plate I.

‖ Near to the baſe of D, at the diſtance of twelve feet from the mill, I cauſed a deep and long trench to be ſunk, conceiving the mill to have ſtood near the center of this range of *tumuli*; but I was not ſo fortunate as to meet with a grave. Behind this mill there are ſome gardens, one of them is bounded by the ſand pit, cloſe to which ſome magnificent relics had been from time to time diſcovered in digging ſand; this cauſed me to open a trench in the garden for a conſiderable length down to the native ſand, but without ſucceſs. I have made this obſervation for the guide of ſucceeding antiquaries, who may be inclined to explore this ſpot with more leiſure and perſeverance than I could poſſibly undertake.

and round, *one* of a *reddish* brown opaque glass, small and round, *one* of a *deep blue transparent glass*, small and round, *one* of a rayed light blue transparent glass, small and round, one of a circular flat deep-coloured amber, and so expressed in the drawing The whole, when strung, forms a diameter of about five inches, which will naturally correspond to the circle for the human neck, and therefore admits of the supposition that the beads were used for a necklace.

By comparing the nature of the beads found in this tumulus, with those found at Chatham, Tum XII. N° II. fig. 2. the greatest possible similitude will be found

Fig 2 CIRCULAR FIBULA*, inlaid with *garnets*, ivory, and gold, two and not quite $\frac{3}{8}$ inches diameter, about $\frac{1}{10}$ of an inch in thickness. The ground appears to have been a soder, composed of silver and some other metallic matter. On handling the gem, it fell to pieces, owing to the perishable substance of the metal, and to the nature of the soil, which at Ash is found to be remarkably incongenial for the preservation of relics As this fibula might have been mutilated by handling to such a degree as not to admit of a faithful representation, I designed it on the spot, and with the greatest accuracy, while its parts were discernible, I produced the annexed drawing The metallic substance which composed the ground † was worked with astonishing neatness The light circles were very thin plates of gold milled upon the soder, the parallelogramical small stones between the second and third small white circles from the rim were of garnet, on a gold chequered foil, similar to the foil of the *fibula*, fig 1 of Plate VIII, between each garnet a small silver partition The small hemispheres appear to have been ivory, and were almost perished, alternatively enchased between the hemispheres were *garnets* on a chequered gold foil; on each side of which was a raised ornament in the form of an S in gold milling, the first light center circle is a silver projecting *umbo*, which is set with ivory, and ornamented with a corded ring of the same metal The drawing the exact size

The reverse the same as the circular fibula before described, with this difference, the *acus* appears to have been silver instead of iron Some small portion of fine linen cloth was accreted to the soder of the jewel The *fibula* was found in the center of the beads, and appears to have been connected with the said ornament in the female attire

Fig 3 A FRAGMENT OF IRON the metal quite perished.

Fig 4 A KNIFE the metal of iron; entirely corroded and covered with the remains of wood, the indication of its having been deposited with its sheath Impressions of coarse cloth in the rust.

Fig 5 FRAGMENT OF CORRODED IRON, with impressions of coarse cloth.

Fig 6 A VESSEL of dark grey earth, slightly baked, 3, inches diameter at the mouth, about five inches in the belly part, and 5, in height. Found at the feet of the skeleton

For further particulars, see OBSERVATIONS on Tum XIII

* H Godfrey Faussett, Esq, of Heppington, near Canterbury, has favoured me with a drawing of a circular *fibula*, from his cabinet, found in a range of the smaller *tumuli* in the county of Kent, very similar to the one here described The composition is silver very strongly gilt.

The *fibula*, found in a barrow in Derbyshire, and described in the third volume of the Archaeologia by Mr Mander of Bakewell in that county, is of the same class Having had the pleasure of a correspondence with Hayman Rooke, Esq, of Woodhouse Place, Nottinghamshire, whose taste for these pursuits led him to visit this part of Derbyshire, I directed my enquiries to him on the subject of this *fibula* Mr Rooke being acquainted with Mr Mander, and knowing the situation of the place where the relic in question was found, was so obliging, to transmit me further particulars, which confirmed my opinion, that the *fibula* was the produce of a lower British barrow, and interred about the same era as those of fig 1 Pl VIII and fig 2 Pl IX I am here happy to have it in my power to acknowledge the curious information which Mr Rooke has been pleased to transmit me on the subject of our British antiquities, and to express my thanks for the services which I have received from his authentic materials In a future passage of this work I hope to detail upon them with much delight

† I assay'd some of the soder, and found it contain a proportion of silver

TUMULUS

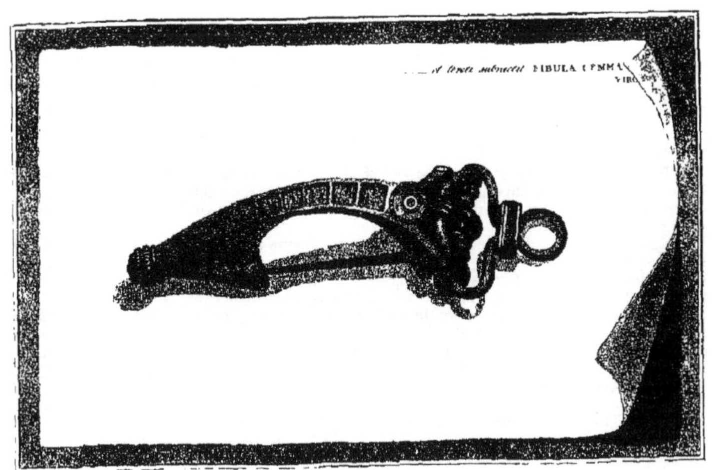

TUMULUS XIV.

I am favoured with the drawings of the magnificent relics found in this *Tumulus* by H. G. Fauſſett, Eſq. of Heppington, near Canterbury, who inherits from his father, the late Rev. Bryant Fauſſett*, a fine collection of ſepulchral remains†, and I may, without any accuſation of flattery, ſay, that the ſon is poſſeſſed of a knowledge and taſte in the ſtudy of the antiquities of this country to render himſelf worthy of ſuch inheritance.

* The late Rev. B. Fauſſett acquired the name of our Britiſh Montfaucon, a title which implies a reſpectful homage due to his diligent and learned enquiries into the antiquities of this country. If his life had been ſpared, and he leſs afflicted with bodily infirmities, he might probably have favoured the world with the reſult of his labours in his ſtudy. I preſume to ſay, if he had done this, he would not have handed his name down to poſterity by a vaſt *amas* of confuſed antique remains as we ſee in Pere Montfaucon, but have concentered a great collection of facts for the advantage of literature, and a more clear expoſition of the antiquities of this country than has been hitherto eſtabliſhed.

† His collection conſiſts of tumuli relics diſcovered chiefly in Kent, and which were elaborately explored; many ſepulchral urns from [illegible] or Long Port Downs, near Canterbury, in Kent, a Roman *burial place*, and which, by a manuſcript in the poſſeſſion of the late Heneage Finch, of [illegible], Earl of Wincheſter, was firſt diſcovered about the year 1703. His Lordſhip opened a few of the interments which were finally and wholly explored by Mr. Fauſſett. The other part of his tumuli collection conſiſts chiefly of the contents of [illegible] found in cluſters ſimilar to the ſpecimens which I have here deſcribed, and to which he had prepared a deſcription neatly drawn up in manuſcript. Beſides a collection of medals, which he had diligently and choicely ſelected at a great expence, and in which he was uncommonly ſkilled, he beſtowed much labour on the eccleſiaſtical hiſtory and genealogical records of families in Kent, which, [illegible] to the beſt of claſſical learning, accompliſhed him for an excellent antiquary. Theſe particulars I have taken the liberty to record, leſt accident, or the many [illegible] of life, ſhould conceal the name and abilities of a learned and diligent Antiquary from public memory.

This Tumulus was opened at Kingston, on Barham Downs*, near Canterbury, anno 1771, by the late Rev Bryant Faussett, of Heppington, in that neighbourhood

The

* It formed one with the groupe at the end of the race-course, to the left of the high road to Dover, the Old Watling Street, or *Via Originaria*, as you ascend the hill from Bridge departing from Canterbury *Three hundred* of them were opened by the above antiquary The bodies chiefly lay in an east and west direction

Barham Down or Barham doune, in the Saxon, according to Lambard (see his Peramb of Kent), is derived from the *hill where bears frequented* As this appears to be rather a *wild* derivation, I shall take the liberty to offer one that is more appofite and consistent with the nature of the place The soil of the Down is chalk, and appears to have been always barren of trees, or the necessary harbour for this kind of animals, and as there are great numbers of *tumuli*, or *barrows*, on it, so the Saxons have prefixed the name Byrgen to the Downs, *Burgham*, or *Burham*, as it has been variously written, as being a place where the dead were interred Burg, Berg, Berig, Beorg, the Saxon for *town*, *city*, *hill*, or *barrow* See Spelman Hinc etiam byrgen *sepulchrum*, et byrigean *sepelire*, quod aggesto in collem cespite olim tumulabant mortuos, ut per agros hodie cernimus This is to be observed in the most conspicuous places on the Downs, and which doubtless must have caused the name of *Burham*, or *Barham*, to be prefixed to them, especially as these grassy *tumuli* were evidently raised antecedent to the effectual conquest of this island by the Saxons, when these people began to change the names of British as well as Roman places, and to give names to others The adjoining village of Barham may have had its name from the Downs Philipot, Vil Cant p 60 writes it *Barham*, Kilburn, *Barban*, and *Berclam*

These burial places have been described by *some modern* writers as tumuli raised over the soldiers who fell under Julius Cæsar See Mr Packe's Map of the Country round Canterbury, and *Gostling's Walk in and about the City of Canterbury*, p 5, where they are called Burying-places of the *Old Romans*, thereby implying, the Romans on their first arrival in Britain It has been from the want of proper information on the nature of the discoveries made in these tumuli, that other antiquaries, as well as the gentleman above cited, have been misled on the subject of Cæsar's march from his fleet on the second *progress* he made in Britain, as well as then being mistaken in the æra, and in the people to whom such interments should be ascribed it being premised, that Cæsar on his first march advanced twelve miles in the night when he discovered the Britons See his Commentaries, lib v § viii Illi equitatu atque essedis ad flumen progressi, ex loco superiore nostros prohibere et prælium committere cœperunt which implies, that the Britons had taken post on the high ground, and that the Romans were in the vale on the banks of the river, which I conceive, without a doubt, to have been the *Stour* From this attack the Britons were repulsed, and pursued to their strong hold, egregie et natura et opera munitum, where they made a stand, and which being forced, Cæsar would not permit his men to pursue the Britons, being unacquainted with the country, and, like a prudent general, desirous of securing a post, to which, in case of defeat, he could make a retreat, he assigns this reason Et quod magna parte diei consumptâ munitioni castrorum tempus relinqui volebat This, therefore, was Cæsar's first position in the valley after his twelve miles march, and which kind of position the Romans generally took on their marches in a war of attack, as well for a supply of water, as to sally forth with their legions on the plain, and for the manœuvres of their cavalry, in case of any temporary repulse, to their camp Cæsar's post must not therefore be supposed to have been on the high ground of Burham Downs, where some antiquaries conceive they have discovered the remains of his encampment Cæsar, hearing of the disaster which happened to his fleet, returns to it, and, after ten days absence, proceeds to his inland camp, which was not yet finished, and, to justify my argument on the nature of this encampment, as being raised for a post from which he planned his offensive operations on the high grounds commanded by the Britons, so we find his cavalry were advancing to the enemy when they were attacked, and suffered some loss Soon after, the Britons, though driven back to the woods and high grounds, made a fresh attack on the Romans employed on their fortifications, and who suffered some loss, the Britons having cut their way through and retreated with safety Per medios audacissime proruperunt, seque inde incolumes receperunt Hence this defeat gave rise for the conjecture, that Cæsar buried his men on *Barham Downs*, and which idea was also transferred to Chartham Downs by Dr Mortimer, where another similar range of *tumuli* had been discovered, and which I have before cited

This short digression, I trust, will clearly point out Cæsar's encampment to have been on the banks of the Stour, and not on the high grounds of Barham Downs, and the relics discovered in the *tumuli*, compared with similar ones found in others of the same structure, with coins of the very lowest of the empire, such as *Tl Julius*, *Constantius*, *Valentinianus*, *Anthemius*, *Justinianus*, &c will doubtless establish the period of these interments It should here be remarked, that the *agger*, or ridge of earth, thrown up at some little distance from these tumuli, and which has been called the remains of Cæsar's camp, is apparently of a less antient date At one end, near a road which traverses it, I dug a little into the base of the bank, and, on coming to the native chalk, I found the bones of a child, incisted in clay or loam, no unusual mode of interment in the above æra of the lower ages Mr Faussett, as well as myself, have had occasion to remark a deposit of clay near these tumuli, from

which

Pl. 10

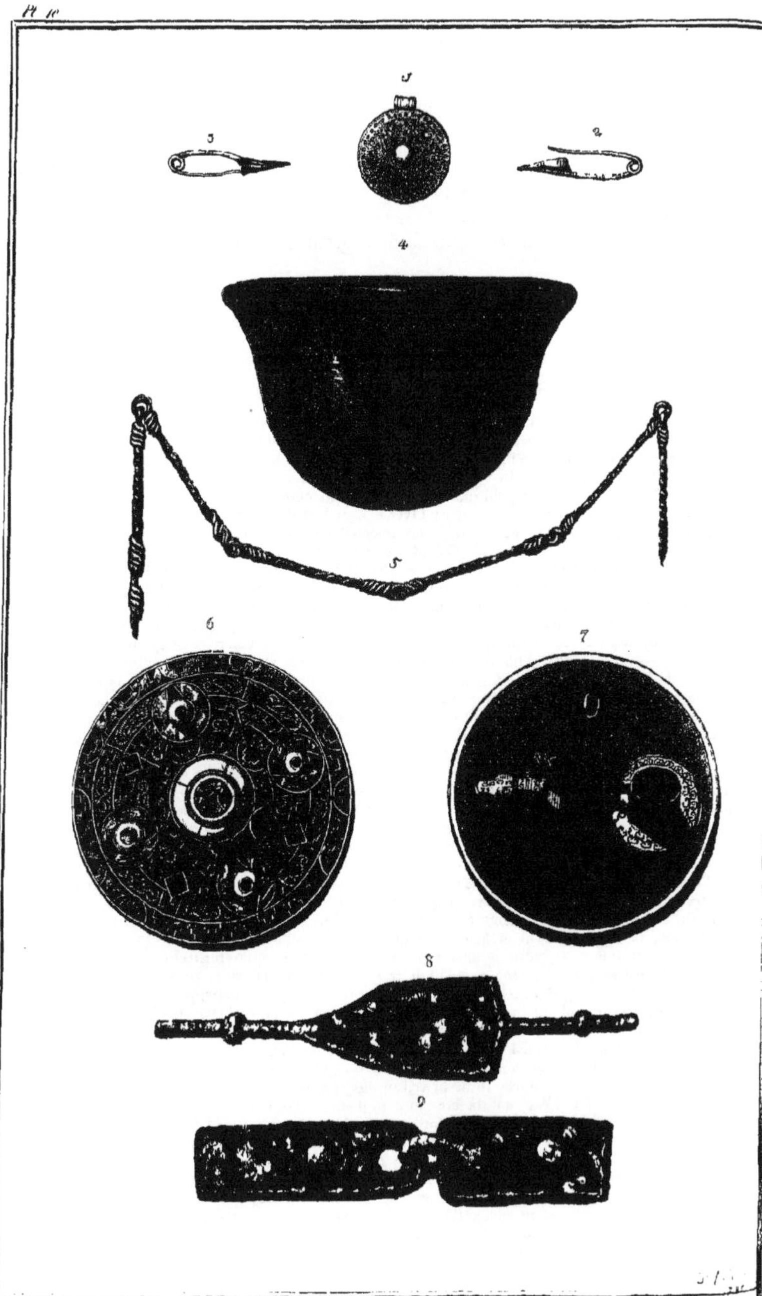

The cone larger than the medium ſize, which, in p. 1. of this work, are deſcribed to be about 23 feet in diameter. The apex very much compreſſed, probably occaſioned by the capacity of the ciſt, which in depth exceeded *ſix*, in length *ten*, and in breadth *eight* feet. There ſeemed to be the appearance of a coffin much burnt or ſcorched, very thick, and ſecured at the corners with large claſps, and rivetted pieces of iron. The *bones* much decayed; the *ſcull* remarkably ſmall.

Pl. X. Fig. 1. A Pendant Ornament of fine gold, 1[illegible] of an inch in diameter, weight 2 pennyweights and 7 grains, found near the neck of the ſkeleton.

Fig. 2 and 3. Two small fibulæ, near the bone of the left thigh.

Fig. 4. A Glass Vessel, or Patera*, 4½ inches diameter, and 2[illegible] in depth, of

which a portion of it was taken to ſheet the ciſt of the grave, and which ſerved, as I apprehend, the purpoſes of a coffin.

King John, on his baſe humility to the pope, muſtered a large army on *Barham Downs*, as alſo Simon Mountfort Earl of Leiceſter (ſee Lambard, p. 273), againſt Henry III., which armies may have cauſed ſome military works to have been thrown up. As the Earl ſeemed to apprehend an attack, on the ſide of the King's party, by Queen Eleanor, who appears by hiſtory to have prepared a defenſive poſt on the Downs, I ſhould therefore attribute this raiſed ground to the latter army.

Near Broom, the reſidence of Sir Henry Oxenden, at a ſmall diſtance from this group of barrows, is a ſmaller one, conſiſting of about *fifty*. My interceſſions could not prevail on Sir Henry to forego a pious veneration which he and Lady Oxenden entertained for the aſhes of the antients. A ſpirit of enquiry of this nature inclined Dr. Battely to adviſe all antiquaries to ranſack theſe ſepulchral depoſits; and, to apologize for the trouble I have given the Baronet on this occaſion, I muſt ſay, that ſince I firſt found ſuch remains were unexplored on his eſtate, this ſpirit has ever been reſtleſs within me. I confeſs with Browne, in his Hydriotaphia, "to be gnawed out of our graves, to have our ſculls made drink-"ing bowls, and our bones turned into pipes, to delight and ſport our enemies, are tragical abomi-"nations."—but,—"He that hath the aſhes of his friend, hath an everlaſting treaſure." Wherefore, had the hoſpitable Baronet, of Broom, permitted my antiquarian ſpirit to have been appeaſed by the opening of theſe barrows, no *drinking bowls*, no *tobacco-pipes*, would have been made of their contents, no abominations of this nature would have been committed on them. On the contrary, had he deſired they ſhould have been made, as the above learned old writer ſays, *everlaſting treaſures*, I would have placed them in my cabinet, a more honourable and comfortable ſecurity for rotten bones than a bleak cold heath, expoſed perhaps, when time ſhall ſo order it that the worthy guardian of their duſt ſhall be mouldering in his own ſepulchre, to ſome ignorant and incautious *virtuoſo*, leſs ſcrupulous than I ſhould have been in committing them piouſly to their own interments again, having firſt diveſted them of a little ſuperfluous treaſure, in which the dead could find neither profit nor delight; for if we believe Ulpian, l. 14. D. De Relig. et ſumpt. "Non autem oportet ornamenta cum cor-"poribus condi, nec quid aliud hujuſmodi quod homines ſimpliciores faciunt."

The following extract relates to a *Tumulus* opened on Barham Downs, which I apprehend to be an exaggerated account of the contents of one of theſe ſmall barrows. "Henrici noſtri temporibus, "paucis elapſis annis, ex frequenti paſtorio ſomnio eidem Regi indicato, ab eodem imperatum eſſe "recordor, ut agger quidam inuſitatæ magnitudinis Barhamdune effoderetur. Quod cum impenſis "Chriſtophori Halesii equeſtris ordinis viri, et ſacrorum ſcriniorum præfecti, cura vero Gulielmi "Diggeſii generoſi, fieret, ſub incredibili terræ acervo *ingens urna, cinere oſſibuſque maximorum "fragmentis plena, cum galeis ac cupreis* [illegible] *et ferreis* rubigine pene conſumptis, eruta eſt, ſed nulla "inſcriptio, nomen nullum aut teſtimonium tempus aut fortunam exponebat." Twine de Rebus Albionicis, lib. 2. p. [illegible]. It has all the air of deception and exaggeration.

* The faſhion of this veſſel muſt ſhew the intent of its uſe, that it was deſigned for ſepulchral and not domeſtic uſes. The ſepulchral veſſels of the antients being rounded at the bottom, as is the caſe with *urns*, having no baſe to be placed upright on, is not uncommon. See the analogy of this *cup* with fig. 5 of Plate IV., and the note to it in p. 1[illegible], alſo a more perfect one in Plate XII. fig. 13. found in ſimilar *barrows* in different places. I am therefore ſtill firm of opinion, that they contained a luſtral water which the antients believed would preſerve the *manes* from any future ſpell or incantation to diſturb them. Propertius, in the firſt elegy of his fourth book already cited, is not the only antient poet who mentions this cuſtom; we find it deſcribed by ſeveral of the Roman poets. See Lucan, lib. 6. of the ſpells of the Emonian Witch, Erictho, beſtowed on the dead body ſhe raiſed to life, and to which ſhe promiſes charms to ſecure it from any future incantation.

——— *tali tua membra ſepulcro,*
Talibus exuram Stygio cum carmine ſylvis
Ut *nullos cantata magos exaudiat umbra.*

Si

of a greenish colour, and beautifully coated with the *armatura*, which it has acquired by laying a length of time in the earth. Found, as I apprehend from Mr. Faussett's description, at the foot of the grave.

Fig. 5. SIX LINKS of an *iron chain**, *twenty* in number, and each link two inches long: near the foot of the grave.

Sit tanti vixisse iterum: nec *verba*, nec *herbæ*
Audebunt longe somnum tibi solvere Lethes,
A me morte data. Eiz. Edit.

Also where she is described to have the power of tormenting the *manes*

——— per busta sequar, per funera custos
Expellam tumulis, abigam vos omnibus urnis.

This poet in the same book has another passage on the subject. See Tibullus, lib. 1. Eleg. 2.

Hæc cantu finditque solum, manesque sepulcris
Elicit et tepido devocat ossa rogo.

See also Prudentius lib. 1. contra Symmachum de Mercurio.

The Romans had laws as well as enchantments to hinder the violation of their ashes. See Kirchman, C. XXIII. De Contrectatione loquitur L. 4. C. Sep. Viol. jubens x pondo auri fisco inferre eos *qui corpora sepulta aut reliquias contrectaverint*. See also Seneca, lib. 4. Controv. 4. Sepulcri violati sit actio. The Cod. Theodos. tit. 5. de Sepult. Paulus, lib. 11. D. de Sep. viol. & Ulpian l. g. 3. § 7.

Magical enchantments to disturb the manes are also mentioned by Quintilian in his *Declamat.* 15. Apuleius libro 2. Miles. & lib. 3. in descriptione Magicæ Officinæ. Statius, lib. 4. Thebaid. Various other antient writers mention the same.

Cæsar says, lib. VI. the Gauls were accustomed to cast into the fire the things which the dead delighted in when alive. "Omnia quævis cordi fuisse arbitrantur in ignem inferunt." And hence, it may be concluded, these vessels might be applied to domestic as well as sepulchral uses. Possibly they might have been so used. But when we know the antients, even the Christians, as well as the Pagans, were much given to the superstitious use of exorcism and incantation, and when we find relics evidently appropriated to magical ceremonies, as in the instance of the CRYSTAL BALL, fig. 8. pl. 4; the SPOON, fig. 9. pl. 2, can we have any reason to doubt the truth of this observation, "Manes temerare sepultos?" and especially when they are the remains of a people which consecutive facts will show were highly devoted to these superstitious rites, and to Druidical ceremonies, which were still exercised for many ages after Christianity, even when the Christian religion in many places and particularly in Gaul, became general? See Concil. Nantenens. Labbe, Tom. IX. p. 474, the ceremonies of which (see p. 956 of the above work) were in Gaul commanded to be suppressed by the order of this council. This idea of the body being disturbed after death has been handed down to the lowest ages of Pagan superstition, and in many instances is found to prevail among the Roman Catholics to this day. What is their Requiem, their peace to departed souls, the aspersions of holy water bestowed on the dead, and the suffumigations which we read of in monkish writings, but relics of these mysteries?

* I am far from attempting in this place to wrest an argument to any favourite point, nor does it follow, as having before remarked that several relics found in these *tumuli* are of mystic or magical significancy, that I now see with mystic or magical eyes such virtues in every relic before me. I shall, however, beg of the reader to suspend his judgement, till, from an assemblage of facts, he is more enabled to pronounce on the truth of these remarks, and proceed to shew, that fig. 8 has a right to claim some relation to such superstitious ceremonies of the ancients in their interments. Twenty of the *links* as above described in the above *fac simile* drawing of the chain will more than suffice to encircle the human body of the largest dimensions; to what purpose, therefore, could this *chain* have been applied, but to some mystic purpose by the wearer? Women have been supposed to be more easily deceived into these rites than the men (see Wecker de Secretis, p. 518). Strabo says, Geogr. lib. 7. that the Druidesses, whom he calls Fatidicæ, had white gowns, linen cloaks joined *together by clasps* (see fig. 6 and 7. pl. X.) *girdles of brass work* (see a *brass* girdle which I have described in pl. VI.) and which, though descriptive of the dress of a Druidess in the higher times of antiquity, may, notwithstanding, relate to the lower. Tacitus says, the Germans, in reverence to the sacred grove of their druid worship, wore, out of humility, and a confession of their deity's power, a kind of *fetter*, or shackle, about the leg. See fig. 3. pl. VIII. where links of an iron chain were found in a *tumulus*. Lucan, lib. III. says, the priests themselves trembled on these solemn occasions, and doubtless had some symbol of their humility about them. See Borlase, ch. xviii. p. 119. from Alex. ab Alexand. p. 153. where the Britons initiated their women into their religious mysteries, and also Ch. IX. the female druids of Gaul, who were married and brought up children, and entered into the domestic cares of life. That the Britons, in the age I am alluding to, had the same rites as the Gauls, there can be no doubt, and, without entering further into a dissertation on female druidism, where so many materials are at hand to prove, I shall close this note with observing from the above comparative facts, that this *chain* or *shackle*, might have been worn by the female interred in this tumulus on some solemn religious ceremony, and which most probably answered the purpose of the fetter, or shackle, described by Tacitus, affixed to the leg, but in this case also fastened to the waist, and to which purpose, by its proportional length, it seems perfectly to answer.

Fig. 6

Fig 6 A Gold Fibula*, elegantly enchafed The ftones within the femicircles of the outward circles are *garnet* and pale blue *tourquoife* The ftone, like

* As various opinions might be entertained refpecting the part of the drefs to which thefe circular *fibulæ* fhould be applied, to afcertain this, I have here given the reprefentation of an antient buft of Queen Ultragotha, wife of King Childebert, on the Old Tower of St Germain of the Meadows in Paris The church was built anno 546, by Childerbert (fee Montfaucon) From the proportion which the *fibula* under the neck of the Queen has to the buft, we may conclude it to have been of the fize of fig 6 and which perfectly agrees with the pofition where it was found in the tumulus It feems, therefore, to have been connected with the fuperior part of the *tunicula*, or under garment, which may be noted in the buft of the Queen, and which appears to have been bordered with jewels The date of this church will agree with the coin of Juftinian found at Afh the reign of this Emperor being in 530, the difference will be only 16 years, therefore, as the contents of the tumuli at Afh (fee pl IX and pl. XII) are evidently fimilar to plate X, we are permitted to eftablifh a coeval date of interments, efpecially as it naturally follows, that the relics in pl XII may have been depofited fome years after Juftinian's reign In a future paffage of this work, fome account will be given of a gold Coin of Clovis, found with other relics in a barrow of this clafs, and other proofs that will effectually eftablifh the period of interment the fame as above defcribed Many bufts of the Emperors fhow the Sigum and Paludamentum connected with a fibula (fee Octavius Ferrarius De Re Veftiari, p 30, where the ufe of fibulæ are defcribed) In the lower empire the ufe of thefe decorations appears to have been more common than in the higher, if we may judge by the fculptures and coins of the Emperors, but we may conclude, from the analogy of the difcoveries made in thefe *tumuli*, where the circular *fibulæ* have been found (fee pl V No 1 fig 1, pl VIII No 2 fig , pl IX fig 2, pl X fig 6, and pl XII fig 1) that they were the ornaments of the women Kirchman de Funer Rom in pl I of his work has produced a female figure with a circular fibula of this nature apparently connected with a double row of beads, under the neck of a figure as above defcribed Whether it be the tafte of *Hooge*, the engraver, a very fkilful artift, who has etched his defign with great tafte and knowledge of antient apparel, or of the author, may be difficult to afcertain, but it fhould appear they muft have had authority for the fame efpecially as it correfponds with the [illegible] of these ornaments I fufpect a kind of circular *[illegible]*, in the age of Conftantine were worn on the *paludamentum* or long robe of generals and great men, and which may probably ferve to explain the coloured emblems, or allegorical figures, of the provinces defcribed by Pancirolus [illegible], before noted in *Tom* XII and which were attached to their dignity, but by fucceeding Emperors who [illegible] this mode of government were transferred as ornaments to the other degrees of the people I have beftowed no fmall pains to enquire whether they have been difcovered in Italy but I do not find from the accounts I have received that they are in any of their cabinets and I apprehend not in any of their publications, fome of which I have examined The fafhion of fig 6 has all the character of the *Pierre Gothic*, fo much adopted in the Eaftern Empire, and from whence, probably by the legions thefe kind of ornaments were tranfported into Gaul and Britain by way of [illegible] which many concurring arguments will prove In Mr Dumes's fale, anno 1786, a circular gold fillagree brooch, or fibula, about the dimenfions of fig. 2 pl IX was purchafed by Mr Jackfon, a wine-merchant, in Clement's-Lane, Lombard Street, who has a collection of Roman relics It appears to be of the lower empire, but fomewhat antecedent to the age of the one as above cited

This rich and fuperb Jewel, fig 6 was doubtlefs a mark of the diftinguifhed character of the perfon interred with it For fize and magnificence, it excells all the antient jewels of this nature I have feen or heard of When they occur in *tumuli*, the fmall ones are found in the proportion of [illegible], fuch as fig 1 pl XII of the richer order, and this in clufters of *tumuli* that exceed [illegible] [illegible] but it generally happens, if the place of interment be extenfive, and crowded with [illegible] the contents are more curious and valuable

M I.

like the superior part of a cross, is the *tourquoise*, and one of the same form alternately enchased between the semicircles. The vermicular gold chain in the

It was the custom, from the remotest period of time, to inter rich ornaments with the dead The earliest account I find of this custom is in Herodotus, lib II p 136 Edit Lugd Bat 1751, where Micerin, an Egyptian king, caused sumptuous decorations to be bestowed on his daughter's tomb See also, p 244, a description of the Scythian mode of interment of their kings, in which a proportion of *gold vessels, furniture of various kinds, are deposited* The speech of Indathyrsus to Darius (see lib IV p 262) inclines me to believe the very rich sepulchral ornaments within these few years, taken out of the tombs of the antient Tartars, were the same as this old Historian describes as Scythian That this conjecture may appear well founded, and therefore this discovery of the antient Tartaric sepulchres interesting to antiquaries, who are hereby desirous of rescuing the name of Herodotus from an imputation of falsity in some of his narrations, independent of the wonders which he recites, and which he certainly did not believe himself, I have thought proper to insert it εἰ δὲ δέοι πάντως ἐς τοῦτο κατὰ τάχος ἀπικνέεσθαι, τυγχάνουσι ἡμῖν ἐόντες τάφοι πατρώιοι, [illegible], ἀνευρόντες, συγχέειν πειρᾶσθε αὐτοὺς Καὶ γνώσεσθε τότε εἴτε ὑμῖν μαχησόμεθα περὶ τῶν τάφων, εἴτε καὶ οὐ μαχησόμεθα In the sentence before this passage, he says, "we have no towns nor cultivated lands which "we dread the plunder of;" therefore, conceiving the Persians came for plunder, he very naturally said his countrymen would, as much out of respect for the repose as for the tomb of their ancestors, defend them to the last "*Give us cause for fighting*," says Indathyrsus, "by the outrage you offer to "them, and then you will prove our courage" Why this reply, unless he fancied the Persians intended offering violence to the tombs of their ancestors by despoiling them of their treasures? To return from this digression.

The Romans, by the laws of the XII Tab were interdicted the antient custom of interring rich ornaments with the dead See Cicero, lib 2 Legg In the lower empire this law seems to have been neglected, as many valuable relics have been discovered in tombs at this period (See the tomb of Maria wife of the Emperor Honorius, p 18 of this work) The Romans framed this law on that of Solon, which retrenched the magnificence of the Greeks in their sepulchral ceremonies Marcianus L Julia, 4 D ad leg Jul pecul Non sit locus religiosus, ubi Thesaurus inventus, nam etsi in monumento inventus fuerit, non quasi religiosus tollitur Quod enim sepelire quis prohibetur, id religiosum facere non potest. At *pecunia* sepeliri non potest, ut et mandatis principum cavetur Guichard, Fun des Grecs et des Rom takes the word *pecunia* in the sense of any treasures, jewels, or ornaments of value (see p 91), and Kirchman (p 448) understands by it apparel of any sort. Bologninus ad d l D de Legib cited in Guichard, reproves the extravagance of the Christians in this instance of decorating the dead with rich ornaments The antients, in their wills, were solicitous of bestowing this posthumous splendour on their remains (see L Servo alieno 113 § fin ff de Legatis 1 the testament of a woman) Funerari me arbitrio viri mei volo, et inferri mihi quæcunque SEPULTURÆ MEÆ causa feram EX ORNAMENTIS lineas duas ex margaritis (*two rows of pearls*), et viriolas ex smaragdis Concerning this custom a controversy was originated See 1 Scævola l Medico 40, and Ulpian, l 14 ff de Rel et Sump

Origen, lib 1 in Job says, the primitive Christians interred their dead with sumptuous apparel, doubtless from the Pagan custom, that their parents and friends lavished rich ornaments on them Eusebius, lib 7 cap 16 de Marino Martyre, confirms this in his Ecclesiastical History, and in other places of his work. Prudentius says, this was also a custom in his time (See Hymn in exequiis defunctorum) The custom also prevailed in the time of Pope Gregory (see *In Cant* [illegible]) and it was finally abolished by the Council of Auxerre Mr Sharp, in one of his letters from Naples, mentions the body of a boy, about eight years old, carried about the streets for exhibition He was ridiculously dressed in a fine laced hat, bag wig, blue and silver cloaths, and a sword by his side — he finds himself at a loss to account for this extraordinary spectacle Doubtless the remains of the custom is above referred to, and which, according to Guichard, anno 1[illegible], was still used by the princes, nobles, and extraordinary personages of his time

Tillet, in his Collections of the Kings and Queens of France describes the magnificence of their funerals, and explains the nature of their pompous effigies as something similar to those of wax, a substitute for the actual deposit of the regalia, which are now to be seen of a few of our modern kings and Queens in Westminster Abbey, and a relic of the custom used in former ages of entombing the regalia with the dead, which appears in later times to have been disused, in some respect on account of the violation of their remains for the sake of such plunder See Guichard, p 9, who cites Comm lib 4 cap 1 num [illegible] and which is confirmed by the late experiment of our modern [illegible] on the sacred ashes of King Edward the First These gentlemen, I flatter myself, will excuse the freedom of a brother's jocularity, especially as I am informed some little pleasantry transpired on this occasion

Sidonius Apollinaris, lib 3 Ep 12 who wrote, anno 486, near to the æra to which [illegible] should be assigned, says, in Gaul the bodies of the Pagans were burnt, and the bodies of the Christians inhumed That a union existed between the Britons and Gauls about the period of this interment, [illegible] no doubt See the Abbé de Vertot, Hist Critique de l'Etablissement des Bretons dans les Gaules Vol VI p 389 oct Procopius and Gregory of Tours authenticate the [illegible] which is also [illegible]

the compartment of the second circle is delicately milled with notches, and ENCHASED ON THE GROUND OF THE FIBULA; the alternate square setting is *garnet*, the four small circles on the third contain in their center a white hemisphere of a shelly substance, with a circular garnet, the triangular enchasement, and the one in form of the head of a cross, *tourquoise* stones, and the intermediate garnet, the fourth circle like the second, the fifth like the first; the sixth forms the umbo which protrudes from the ground of the *fibula*, and is of a white shelly or *coque de perle* substance, divided into right angles, with a gold enchasing, the next, or seventh, is gold milled in notches, the light circle next to this is plain gold, which rises higher, and receives the central enchased ornament, the small heads of crosses of a dark tint are *tourquoise*, the rest *garnet*, excepting the central stone of all, which is lost

Fig 7 THE REVERSE of fig 6 The clasp which receives the acus of this *fibula*, or broach, is in the form of a *snake's head*, the circle round the eye, which marks the nostrils, and beading round the neck, is a neat fillagree work; the same may be observed at the base of the vertical hinge of the *acus*, which hinge is ornamented with garnet and tourquoise stones, the cross describing the latter, over the *acus* is a loop which evidently secured the *fibula* to the dress, lest, as being a valuable ornament, it might be lost from it. See a loop of this nature to a *fibula*, in the *vignette*

This curious Jewel, which I apprehend to be the most elegant sepulchral relic discovered in Britain, is $3\frac{1}{2}$ inches in diameter, and weighs 6 ounces, 5 pennyweights, 18 grains, and $\frac{1}{4}$ of an inch in thickness. It was found near the neck of the *skeleton*

confirmed by the subscription of a bishop of the Britons to the first Council of Tours, A D 461, or rather 481, according to Mr Gibbon Gildas says, on the dispersion of the Britons by the Saxons inroad, alii transmarinas petebant regiones, c 25 p 8, and this loose declamation, with the army of Riothamus, Mr Gibbon thinks, may countenance an emigration as early as the middle of the *fifth* century the exact æra to which I have ascribed the erection of these small *tumuli sepulchrales* When Aurelius landed from Armorica, aided by Aldroen king of that country, to take the command of the Britons, (Stillingfleet Orig p 319, M Westm p 82), he was doubtless accompanied by many of the Gauls, and hence, from the expedition, the revolution in the affairs of the Britons, and the establishment which took place, we might be led to conclude the tumuli, as above described, were erected by the Britons at this period, or perhaps by the Pagan Gauls in this expedition That we may not lose sight of facts in our argument, let us advert to the analogy of relics found in these barrows with those in the interment of King Childeric, a Pagan Gaulish king (see Chiffletius, p 210 p 2[illegible] p [illegible]), the *Chrystal-ball, axe* and *spear*, found in his grave, are exactly similar to the CRYSTAL BALLS, fig 8 pl IV and fig 3 pl V and the AXE, fig 5 pl 12 Here will be found also a strong similitude in the other relics, if the reader will give himself the trouble to compare them In the laws of King Pharamond, concerning the decoration of sepulchres, there is nothing relative to Christianity, and no mention made of burning the bodies of the dead, but only of inhumation. Pharamond died a Pagan, A D [illegible]8, and was buried after the Pagan custom Sepultus est BARBARICO RITU Rhenus extra urbem [illegible] versus in monticulo, qui Latine PYRAMIS dici potest Ex MS cod Bruxell Palatin, cited by Chiffletius, p 5, that is, he was buried under a BARROW, or TUMULUS, similar to those we have described Also, from the Genealogia Bruxellensis (see Chiffletius, p 81) Pharamond Clodovius, Merovee, and CHILDERIC, are thus mentioned "Tous ces quatre devant "dits estoyent Payens, et furent enseveliz a la mode Barbarique," which according to Chiffletius, implies an external regal form of interment, with sumptuous apparel, as I have before remarked It follows therefore from the above comparative facts, that, in or about the middle of the fifth century, the Pagans adopted inhumation in Britain, the cause of which, whether by their own election or [illegible] of Christian princes, will require a separate discussion, and which will apply to those [illegible] *[illegible]* with circular trenches, found in clusters in various parts of this island

[illegible] here explained a similarity of sepulchral rites in respect to the decorations of the dead [illegible] between the Christians and Pagans at this era [illegible] arguments can be deduced on both sides, [illegible] can only be from the result of combined facts as the reader proceeds in the examination of this [illegible] he will be enabled to form a decided opinion on the nature of these interments

It is

Fig. 8. An Iron Fragment which appeared to have been rivetted to a box: found at the feet.

Fig 9 One of two Iron Hinges of a box, to which fig 8. was apparently attached

Pl. XI. Fig 1. A Gilded Brass or mixed Metal Vessel*, $5\frac{1}{2}$ inches diameter at the mouth, and $2\frac{4}{10}$ inches in depth It has *three handles*, and each handle

* As the zeal of an antiquary may possibly incline him to survey the customs of the Romans in their interments, to enable him to form a comparative view of the customs of other nations in some respects allied to them, it would be necessary to advert first to the Roman order of funerals as to what regards our present object of interring *vessels* with the dead

Few of the antient writers have mentioned these *vessels* in tombs The Abbe Winkelman, on the Etruscan Pottery, cites Aristophanes as the only writer (see his Eccles v 535), and the vessels which are here mentioned are said only to contain *Oil* Tertullian, in Apologetica, cap 13 mentions a vessel with a big belly, which the Romans called *Obba*, as used in the funeral feasts Quid differt ab epulo Jovis Silicernium? a simpulo *Obba*? ab aruspice pollinctor? nam et aruspex mortuis apparet I am surprized the acute Winkelman has suffered this to escape him, particularly so, as the *Obba* and *Simpulum* were the sacred vessels of the Etruscans, and which the learned Scaliger derives from Hebrew origin *Simpulum* from SOPHEL, and *Obba* from OB, a big bellied vessel (see a *Simpulum*, and several of these vessels called *Obbæ*, in the Etruscan tomb, in the neighbourhood of Capua, opened by Sir William Hamilton, anno 1757, now in the British Museum), the particulars detailed by Winkelman, p 199 See this tomb described in the *vignette* to p 13

It is the opinion of Wolphgangus Lazius, Comment Urb Rom that these vessels found in tombs contained the libations of wine, milk, &c but which idea Guichard, p 82. Fun des Rom transfers to the *lacrymal* vessels of the Romans I think there can be no doubt but they were applied to both the uses of libation and lustral purification *wine*, *milk*, *blood*, *pulse* of various kinds, *honey cakes*, &c being used in the former rites, *water*, *gums*, and *oil* in the latter. I make this distinction from the variety of vessels found in tombs, and from the distinction of the above rites Though the ancients are not explicit in the actual deposit of the vessels with the body, they particularly express the nature of the *liquors*, *unguents*, *balsams*, and *viands*, which were used in the sepulchral ordinances, and it should be from these facts, corroborated with the discovery of the vessels in their sepulchres, that a decided opinion can be formed on any particular species of interments, and also, by the forms of the vessels, to what uses they might be applied. The libation of water was called Arferia (see Festus) Arferia aqua quæ inferis libabatur

All kinds of liquors bestowed on the Inferiæ were by the Greeks called χοαὶ, from shedding or pouring out Aristot Θεοῖς τε θυσίαι καὶ ἡρώων θεραπεῖαι καὶ χοαὶ κεκμηκότων. which is thus translated by Apuleius, *Diis sacrificatur, geniis ministratur, obitis libatione perfunditur* Before the body was interred, it might have undergone the ceremony of purification, being sprinkled with consecrated water in the vessel, and which vessel, as being sacred to the purposes of the dead, might have been interred with the body See Festus on the libation of *Wine* Respersum vinum significat apud antiquos, quia in sacris Novemdialibus, *vino* mortui sepulcrum spargebatur

Blood and *Milk* Virgil, Æneid 3

Inferimus tepido spumantia cymbia lacte,
Sanguinis & sacri pateras

Servius, explaining this custom, says, the soul after death delighted in this offering of blood and milk, milk being the natural nourishment of the body, and blood the union of the body and soul, without which the soul could not exist

Balsams and *Unguents* Ausonius in Epitaph Carm 36

Sparge mero cineres, et odoro perlue nardo
Hospes et adde rosis balsama puniceis,
Perpetuum mihi ver agit illachrymabilis urna,
Et commutavi secula, non obii

Anacreon

[illegible] λίθον μύρα [illegible],
[illegible] γῇ χέειν μάταια,
[illegible] μᾶλλον, ὡς [illegible]
Μύρισον, ῥόδοις δὲ κρᾶτα
[illegible], &c [illegible]

The extravagance of these rites was restricted by the law of the XII Tables [illegible] made of the suppression of the *Murrhina potio*, at the Silicernium, or funeral banquet [illegible] and I have little doubt, as the exterior ceremonies were in a great measure interdicted by the ancients [illegible] to their superstition inclined them to add some symbol of their pious intentions toward the dead by entombing with them the vessels appropriated to such uses [illegible] this appear to have been [illegible] custom the recent discoveries of these kind of vessels in tombs, after the [illegible] sufficiently evince, and no other can be admitted when the question [illegible]

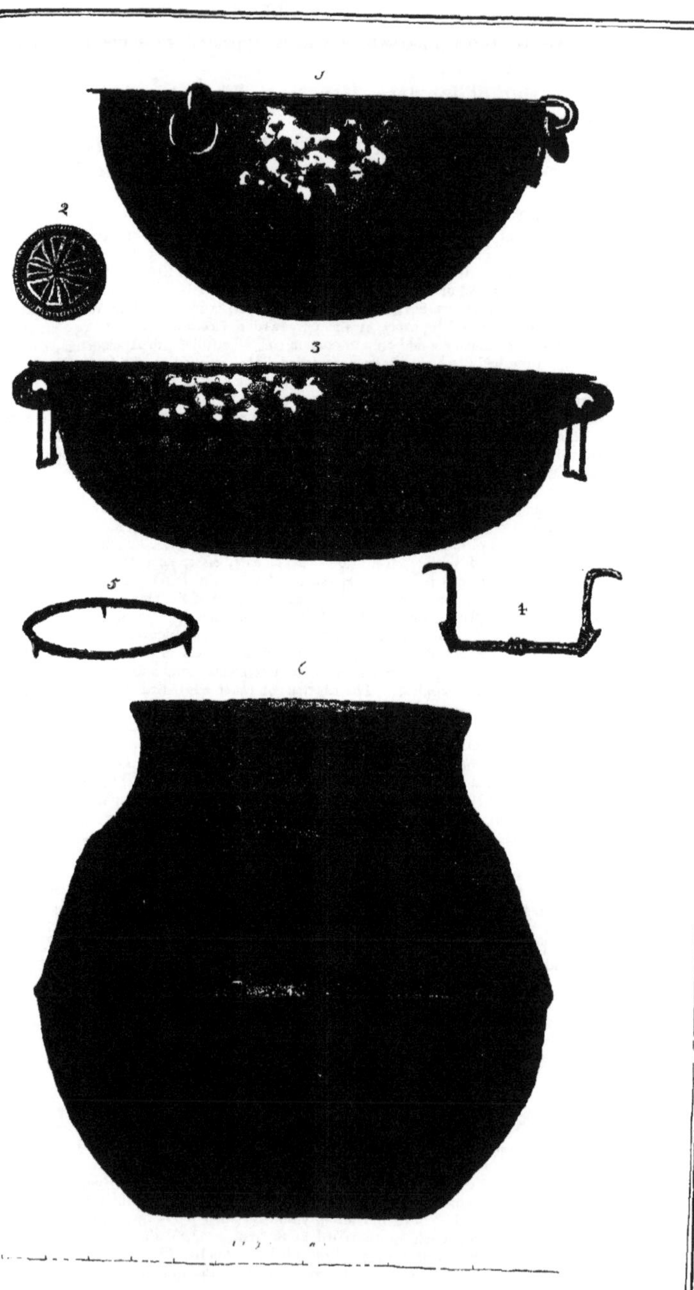

handle ornamented with a circular piece of white metal, probably silver, as expressed under the ring of the handles: the ground of which is of a red composition,

a Roman interment. Guichard, p. 158, from Pomponius Lætus de Rom. Antiquitat. says, that on the interment of the unchaste vestals (see Servius, lib. 9. Æneid. Festus, Plutarch, and Dionysius of Halicarnassus, lib. 2.) they were entombed with a lamp, a little bread, *three pots of water, milk, and oil*. As this is part of the rites of the *inferiæ*, it was doubtless adopted in the sepulchral ceremonies of other individuals, especially as it is common to find lamps interred with vessels suitable to the above purposes in many Roman interments. Muret, no bad evidence, though he does not assign his authority, p. 26, on the funeral of the Romans, says, a perpetual lamp, small vessels full of several sorts of drink, viands, and a piece of money, the Naulum Charontes were interred with them. I repeat, it is no bad authority, since modern discoveries in antient tombs seem to authenticate the same.

The custom of placing vessels of various kinds with the dead was common to many nations besides the Romans. (See Nicolo [illegible] on the customs of the Indian Tribes, and Bellefoeft's Cosmography, vol. II. book III. cap. 29. Ferdinand Lopez *Hystoire de l'Inde*, liv. 1. ch. 14.) Muret says, the Maldivians, the Caribbees, and other people, used this custom, and modern history tells us the Chinese and Peruvians adopt it.

In the great variety of superstitious customs adopted by the antients, it is, and ever must be, extremely difficult to arrive at a perfect knowledge of any particular enquiry which depends on them. It is flattering to human curiosity to solve a complicated enigma, and though the momentous concerns of social life do not depend on this kind of solutions, the mind derives a pleasing satisfaction in the pursuit, and perhaps not much inferior to what is wantonly and ignorantly called more useful enquiries. L'ame veut etre nourrie comme le corps.

Though we have found, in many instances, a great analogy between Roman relics deposited with the dead, and those the subject of this enquiry, yet, as many of these relics have been apparently adapted to other uses than those merely sepulchral, so we are not to confine ourselves to the forms of sepulture as above described, but we should consider whether fig. 1. and fig. 3. were not interred with the dead from some different motive of antient superstition.

Pliny denotes seven ways of divination, lib. xxx. cap. 11. Ex aqua, et ex sphæris, et ex aere et stellis, et lucernis, ac *pelvibus* securibusque, et multis aliis modis divina promittit: by water, globes or balls, air, stars, fire, *Basons*, and axes, &c. Some of these are described by Godelmannus, lib. 1. cap. 5. p. 45. The one which he calls *Lecanomantia*, or divination by *basons*, (which, he says, was practised by the Egyptians, Chaldeans, and Assyrians), or vessels capacious at the mouth, I shall here transcribe. In *pelvem* aqua repletam imponebantur *aureæ et argenteæ laminæ*, lapidesque pretiosi, characteribus certis signati, et postquam connecta essent verba pronunciata, quibus Dæmon advocabatur, proferebatur quæstio. His peractis, tenuis atque exilis vox instar sibili ex aquis emergebat, referebatque, quæ exposcebat quæstio. He then explains the Hydromantia magica, or divination by water, which, he says, is variously performed. It is here necessary to remind the reader of a curious fact which occurs in the discovery of a golden plate, with the names of Michael, Gabriel, Raphael, Uriel, engraved upon it in Greek letters, found in the tomb of the Empress Honoria, cited in the note of p. 18 of this work, and which seems to relate to the *aureæ et argenteæ laminæ—characteribus certis signati* of Godelmannus.

It will not perhaps be unacceptable to the reader, in this place also, to note a curious magical experiment, which this author describes to be performed with a *glass vessel* of the shape of fig. 4. He calls it *Gastromantia*, which may be derived from Γαστρος [illegible], ventre vaticinor. This kind of prophecy, he says, is not performed by a voice, but by pictures, which, I think, should be translated *shades*, shadows, forms, or images. [illegible] *vasa vitrea*, rotunda, aquis confecta limpidissimis, et circum collocabantur accensi cerei [illegible] evocatio Dæmonis occulte [illegible] et quæstio recitata esset, adhibebatur *puer impollutus*, aut *mulier prægnans*, quæ [illegible] diligenterque intuetur ac circumspiceret, rogaretque imperent, & flagitaret responsa [illegible] tandem *imagines*, quæ per [illegible] speculo [illegible], ex aquis quadam [illegible] fulgebant, diabolus exprimebat, lib. 1. ut sup. This kind of magic, he says, was of the same nature of the [illegible].

In Keating's Irish History, translated by O'Connor, there is an Irish poem, describing the magical things brought over by the Tuatha Dadanan, among them is a brass vessel, or caldron. The Tuatha Danan, in Irish, are magicians, sorcerers, priests, or [illegible]. *Danan* signifies [illegible] —*dana*, in Old Persic, doctors— [illegible] Tuath [illegible] Chendh [illegible] Tuath [illegible] and Chendh, is sorcery, [illegible] *Du* is also the [illegible] sorcerers, and *Du* is the Arabic [illegible], to augur. See Vallancey's Pref. to his Coll. Hib. [illegible]

Aristotle says, there were two pillars at Dodona, upon one a *brass bason*, and upon the other a child holding a whip, with cords made of brass, which occasioned a noise when the wind drove them against the *bason*. The Abbé Banier, by way of interpretation perhaps, says, a number of *brass kettles* were [illegible] this oracle, which, being [illegible] with a whip, clattered [illegible] another, and so pronounced the oracle, for he says *Dodo*, in Hebrew, signifies a *kettle*. Perhaps, as the learned Vallancey says, the Abbé's genius in this is a little too lively; but what can be opposed to Aristotle's authority on the subject of the [illegible] *bason*? Fig. 1. has *three handles*, and which, for a true equipoize, are perhaps so applied to suspend it. It was found with fig. 3. thereby shewing,

N

from

composition, apparently in imitation of the garnet, cornelian, or beryl, and enclosed in a border of the same metal as the vessel. This kind of composition may be observed on a Roman curvated *fibulæ*, engraved in the vignette over Tum. XIV and which is an evidence that the above composition was used as an imitation of some kind of stones.* It is engraved to shew its analogy with fig 2 and 3, and to shew the probability of their being of a cotemporary deposit.

Fig 2. One of the CIRCULAR ORNAMENTS, as described at the handles; and which, within and without, is sodered † to the center of the bottom of the vessel.

Fig 3.

from a natural inference, the nature of its use or connection with it. Fig 3 was placed on the trivet, fig 5 which would produce, were any thing to be stricken against it, a full and clear reverberation of sound. It should therefore seem, from a probable inference, that fig 1 was suspended within fig 3. and by some accidental percussion a sound was produced whereby a species of divination was performed. At this day there is an idle fancy of young women, who pretend to draw forth a divination from the suspension of a ring in a glass. I shall here just drop a hint as I proceed, that it appears very presumable, from the nature of the workmanship of these relics with many similar found in *tumuli*, that they were fabricated in the East, and introduced by way of traffic among the Gauls and Britons, who, strangely affecting magical customs, could not fail to afford the highest encouragement to all the absurd apparatus which they would possibly procure of this nature. Dr Borlase is also of opinion, that the Phœnicians, and after them the Greeks, finding the Druids beyond all others devoted to superstition, would naturally court that powerful order, by bringing them continual notices of the Oriental superstitions, in order to promote and engross the lucrative trade which they carried on in Britain for so many ages. (Hist of Cornwall, p 146) In Justinian's time, the period I have affixed to these relics, Marseilles imported from the East paper, oil, linen, silk, precious stones, spices, &c. The Gauls, or Franks, traded to Syria, and the Syrians were established in Gaul. (See M de Guignes, Mem de l'Academie des Insc &c tom XXXVII p 471—475, cited by Mr Gibbon) Is not this a confirmation of the truth of the above remark, and may it not account for the introduction of many Eastern commodities into this island, especially as I have before remarked, that a coin of Clovis was found in a barrow in Kent, whose sons, twenty years after his death, entering into a treaty with Justinian, had the sovereignty of the countries beyond the Alps yielded to them, consequently Marseilles then became subject to the Merovingian kings? The magic of the Druids, according to Rowland, p 140, remained among the Britons after their conversion to Christianity, and is called *Taish* in Scotland, the same as *Tuatha* in Irish, signifying sorcery, or prediction, and which by the inflection of the Scotch dialect, is so pronounced, also by them called second sight, and which Mr Rowland conceives to be a relic of Druidism.

Pliny on magic says, *Britannia* hodieque eam attonite celebrat tantis ceremoniis ut dedisse Persis videri possit, lib xxx cap 1. The vain pretence to this art was, I apprehend, the same as it is this day, common to every uncivilized as well as civilized country of the universe. Human beings of all denominations, from a natural consequence of the feebleness of their nature, are ever desirous of seeking consolation in a supernatural power, and those, who are not so fortunate as to find it in revealed religion, are tempted to seek for it in some species of fanaticism, or some barbarous pretence to sorcery. It is a gloomy retrospect, to think that every age has marked the progress of men in the pursuit of some palliative, to calm the miseries of life, and to confirm them in the necessity of looking up to some supernatural power for consolation.

Dii sic voluere, oraculo monitum est. Sibyllæ prædixerunt, populus vult decipi, et decipiatur—it always was and ever will be so.

N B These vessels have no appearance, by the delicacy of the metal, and the ornaments sodered on the outside and inside of one of them, to have been used in culinary offices with fire. No I is also too small to [illegible] uses, nor do they seem to have been adapted to ordinary uses, for the same reason why the three rings to suspend one of them, if intended for the services of common life, and why the trivet on which fig 3 was placed.

* The *fibulæ* came from an antient place of interment lately discovered at Kings Holme, near Gloucester, in a sand-pit. The composition has fallen out of several of the sockets, which are cut out of the solid metal, and shew plainly the use they were designed for. It is apparently a vitrified substance, and enamelled upon the buckle, the bottom of the socket is crenulated, to make the substance adhere.

† There can be no doubt of the antients having the art of sodering metals, perhaps in as great perfection as the moderns. Their skill in this may be observed in the detached ringlets of antient hair, applied to the head among the bronzes of the remotest ages of the art. The most antient [illegible] of this nature is the bust of a woman in the cabinet at Portici, the forehead to [illegible] is decorated with fifty ringlets, worked like wire, of the thickness of a quill, sodered to the

side

Fig 3 A GILDED VESSEL of the fame metal as fig 2, 13 inches in width, and 4½ inches in depth, and which contained the fmaller veffel, fig 2. Found, as I apprehend from Mr Fauffett's defcription, at the feet of the grave

Fig 4 The HANDLE to *fig* 3

Fig 5 A TRIVET †, about 4 inches in diameter, on which was placed the larger veffel, *fig* 3, and of the fame kind of metal

Fig 6 A VESSEL OF COARSE RED EARTH ‡, 6 inches in height, and 6½ in diameter Found at the feet of the coffin, and near to it the bones of a child placed in a heap, well preferved, and which appeared to have been interred prior to the other fubject §

fide of the head, and arranged one upon the other, having each four or five curls The fame cabinet alfo exhibits a youthful head with fixty-eight curls fodered upon it An ideal head of bronze, known by the name of Plato, one of the fineft fpecimens of the art in the fame cabinet, has ringlets fodered upon the temples Winckelman, tom II p 294 Pliny is explicit in the art of fodering in his time. Auri glutinum eft tale Argilla ferro, cadmia æris maffis, alumen laminis, refina plumbo et marmori, fed plumbum nigrum albo jungitur, ipfumque album fibi oleo Item ftannum æramentis, ftanno argentum Lib xxx iii cap v From the fpecimens of the metallic ornaments of the antients feen in cabinets, they feem to have underftood the management of metals in all its cafes

* The antients, from an early period of the empire, had the art of gilding This may be noted on the equeftrian ftatue of Marcus Aurelius, on the remains of the chariot and four horfes which ornamented the front of the theatre of Hercules, on the Hercules of the Capitol, in the ornaments difcovered in the fubterraneous chambers of the palace of the Emperors in the villa Borghefe, on the Palatine Mount It has alfo been preferved in the ruins of Perfepolis (Greave, Defert des Antiq de Perfep p 23) It is alfo confpicuous on a variety of other ornaments of the antients their marbles were gilded, as may be feen on the head of Apollo at the Capitol; and in the fine Pallas when difcovered at Ortic Cabinets of note produce many inftances of this nature on the inferior as well as the moft admired relics of the antients M. Legaier's cabinet at Nimes has many *bronze veffels* ftrongly gilt within and without (*Thicknefs's Journey*) By the following paffage of Pliny, it does not feem the antients knew the modern art of gilding by amalgamation Namque æs cruciatur in primis, accenfumque reftinguitur fale, aceto, alumine Poftea exarenatur, an fatis recoctum fit, fplendore deprehendente, iterumque exhalatur igni, ut poffit edomitum, miftis pumice, alumine, argento vivo, inductas accipere bracteas Lib xxxiii cap iii This procefs of gilding with leaves has doubtlefs been the caufe of its prefervation through fo many ages many layers of thick leaves, the Abbé Winckelman fays, are apparent on the horfe of Marcus Aurelius From the various fpecimens of very thin antique gilding, many of which I have in my collection, I fhould be inclined to queftion whether the antients in the lower empire may not have known the modern way of tinging metals with gold It would afford a long and improper digreffion in this place, to treat chemically and demonftratively on the fubject, much matter may be collected from reading, and much from relics handed down to us, to render the conjectural part more refpectable than is generally the cafe with thefe kind of ftudies

† See PLATE XII fig 12 where a fmall metal gilt *patera* was reverfed, and ferved as a bafe to the large *veffel* FIG 4 defcribed in the fame tumulus

‡ I conceive this veffel to have been depofited with the child, and to have contained the *aqua magica*, or perhaps the luftral water as before remarked, and which cuftom of ufing luftral purification feems to have been common to moft nations, as well as the Romans

§ It is not improbable but thefe bones were the remains of a child of the female fex buried in this *tumulus*, and which had been taken up when the mother was buried, and placed at her feet This will account for the ftate of prefervation in which the bones were found, for not having been expofed to the quantity of putrefcent matter as the body of the mother, they would naturally be lefs fubject to diffolution in their parts, whereas the bones of the mother were almoft perifhed

TUMULUS XV.

I Have here assembled several relics apparently the contents of the same TUMULUS, but which have been casually scattered among several gentlemen in the neighbourhood where they were found, some are now in my possession; some in the cabinet of Mr. Faussett. Their analogy with those of *Tumulus* XIV. have induced me to introduce them in this place. They were discovered, anno 1771, at Ash, in Kent; and, as I apprehend, by labourers digging of sand. A Mr Hayward of the faculty, residing then at that place, collected them; some of which, I believe, he presented to Mr Jacob of Faversham, through whose hands I received those which are in my possession. As no notes were taken on the spot, I am obliged to be satisfied with the information I could gather, and which I shall here set down with fidelity

Pl. XII. Fig. 1. A CIRCULAR ENCHASED FIBULA composed of a plate of gold

* This Jewel was in the possession of Mr Jacob, who, I apprehend, received it from Mr Hayward at the same time he received the other relics, and wherefore I conceive it to have been the produce of the same *tumulus*, especially as there is an evident analogy in the contents of this and *Tumulus* XIV. It is now in my possession, with fig 2 3. 4. 5 the fragments of fig 11 and fig 12 and 1,

These kind of funeral gifts bestowed on the dead were called δῶρα and [illegible] by the antients See Nicarchus cited by Kirchman, p 296

Ἄλλαι [illegible] δῶρα φέρουσαι
[illegible] δάκρυα χεῦτε [illegible]

And [illegible], see Xiphilinus in Severo, [illegible] In hunc rogum conjectis iis, quae pulcritudinis causa allata fuerant, lectus impositus est

See Lucian, in his Life or customs of a philosopher, [illegible] Alii vestes, alii aliud quippiam earum rerum, quas olim in delitiis habuerint, eodem rogo secum cremari mandant Suetonius in Caesare, cap 84 Tibicines et scenici artifices vestem, quam ex instrumento triumphorum *ad praesentem usum induerant*, detractam sibi atque discissam injecere flammae I have cited this full passage to confirm what Caesar says of the Gauls. In the same chapter also, Matronae etiam PLERAQUE ORNAMENTA SUA, quae gerebant, et liberorum bullas atque praetextas *But this extravagance was retrenched by the law of the XII Tables*, which I have before remarked, and which I have thought proper here further to explain It is evidently founded

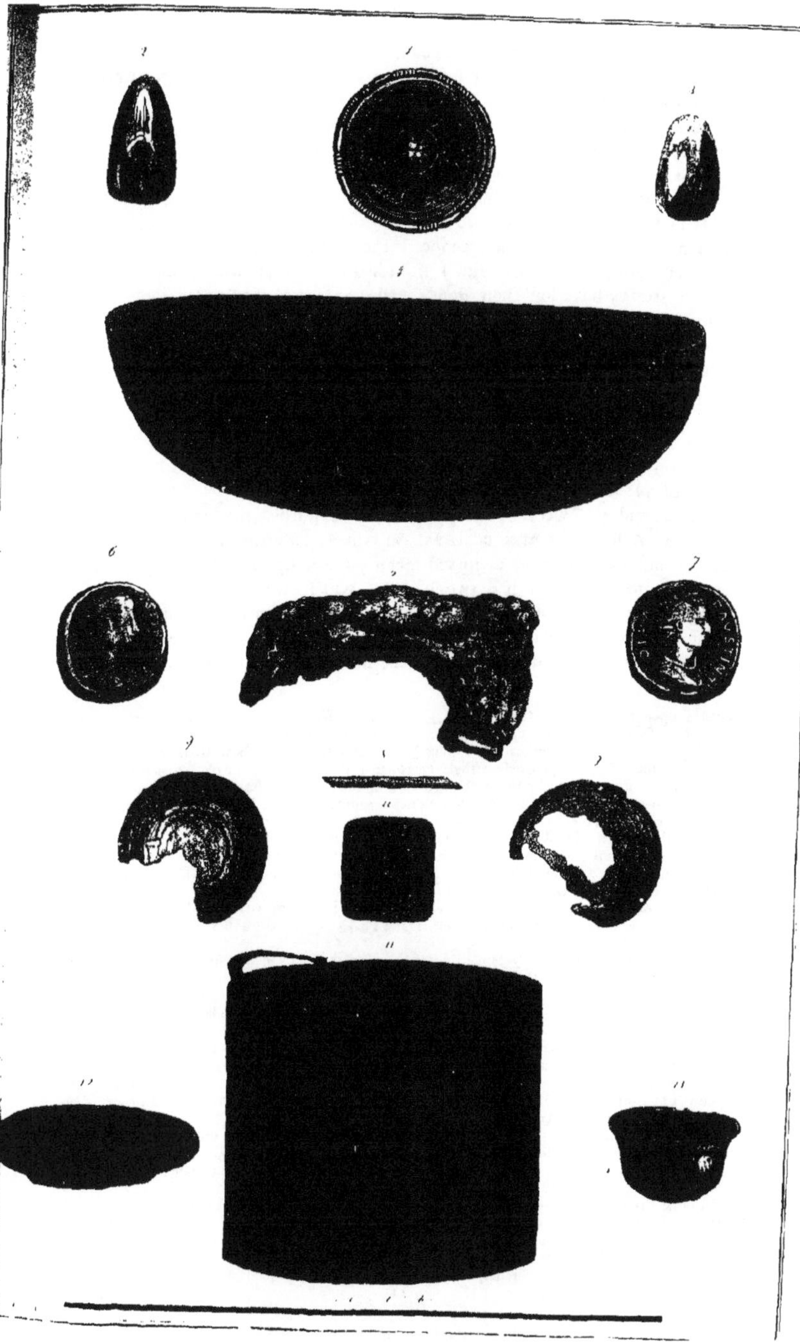

gold on a ground of ſilver. The chain work on the third circle is more delicately executed than expreſſed in the drawing, as alſo the fillagree work between the ſix projecting parts where the enchaſing commences. The three intervening ſmall circles were moſt probably ſet with an hemiſpheric pearl, ſhell, or ivory, as in thoſe of *fig.* 6. Pl. X. and now loſt from the ſockets. The three angular compartments between the hemiſpheres are ſet with garnets. The ſockets at the points of the angles deſcribed by a dark tint, being ſhaped like thoſe in fig. 6. Pl. X. which are of [illegible] ſtone, appear to have contained the ſame. The circle which connects the hemiſpheres and angular ſetting, is enchaſed with garnets; the ſmall ſockets between each [illegible] line where the garnets are ſet, have loſt their ſtones, and which, for the reaſon above ſtated, ſeem to have been [illegible]. The next circle deſcribed with a dark tint [illegible] to the ground of the fibula, which appears to have contained a [illegible] ſetting, the ſame being loſt, perhaps [illegible] or [illegible]. The central ſetting [illegible] compoſed of four white, and eight green ſtones. I do not pretend to [illegible] of what nature. The garnets have, as in the enchaſed *fibulæ* before deſcribed, a gold chequered foil under them to add to their colour and luſtre. The [illegible] on the reverſe is ſilver, and was connected in the ſame manner as [illegible] in fig. 7. of pl. X. The drawing is the exact ſize.

Fig. 2 and 3. TWO AMETHYSTS [illegible], of a fine purple, perforated.

Fig. 4. A BRASS OR MIXED METAL VESSEL †, 16 inches diameter, extremely thin. Found on the *braſs* or mixed metal *patera*, fig. 12. which was inverted for a baſe to *fig.* 4. It had two handles, which are now detached from it, owing to the periſhable quality of the ſoder. The metal is much corroded, and in ſome parts has loſt its tenacity, yielding and becoming brittle to the touch.

Fig. 5. IRON HEAD OF AN AXE ‡, the metal entirely corroded, 7½ inches in length.

founded upon that of Solon (ſee Plutarch,) [illegible Greek] Nec ſinit ammo in taurum, aut plus tribus *palliis* in funus imponere. (See further in [illegible], and the interpretation by the learned Lipſius.) It muſt therefore appear from theſe facts, independent of the low date prefixed to theſe *tumuli*, that they could not be of Roman ſtructure. In the fourth century we find, by the tomb diſcovered of Honoria, Stilicho's daughter, and wife to the Emperor Honorius, that the cuſtom of [illegible] rich ornaments with the dead prevailed among the converted Romans, (ſee [illegible], p. 18. of this work.) In the [illegible], and beginning of the ſeventh centuries, it prevailed among the Franks, but was aboliſhed by their eccleſiaſtical councils ſhortly after.

See Gregorius Turonenſis, lib. viii. cap. 2. deſcribing the rich ornament of an illuſtrious French woman, Ante paucos autem dies, mortua propinqua uxoris [illegible] in Baſilica urbis [illegible] ſepulta eſt cum [illegible] et multo [illegible].

* In my poſſeſſion, from Mr Jacob of Feverſham, who had them with the *fibula* and other relics I ſuſpect [illegible] were found. See Pl. VIII. N° II. and Pl. IX. fig. 2. [illegible] have been found with ſimilar *fibulæ*.

† In my poſſeſſion, from Mr Jacob. I was favoured with [illegible] drawing of this veſſel and [illegible], with ſome others from Mr Boys. "These two utenſils," he ſays, "were found in one grave, the [illegible] placed "on the bottom of the ſmaller," which he alſo enumerates with ſome of the other relics.

The moſt early account [illegible] have of the myſtic or conſecrated uſes of braſs veſſels, [illegible] authority. "And the king commanded Hilkiah the high prieſt to bring forth out of the temple [illegible] "[illegible] all the *veſſels* that were made for Baal, and for the grove, and for all the hoſt of heaven." 2 Kings, ch. xxiii. See a conſecrated veſſel alſo in Herodotus [illegible Greek]. Hoc in loco [illegible] *ahenum* ſextus tantum quantus *crater* qui eſt in oſtio Ponti a Pauſania Cleombroti filio *conſecratus* [illegible] lib. iv. p. 248. Edit. Jacob Gron. Fig. 4. may therefore be eſteemed to form ſuch conſecrated uſes as was before remarked on [illegible] pl. IX. and where the matter is ſufficiently explicit to induce me to adopt the ſame ſignification to it.

‡ See Chifletius, the Plate of an IRON AXE, p. 210, exactly ſimilar to *fig.* 5. found in the grave of king Childeric, with a CRYSTAL BALL and other relics as before deſcribed.

An IRON AXE HEAD, in ſhape like the *bipennis* of the Romans, one end like a hammer, the other [illegible] towards the gripe or handle, in my poſſeſſion, was lately found in the ſand pit, at King Holme, near Glouceſter, an ancient place of interment. Several relics have been ſent me from thence, conſiſting of a ſword blade (ſee Archæologia, vol. VII. p. 3[illegible]) [illegible], coins from [illegible] to [illegible], Roman earthen ware, and other relics, which atteſt the age of its [illegible].

O Charles

Charles White, Esq, of Manchester, a gentleman well known in the circle of physic, by his great skill in extraordinary chirurgical cases, has favoured me with a curious relation of the discovery of an iron *axe head* in his possession. It was found, anno 1739, at a place called Walton near the confluence of the rivers Ribble and Darwen, at the depth of ten feet, with or near to *a human skull*, and, as reported, accompanied with the *os frontis* of a bullock, both apparently fractured near the same place, also with the *sandals* of an adult and young subject, *the bones of a child*, a coin of the small bronze of Trajan, *lamps, small vessels*, and a quantity of Roman *exuviæ* among which was the red *coralline ware*, known by the name of *Samian*, and other fragments of pottery. As this discovery has been rendered interesting, from a supposition that the human skull, that of the bullock, and the *axe*, were sacrificial remains, I shall here take the liberty to intrude my remarks upon them.

Human sacrifices were abolished in the Roman empire, by a decree of the senate, under the consulship of Cn Cornelius Lepidus and P Licinius Crassus, anno 657, after the foundation of Rome. (See Pliny, lib xxx cap 1.) This decree passed 95 years before Christ, and the Romans had not then made their invasion in Britain. Cæsar landed in the joint consulship of Ca[illegible] Bibulus Anno 57, ante Christum. Bede states it, anno 60, and anno 693, U C Rom, but which should be anno 694 (see Helvicius, Chronologiæ Systema), no great difference—but it is right to approach as near as we can to the truth. The intervening time was near 127 years from this invasion to the landing of Claudius, anno Domini 47, therefore, supposing a Roman establishment had actually taken place at this period, and the relics in question coeval with the same, it is certain the Romans could not have performed human sacrifices in Britain, since, from the above historical fact, they had been interdicted this custom 142 years. Were we also, only for the sake of argument, to consider these remains *Druidical*, as was suggested at the time of their discovery, still we should find, under Trajan, these inhuman sacrifices were also effectually abolished in Britain. (See the Honour of suppressing the Gaulish Druids, attributed, by Suetonius, to the Emperor Claudius.) "Druidarum Religionem apud "Gallos diræ immanitatis et tantum civibus sub Augusto interdictam penitus abolevit, viz Clau- "dius." Suetonius in Claud cap 25.

The discovery of the coin of Trajan will therefore, with the other Roman relics, indisputably serve for our effectual enquiry into their age, since no surmise of an antecedent date can, from this argument, be permitted.

As these bones had no signs of fire upon them, I apprehend they were the remains of an inhumated body of the lower Romans, or Britons, after the general assent to Christianity under some of the Christian Emperors, when burning the dead was disused. Or perhaps Pagan and Christians were indiscriminately inhumated as at Crundale, in Kent. (See note, p 37.) Inhumated bodies having been found in the same ground with ossuaries, or urns, containing the ashes, and this I have also had occasion to observe in several places. This will account for the Roman *exuviæ* found on the spot, which are always noted near their *cubiæ*, and which might be considered as belonging to their animal sacrifices and libations performed at their inf[illegible].

Had this burial place of Walton been curiously examined, more sepulchral remains would doubtless have been, and perhaps might now be, discovered. The Romans were accustomed to bury their dead on low as well as high ground; their *cubinæ* were at no great distance from their encampments, and their *Castra stativa*, which, unless on any material expedition, were stationed in places near rivers or rivulets, and their exploratory posts on commanding eminences at no great distance.

I have frequently had occasion to remark, on opening of barrows, the eagerness of bystanders to ascribe the *exuviæ* of the factitious soil falling in among the earth, or materials of the grave, to relics deposited in it; hence I should conjecture the potsherds small animal bones, and the *skull of the bullock*, to have been in that soil, and the *axe* to have been interred with the body. It is impossible, on these occasions, to be too careful of minutiæ, as much literary fact may depend upon the accuracy of such observance.

From the passages I have before selected from ancient poets, we may naturally conceive that the utensils adapted to their magical rites would be also efficacious in their sepulchral rites.

——— Sæpe animas imis excire sepulcris,

which Virgil, Eclog viii says of the witch Mœris, another proof that the dead were supposed to have been tormented by evil spirits. This species of magic was called *Goetica*. (See *Hecker de Secreti*, p 516.) Hi sunt ergo qui *defunctorum reclamant animas*, &c. Which rites, he says, were confounded and blended with the Christian, and which remark we find confirmed by the history of the primitive converts, who were in many instances permitted to follow several of their Pagan customs.

It has been observed, that many relics in these graves are magical, and it may perhaps be an addition to the interest which the curious reader may take in this enquiry to consider the *axe* as such.

Divination by these instruments is called *axinomantia* (see Pliny before cited, cap xxx lib ii), and is thus explained by Godelmannus, lib i cap 5 p 45.

Koskinomantiæ et *Axinomantia* qui ad pervestigandos atque apprehendos occultos scelerum autores et res alias obscuras explorandas et proferendas, incantatores utuntur. Hinc *securi* expedimi rotundo palo infixa, aptaque, ad normam ac perpendiculum et cum prefatione, ordine enumeratis nominibus eorum,

Fig 6. *A Coin of* FAVSTINA wife of MARCUS AURELIUS

Fig 7 A *coin of* the large BRONZE of FAVSTINA wife of ANTONINUS PIUS

The reverses of these *coins* have been ground smooth to make them of a certain weight, and which is probably denoted by the *single* point before the mouth of *fig* 6 and the *six points* on the head of *fig* 7 They were found, with other plain brass weights and one of lead, piled one upon the other, gradually lessening to the top to the number of eight *

Fig 8. and 9 REMAINS OF A PAIR OF SCALES Found close to the weights The drawing the exact size

Fig. 10 A TOUCH STONE † Found with the scales and weights Near the real size as described in the drawing

Fig 11 A VESSEL IN THE SHAPE OF A PAIL ‡, 8 inches in diameter, and

corum, qui in suspicione haren Ad cujus [illegible] *[illegible]* vel [illegible] ulum [illegible] nutat, cur culp [illegible] pergunt

We have seen in King Childeric's grave the instance of the *crystal ball*, a magical implement deposited with the *secures* or *axes* Pl XI fig 5 may also possibly shew an *axe*, companion to a magical vessel, fig 4 engraved upon in the *note* to fig 1 and fig 3 of Pl XI and is this [illegible] was doubtless interred with the remains of a female subject, obvious by the [illegible] in [illegible] So the same deduction of sepulchral custom, as stated [illegible] Chifletius on the tomb of King Childeric would at first sight seem inadmissible Arms we know, were an honourable symbol of military exploits buried with the defunct Vir fortis, [illegible] ARMIS, [illegible] fortis [illegible] fuit, fortiter pugnavit et reposuit, says Seneca lib 4 Contro apud Quintil Decl 369 See also Virgil, Æneid 6, also the tomb of Deiphobus in the same author See also Sacred Testament, which I should have first cited "And they shall not lie with the mighty, that are fallen of the uncircumcised which "are gone down to hell with the weapons of war and they have laid their *swords under their heads*" Ezekiel ch xxxii v 27 Childeric had his *sword*, with sumptuous ornaments, buried with him as an honourable symbol of this nature Why then the crystal ball and the *axe*? It might be said, the latter is an arm peculiar to the Franks, called the *Francisca* [illegible]—but why do these instruments occur in other tumuli also, under circumstances peculiar to apparent different forms of interment? Flodoardus, in *Historia Remensi*, lib 1 c 1 has this remarkable passage of Clodoveus I son to Childeric Quidam Francus *Bipennem* [illegible] *[illegible]*, nihil [illegible] *[illegible]* tollendum [illegible] Here is a mystic signification prefixed to the *axe*, the *bipennis*, or *securis* further, Ad cum, qui dudum percusserat *[illegible]* pervenit, spretisque [illegible] armis, ejus tandem *[illegible]* projecit in terram, ad quam recipiendam inclinato milite rex in caput suum defigit *bipennem* [illegible] recepit omnibus acerbitate, rememorans præsumptionem Here we find a kind of expiatory ceremony performed by the King with an AXE and a VASE, chastising himself for some mortal misdemeanor See Gesta Regum Francorum, cap [illegible] by an anonymous author, cited by Chifletius, p 211 Sepulc Child [illegible] I [illegible] of this King [illegible] about the [illegible] *[illegible]* here [illegible] of the contents of which have been shown to bear a great resemblance to what was found in his tomb

At a glance the reader will here see ample field for argument and the many curious deductions possible to be drawn from the above facts The matter advanced, I hope, will not be thought an intention to flatter the vanity of conjecture or to display the above relics in a light beyond their most natural interpretation

* One of these coins of FAUSTINA the younger is in the possession of Mr [illegible], with the *scales* and *weights*, and the *touch stone* Were these relics compared with our weights, and were they evidently Roman, possibly the points on the coins might lead to some illustration, and render the knowledge of the Roman weights more satisfactory than is to be found in Budæus, Scaliger in the [illegible] of Peireskius by Gassendus and other writers I suspect they were money-weights and scales used to essay the base gold coined in the lower Empire, and which the *touch stone* actually seems to indicate

† This is evidently the *coticula* described by Pliny, l 33 xxxiii cap viii He says [illegible] kind of stones are but small not exceeding four inches in length, and two in breadth They were used in his days in the same manner as among the [illegible] His *cotibus* [illegible] [illegible] experimentum, [illegible] quantum [illegible] [illegible] non fallente

‡ The size of this vessel, the care of its preservation, as may be noticed on the [illegible] and the custom of the ancients to throw into the funeral pile, or to inhume with the body, things *esteemed* by the person when living, Kirchman, lib [illegible] who has enumerated all the ancient writers on this subject, naturally inclines me to attribute it to a use of some mystic nature I do not here pretend to determine the particulars of this use, but I should apprehend it to have been attached to some such as were the *brass vessels* and the *axe* I should think it was dedicated to some other more uncommon than that of holding liquids for domestic use

$7\frac{1}{2}$ inches in hight The drawing is accurately taken from a model of thick paper, which Mr Boys of Sandwich made when the relic was found Many fragments of this veſſel are in my poſſeſſion, and which ſtrictly correſpond with the model The handle, I think Mr. Boys ſays, was of iron, but I am not certain It is not preſerved among the fragments The upper rim is very thin braſs, which connects the ribs and other component parts. The perpendicular plate, which connects the handle, is of iron; a fragment of which is now adhering to the rim, and to a wooden rib, which is faſtened with a rivet of the ſame metal. The ſecond rim is compoſed of angular plates of very thin braſs, connected to the wooden ribs, and decorated with ſmall punched holes The third rim is a thin plate of braſs, or ſome mixed metal. The fourth ſhews the wooden ribs of the veſſel And the fifth a band of thin braſs like the former. I have no deſcription of the bottom; nor does it appear that any one was found; perhaps the ſame was periſhed, being of wood The perpendicular plate from the rim to the bottom is of braſs, and ſerves as a band of union to the whole · on the oppoſite ſide was another of the ſame metal. The remains of this veſſel, which now conſiſt of ſome of the plates of the rims, and the wooden ribs connected with other pieces of braſs, and ſeveral mendings diſcovered upon it, are proofs that it was preſerved with much care The wood ſeems to be of aſh, or of the plane tree, the grain is very fine, and where the wood is much ſaturated with verdigreaſe and iron ruſt, it is well preſerved, and the pores and textures very diſcernable It was found with fig. 4. 5. 6. 7 8 9. 9 10. and 12

Fig. 12 A BRASS OR MIXED METAL PATERA*, near 6 inches in diameter, and rather more than half an inch in depth Found inverted as a baſe to fig 4. The bottom, which adhered to that of the large veſſel, has ſome remains of gilding upon it, and which, by being leſs expoſed to the moiſture of the earth, is preſerved in its natural ſtate The other parts are covered with a fine variegated deep *patina*, the ſame as on fig 4

Fig 13. A GLASS PATELLA †, 3 and [illegible]/10 inches in diameter, and $2\frac{7}{10}$ inches in depth; in ſhape exactly like the one in fig. 4 Pl X. The colour is of a bright yellow green, and has little or no coating of the *electrum* or *armatura* upon it It was preſented to me by my good friend Mr. Jacob, of Faverſham, who received it with fig 1 2 3 4. 5 fragments of fig 11 and with fig 12. I have therefore preſumed it was found in the ſame grave, and which ſtrictly confirms the analogy with Tumulus XIV See OBSERVATIONS

* This is the form and the ſize of the libatory and ſacrificial *pateræ*, which may be ſeen on antient ſculptures and coins See a gold patera of the exact ſize in the Britiſh Muſeum, from the collection of Sir William Hamilton The rims ornamented with bulls, the emblem of Bacchus, and therefore apparently uſed in libations for his rites It is ſaid to have been found at Agrigentum in Sicily I have a coin of the large bronze of DIDIA CLARA, in very fine preſervation, on the reverſe a female figure, pouring out a libation on an altar, with a ſimilar kind of *patera*, the inſcription, MATRI CASTROR, alſo ſome of the FAUSTINÆ, one of SABINA, and CRISPINA, with ſacrificial figures of this nature See Octavius Ferrarius de Re Veſt p 85 A figure holding a patera of the exact form of fig 12 pouring out a libation over a tripod altar

† See the note on theſe patellæ, p 15, and the ſame on fig 4 Pl X A *green glaſs veſſel*, of a ſmall faſhion, like *fig* 13 five inches in diameter, ornamented with raiſed cords on its ſurface, was found, with a human ſkeleton, ſeven feet deep, in digging a grave in Minſter Church Yard, in the Iſle of Thanet, ſome time in November, 1786 The account, in the St James's Chronicle, aſcribes the body to ſome *Dane*, who was interred Anno 990, when the Danes demoliſhed St Mildred's Abbey at Minſter Is it preſumable the *Danes* would have interred their dead in a conſecrated ground where they ſhewed ſo much of their unconverted rage? See *Roma Subt* where glaſs veſſels have been found with the remains of the Primitive Chriſtians in their catacombs. The *veſſel* is doubtleſs ſome centuries older than has been ſuggeſted

Pl 13
1
2
3
4
5
6

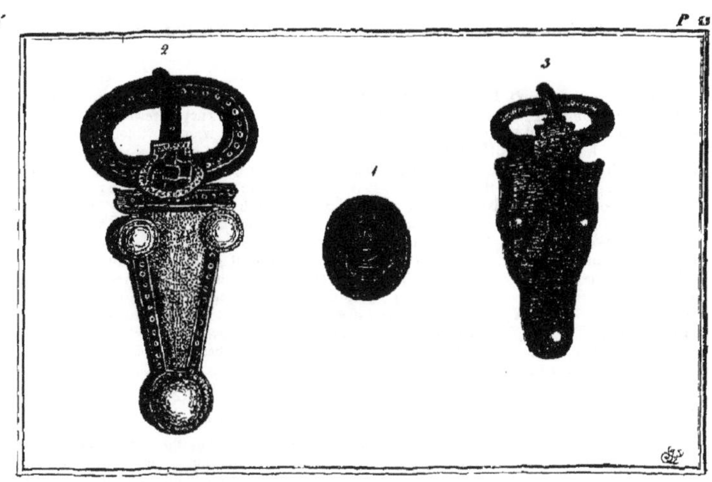

T U M U L U S XVI.

On CHATHAM LINES, 1780

THE bones in this ſepulchre were in their texture more delicate and friable than are uſually found with the arms appropriated to male adult. I opened it with tolerable accuracy as to the poſition of the head, and found the mouldering remains of the *ſcull*, with ſome few of the teeth. This being the uſual method I purſue when I have firſt defined the contour of the cist from the factitious ſoil or mound thrown over it, I then proceed to remove the ſoil from the head, keeping in ſight the line of the ſkeleton, to be more accurate in aſcertaining the poſition of the relics which are inhumed with it. On proceeding therefore with this caution, I am enabled to examine the remains of the bones with critical minuteneſs, and had, from repeated obſervations of this nature, the greateſt reaſon to believe it was the grave of a young ſubject.

PL. XIII. FIG. 1. and 2. The reverſe and head of a ROMAN COIN of the middle bronze, and which I conceive to be of the higher empire, but not ſufficiently diſtinct, either by legend or compariſon, to offer a conjecture as to the Emperor. It was taken from the looſe ſoil without any regard to its poſition, having been thrown up by the labourers, and it is for this reaſon I am doubtful whether it was depoſited with the body, or only in the factitious earth.* Had it been placed in order with the other relics, I could not have failed to have ſeen it.

Fig.

* Want of attention to this caution has frequently led antiquaries into the greateſt of errors. This was the cauſe of Chiflet's incorrect account of the reputed celebrated tomb of King Childeric, opened

P

Fig. 3. A BUCKLE, with an appendage to fasten on the girdle. The metal,

a

opened at Tournay, anno 1653. see his Treatise, Caput II. p. 57. Anast. Childerici Franc. Regis. Labourers were digging at the depth of seven or more feet, when they threw up, in a promiscuous manner, most likely from the artificial incumbent soil, a horse shoe, which, without considering other facts, such as the discovery of the bones of the animal, the quality of the iron, whether corroded sufficiently by age to admit of his conjecture, produces learned arguments on the subject, and endeavours to prove from this discovery, that, according to an ancient custom of the Gauls, this relic belonged to his Majesty's favourite war horse, which had been entombed with him, and as there were two skulls thrown up with other human bones, he assigns one to his Majesty's equerry. Had Chiflet been present, and received more critical information, he doubtless might have considered this fragment of a horse-shoe (see the engraving, p. 224. in Chif.) to have fallen from the upper coating of the earth: he would also perhaps have found the iron in a great degree to have preserved its tenacity and magnetic virtue, a property which this metal by lying a length of time in the earth, generally loses, unless the soil be uncommonly dry, and which was not the case in this instance, by these words in Chiflet, *Effossa multa ferramenta, vetustate exesa et consumpta* [illegible] HUMECTI VITIUM. From these and several other passages, I have been led to consider this work as a pompous production to add consequence to the discovery of the tomb, and built on imperfect, as well as in other respect fallacious materials. I have therefore thought proper, in this place, to offer my remarks upon it.

The labourers, being employed on some occasional work not specified, first threw up a gold fibula, or broach, and in a round hole, as if inclosed in a decayed leather bag, upwards of an hundred gold coins of the Roman emperors. This being reported in the neighbourhood, some learned men resorted to the spot, and other discoveries were afterwards made. They then found upwards of two hundred silver Roman medals or coins, much corroded, and many remains of ancient arms, not engraved in Chiflet, particularly a hatchet and spear head: but from his expression, *multa ferramenta*, I have not a doubt but several others were also found, the produce of more graves than one. Two skulls were also found, one greater than the other, with many other human bones. Then, digging *at the distance of five feet*, a *sword* was discovered, the blade of which fell to pieces, which he proves to have been of good tempered steel, *tam bono chalybe*, because it was so very brittle to the touch, having laid some hundred years in a moist soil. This line of reasoning brings to my mind the two handed sword, used by armour bearers in King Henry the Eighth's time, found in Castle Field, near Manchester, recorded in Mr. Whittaker's learned antient history of that great commercial town, vol. I. p. 78. 8vo edit. who supposes the sword to have been Roman, because it was found on a Roman station: not considering that length of time would have destroyed the *Aurea ferrea* [illegible], which on inspection, I found it to possess, when it was deposited in Sir Ashton Lever's Museum; that the blade was four feet in length, and the sword altogether upwards of five, a size which the Romans were never known to adopt; and that the handle of wood was preserved and *covered with leather*. Such an instance of durability of perishable substances, I believe, was never before attested. To return to Chiflet. There was found also the pummel of the sword, and decoration of the scabbard, some rings, fibulæ, tablets, a pen case, a bulla, and three hundred bees, all of pure gold, with a quantity of gold threads, the remains of some rich vestment: most of the ornaments, he says, were inlaid with the *pyropus*, or carbuncle. A crystal ball and an *horse shoe* were also found; but these do not enter into the general description as above, therefore it is difficult to say, whether they were found near the arms, or five feet distance from the spot, with the gold relics: but mark the result of this sepulchral discovery. The learned *Dean*, *Abbe's*, and many other respectable persons of Tournay, who were present, were naturally at a loss to whom they could ascribe this burial place; but having *afterwards fortunately discovered* a gold ring, on which were engraved the head of a prince, and these letters, CHILDERICI REGIS, they had no difficulty to find an owner. Chiflet, physician to the Archduke Leopold of Austria, was fixed on to be consulted on this interesting treasure of antiquity; and his son, a canon of Tournay, dispatched to him, to inform him of it. On the *undoubted* testimony of these people present, with *the fact* of the ring, he composes a learned book in Latin, to prove these relics to have appertained to King Childeric, one of the first kings of France, interred in that place Anno 481.

From the similar relics which I had collected from sepulchres in this country, I was thus inclined to consult M. Chiflet's work with critical inspection; and, by comparing my own discoveries with many others of this nature, it appears, that all the relics could not be ascribed to the same grave; and, in consequence, much of Mr. Chiflet's ingenious work fabricated on very imperfect and incorrect information. The labourers, who first discovered the *gold broach* and coins, threw them out of the ground in a promiscuous manner, careless to observe how they were deposited; it seems therefore uncertain whether they were actually found in the same grave with the hatchet and other arms, *multa ferramenta*. But wherefore should King Childeric be so well provided with military weapons? A sword, a hatchet, and a spear, would be sufficient for any reasonable *shade* to defend itself against the evil spirits which by it he might troubled: and more weapon than a *sword, shield, spear head, and a knife*, I believe, have never been noticed in these kind of lower tumuli. Two skulls were thrown up, and other human bones: it was but reasonable, in this case, that one of the skulls should have had part of the armoury assigned to it: but when the news of this discovery was spread abroad, the

learned

a composition of *tin* and *copper*. The whole cast in a mould and embossed with

learned assembled on the spot, and this implies an interval of time, [illegible] natural to suppose the labourers had profited as much as they well could in their first digging, [illegible] many relics were sold among the inhabitants. The ground was [illegible] the distance [illegible], when the *gold hilted sword* and all the other treasures were explored [illegible] doubtless [illegible], which could not have any connection with the former, [illegible] place.

This discovery of valuable treasure was published [illegible] *Dell* [illegible], and the magistrates undertook the custody of some of the relics [illegible] now deposited in the King of France's cabinet of medals, [illegible] in the month of April 17[illegible] I visited and took a close inspection of [illegible] I was favoured by M. [illegible] Abbe De Courcy [illegible] of the ring, to whose custody this immense and valuable cabinet was then entrusted, and whose friendly attentions, the short time I was with him there, to communicate every information in his power on the subject, I am here happy to acknowledge. Many of the relics were not to be found [illegible] the horse shoe, the spear, a fragment of [illegible] *gilt vase*, not in Chiflet's general description, p. 37 [illegible] mentioned [illegible] he had purchased, p. 47 and several of the gold ornaments and coins. These relics I suspect, [illegible] industry of Chiflet, his son, canon of Tournay, being empowered [illegible] as many as he could, perhaps with the Archduke of Austria's money, from whom I conjecture [illegible] came into the King's possession were preserved from the [illegible] of the rest, consigned very probably to the melting pot [illegible] relics were also there, not noted in Chiflet, several gold inlaid ornaments, and amongst them [illegible] head of a fish of gold inlaid with stones. The latter, instead of Chiflet's *pyropus*, I found were of garnet, set on a gold foil, which gave them the carbuncle lustre, and in every respect similar to the workmanship of the ornaments in Plate X. fig. 6 and Plate XI. fig. 1 of this work.

Among the gold coins there were several [illegible] Valentinian, Marcianus, Leo and Zeno, Basiliscus and Marcus. As Childeric died in [illegible]471, and Basiliscus in 476, Chiflet makes the discovery of the ring accord with chronology. But this ring was [illegible], and he himself confesses the inscription was suspected as a forgery. "Scio non nullis [illegible] "[illegible] suspectam [illegible] ob Romanos characteres," [illegible] to prove [illegible] was well known by the French Kings, and that this alone would remove the objection, which [illegible] tion, in other respects, insisted on the inscription to be written in [illegible] characters. [illegible] any suspicion of forgery, and why should Chiflet attempt to clear the matter up by [illegible] harangue? He could have procured the undoubted testimony of those [illegible] the actual finding of it. This he does not dwell upon, but flourishes [illegible] all the [illegible] on the various writing of the name, citing passages from authors, without [illegible] discrimination of typical proofs. If there has been no similar specimen of [illegible] name, of the æra of the fifth century, with the genitive case in Latin, [illegible] or any century, either before or after it, I believe Childeric's ring will [illegible]. Had the letters been simply written CHILDERICVS REX, [illegible] would [illegible] the head to have been the head of King Childeric, in like manner as the letters on the coins [illegible] the head to have been of that emperor. But this would not have answered the purpose of the antiquary; the ring must indicate that Childeric was the absolute owner of it. The covering of a coffin, or a sarcophagus, would have answered the purpose better, with [illegible] inscription, but no such thing being found, an Antwerp artist, I suspect, must have been employed for the forgery, and the seventeenth century being fertile in the best artists of Holland, [illegible] one of which would have been equal to the execution of [illegible] coin of the lower empire, which the most [illegible] pupil in the arts could have imitated. But the letters on the [illegible] ring, themselves establish the forgery. Their structure is not similar to those used at that time. The [illegible] and the rest of the letters would have been engraved much thicker at the [illegible] very probably copied from those of the time, but not with art enough to conceal the [illegible]. They are not sufficiently embossed, and some of them towards the head take an irregular inclination, which a little care would have made otherwise, and which [illegible], would have been contrived by the artist who was working for a sovereign prince. It is further natural to suppose, if Childeric was in actual possession of this ring, having either an artist in his dominions, or in [illegible] at Constantinople, where, history [illegible] some time resided, that the [illegible] could [illegible] made [illegible] for his mintage; but in the French coins, I believe, of this [illegible], Le Blanc does not exhibit an instance of a coin that has sufficient analogy to admit of such a supposition, and I believe no coin of Childeric was ever found, to put the same beyond a doubt. It is also natural to suppose some of his mintage would have been found among his regalia, or otherwise some Gaulish coin of other princes.

Several of the gold and silver coins in this grave were perforated, like those in Plate II. of this work, and used as female decorations, like the one of the [illegible] mentioned in the note of p. 8. Suffice it barely to say, that the crystal ball, in the numerous instances which can be cited, (see the note p. 1[illegible]), only occurs in the tombs of females, or young women, who at this period were, as in the time of our King Charles, and to this hour in several parts of Scotland, supposed to have the gift of *second sight* by inspection of this stone. See this more fully explained in the above note of p. 1[illegible]. Therefore the *crystal*, the [illegible], (see p. 1[illegible] and 49) the [illegible] *cup*, (see p. [illegible]2) may be considered as magical relics, deposited in a tomb with one of the female sex, and which cotemporary discoveries have sufficiently attested.

The

with the small circles and beading described on similar relics of the æra of the lower empire.* Found on the left side of the skeleton.

Fig. 4. A KNIFE of iron, the metal entirely corroded. The handle of wood, part of which is accreted to the rust. Near the side, and found with the buckle.

Fig. 5. The HEAD OF AN IRON SPEAR. It has lost its magnetic virtue by laying in the earth: has in several places the fair impression of a coarse cloth † accreted

The ornaments of gold inlaid with garnets, which Chifflet calls *Phaleræ Regii Equi*, p. 226, horse-trappings of the King, most probably were only the personal decorations of the owner of the sword and the other regalia, similar to the workmanship of the former. There were doubtless several graves opened, and I am persuaded, if fresh digging was made on the spot at this time, more bodies would be discovered. The sword and the other rich ornaments may have been of some distinguished personage; but I am convinced no proof is sufficiently established to admit of their belonging to King Childeric. Perhaps the crystal ball might have been found in the grave with the sword, but no proof of which can be sufficiently ascertained, and, were it to be sufficiently established, it might have been used by a female in some rights of magic with the crystal. This may be thought perhaps *too refined*; but I am nevertheless persuaded, even in this case, it is nearer the truth than M. Chifflet. In short, the whole argument can only be deduced to these few words, that several graves were opened at Tournay in a very careless desultory manner, and some rich relics promiscuously found in them, as delineated in the above work: the ring I believe to be an ingenious forgery; but the relics in general, are the mode of inhumation, coeval with the æra to which they have been assigned: which credit is due to the learned author, for the pains he has taken to transmit the account of this sepulchral treasure to posterity for the inspection of antiquaries, and we can only say, we lament he was not present himself at the discovery, and sufficiently guarded against the imposition of the ring, or as sufficiently honest in his declarations if he had truth for his argument.

I have given in the VIGNETTE to p. 53, as correct an imitation of the impression of this ring as possible.

* Mr. Boys, of Sandwich, engraved a plate of antiquities found at Ash, anno 17[illegible]1, in which (see *fig.* 3 and 5.) is represented two gold buckles of a similar shape, inlaid with garnets on a gold foil, ornamented with a milling and filligree work. To establish truth by analogy in this kind of enquiries, this buckle is re-engraved in the VIGNETTE, p. 2, fig. 3, also another of a similar form, fig. 53, of brass, or a metallic composition, from Sir William Fag's cabinet, taken from the tumuli on Chartham Downs.

† The preservation of cloth by the rust of the spear is a proof that the body was buried with a vestment: the several specimens of relics, which have impressions of linen, woollen, and silk, of different textures and fineness, indicate that the dead not only had a funereal garment to cover them entirely, but that they were also entombed with their accustomary apparel when alive; and which perhaps, as in the instance of modern inhumation at Naples thus buried (see note, p. 42,) was more profusely lavished on these occasions. See the curious paper of the Countess of Moira, p. 90. vol. VII. of the Archæologia, which describes the vestments of a skeleton found in a bog in Ireland, and which the elegant pen of this lady treats of, as similar to a Gaulish dress. There is no doubt but the body had been interred many centuries, and that the gravelly soil in which it was found seems to have had a peculiar property in preserving all kinds of apparel in a different manner to the rust of iron, or the copperas from brass, or similar metals. This remark I have corroborated by the contents of graves in Greenwich Park. In January, 1784, by favour of leave from the Hon. John Pitt, of Arlington Street, surveyor general, &c. of the royal domains, I there visited a range of barrows, situated near the gate that leads to Crombs Hill, to the amount of about *fifty*, which I conceived to be lower British; and on opening of one, in which were similar beads to those wherein I have found coins, dating their age to be of the fifth and beginning of the sixth century, I discovered the remains of a garment, and a braid of human hair: the braid tenacious and very distinct, and the hair itself, which was of an auburn colour, contained its natural phlogiston. This curious fact of hair lying so long undissolved in the earth, made me cautious in examining the contents of this grave with great attention, when I plainly discerned throughout the whole of the cist very distinct appearances of cloth; which the fire soon proved to be both of woollen and linen. They were of different fineness and textures: some wove in the herring-bone, and others in the usual square pattern. I have preserved many remains of the cloth, and have the braid of hair as perfect as when first taken out of the earth. On repeated discoveries of this nature in these graves, Sir Joseph Banks and Dr. Blagden were pleased to honour me with their company, and were fully satisfied, when I opened one in their presence, of the truth of this phenomenon. As the graves were very shallow, several not exceeding three feet in depth, I imagined the vegetable juices, from the incumbent soil, might have been the cause of the preservation of this hair and cloth, as in the case of our peat mosses, and which appears to be also the case with the juices of the bog, under which, in a gravelly soil, the skeleton and its vestments were preserved, as described by Lady Moira.

There

accreted to the iron. The remains of wood, apparently of ash, is preserved in the socket. Found close to the *os humeri* of the right side.

Fig. 6. A Tweezer †, the metal of bronze, and the size represented in the drawing. On the left side near the *pelvis*, and close to the buckle and knife.

The relics in this grave are singular, and seem to denote the person to be of a more effeminate order than is usually the case when I have opened graves which contained warlike instruments. The delicate appearance of the bones, the size of the spear, which is smaller than usual, the tweezer and the buckle, are in general found in graves of the women, which are critically denoted by beads in the same graves near the neck, and in which no military weapons are found.

For further particulars, see OBSERVATIONS.

There is now deposited in the Vatican a skull with hair; which, by the braid and the ornaments upon it, appears to have been of a female, and to have been interred 1400 years. It was found not far from the Tyber near Rome. Human hair, after death, is known on some bodies to increase greatly. Mr John Pitt assured me, that on visiting a vault of his ancestors in Farley chapel, in Somersetshire, to give orders for some necessary repairs, he saw the hair of a young lady [illegible] which had in a most exuberant manner, grown out of the coffin, and hanging down from it, and by the inscription she was buried considerably upwards of an hundred years since. But this instance is essentially different from the above: the body was not exposed to the continual moisture of the earth, but entombed in a dry vault, the proportion of years besides bears no affinity with the former.

* I have frequently been at a loss to decide, whether the spear was buried entire with the body, the earth decaying the haft, and leaving the iron, or whether the head was broke off, and in this state buried with the body. In some graves it should seem the spear and other arms were enclosed with the body in a sheet, as was in antient times, and is now the custom in some countries. The head of the spear in general is found close to the bones of the arms, as if placed designedly, the other remaining parts of the haft (excepting once the specimen of a stud, which seemed to have been driven in at the head, and engraved in PLATE I. fig. 5.) I have not discovered, though I have repeatedly pryed narrowly into the adjacent soil in the cist, chalk being an excellent material for making these discoveries in. Had the spear, sword, or shield been deposited on a coffin (for coffins in several instances, by the look of the soil and the discovery of nails, appear to have contained the dead buried in these kind of tumuli), they would, when the coffin by decay had fallen in, also have taken in promiscuous and irregular positions, and thus have been discovered on or near the skeleton; but, in almost every instance, the spear is methodically placed, the sword, and almost always the shield, the same. When I have found the spear on the right side, it has been placed in as much order as on the left. There is one circumstance which inclines me to believe that some of them had no coffins, the shield could not, from its orbicular shape and being upwards of two feet and an half in diameter, be placed in one. At least I apprehend not.

† This instrument was called by the Greeks παρατιλτρον, and by the Latins *Volsella*. There were men employed in the office of plucking off the hairs of effeminate persons, who frequented the baths, and this custom prevailed among the Greeks, as well as the Romans: the latter people, in all their customs, evidently imitating the former. The Greeks had their δρωπακιστας, and the Romans their *alipilarios*. Among the Greeks, if a man was candidate for a public office, he was obliged to give a testimony of his manhood and virtue, by lifting up his arms, and producing his hair under them.

——————— Δημοσιᾳ [illegible]
Ἐξεπιτασας τὸν [illegible] Βραχιονα. Aristoph.

See Juvenal, Sat. ii.

——————— Dura per brachia setæ
Promittunt atrocem animum.

The above passage alludes to the abominable *Socraticos Cinædos*. There were a set of people, whom Juvenal satyrizes, at this time in Rome, who, in imitation of the infamous *Cinædi* of Athens, avoided this athletic appearance, and used all kind of artifice, in diets and in their bodies, to shew their effeminacy. This is also satirized by Martial, Lib. ii. Epig. 62. v. 1.

Quod pectus, quod crura tibi, quod brachia vellis.

It is evident from the reply of Cappadox, the pandar in Plautus, see act IV. sc. 4. Curculio, that these instruments are peculiar to effeminate, and such persons as I have above hinted at.

At tu me *volsella*, pecten, speculum, calamistrum meum
Bene me amassint, &c.

And with the ornaments of women they are chiefly found; several specimens of which will occur in the description of that kind of sepulchres. Mr Faussett found one in a woman's tomb at Sibertswould in Kent. They have been found at North Elmham in Norfolk, 1786. Five graves I have opened with these *nippers*, or *volsellæ*, which contained female ornaments; and from what I can possibly collect on the subject, they appear to me as instruments peculiar to the female sex; wherefore my conjectures on TUM. XVI. are not the most favourable to the male subject interred in it.

TUMULUS XVII.

OPENED the 18th of May, 1780, on Chatham Lines, on the same ground as described in note to p. 3. The bones imperfectly preserved, excepting the large fistular bones, it was with difficulty I could trace the mouldering remains of the body. The *radius* and *ulna* of the left arm, the extremities of the right, and the two last joints of the little finger of the left hand, were the only parts of the body distinctly preserved: their preservation was owing to their position near metallic ornaments, such as *armillæ* and a ring. By an accurate and near inspection of the chalk, in which soil these tumuli were situated, the mouldered remains of the bones could be traced, discernible by a brownish tinge, and at times very small particles of them could be seen in it. This grave or cist contained two female bodies: the companion to it was the following, described *Tum* XVIII. Their proximate position by the side of each other appears to have arisen from a reciprocal tie of consanguinity or friendship of the parties. This body I conjecture to have been buried earlier than the companion to it; not so much from the few remaining parts of the skeleton, compared with the almost total preservation of the other; as a few years, or the natural course of human life, would make but a small difference in this soil, but from the greater portion of corruptible matter received from the other later buried body, which seems to have accelerated the dissolution of the bones *. The position of both these bodies was meridional.

* I have made this remark from a supposition that carneous subjects have their fibres or bones sooner dissolved in the earth, than others of a different temperament. There is no doubt but the quality of soil will in many instances cause this observation to vary: however, as a fact to substantiate my remark, I can attest the truth of a body, which was interred in Rochester cathedral, having been, in point of corpulence, of a dimension which required the casement of a window to be taken out to receive the coffin, and that twenty or thirty years afterwards, one of the same family dying, the same ground in the cathedral was broken to receive it, when, to the surprize of the inquisitive family, after the remains of the aforesaid body, there were only found some few fragments of the metal ornaments of the coffin, and a large lump of saponaceous matter, produced by the human fat and its lixivial salts, but no bones whatever were discovered.

PL.

Pl. 14

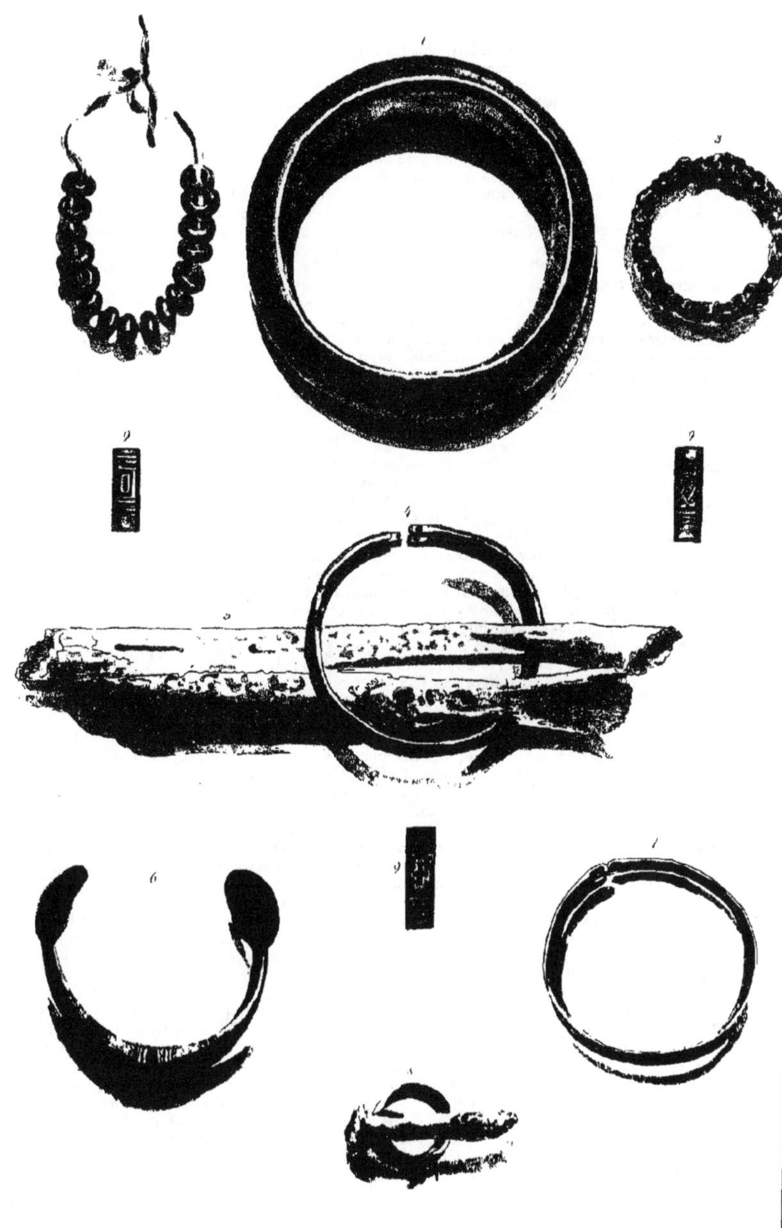

PL. XIV fig 1. A GLASS ARMILLA* of a transparent light green colour. At the extremity of the left arm on the right side

Fig.

* Bartholine *de Armillis veterum* says, the word is derived from *armus*, and which [illegible] from Festus *quod antiqui humeros cum brachiis armos vocabant* This is undoubtedly the true meaning of *Armilla*, and whether the ornament of the wrist or arm, the application of the word is in [illegible] this sense by the antients When it occurs as a military [illegible], donative, or reward, in Roman [illegible], or as an ornament of women, it has the same appellation, but, I think, not with [illegible] or just discrimination Sometimes, indeed, it is called a *fibula*, or clasp, see Pitiscus, lib [illegible] or buckle Festus also calls *spinter*, clasp, a kind of *armilla* Among the number of these kind of [illegible], many occur to prove they were used as such, for if we may [illegible] to be that of collecting the folds of drapery, then *spinter* is applicable enough, [illegible] Fig 1 which could not serve only as an ornament, but also as an instrument to collect the loose plaits or folds of the [illegible] or upper garment when the flowing parts became troublesome and which were loosened [illegible] for [illegible] of appearance and parade Antient marbles will prove the truth of this remark This ornament is also called *spathalium* by Pliny and Tertullian, from the Greek [illegible], volupt[illegible]ous ornaments of the female sex, called [illegible], [illegible] bracelet, also [illegible], *cubiti*, [illegible], *dextro cheria* the latter from the ornaments of the right arm All ornaments for the arms, according to Suidas, were called *βραχιόνια*, afterwards changed to *βραχιάλια* so that bracelet in this sense, should be the general term for the decoration of the arms and *armillæ*, when it occurs as in Fig 1, the diameter of which being suited only to the more fleshy and upper part of the arm When the ornament is made of beads or pearls, as in *fig* [illegible] *pl* XIV they are then called *viriolæ*, see Ulpian, Leg XXV *de auro* et argento In aures, armilla, *viriolæ* [illegible] [illegible]torios Pithonius thinks *viriola* does not occur as a neck ornament, and cites Juvenal to prove it But [illegible] occur in Latin authors in both senses

Armillæ have been the ornaments of the human species from the very earliest [illegible] of antiquity and indeed, from the natural attention to personal decoration, they seem to have originated [illegible] with the creation of man Rebekah, Gen xxiv—v 22 was ornamented with the [illegible] צמד, [illegible] the Septuagint, translated [illegible] The people of the new discovered islands (see Cook's Voyages) Peruvians, Africans, Asiatics, Europeans, all the known inhabitants of the globe [illegible] have used them from an unknown period of time It is absurd, therefore, to [illegible] citation upon citation to explain their use as common ornaments it [illegible] to say, among the Greek and Roman writers, they are often mentioned with their dress, among their vestiges [illegible] and tombs, they are daily found, and in most cabinets they are deposited GLASS ARMILLÆ must have been invented from the first discovery of glass, and continued in that [illegible] nations. I have several fragments of glass bracelets in my cabinets for the [illegible] and doubtless many must be noticed in others yet I believe the *armilla*, *fig* 1 though it is reasonable to apprehend many more such must have existed, appears to be hitherto single in its kind.

As many of these glass relics have been found in tombs, and accompanied with a [illegible] of the time of their deposit, it would perhaps be a curious subject of enquiry to [illegible] of the invention of glass, its introduction into this island, and whether the ancient Britons were [illegible] with the art? Pliny has recorded a tale, which is sufficient to attest that the [illegible] the remembrance or positive testimony of his contemporaries "Certain merchants having landed on the "borders of the Lake Cendevia, at the foot of Mount Carmel, in Syria who, having a quantity of nitre "on board their ship, used some lumps of it as props to support their vessels over a fire to prepare "victuals in, which, incorporating with sand, was the first cause of this discovery" And he further observes, that the lake or the mouth of the river Belus, during [illegible], furnished many places with material for this purpose, *multa per sæcula* is their expression [illegible] xxxvi [illegible] xxvi [illegible] evident proof enough that the art of making glass was of [illegible] the written testimony of Pliny's time who, having ransacked 2000 manuscripts of [illegible] to [illegible] his Natural History, and many among them of Greek authors, would doubtless have [illegible] on the subject and have transcribed a more satisfactory narrative of its first discovery, if [illegible] could have been found in any prophane writings Strabo, who flourished 52 years before Pliny speaks of it p [illegible] 7, [illegible], *vasa vitri*, and which he says was introduced into [illegible] by traffic from Tyre [illegible] with decision on the discovery, and to prefix it to any particular [illegible], will be absurd, unless we could find more decisive proofs, but as, from the undoubted relation of the old Roman naturalist, we may safely trace it to a remote period beyond his time, we may be permitted to shift our ground to other sources of greater antiquity I shall therefore consider the name of *Glass* in the Hebrew, and endeavour to approach as near to the period of its discovery as truth will admit In the third chapter of Isaiah, ver 23 we read of גליונים *gilionim*, glasses in Lexicons we find גליונים *gilionim*, evidently *Glasses*, but whether reflectors of the face, or transparent utensils, is not sufficiently [illegible] The interpreters absurdly explain away the meaning thus *Nam specula reddunt [illegible] facies, vel [illegible] in corpore ejusve amiciendi modo [illegible] ut de more corrigatur* Kimchi and others, still more absurd, render it more *transparent*, and will have *gilionim* to signify *transparent linen*, keeping in view the expression of *fine linen*, which in Isaiah follows the word *gilionim*, glasses, and Horace's description of the Lacedemonian women, "Ne corpus pene nudum videri queat," therefore they explain the word, which

truly

Fig 2. TWENTY BLUE GLASS BEEDS. Near the extremity of the *radius* and *ulna*

truly signifies glasses, by *interulas, sive sabuculas, tenues ac subtiles, per quas corpus transparebat* This is sufficient to shew the word is adopted, and not of Hebrew origin Pliny says, the *Sidonians* were in *antient times* famous for various devices in glass, and seems to infer, that the perfection of it was centered in them, and still observing it was of antient date, *Hæc fuit antiqua ratio vitri* The above cited passage in Isaiah alludes to the daughter of Zion, to the town in its flourishing state before the first captivity. This was the period of the Phœnicians, when Tyre and Sidon were in their prosperity, when all the arts of merchandize were cultivated to the greatest height of perfection it is to this period then, 768 years before Christ, we are to look for the existence of *glass*. This is the period which has been marked by Ezekiel, who, concerning the opulence of the Tyrians, is remarkably explicit, describing many of their branches of commerce which excelled in the greatest degree of magnificence This discovery therefore pre-existed any tradition of the Greeks, being only in the second Olympiad, before which, according to Varro, 21 apud Censor de die natali, cap 21 all was error and uncertainty, and Plutarch, in his life of Theseus, compares the early history of Greece to geographical maps, where regions that are known are bounded by uninhabited countries, deserts of sand and frozen seas It is not in the prophane history of the Greeks we can then trace the early discovery of glass; but, as Pliny says, the Sidonians were famous for the art of making glass, and particularly specifies their having been inventors of looking-glasses, *siquidem etiam* SPECULA *excogitaverat*, so we may, by a correct affinity of the æra, prefix the גלינים of Isaiah to *reflectors of glass*, and thus establish a certain date for its existance, anno 768 ant Christum, for it is unequivocally certain, that Pliny would never speak of Sidon after the captivity of Nebuchadnezzar, when this town and Tyre were absolutely rased to the ground, when their splendor, their arts and commerce, were transferred into other regions

Pliny says, the Germans called amber *glessum*, c xxxvii c iii This was the Scythian name for transparency In the British *glaine*, in the Irish, *gloine*, glass, hence *glain naroith*, glass-adders, absurdly called the *anguinum* of the Druids by bishop Gibson, see his notes to Camden There is a *glass bead* found in Scotland, which that people call *glain naoroth*, and which vulgar and superstitious appellation has been received into the serious arguments of the learned A bead of this kind is engraved in Camden, but which, we shall soon have occasion to see proved, was not the Druids charm here referred to but of a date much posterior. *Glaine* therefore, a Scythian or Phœnician name for glass known by these people, who were seated at *Dor* near Tyre, has been received into the Hebrew, and hence we read גלינים *glinim*

By comparing the vitrified ornaments found on the coverings of mummies, such as beads, scarabei instruments, hieroglyphic figures, and the small deities encloled in the wrappers of the dead, or a blue opaque vitrifaction, to the reputed time of the Ægyptian custom of thus interring their dead; the antiquity of this invention may be carried to a certainty to the age of Solomon, 1019 years before Christ Whether the Egyptians were proficients in the art of forming their glass into the useful purposes of vessels, would be a pleasing question to answer in the affirmative As I have not had any information that glass vessels have been found among other relics of these very antient people, so I can only reply by a reasonable conjecture, that, on such an important discovery, they would be naturally inclined to render it serviceable to the domestic duties of society, and not remain satisfied with it as a decoration of attire, and an art conducive only to purposes of traffic If they did not understand the use of the lathe or blaste, as described by Pliny, they would doubtless have thought of the mould common to all metallic smelting arts, and, in this case, I say, it is reasonable to conclude they made drinking vessels of it Happy am I therefore, in this place, to reply to that very trivial, careless, and superficial remark of Voltaire, "that the invention of drinking glasses is but modern," see his Philosophical Dictionary, Chap "On Solomon," and this he applies as sufficient grounds to accuse the book of Proverbs, as the production of some Alexandrine Jew, much subsequent to the æra of Alexander He surely had never looked into Pliny, Strabo, or any modern cabinet of antient relics, otherwise he must have conceived this passage in Proverbs, "*Look not on wine when it appears bright* "*in the* GLASS, *and its colour shines*," not in the light of anachronism, but which might correctly be applied to the illustration of the use of *glass* in the time of Solomon

Many glass antient relics have been found in Britain, such as beads and vessels, some in tombs, some by casual discoveries Those in tombs, by Dr Stukeley, have been pronounced British (see Stonehenge, p 45) Camden has also called them British, p 684 c. 815 The country people, in some parts of Britain, who find antient glass beads, call them amulets or charms Mr Edward Lloyd, in his Observations on Wales, writes, that in his travels through Scotland, *glass beads* were used as amulets, and that they have been handed down from parents to children as such from the time of the Druids *There is no accounting for the superstitious ideas and romantic notions of a modern, rude, and unpolished people* The most specious tradition on striking subjects of history are frequently tinctured with the most glaring colours of extravagancy Mr Whitaker, following the observations of Dr Stukeley, and the occasional remarks of other writers, has decided on glass being the manufactory of the antient Britons before the invasion of the Romans, and which he chiefly rests on the glass relics found in a barrow on Salisbury plain by Stukeley, and the glass amulet mentioned by Camden, called glainen nadroedh See the History of Manchester, vol II p. 25 The barrow on Salisbury Plain I have evidently demonstrated (see note, p. 24) to have been of the age of the fifth century The *glainen nadroedh* is a rayed coloured glass bead, cut from a rod of glass, a specimen of

ulna of the left arm, and which denoted their use as a bracelet.

FIG 3. AN IRON RING, too small for a bracelet, and apparently used as an amulet †. On the side, near to the beads, *fig.* 2.

FIG.

of which may be now seen in the British Museum, and which was there deposited by Sir William Hamilton from Italy; the manufactory of the lower Romans, many specimens of which I have in my cabinet. They were introduced into Britain by traffic and, being found in Scotland, they have given rise to the ridiculous opinions and name of *snake stones*, mentioned by Mr Edward Lhwyd (see the *Observations* on the plate of miscellaneous beads engraved in this work). It is impossible to deduce from the [illegible] σκευη, *vasa vitri*, of Strabo, p. 3[illegible]7, speaking of imported articles into Britain, that glass was the manufacture of the Britons; it is idle to suppose it. The importation was from Tyre, and in after-times, when the change of empires decreed the Romans to be possessed of the commerce of the Sidonian coasts, Britain received all her glass wares to the very declension of the empire from Italy, and perhaps from some few places in Gaul.

On the [illegible]2th of May, 17[illegible], Dr Stukeley presented a *glass vessel* to the Antiquarian Society, taken from a barrow in the Isle of Ely, near Chartens (see this barrow mentioned in *note* of p. 11, where the *glass vessel* is also mentioned) and endeavours to prove, from this relic, that the antient Britons were famous for glass manufactory, and that this country was originally peopled from Tyre. Compare the relics from this barrow with the relics in Tum. I and IV and the period of their inhumation will be found to correspond with the fifth or beginning of the sixth century. The glass vessel from Charteris most probably was not found in the same sepulchre with the [illegible], *spear*, *[illegible]*, and other relics; more graves than one were opened; and, as Stukeley's information was on hearsay only from the report of ignorant labourers, we must take our argument from the agnation of similar relics, found in similar tombs, and which agnation I have, in the course of this work, sufficiently attested. What grounds, therefore, have we to conclude on, that the antient Britons were instructed in the art of making glass from their friends the Phœnicians? It is doubtless natural to suppose that most, as a barbarous people, have been pleased with an art so calculated to awaken their curiosity and admiration, as we have found, in these our days, to be the case with the African slave trade. In the course of time, some secrets of the art might transpire, or chance might have occasioned some discovery in it, by the vitrification in the process of making bricks, or any process in which the furnace was concerned, or perhaps from the ordinary uses of fire; but an attempt to establish a manufactory of glass among the Britons, prior to the Roman invasion, to equal the many beautiful antient specimens of the metal found in this island, inseparably allied with other arts, and other refined conveniencies which we cannot suppose the antient Britons to have accomplished, must be utterly ineffectual and unsatisfactory. The variegated colours on the glass relics of the antients shew a knowledge in mineral compounds, and a chemical process, which a primitive people could not attain to. But why do I dwell on this impossibility? Had the Britons ever the art of making glass, whatever their changes may have been by the hostile invasions of foreign enemies, and other incongenial events to the arts, they would never have lost it; but Bede assures us, *they had not that art*. "Anno 4° Egfridi Regis, A. D. 674. Benedictus Biscop Abbas Minumathensis, Galliam petens, cæmentarios abstulit, qui lapideam sibi ecclesiam juxta Romanorum morem facerent. Perfecto opere, misit legatos Gallias qui VITRI FACTORES adducerent, *Britannis incognitas artifices*, ad cancellendas ecclesiæ fenestras." And Stubbs, in his Acts of the Bishop, says, that Wilfred, junior, who died A. D. 711, was the first that brought *[illegible]* into England.

* This bracelet was in imitation of the gem or precious stone bracelets of the antients. Manilius, Lib. v. de Cassiope,

Perque caput ducti lapides, per colla manusque.

See Bartholine de Arm. Vet. p. 37. See Q. Curtius, Lib. IX. cap. 1. on the habits of the Indian Kings. "Lacerti quoque et *bra[illegible] margaritis* ornantur." The Persians had that kind of ornament though of a more sumptuous nature. See Ammianus Marcellinus, Lib. xxiii. Armillis uti monilibusque aureis et gemmis præcipue margaritis. Athenæus Lib. [illegible] speaks of their being worn on hands and feet: ψέλλια περὶ τὰς χεῖρας καὶ [illegible] πόδας, Armillas circum manus pedesque. Antient marbles frequently exhibit the gemmated bracelets on the wrist.

† Dr Plot, in his Hist. of Oxfordshire, p. 3[illegible]5, first edit. mentions an antient bracelet with a small *iron* and small green glass *ring* pendant to it; he very properly cites Bartholin *de Armil. [illegible]* § [illegible] p. 41 to shew that the *iron* and glass ring were prefixed to them for some mysterious purpose. "Illum vero quod annulis armillis fere jungeretur *non caret mysterio*, [illegible] illorum formam [illegible] in brachio præstent, quod digitis annuli." See the ivory armilla with the silver rings and beads pendant to it, described in the note to p. 7. *Iron rings*, apparently worn as amulets on some part of the body, I have frequently found in these lower tumuli. They are more common in the graves of the women than in those of the men. See Pl. VIII fig. 7. One of which was prefixed to a long piece of iron having a loop at the end to hang it to the side, and indeed seemed to answer no other purpose whatever. It was found with beads, two small brass coins of the lower empire, a small drop of silver, brooches and other relics. Lucian, in his dialogue between Philocles and Eucrates, ridiculing the superstitious credulity of his contemporaries, makes the latter say, "that he used to be much frightened at the "frequent sight of demons and spectres, but when a certain Arabian had given him an *iron ring* taken "from a cross, by which the criminal was fastened, and had taught him to repeat a verbal charm "composed of several proper names, he found his fears had vanished." *Iron rings* also occur in these

R

small

FIG. 4. and 5. A BRASS GILT ARMILLA*, with the two bones of the arm on which it was found, the *radius* and the *ulna*. It ſeems to have been rivetted on the wriſts of the wearer.

FIG. 6. A braſs or mixed metal GILT ARMILLA, of a lunar ſhape.

FIG. 7. A braſs or mixed metal GILT ARMILLA, worn very thin; and which appears to have been rivetted as the one of *fig.* 4. found near the right arm fig. 6.

Fig. 9. 9. 9. The *Ornamental Marks* of fig. 4. diſplayed.

FIG. 8. A MIXED METAL RING, and two bones of the little finger on which it was found. The ring was ſet with a ſtone which dropped out. It is remarkable, that the two joints of the extremity of the finger have been oſſified; and formed what ſurgeons call an *anchyloſis*, probably from injury which the finger had received, or from diſeaſe.

For further particulars, ſee OBSERVATIONS.

ſmall lower tumuli; ſee a ſmall one in plate XV. In the courſe of this work larger ones will be produced, and which will appear alſo to have been uſed in ſome myſteries by the antients. See Theocritus Lib. β. ΦΑΡΜΑΚ.

Χ'ὡς δινεῖθ' ὅδε ῥόμβος ὁ χάλκεος, κ' Ἀφροδίτας,

Utque volvitur hic æneus orbis, ope Veneris

The Greeks had an inſtrument of this nature, with which they operated a love ſpell, placing the effigy of the object on the wheel, and whirling it round. The expreſſion ſomewhere occurs in their writings, [illegible] τροχῶ, they uſed a verbal ſpell in turning it. Sometimes the object was prefixed to τροχος, or a wheel of wax, and both conſumed in the fire. Lælius mentions a magic ring of this kind.

Trochiſcili, ungues, Tæniæ,

Auieæ, Illices bitortilæ

Some commentators, on this magical *Trochus*, conceive it to be the muſical trochus, which charms or operates as a magical ſpell by its tinkling; but, as this *trochus* is evidently uſed in the ſame act of working magic ſpells as the *[illegible] lacertis* of Horace, Lib. 1. Sat. viii. and the σαῦραι, *Lacertæ*, in Theocritus, ſee his ſecond Idyllium, I think it muſt imply the ὄφεις τῶ χαλκεῶ, *bracelets or rings* worn about the wriſts. The muſical *trochus* referred to is, perhaps, a kind of *crotalum*, bracelet, with gingling rings fixed to it, one of which is engraved in the work of the Rymſdyks, which contains ſome of the curioſities of the British Muſeum, Tab. xxiv. When Count Caylus (ſee Pl. LXXI.) deſcribes a bracelet with rings to be the *trochus* of Mercurialis, p. 219, he certainly muſt have meant the *crotalum* of the Romans. But to explain the caprice of the antients in magical inventions would exceed the bounds of the readieſt pen, and the moſt patient reference to antient authors. From the frequent diſcovery of ſuch relics in the ſepulchres of the antients, I think it almoſt beyond a doubt that they were fabricated as articles of traffic, and circulated over Europe, in that ignorant and unlettered period to which I have aſſigned them, the latter end of the fifth and beginning of the ſixth centuries.

* Bartholin, p. 33. ſays, braſs *armillæ* were the ornaments of the common people. Plebeiæ plane cenſendæ æreæ. There is no doubt but ſuch metals were diſtinguiſhing marks in thoſe days as in the preſent. He might have ſpared his remark in compliment to the common ſenſe of his readers.

TUM.

TUMULUS XVIII.

THIS was the companion to Tum XVII and evidently contained the remains of a female ſubject The bones more perfect than the preceding one, but much inferior in ſize and ſolidity to thoſe which on repeated obſervation I have examined in thoſe graves which contain arms and other inſtruments peculiar to the men. The head to the north; the poſition of moſt of the ſkeletons found in this place of interment *.

* In ſome places of interment, the chief part of the graves are in an eaſt and weſt direction, as on Chartham Downs, near Canterbury, Kingſton on Barham Downs, Sibert's Would, near a ſeat of Lord North's in Kent, where two hundred and more have been explored

The Chriſtians, from the firſt æra, interred their dead in an eaſt and weſt poſition it may hence be inferred, that, as ſome graves are in an oppoſite direction, an alteration of ſepulchral rite was [illegible] in conſequence of a different religious perſuaſion of the defunct Many relics interred in theſe ſmall tumuli would alſo incline an antiquary to conſider them [illegible] to Pagan ceremonies, particularly when veſſels have been found in them, but, as many Chriſtian rites are [illegible] on the Gentile and in the early ages of Chriſtianity ſeem, in a variety of inſtances, to be blended with each other [illegible] will be difficult, at a firſt glance, to fix whether the people inhumed in theſe ſepulchres were Chriſtian or Pagan and, till a greater aſſemblage of facts make their appearance in the courſe of the work [illegible] give a poſitive proof, I ſhall decline to aſſign them either to the one or the other, [illegible] to argue with my [illegible] on their hiſtory It is evident, as Chriſtianity gained ground the Pagan cuſtom of burning the dead was by degrees [illegible] aboliſhed, and both the one and the other people adopted a ſimilarity of cuſtom in their inhumation This period may be [illegible] to the time of the Emperor Theodoſius (ſee Macrobius, Saturnal [illegible]), but theſe tumuli are conſiderably of a lower date

The dead were in theſe ſmall tumuli interred in their apparel, and ſome more decorated than others Tertullian (ſee his Apol [illegible]) ſays, Chriſtians in his time were ſumptuouſly entombed, perfumed, and richly apparelled Origen, [illegible] in Job, mentions the [illegible] of the primitive Chriſtians in the decoration of their dead S Gregory of Nyſſen beautifully attired the body of his ſiſter Macrina, who died in a monaſtery but from the [illegible] of Pope Gregory, this honour in a time was only due to [illegible] which it was doubtleſs [illegible], afterwards reſumed perhaps by ſome ſtate regulation, and finally aboliſhed by the Council of Auxerre See Guichard, p 518 *Fun. des Rom*

PI

PL. XV Fig. 1. A CHAPLET OF BEADS: forty-one in number; for the most part of *amber* *, worked and polished, to humour the fragments of which they are composed; consequently they are of various shapes; some round, others oblong, flat, square, and angular. Eight of the chaplet are of glass: one of which, a pellucid vitrifaction, emits many beautiful and variegated colours; two are of a straw-coloured opaque vitrifaction, with wreathed pea-green stripes; the size of the smallest described in the drawing, one of a most beautiful sky-blue colour of opaque glass: the others white, red, and straw-colour; also opaque. Near the position of the neck of the skeleton.

Fig. 2. Fragment of an IVORY ARMILLA † near the left side, apparently the ornament of the arm. It was entire in the grave, but broke in taking up.

Fig. 3. A spiral SILVER RING ‡ for the finger, which can be extended to fit one of any size.

Fig. 4. BRASS RING; much worn on the extremities, where it seemed to have been attached to some part of the dress. Under the *pelvis*.

Fig. 5. SILVER BROACH: gilt and enchased with garnets, with a kind of a delicate inlaid milling, as described in *pl.* XIV. fig. 7. The reverse has a clasp, which received an iron *acus*, part of which is now remaining, and accreted to the silver. On the *os pubis*, and which seems to have been an ornament of the zone or girdle.

Fig. 6. CIRCULAR PIECE OF BONE §; evidently turned in a lathe, ornamented with circles, perforated in the center, and served to unite the loops of the dress, which were introduced through the center, and turned over the instrument; which answered the end of a broach, or such like devices, to compress the fore parts of the apparel ‖.

Fig. 8. A FRAGMENT OF GREEN TRANSPARENT GLASS **.

Fig. 9. Two BRASS CLASPS, or TONGUES; perforated on the reverse, apparently sewed to the drapery, and used as broaches. Near to fig. 5.

Fig. 10. A SILVER-GILT BROACH, ornamented with a metallic composition, inlaid in the milling, as before described. As a Gothic ornament, the workmanship is extremely beautiful. Found on the first *vertebre*, and may have served to compress the upper part of the apparel.

Fig. 11. A GOLD FLAT WIRE, which appears to have been woven with some kind of stuff, by the breadth, as described in the drawing, quantity, and position, where it was found near to the armilla, fig. 2. it appears to have been a BRACELET.

Fig. 12. CIRCULAR PIECE OF PERFORATED LEAD, used as fig. 6. for the purpose of closing the dress.

Fig. 13. A PIECE OF CLIPPED SILVER. Near the side, close to the fragment of glass, and perhaps inclosed in the zone or the pocket.

Several fragments of IRON RINGS were also found in this Tumulus by the side of the skeleton, most probably answering the purpose of amulets (see note, p. 61.)

* The AMBER of these beads is considerably more brittle than the native amber found on the British coasts.

† See this armilla mentioned in *note* to p. 6.

‡ A similar ring occurred in this range, in another grave, with female ornaments.

§ See a similar instrument engraved in the plate of *Miscellaneous Relics*.

‖ A similar kind of contrivance to answer the purpose of a broach, or buckle, is described in Rubenius.

** At the Kingston range of tumuli on Barham Downs, Mr. Faussett found a *fragment of green glass*, with other female trinkets, somewhat about the same size. It is evident, from these fragments, that the ancients ran their glass into plates of considerable thickness. They do not seem to have been the remains of any vessels, but broken off from plane and horizontal surfaces of large dimensions.

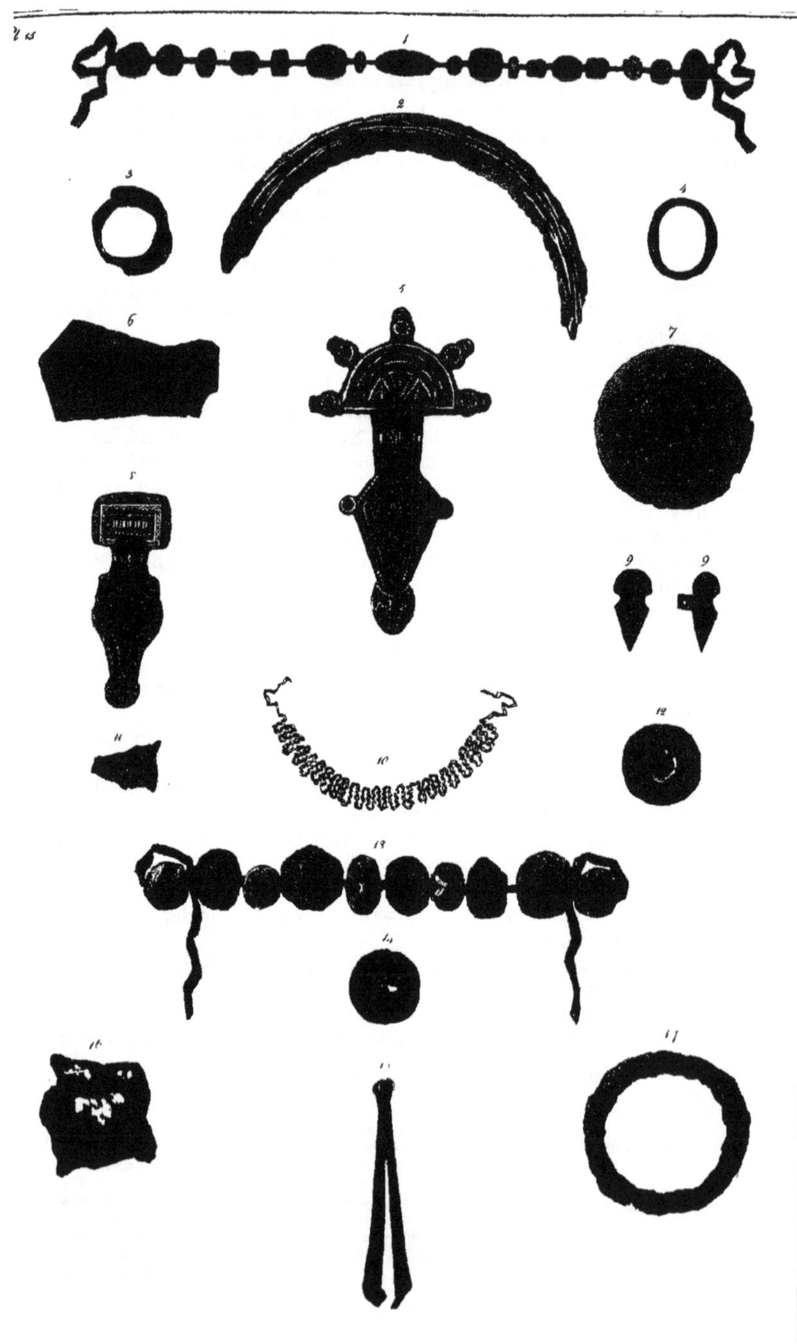

TUMULUS XIX.

On CHATHAM LINES, the bones small, and much perished.

PLATE XV. Fig. 13. EIGHT AMBER and TWO VARIEGATED GLASS BEADS. Those of glass are described in the drawing with convoluted stripes. The stripes yellow, on a black opaque ground. Found near the neck of the skeleton.

Fig. 14. A PETRIFIED ECHINUS LATOCLYTHUS, or button-stone *. Found with an amber-bead on the side of the skeleton.

Fig

* On the first discovery of this fossil, I considered it as having been thrown into the grave with the adventitious soil, but as it was a petrifaction of the *yellow flint*, and therefore heterogeneous to the black siliceous and white sparry echinites found in chalk, its native bed having been of loam and gravel, and from its position also in the grave, among other relics deposited with the body, I am inclined to believe it was carried about the person when living, as an *amulet*, and to which uses they seem to have been applied by the ancients. Pliny says, if this shell-fish be worn on the neck, arms, or any other part of a pregnant woman, it will hinder abortion, and be productive of other favourable effects; and, if preserved in salt, and used as an *amulet*, it will cause a [illegible] labour; to which virtue it was called by the Greeks *[illegible]* (Lib. xx[illegible]) In Scotland, the peasants have at this day a belief in the virtue of these fossils. They are called by them *cock-knee stones*, and mentioned by Lhuyd in his Observations on Wales, who saw them in Scotland. [illegible] they [illegible] called *[illegible]*. Naturalists enumerate fifty species of this fossil, [illegible] petrifaction of the [illegible] *[illegible]*, and of various sizes, from a large orange to the specimen described in the [illegible]. In their natural state they are armed with spines, and which differ in length and shape according to the nature of this kind of shell-fish. The *[illegible] mammillaris*, with hemispheric eminences in the form of nipples, is brought with spines three inches in length, and the sixth of an inch round. Some of the other kinds have them not exceeding half an inch in length, sharp, and thin.

They were also called by the ancient *remora*, or ship-stays, and Pliny (see the stone [illegible]) relates a story, that Antony was retarded in a voyage by it [illegible] in a ship with an hundred

rowers,

Fig 15. A Brass Tweezer On the right ſide near the pelvis, and with Fig 14 16 17. The body in the meridian.

Fig 16 A Piece of Lead adhering to ſome fragments of iron. the end curvated, to ſerve the purpoſe of a hook

Fig 17 An Iron Ring *. On the right ſide near to fig. 14

rowers, in which was the Emperor Caligula, was withheld in her courſe, when the reſt of the navy proceeded with conſiderable rapidity Abbe Fortis, in his Travels into Dalmatia, where the mariners ſtill entertain the ſuperſtitious belief of the antients on their power of retarding a ſhip on her paſſage, ſays, they are called in the Archipelago *Paklina*, and attempts to aſſign ſome reaſons why there may be ſome truth in Pliny's wonderful relation, but I think very unſucceſsfully The *echinus*, if the ſame kind of ſhell-fiſh ſo named by the moderns, is alſo called *remora* by Lucan, lib. viii who, like Pliny, attributes the ſame property to it

Non puppim retinens, Euro tendente rudentes,
In mediis echeneis aquis——

Pliny ſays, the Greek writers have ſaid much on its medicinal property,

* See ſimilar ſpecimens Pl. VIII. N° 2. Pl. XIV. fig 3.

TUMULUS

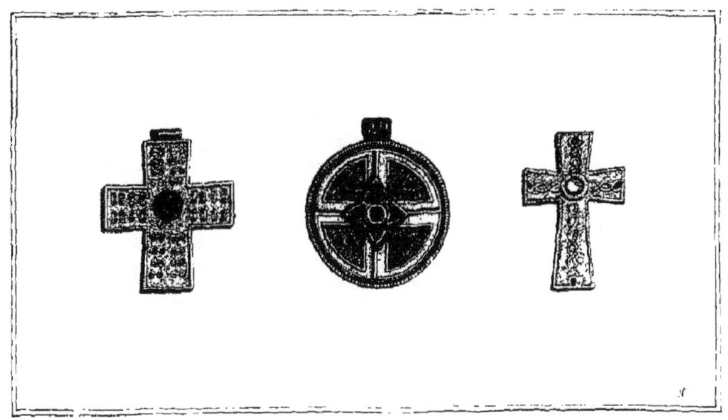

MISCELLANEA ANTIQUA; VETERIS AEVI MONUMENTA

——CARPAMUS DULCIA, NOSTRUM EST,
QUOD VIVIS, CINIS, ET MANES, ET FABULA FIES.
PERSIUS

THERE is here aſſembled a variety of ſepulchral relics, ſimilar in reſpect to their workmanſhip, and which were deterred from *tumuli* of ſimilar conſtruction to thoſe deſcribed in the foregoing ſheets The curious reader will conſequently be enabled to form comparative deductions; his eye gratified by a repreſentation of the relics themſelves, in contemplating ſome particulars of the art and cuſtoms of the antients in reſpect to their modes of common life, as well as to their funeral ceremonies

Drawings muſt always ſuperſede a verbal deſcription, but it would be an endleſs labour to exhibit every antient relic under this feature, which are produced from ſepulchres; ſome repetition might alſo occur, and, unleſs a proper ſelection be made, time and trouble may be diſſipated Such things therefore, under the head of MISCELLANIES, will be produced as will only ſuffice to explain and perpetuate the ceremonies of interment of an antient race of people, to whom theſe ſmall conic ſepulchres are attributed.

PLATE XVI

Fig 1 A SILVER CROSS * from a barrow at Kingston Barham Downs, near Canterbury The drawing is made from one side of the cross, there being a similar face connected with it by a frame, and filled with some kind of cement it had a loop at the top similar to the pendant ornaments, *fig.* 1 in the

* This cross is drawn to show its analogy with *fig* 2 and [illegible] in the *vignette*, and also to explain some particulars relative to the discovery of *fig* [illegible] (see *vignette*) which was apparently a relic from the same barrow as the one described in vol III p 274, of the Archaeologia The barrow in question made one of a groupe situated on the commons of Winstor, a village within the King's great manor, de Alto Pecco, in Derbyshire, which have been lately enclosed. Having directed some enquiries concerning this barrow to Mr H Rooke, of Woodhouse Place, near Mansfield, a member of our society, and a gentleman who had frequently visited Derbyshire, to explore many curious British remains of great antiquity in this county, I received from him the following information "About twenty years ago, a "woman picked up in a field near Winstor, and not far from the barrow which contained the orna-"ment in Mr Manders possession, (see the Archaeologia above cited, a small brass cross of fillagree-"work, (see *fig* 2 in the vignette), in the middle is a socket, which probably contained a stone It "is now in the possession of Mr Mason of Winstor " This cross is evidently of the same workmanship as the gemmated circular *fibula* engraved in Mr Manders paper, which being found with two glass vessels, and *fig* 1 Pl XVI taken from a barrow in a range of tumuli on Barham Downs, which also had been productive of similar glass vessels see *fig* [illegible] and *fig* 3 of Pl XVI the latter having also been found with a *cristal ball*, will doubtless demonstrate strong analogy of facts, and greatly tend to prove that these ranges of *tumuli*, situated at those remote distances in Britain, did appertain to a similar people See the striking analogy also of these vessels, and a *cristal ball*, in Pl V. N 2 fig [illegible] and 7

Crosses, doubtless, are very presumptive emblems of Christianity, and though it can be proved that the antients, particularly the Greeks, used them on their coins and as [illegible], emblems of the *deus regenerator*, or great prototype of Bacchus, yet we should not enter into an enquiry which may possibly lead us into a disquisition too complicated to throw light on the subject, and do injury to the most natural way of accounting for the discovery of them in tombs Fig 1 *Pl* XVI was a pendant ornament most probably of the neck, like *fig* 1 2 3 in the *vignette* Monetas Helenæ Augustæ, et *inventæ crucis* antiquitus cusas præsens esse remedium *adversus* MORBUM COMITIALEM T Bosius, lib xv cap 12 Here is the *cross* adopted on the coin of Helena, the mother of Constantine, as a charm or preservative against the falling sickness See a perforated coin of Constantius, in Chifletius, p 271 the reverse a cross between two figures with crosses on their heads, and the same in their hands, also a coin of Heraclius, the reverse a cross of the exact form of fig 2 in the vignette, which will serve to explain the two pensile ornaments found in a tomb, (see the [illegible] p 271) This coin was evidently worn as a neck ornament, it is incased with a corded hoop, and a loop at the top to hang it by Veteres nummi gestabantur e collo, ut pretiosa monilia, quod [illegible] circulo quo includebantur, *aut foramine* quod erat in summa eorum parte Multi [illegible] nodique reperiuntur, qui aut *limbo circumdati sunt, aut perforati* Ludovicus Savotus, [illegible] part I See those found in *Pl* II of this work Marcarius de Gemmis Basilidianis says, they were suspended at the neck, not only to *avert the evil, but to effect the good* Bartholine says, that the primitive christian women suspended the cross to the neck of their children, as a charm to remove evil from them The Pagans had obscene amulets for this purpose, sacred to their *[illegible]*, or [illegible] gods All relics of this nature may therefore reasonably be esteemed as *amulets* as well as ornamental Constantius Presbyter, in the life of St Germanus, anno 429, says, "casting his eye on the "ground, he saw a brass coin with a *cross* upon it, which, gathering up, he wore it suspended round "his neck, in commemoration of St Genoveve, who had endowed the spot " Most probably a coin of the lower Empire, which have frequently crosses upon them We may hence infer, that *crosses* were worn as types of Christianity, that *fig* 1 2 and 3 (see VIGNETTE) were relics of a people devoted to it, answering the purposes of religious as well as ornamental purposes, and in some cases used as amulets They have frequently been found entombed with dignified ecclesiastics [illegible], in the funerals of the antient Kings and Queens of France, says, the *cross* was laid at the feet, and entombed with the [illegible] In Westminster Abbey, in the reign of James I were found a gold *cross and chain* in a tomb It is a custom at this day in catholick countries to deposit crosses with the dead, as well with the clergy as laity It would be useless to enlarge on this subject, as many discoveries and books concur to prove the custom of entombing *crosses* with Christians, and therefore, whenever they occur in barrows or tombs, we may naturally be inclined to judge them of christian origin The Pagans also may possibly have worn them as amulets or ornaments, and traders may have introduced them from the places where they were manufactured for by the style of workmanship, it appears that these relics *fig* 1 in Pl XVI and *fig* 1 2 and 3 in the *vignette*, compared with many others from these small conic tumuli were the manufacture of some particular country

VIGNETTE, Fig 1 is gold, set with a carbuncle, or ruby, in Mr Faussett's cabinet, found in a barrow at Sibert's Would or Shepherd's well in Kent, with other relics Fig 3. is a *silver cross* from a barrow at Chatham, also in Mr Faussett's cabinet, found with other relics

vignette The contents of this grave conſiſted of beads, twelve of which were amethyſts, two pendant ornaments, one of which was a garnet in gold, the other a purple ſtone ſet in ſilver, perhaps *lapis lazuli*, a gilded pin and inſtrument like an ear-picker These relics are in the cabinet of Mr Fauſſett, of Heppington See the plate of MISCELLANEOUS pendant ornaments

Fig 2 A GLASS VESSEL, from a barrow at Kingſton Barham Downs In the poſſeſſion of Mr Fauſſett, found with a knife and a few nails of iron

Fig 3 A GLASS VESSEL, from a barrow of the ſame place, with another of a ſimilar ſhape, a CRYSTAL BALL, *ſome beads, a ſilver pin, two ſlender knotted ſilver wire rings,* having a blue glaſs bead ſtrung on each, ſimilar to fig 10. of *Pl* II.

Fig 4 AN IRON SPEAR-HEAD *, from a cluſter of barrows opened on the eſtate of the late Sir John Vanhattem, of Dinton Hall, near Ayleſbury, in Buckinghamſhire The drawing the exact ſize

Fig 5 A GLASS VESSEL, from Dinton

Fig 6 A ſmall IRON SPEAR-HEAD, from Dinton

* I was favoured with the drawings, fig 4, 5 and 6 from Mr Claxton, of Great Ormond Street, who informed me, "they were dug up, together with human bones, in a field adjoining Sir J Van-"hattem's Summer houſe, near the road from Dinton to Thame, in 1769"

Having acquaintance in that neighbourhood, and from the nature of theſe relics conceiving they were the produce of ſeveral *tumuli*, I was determined on a viſit to the ſpot, to proſecute, under favour of leave, a further reſearch, but my abſence from England on the continent prevented me ſince which, the death of Sir John has made me give up all further views I ſhall here introduce the eſſential of a letter which I received from this gentleman, which will ſhow theſe relics to have been the produce of more than one grave, and alſo afford a ſtrong reaſon for preſuming that *fig* 5 was not depoſited with fig 4 and 6

"*Dinton Hall*, 21 *Feb* 1786

"With the *cup* repreſented by Mr Claxton's drawing, I found one perfect ſpear, and ſeveral pieces "of iron, ſo corroded with ruſt, as to make it difficult to ſay what they were but from their ſize, I "conclude them to be ſpears, and eſpecially as I took one of them out of the neck of a ſkeleton, "*dug up near the ſpot where the cup was found* In the ſame place I found many, twelve bodies at "leaſt the bones of three entire, and many ſculls and parts of other bodies If you will do me the "honour of a viſit, I will reſume my ſearch, which I have diſcontinued ſome time If you could "make it convenient to come ſoon, we might probably make ſome diſcovery worth your notice"

As ſeveral ſkeletons were found, and, as Sir John obſerves that the cup was diſcovered near the grave which contained the ſpear, I ſhould apprehend it was depoſited in the interment of a female body, ſuch relics being uſually found in theſe caſes, and that other relics were ſcattered by the workmen, or perſons preſent, through the want of care and diligent attention ſuch as *beads*, *fibulæ*, &c The *ſpear head*, uſually depoſited near the neck of the body, cauſed Sir John to apprehend the weapon was ſtricken into the perſon when alive, and hence an inference might be drawn to prove their remains to have been interred after ſome hoſtile event But frequent diſcoveries of this nature already delivered in the courſe of the work, will doubtleſs ſatisfy the reader that they ſhould be aſſigned to ſome nation or clan of people of a peaceable æra in hiſtory, or rather, that they are not with propriety to be aſſigned to honours ſhown the dead on any warlike occaſion A people in a ſtate of peace do neceſſarily bury their dead as well as thoſe in a ſtate of war This remark would be an inſult to the good ſenſe of the reader, was it not a conſtant, I may ſay almoſt a general maxim, for perſons to favour the opinion of warlike diſaſters being the cauſe of theſe kind of interments On ſuch conceptions hiſtory is conſulted, and a page produced, to prove that a battle had been fought at ſome diſtant period in the Annals of Britiſh hiſtory, on or near the ſpot where the caſual diſcovery was made.

Fig 5 has convoluted raiſed cords upon it, ſimilar to the glaſs veſſels, *fig* 2 and the veſſel, *fig* 7 No 1 *Pl* V The ſpears are evidently of the ſame ſhape and ſize of a conſiderable number which I have taken out of tumuli, and ſome of which have been engraved in this work The cones of the barrows at Dinton have been levelled by tillage they were once raiſed in a bell-like faſhion, like thoſe deſcribed in the firſt page of the work, and of the ſame ſtructure they are therefore evidently claſs with thoſe heretofore deſcribed, and refer to a ſimilar race of people The barrows at Winſter, in Derbyſhire, have the ſame analogy, and will admit of ſimilar deductions

PL. XVII. Fig. 1. 2. 3. and 5. GLASS VESSELS*, found in Roman urns, placed in the ashes. The drawings the exact size.

* I have thought proper to select, from a variety of antient glass vessels in my cabinet, a few specimens, which are usually called by antiquaries *Lachrymatories*, which may possibly throw light on the nature of the *glass vessels*, heretofore described as peculiar to the small *tumuli* of a conic form found in clusters. *Fig.* 1. was taken out of an urn with ashes, and evidently placed in it to contain some liquor. The shape is very singular, as it resembles very much a modern tumbler. Fig. 2, 3, and 5, of very thin glass, found with ashes in urns, must have also contained liquors; but whether tears, unguents, or balsams, seems to be the question. As the forms do frequently vary, it would be reasonable to conclude their contents did also vary. No passage in antient authors, or sepulchral inscriptions, has hitherto come under my observation to justify an assertion, that these vessels contained *tears*. The only passage to be cited for this purpose, is from the 56th Psalm, "put thou my *tears* into thy *bottle*." Whether the passage is to be apprehended allegorically, or applicable to the custom of depositing tears with the dead, is not yet satisfactorily explained: but, if referable to a ceremony of burial, the custom of putting tears into a bottle must have existed 300 years before the foundation of Rome, and 1048 before the Christian æra, and in this case must not be considered as Roman. I am chiefly governed by Kirchman De Fun. Rom. who has cited no passage relative to the actual deposit of these tear bottles. The antients often speak of tears being shed over the dead and their ashes, but do not mention these vessels as applicable to such uses. In cap. VIII. p. 321. he says, Collecta igitur ad hunc modum ossa ac cineres, vinoque et aliis odoribus [illegible] lacrymis *perfusa* et *irrigata*, in monumentum condebant. Wine, sweet odour, and tears, are here only said to be shed and sprinkled over the ashes; urns have also been found with perforations on their lids apparently for these purposes.

Mr. Whitaker, in his History of Manchester, says, a lachrymatory with an urn, a Roman coin, and a clasp, were found anno 1765 and 1766 in the artificial bank at Castlefield. The *lacrymatory*, he adds, *was half filled with tears*. The lenity of Fabricius, a celebrated antiquary of the last century, (see his life by Gassendus), inclined him to wish that authors should speak with forbearance of each other—indeed no detraction is here meant from Mr. Whitaker's merit as an antiquary: but it is absolutely necessary, though a matter of no great literary moment, to dispute the assertion, that Roman tears could be preserved to this day in a bottle. Even the Roman *Cœcuban* and *Falernian* would lose their characteristic flavour, if not be wholly evaporated, as was the case of the wine supposed to have been contained in the large *amphoræ*, jars, and other vessels, found in the ruins of Pompeia. Surely in this case human tears would lose their briny quality also. Several specimens of these vessels, in my cabinet, seem to have contained incrassated substances: an opaque or cloudy coating is adhering to the insides, but evidently not the *armatura* or *electrum* found on specimens of antient glass. Phials, or vessels of this nature, contained lustral waters, as well as aromatic liquors, and were used by the Romans as amulets, and carried about them in superstitious ceremonies, to avert the effects of accidental contaminations. *Præficæ*, or hired weepers, were doubtless commonly attendant on these obsequies, and tears were perhaps shed in abundance; but it appears rather extraordinary to [illegible] should introduce them into the apertures of these phials. *Fig.* 1. would likely be attributed to an unguent or lustral vessel. *Fig.* 5. the same: they were found in the ashes like *fig.* 2. and 3. which possibly, notwithstanding the ordinary acceptance of them, might also be adopted for such purpose. When burning the body was disused, on the introduction of Christianity, the same kind of rites were continued among the early Christians: see Eusebius, lib. II. cap. 16. de Martyr. Mar. before cited, and Prudentius hymno in exequias defunctorum. Holy oil and holy water were occasionally used, and most apparently deposited with the body; hence these vessels, originally invented by the superstition of the Pagans, and continued many centuries after the Christian æra in the customs of the converted. See further particulars relating to vessels found in tombs in *note* to p. 44. From these collective arguments, it will be natural for the reader to conclude, that no. 5. and 6. were vessels expressly fabricated for funereal obsequies, and interred with the dead replete with lustral water, oil, gum, sweet odours, and *possibly*, in some cases, tears also. When they occur, as in no. 5. Pl. XVII. fig. 2. and [illegible] Pl. XVI. they may be supposed to have contained balsams; and Doctor Mortimer, in his Manuscript, which will be printed in the course of this work, whether fancifully, or in reality, has asserted that fig. 7. N° 1. Pl. V. did emit a perfume when first taken out of the barrow. It has been said, that no mention is made, either in the writings of the antients, or in any of their inscriptions, of the actual deposit of tears in a bottle with the ashes. In [illegible], I believe the expression occurs, [illegible] *posuere*; but this does not imply the actual deposit of the tears. It is a figurative expression of grief, and means interment accompanied with the sorrow of surviving friends. Tears were evidently shed over the ashes, and possibly might also have been inhumed with them in phials, Roman superstition being adapted to any such purpose; but the assertion is, that no strict authority is at hand to prefix such bottles to such uses. Dr. Brown, in his little elegant treatise on Urn Burial, p. 53, cites [illegible], who says, that sepulchral vessels have been found with a vinous spirit in them, more possible and probable than the preservation of Roman tears in a phial, which must lose all saline flavour, and render it extremely difficult for any palate to ascertain whether the liquor in the phial heretofore cited actually contained human tears, or only a little lymphid water [illegible] through the circumbient soil. The Opimian wine of the antients, which Petronius Arbiter asserts will hold its quality a

hundred

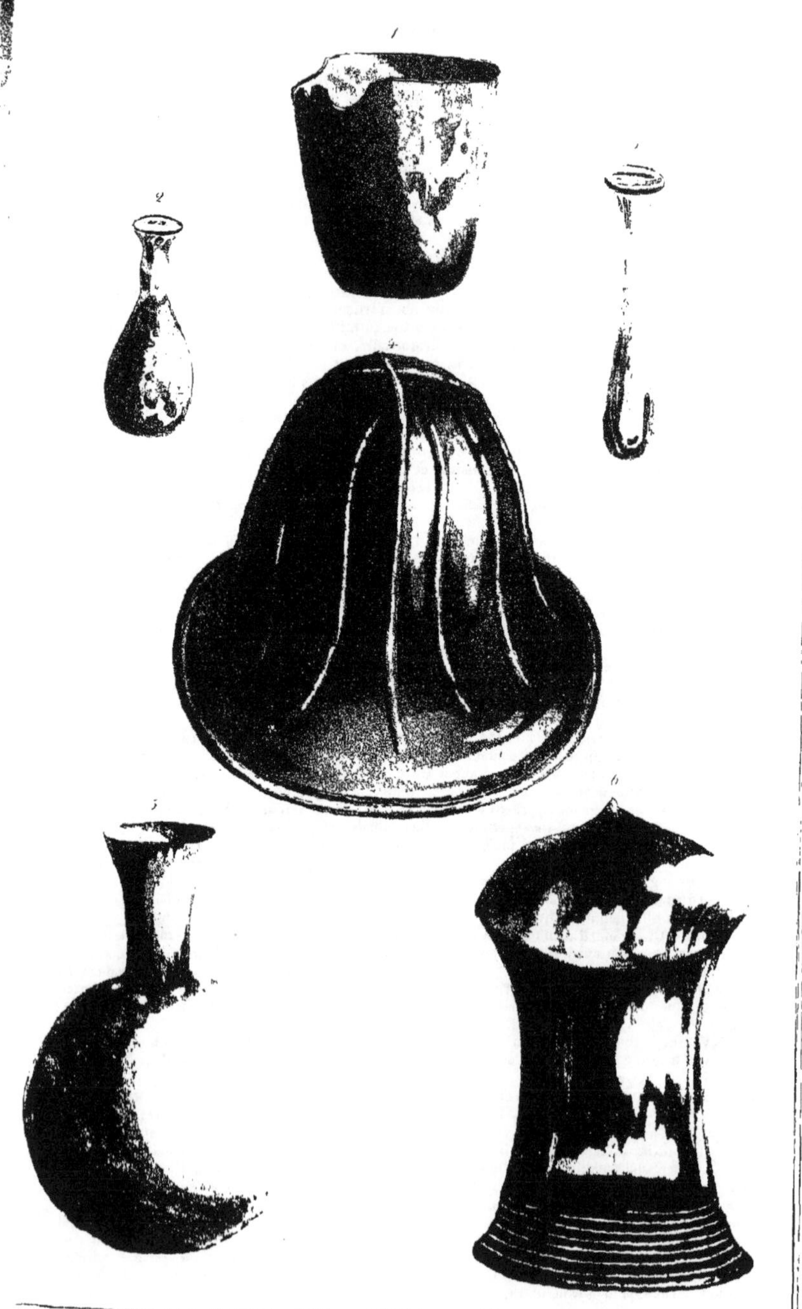

Fig 4 A Glass Vessel, five inches in diameter, the ſame in depth, found in a grave in Minſter Church Yard in the Iſle of Thanet, at the depth of about ſeven feet From the account in the St James's Chronicle, in November, 1786, it appears, that the ſkeleton was near eight feet in length, and the veſſel placed on the ſkull It is of green glaſs, and has ſixteen ornamental cords upon it, ringed or convoluted like the glaſs veſſels, *fig* 2 5 Pl XVI and other veſſels diſcovered in the ſmaller tumuli I was favoured with the drawing by Mr Boys, of Sandwich The glaſs is in the poſſeſſion of a bricklayer at Minſter The ſize of the ſkeleton ſeems to be exaggerated, the wonderful is too apt to intrude itſelf in theſe kind of diſcoveries It is called the grave of a Dane but from ſimilar diſcoveries, the grave moſt probably exceeded the date of the church and therefore ſhould by analogy claſs with thoſe deſcribed in Pl XVI See a note on this veſſel, p. 52

Fig 6 A Glass Vessel, from Woodneſborough, near Sandwich The drawing ſent by Mr Boys, who has lately received a *fibula* from thence Thirty of theſe kind of veſſels were found very near the conical hill there ſome years back

As theſe veſſels bear ſo ſtrong a reſemblance to each other in their workmanſhip, and as they ſeem to have much peculiarity in their ſhape, they will doubtleſs be acceptable to the curious antiquary

hundred years, might induce Wolfgangius Laſius to talk with ſome authority of veſſels containing [illegible] odours but I very much doubt that any precedent can be found to vouch for the poſſibility of preſerving the flavour of ſepulchral tears in a bottle fourteen hundred years, which Mr Whitaker has aſſerted in his Hiſtory of Mancheſter If this gentleman had actually taſted the contents of the phial we ſhould rather incline to think ſome wicked byſtander had been ready with a little ſalt and water to put into the Roman phial tricks of this nature are not unuſual with perſons who are curious after antient reſearch I myſelf was once directed to a pretended [illegible] tumulus, which I opened in the preſence of ſome friends, and to their great ſatisfaction produced the bones of a horſe The gentleman at whoſe houſe I was viſiting, had directed me to a ſpot where a favourite old hunter had been buried I had anticipated the jeſt and was equally pleaſed to favour their laugh by giving into it On a ſearch into a grave at Ash, in Kent, a friend and antiquary, then preſent [illegible] a modern bead, manufactured for the African ſlave trade, and like the one engraved in Camden called the Glin Naderoth, or Druid's chain to me conveyed into a cluſter of antient beads in the grave [illegible] on the ſpot, I was rather ſurprized at the diſcovery, but when he ſees this ſheet, he will recollect, that I inſiſted on a trick being played me, and which made him confeſs the fact before it was his intention to undeceive

THE succeeding plate contains miscellaneous relics from the graves of women, and which seem to have been connected with their attire they will afford a curious retrospect on antient arts and customs, and discover to modern times, that many of its useful and ornamental particulars, relating to personal and domestic uses of women, are of a more remote invention than cursory observation or conjecture have too generally adopted Though the stupendous vestigia of Greece and Rome are not here detailed, antiquaries may derive no small share of curious matter from the inspection of these relics, which, though not of equal beauty to the ruins of Attic architecture, or to the statuary of a Phidias or Polycletus, may notwithstanding establish many interesting facts, which have been long disregarded by the contemplative eye fixed on more striking remains of the antients

PLATE XVIII

FIG 1 A BRASS BOX, containing thread from a barrow at *Shepherd's Well**, found with other relics

Fig 2 INSTRUMENTS apparently for the teeth and ears from a barrow at Kingston, Burham Downs, opened anno 1767, by Mr Faussett

Fig 3 A BRASS INSTRUMENT accreted to a lump of iron apparently used as a clasp to connect a garment From Chartham Tumuli, opened by Dr Mortimer †

Fig 4 A BRASS INSTRUMENT, found with Fig 3.

Fig 5. Found with fig 3 See a FIBULA something similar to Fig. 3 and 5 in Montfaucon, Vol III Tab 29.

Fig 6 A BRASS PIN ‡, set with a garnet Chartham, opened anno 1773

* *Sibertswold*, now Shepherd's-well, in Domesday *Sibertswalt*, Saxon, *Siberts Wald*, Fildo Domain, Siberti Pomerium or Fold, is locus incultus silvæ Planities, a Down This village, which takes its name in part from the Down, and from the name of a Saxon, is in Kent, near Waldershare, a seat of the Earl of Guildford, from which, at about three quarters of a mile distance, is a down, on which are situated, at no great distance from each other, two ranges of *tumuli*, consisting of two hundred In all probability there existed many more, but which are now obliterated in part perhaps by cultivation and the extension of roads which traverse the burial place in several directions These barrows, I am informed were opened by Mr Faussett In the year 1782 I visited this range, and, on a close inspection, found they had all been explored, most probably by the above gentleman, in whose collection of sepulchral relics fig 1 is deposited For further particulars, see the plan and description of these barrows at Shepherd's Well

† See some particulars relating to these *tumuli*, p 70 TUMULUS V

‡ These relics are not unusually found on Roman stations I have seen several from Reculver and other places some I have in my possession See a pin, pl IV fig 4 to shew their affinity, and to assort with fig 1 as an implement of housewifry

Fig

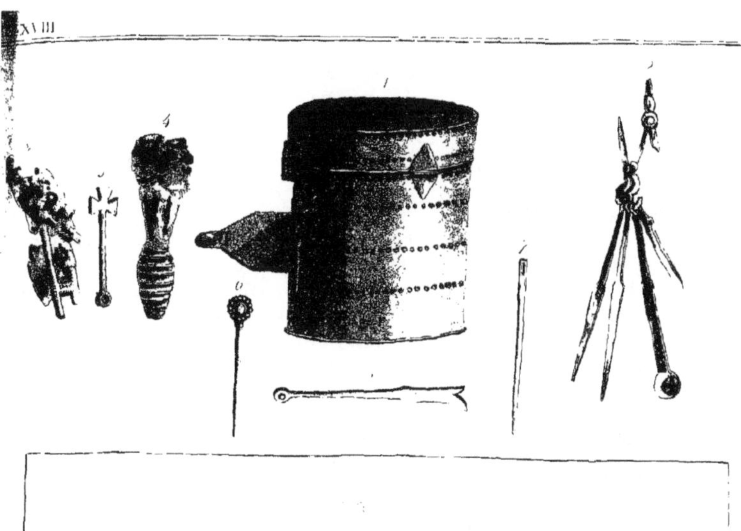

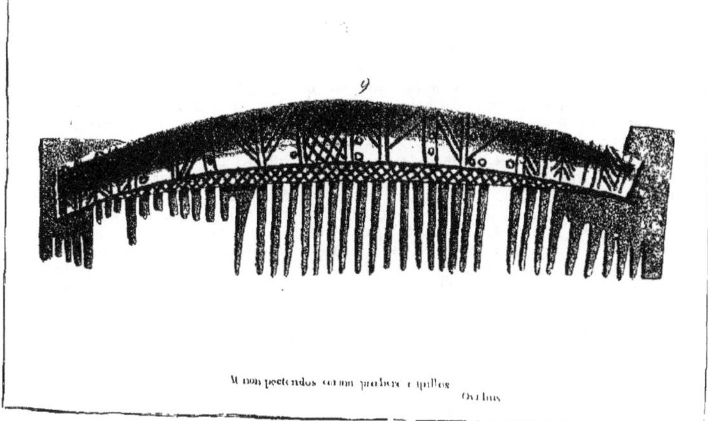

At non pectendos coram praebere capillos
Ovidius

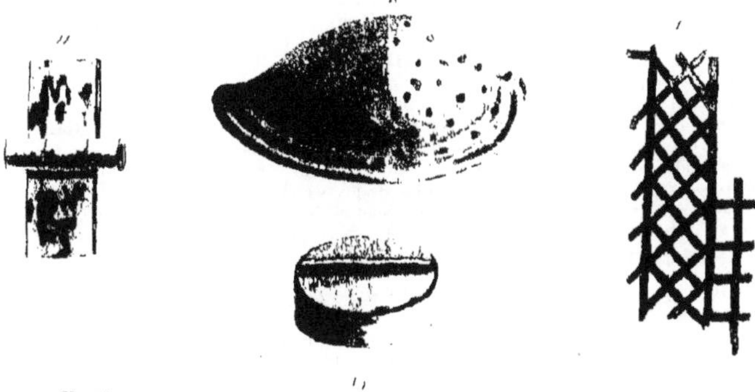

Fig 7 A Brass Needle. Kingston, the barrow opened by Mr Faussett, anno 1771

Fig 8 An instrument, probably for the teeth. Kingston. In Mr Faussett's cabinet

Fig 9 An Ivory Comb *.

Fig 10 Large Indian Cowry †. In Mr Faussett's cabinet, from the ring of barrows at Kingston Burham Downs, opened anno 1771, found near or among *the remains of a box*, with *a fossil screw, armillae, fibulae, remains of iron work*, &c. Mr Faussett has three other specimens of these *shells*, taken from barrows much calcined by laying in the earth

Fig 11. A Brass Hinge of a box, found at Chartham, in the barrow with Fig 3, 4, and 5.

* In Mr Faussett's cabinet, from a barrow at Kingston Burham Downs, anno 1771, with other relics. See Browne's Urn Burial, p 2, combs found in an urn. Also Montfaucon, where a comb is described as found in an urn, discovered near the Vatican, with other relics. Mr Faussett has several [illegible] ornamented with brass.

† This shell found [illegible] with the *[illegible]* of the ancients, worn or carried about the person as amulets by the Romans, called the *[illegible]*, [illegible] one is a pendant [illegible], in a work by the [illegible] some relics in the British Museum [illegible]. They are frequently [illegible] of bronze, and in the acceptance of the high mythology of the Greeks and Romans, [illegible] to be considered as the emblems of the *[illegible]*. How far the mythology has been [illegible] or changed by the succeeding ages of the Romans, will leave room for speculation; but I believe in general it will leave little doubt but the whole is to be conferred on the worship of P[illegible]. The [illegible] emblems and ensigns of this deity are varied in the most whimsical [illegible] figures affixing the dove connected with the [illegible] organ; the latter allotted only, without [illegible] in this case the deity is represented in his active state, and when the Ithyphallic [illegible] wholly the female form, he is considered as passive. From a representation by emblematic figures the great and universal plastic hand of Nature is delineated [illegible] in the human [illegible], and in the shape of [illegible], all denoting the wisdom of the deity, thus sublimely comprehended by the ancients. The Python or the serpent, the ox, the dove, are blended together, and frequently with the *[illegible]*. They are often noticed under the *[illegible]*, the Greek emblem of Bacchus, and is often allied with the Python. Bartholine, de Puerperio Veterum, [illegible], says they are worn as amulets on the [illegible] of children to preserve them from [illegible]. These amulets oftentimes have one end in form of the generative member, and the other [illegible] thumb thrust through the fingers, which indicates an obscene purpose. This seems to supply the female characteristic [illegible], which in form of the [illegible] has the same preference [illegible]. Varro, lib vi [illegible] of them as the amulets of children, and they seem to be mentioned by Plautus, [illegible] Sc I

[illegible]

Bartholine also believes them in some instances to have been [illegible] to the *Dea [illegible]*, or Cradle Goddess, a very learned and very probable conjecture. See a treatise on these ancient amulets, in Recherches sur l'Origine et les Progrès des Arts de la Grèce, [illegible] Cap III, [illegible] 18, and 39.

Sir William Hamilton, in his letter published by Mr Knight, in his account of the remains of the worship of Priapus, [illegible], "that these shells are [illegible] as amulets and as ornaments of dress, at this "day, by [illegible] children of the lower class in Naples. That the modern amulets most in "vogue represent a hand clinched, with the point of the thumb thrust betwixt the index and middle "finger [illegible] *[illegible]*, and the hand is a half [illegible]. These [illegible] *the shell*, which [illegible] "[illegible] are most common made of silver but sometimes of ivory, coral, "amber, crystal or some curious gem or pebble." He also adds, that the shell, *[illegible]* is evidently an emblem of the female part of generation. This shell is called by Sir William Hamilton an [illegible] *[illegible]*, but [illegible] gives it the generic name of Cypræ[illegible]

These shells were evidently introduced by the Romans from [illegible] and thus [illegible] over Europe considerably before the period to which I have prefixed these small conic barrows, from the [illegible] of the fifth to the seventh century. The [illegible] were known to the Romans in Pliny's time, [illegible] when the coast of the [illegible] is mentioned [illegible] the distance of twelve [illegible] called [illegible], famous for shells [illegible]. Many coins of [illegible] have been found in [illegible] and these [illegible] with various other [illegible] of a similar nature, seem to prove that the Romans had an open trade with the Indians; a circumstance which [illegible] mention, and which is here [illegible] by the discovery of [illegible]

Fig. 12. A curious ſpecimen of a fragment of A LEATHER GIRDLE *, from a barrow of a cluſter at Beakſbourne in Kent, opened by Mr. Fauſſett, found with other relics.

Fig. 13. A BRASS BOX †, with a hollow cylindrical piece of the ſame metal traverſing the lid, and ſodered to it, apparently a contrivance to keep it ſhut. Found 1780 on Chatham Lines, in a barrow near the left ſide of the ſkeleton, with an ornamental piece of braſs, amber beads, a buckle, and a knife, cloſe to it. The bones ſmall and ſlender.

Fig. 14. A BRASS PIN ‡, at the back of the ſcull, in the ſame grave with Fig. 13.

* Several ſpecimens of theſe leather girdles, or ſtraps, one with a ſilver buckle connected to it, ornamented with grooves, and ſome of the ſhanks under which the ſtrap was paſſed, were found in the Chatham groupe of tumuli. See leather preſerved in a braſs [illegible], pl. VI. fig. 10. and Dr. Mortimer's Manuſcript.

† I ſuſpect this box was uſed as an amulet, propitious to the favourite wiſhes of the female in whoſe grave it was depoſited.

—— quod nil animis in corpora juris
Natura indulget: *Steriles moriuntur*, et illis
Turgida non prodeſt condita *pyxide Lyde*.

JUVENAL.

The Lydian women ſold theſe kind of boxes, which incloſed an ointment as an amulet favourable to the procreation of children. See Statius. Hoc plaudunt grege Lydia tumentes, &c. conjugal pledges to ſecure eſteem and fertility; many Roman women were diſcarded by their huſbands when proved to be fruitleſs, *Claudian in Eutrop.* This privilege of the huſband was engrafted in the Roman laws, and which cauſed the wives to be deſirous of having children; and to expoſe themſelves naked to the *Luperci*, or prieſts of Pan, in the month of February, with indecent geſticulation, to receive ſtripes with a goat's ſkin. Fortunatus Sacchus, in his Myrothecium, lib. [illegible] cap. 44. ſays, that Lyde ſignifies a ſpider, ſo called from *Arachne*, the Lydian woman, turned into a ſpider; and who, in his Commentary on the words of Juvenal, ſays, *Condita in pyxide turgida*, ſhould imply a *ſpider* that was encloſed in a big-bellied box of a round form, with ointments, and conſidered as having a peculiar virtue againſt ſterility. Therefore in this perſuaſion the Roman women carried a ſpider about them in a box; and to preſerve it from corruption and offenſive ſmell, they incloſed it in ſweet ointment. This confidence in the virtue of fertility attributed to the ſpider may perhaps ariſe from the ſpider called *Phalangium*, which Pliny ſays, lib. II. cap. 24. brings forth 300 young at a time. [illegible] *[illegible]nos*, all ſpiders are prolific. Junius, an old commentator on Juvenal, in his [illegible] on this paſſage, found this *charm* of a ſpider mentioned in a very antient manuſcript; and [illegible], as the ſize of Fig. 13. ſeems ſo little adapted to any other uſe, it may not be unreaſonably [illegible] the LYDIAN BOX, or charm to promote fertility.

‡ Theſe pins when found in tombs, or on Roman ſtations, are often miſtaken for the ſtyli, or [illegible] with which the antients wrote on tables of wax. They ſerved as bodkins to receive the [illegible] of plaited hair. The [illegible], Moravian, and many other European women, at this day have gold, ſilver, and braſs [illegible], at the back of their heads, with the hair twiſted round them.

[illegible] ne madidi violent bombycina crines,
Figat *acus* ſparſas, ſuſtineatque comas.

Martialis, lib. xiv. Epig.

—— *Crinalis acus*, redimicula, vittæ.

Prudentius, Pſychomach.

Ad hunc modum [illegible] mulier, *[illegible] crinali* capite deprompta, Thraſylli conſauciat tota lumina.

Apuleius, Metam. lib. viii.

Coins of the Empreſſes ſhow the hair thus entwined round an inſtrument of this nature, particularly thoſe of the Fauſtina.

SCILICET ET TEMPUS VENIET, CUM FINIBUS ILLIS
AGRICOLA, INCURVO TERRAM MOLITUS ARATRO,
EXESA INVENIET SCABRA RUBIGINE PILA:
AUT GRAVIBUS RASTRIS GALEAS PULSABIT INANES,
GRANDIAQUE EFFOSSIS MIRABITUR OSSA SEPULCHRIS.

VIRGIL. GEORG. LIB. I.

O purſue the connection of relics in our ancient tombs, Pl. XIX. exhibits ſeveral ſpecimens found at conſiderable diſtances from each other. When their ſimilitude be ſtriking, inferences of their appropriation to a ſimilar people may be deduced; and, when occaſionally any diſſimilar relic be diſcovered with relics which have challenged a perfect analogy, it will admit of a decided appropriation.

The Fig. in Pl. XX. have been ſelected for the above purpoſe, and which being in many reſpects peculiarly adapted to the hiſtoric enquiry of the work, they are introduced in this place before the miſcellaneous relics of the ſmall conic ſepulchres are diſmiſſed.

PLATE XIX.

FIG I. AN IRON DAGGER[1]. This dagger was found with a ſpear-head ſimilar to thoſe in PL VII. and therefore it is conſidered as ſepulchral. It was preſented

[1] The ſhifting of the ſands at Weſtram in the Highlands of Scotland has laid open ancient burying places, conſtructed of ſtones, or encircled with them The latter are generally in cluſters, and even with the ſand In the encircled graves, with the bones of men, were found thoſe of cows, horſes, dogs, and ſheep, beſides *warlike inſtruments* of all kinds *battle-axes, two handed ſwords, broad-ſwords, helmets, ſwords made of the jaw bone of a whale*, DAGGERS, &c , *knives, combs, beads, broaches, and chains*, *a round flat piece of marble*, about two inches and an half diameter, ſeveral ſtones, *ſhaped like whetſtones*, but no marks of ſuch uſe, *a very ſmall iron veſſel* like a head-peice, only four inches and an half in the hollow, bruiſed apparently by a ſword or an axe In one of the graves a *metal ſpoon* was alſo found, and a neat glaſs cup, and which might contain about two Scottiſh gills, as the account ſays, or half a pint Engliſh In another, a great number of perforated circular ſtones, which the writer ſays were like ſuch whirls as in Scotland were formerly uſed to turn a ſpindle. In another a gold ring, which encircled a thigh-bone

I have cited this diſcovery of ancient tombs, to apply the DAGGER and SPEARS found near Bolton to ſimilar relics in diſtant parts, thus a chain of argument will follow, and the hiſtoric agnation be evinced

The Weſtram graves are evidently to be appropriated to a ſimilar people adopting the mode of burial peculiar to the ſmall campaniform barrows in cluſters The SPOON will apply to *fig.* 9 PL II, the glaſs cup, to *fig* 5 of PL IV, and *fig* 4 of PL X, and conſecutively the ſame with *ſwords, knives, combs, beads, broaches* or *fibulæ*, and *chains*, which have been engraved and deſcribed in the courſe of this work The *iron veſſel* is doubtleſs the *umbo* of a ſhield, ſee *fig* 1 and 3 of PL VII They have frequently been taken for helmets, though much too ſmall. Mr Groſe, of our Society, ſent

presented to the Author, with the iron spear-head, by the late Sir Ashton Lever, who received it from Mr Rasbotham, of Birch-house, near Manchester, who has had the goodness to inform the writer, that they were found very near the town of Bolton, in Lancashire, in a bed of gravel, as some workmen were *opening* the road from thence to Bury

FIG 2 3 6 and 8 IRON ARROW-HEADS from Chatham-lines[2] Perhaps the bows were also interred, but, being of wood only, were perished

FIG 4 AN IRON KNIFE The sides seem to have been inlaid with horn The bones of a midling size From the Chatham *tumuli* It has been selected from a considerable number, and seems, in point of workmanship, not to be inferior to modern improvements in cutlery

FIG 5 SPEAR-HEAD, or PIKE[3] Like the pilum used by the Romans From the Chatham tumuli Two of these are in the author's collection from different tumuli The graves in which these *pila* were found close 90 and 103 in his note-book There is only mention made of the bones being large Mr Fausset, of Heppington, has a similar specimen in his collection from the small conic barrows in clusters

FIG 7 IRON ARROW-HEAD[4] From a barrow on St Margaret's Cliff, between Dover and Deal.

sent me an account of swords and *umbones* of shields found in Mr Penruddock Wyndham's garden at Salisbury the *umbones*, Mr Grose says, were mistaken for helmets

The bones of quadrupeds were scattered about the adjacent soil, and could by no means apply to this mode of the Westram interments The account, at first sight, appears to have been drawn up by a very inaccurate and incautious observer, and we cannot admit of bones of such animals as *sheep* and *cows* to be deposited with the dead, unless the whole account critically corresponded with this assertion The Westram sepulchres differ very much from the usual mode of interment of the antient Highlanders, and hence we must arrange the former with the small *conic tumuli*, which are here treated of

[2] See *fig* 1 PL VIII An *Iron Bow Brace* Two of these arrow-heads were collected by Sir Charles Frederick in the year 1756, when the vallum on Chatham hill was thrown up by Colonel Desmaretz See note to [illegible]

[3] This military instrument being found in a barrow which could not apply to a higher date than the fifth, or a lower than the seventh century, cannot be considered as Roman To argue from Polybius, or any other classic, would be absurd, unless it could be proved that the head of this spear, javelin, or pile, was of a contemporary age When first the discovery was made of these military instruments, they were conceived to be the heads of [illegible], or something similar to the javelin, which, Polybius says, was shod with iron at both ends but having made no discovery of any other iron point in the grave, they must be considered as the definite head of some military weapon See similar instrument of war in Montfaucon's Antiq Expl [illegible]

[4] *Arrow-heads* are found in most parts of Britain, but, perhaps from their [illegible], are not commonly discovered in tombs Mr Edward Lloyd, in his observations on Wales, writes, that in his travels through Scotland he was diverted with the variety of amulets which were preserved by the inhabitants, many of which he thinks, if not all, were [illegible] by the Druids, and have been handed down from parents to children ever since Among these amulets, he mentions the *arrow heads*, which they ascribe to the elfs or fairies They are chipped flints, with which the Americans [illegible] the points of their arrows In the year 1786, Sir Joseph Banks shewed the author several arrows heads, very similar to those of flint, which he found in our large and antient barrows, one of which he brought from Terra del Fuego, worked by the natives and another of white transparent glass belonging to the ship's company, which the natives chipped and fashioned while he was on the island He has also in his possession the head of a spear of flint, very delicately chipped, which was found in North America in the earth

In reading Ossian constant references will be found to the custom of burial in the Northern nations, which might appear as a strong evidence in favour of the originality of the poems, when subsequent discoveries in antient tombs have proved those references to be [illegible] He talks of warriors being buried with *swords*, *bows*, *arrows*, and *deer horns* [illegible] we have here established as the relics of the dead, also *swords* and *bows* A *deer's horn* the author discovered in a grave on Chatham lines, and which he has now in his collection of sepulchral relics, reduced almost to an impalpable dust. Stags' horns were also discovered on the *cuma* or burial-ground at Chartham, near Canterbury.

The translator of Ossian says, the ancient Scots opened a grave six or eight feet deep: the bottom was lined with *fine clay*, and on this they laid the body of the deceased, and, if a warrior, his *sword* and the *heads* of twelve arrows by his side. Above, they laid another stratum of clay, in which they placed the *horn of a deer*, the symbol of hunting. The whole was covered with fine mould, and four upright stones to mark the extent of the grave. FINGAL, Book I.

On visiting the barrows on Barham Downs, in Kent, the author opened the grave of a child near the *agger*, or bank thrown up at a small distance from the cluster of the campus-dotted *tumuli*, and found the body had been inclosed in a clay coffin; also a grave, at St Margaret's on the Cliff, that was sheeted with clay. A *mound of clay* has also been found in the cluster of *tumuli* to line the graves, and at Chatham, to place this fact beyond a doubt, were actually found the bodies inclosed in clay. So much I think is due to the accuracy of antient customs, described by the translator of Ossian, but whether the same may be admitted into the internal evidence of the authenticity of his poems, is submitted to the better-founded intelligence of his friends or adversaries.

This *arrow-head* was discovered in one of the *barrows* at St Margaret's by a Mr Tucker, an inhabitant of the place, in the year 1775, who opened six or eight of them, and in a very deep one found upwards of twenty beads. On the 21st of December, 1782, the author opened a considerable number of these barrows, and, from his discoveries, their affinity to the same kind of burials in clusters was sufficiently established.

See ITER I of Dr Stukeley's Itin Curios p 126 where these barrows are mentioned.

"About St Margaret's on Cliff, near the light-houses, I saw in two places a great number of little "*tumuli*, of unequal bulk close by one another, and the like I found frequently about Barham Downs, "and between Hardres and Chilham, and other places. I know not that they have ever been taken "notice of; the people say they were burying places of the Danes: probably digging into them might "give us some satisfaction. I believe them Celtic, because I saw many sorts of them, and such as "appear on Salisbury-plain."

It was the misfortune of the ingenious Doctor to see most of our antient monuments with the magnifying lens of Celtic optics. Sufficient proofs, it is presumed, have been established to shew that these small barrows are not Celtic, or what the Doctor more critically should have pronounced Belgic. For, if we are obliged to adopt the *lumen siccum* of a recent writer on Celtic History, we are to conclude the Celts were not inferior to the Hottentots, or any primitive savage tribe, and therefore unworthy the consideration of any learned man. Care should also be taken not to confound the Celtic with the Scythian tribes; the latter a wise and sturdy people, the former a puny, erring, and a stupid race of inhabitants, the descendants of which, by this author, are the Welsh, the vain glory of whose old British descent must now disappear before deep research, dry reasoning, and uncommon accuracy.

MISCELLANEA ANTIQUA.

TUMULUS XX.

Chatham, claſſed N° 65 in the Note-Book

NOT more than a foot from the ſuperfice. The mould of the incumbent earth blended with the bones and cavity of the grave. Working from the feet to the head, about the middle of the ſkeleton on the left ſide, the relics were diſcovered.

PLATE XX

FIG. 1. AN IRON BUCKLE.[1] Under the tongue, which traverſes the angular parts, is a perforation, which received the loops from the two ſides of the garment; one loop through the other was introduced into the hole of the buckle, and lapped over the tongue, by which means the compreſſion of the garment was ſecured. Near the ſhoulder.

FIG. 3. A BUCKLE compoſed of tin and braſs: near or rather above the pelvis, remarkably thick, weight near two ounces.

It appears to have ſerved for the zone or girdle; and by the indent on the tongue ſeems to have ſupported a conſiderable weight. The indent is made by the friction of the girdle, as the aperture for the admiſſion of the girdle does not, in its longeſt oval, exceed more than three-quarters of an inch, the girdle muſt have been of a corded quality, perhaps leather platted, eſpecially as the indent ſhews the purchaſe to have been made on a ſubſtance which occupied

[1] This buckle is ſimilar to one which was diſcovered in the ſame range of graves. As the contents of *Tumulus* XX are ſtrikingly ſimilar, they are here deſcribed. Near the *Os humeri* [illegible] ivory ring, and beads of amber and glaſs, one of amber very large, square buckle exactly ſimilar to *fig.* 1 of Pl. XX. Above the left *femur*, an iron ſtud of a knife, [illegible] and iron [illegible], the braſs ring an inch and a half diameter, that of iron about the ſame ſize. *Two ſmall braſs coins*, the one, legible on the head-ſide, of the Emperor VICTORINUS, the reverſe, a female genius with a [illegible] in her hand, VIRTVS AVGVSTA. The other DN VALENTINIANVS PF AVG, the reverſe a military figure in an offenſive attitude, on each ſide the figure [illegible], the legend not ſufficiently diſtinct, and [illegible]. In this grave, as alſo in N° 65, to which the relics of Pl. XX are applied, was a remarkable bead of glaſs, three quarters of an inch in length, and about the thickneſs of a crow quill, and ſimilar to certain beads found on the veſtment of mummies. The analogy of the relics, on inſpection, will be found very extraordinary.

no great ſpace When taken out of the grave, the metal had received no injury whatever by lying in the earth ſuch an immenſe length of time it preſerved its original poliſh and luſtre.

FIG 6 AN IRON INSTRUMENT WITH A RING AT ONE END[1], near Fig 3 The ſuperior part was compreſſed in the form of a hook, and which ſerved as a pendant, but by handling it was broken off

FIG 8 and 9 The head and reverſe of a SMALL BRASS COIN[2]. VRBS ROMA The exergue under the Wolf and Romulus and Remus T H P

There was alſo another BRASS COIN with a head, and the reverſe a ſheep; but too ſmall and too much defaced for admiſſion.

The other relics conſiſted of an enſculptured piece of fluted braſs, a ſpiral ſilver ring, exactly ſimilar to *fig* 3. PL XV, near to *fig* 3 were two ſmall claſps ſimilar to *fig* 9 9 PL. XV, under the jaw five beads, three of amber, one of a brown and green ſtriped vitrified earth, and one of glaſs, like the one deſcribed in the note to fig 1. of this Plate An iron blade of a knife, and a ſmall piece of iron like the tongue of a buckle. The bones were much periſhed, and very ſmall

FIG 2. A SPECULUM[3], compoſed of tin and braſs

From a barrow at Aſh, near Sandwich, in Kent

I received

[1] This inſtrument may have been appropriated to ſome kind of amulet uſe, or perhaps magical, ſee the note to *fig* 3 p 61. It was apparently affixed to the girdle, perhaps uſed for the purpoſe of a Tintinnabulum, ſee note to FIG 4, or as *Crepundia*, children's play things, ſee Bartholine de Puerperio Veterum, p 63 Women wore rings in token of their freedom, having had three children Crepundia annulos fuiſſe ex Terentio liquet Heautont Act iv Sc I

—————— Hic profecto eſt annulus quem ego ſuſpicor
Is, qui cum expoſita eſt gnata ——————

[2] Theſe coins were ſtricken on the great feſtival of the *Lupercalia*, the ſolemn *Palilia* or birthday of Rome Coins with GENIO POPVLI ROMANI, were alſo ſtricken on this feſtival. The ſtars over the wolf ſhow the twins to have been conſecrated as the *Dioſcuri*, wherefore it is more natural to think with Plutarch, that the Lupercalia were inſtituted from the fable of the Wolf, and not in honour of Pan, which was ſuppoſed to have preſerved Romulus and Remus, ſolemnized on the *Dies Nefaſti* in the month of February Suetonius, in August *cap* 31, ſays, they were reſtored by Auguſtus, and Onuphius Panvinius ſays, they were continued in Rome as low down as the Emperor Anaſtaſius, which remark is placed beyond a doubt by the coins which have been ſtricken for this feſtival, and from the cuſtom of the prieſts, which were called *Luperci*, beginning their courſe from the foot of the Palatine Mount, called by the Romans *Lupercal*, the place where Romulus was foſtered by the wolf

It has been ſhewn that two of theſe barrows contained ſmall pieces of money, that were not perforated, and worn as female ornaments, wherefore they may be ſuppoſed to have an affinity with the Roman mode of interment See a PLATE, which Paulus Petavius has engraved, evidently a Roman ſepulchre, with utenſils, and the *naula Charontis*, Charon's tribute, two pieces of braſs coin in the right hand of the ſkeletons, one of NERO, the other of MAGNENTIUS, the reverſe of the latter having the XP the monogram of Chriſt However ſtrong this coincidence, many reaſons in the courſe of this work will be given why the above barrows are not Roman

[3] See Morant's Hiſtory of Eſſex, Vol I Book III p 182 An urn with aſhes, which contained a metal SPECULUM A leaden coffin, ſituated North-eaſt and South-weſt near the head bracelets of jet and four bodkins of jet, near the coffin, an urn with aſhes, and two braſs coins of ANTONINUS PIVS, and ALEX SEVERVS, alſo another urn, which contained a SPECULUM, a black veſſel of about two gallon meaſure, two bottles of clay, two clay lamps, and [illegible] metal veſſel Many other facts on the diſcovery of metal *ſpeculæ* in [illegible] ancient ſepulchres might be collected Pliny has exactly deſcribed [illegible] compoſed of tin and braſs, ſee lib xxxiv cap ix [illegible] hoc loco optime [illegible] Brundiſium, [illegible] In lib xxxiii cap xvii he ſays there were [illegible] kind of mirror, which Brundiſium was celebrated for, but which were in diſuſe from thoſe invented of ſilver, and which were ſo much in common uſe that the moſt menial ſervants had them In confirmation of Pliny, that [illegible] carried them about them [illegible] Petronius Arbiter to the following ſubſtance "Before Chryſis could return, ſhe [illegible]

[illegible]

I received this sepulchral relic from the late Mr White of Newgate street, who had it from the late Mr. Jacob of Feversham, a very diligent enquirer after the relics of the large burial-place at Ash. Mr Jacob informed me, that he gave it to Mr White, with several other antiquities Mr Hayward, an apothecary of Ash, collected for Mr Jacob, and I therefore apprehend this *speculum* came from that place

Fig 4 A small Bell[5], the exact size of the drawing From Ash, near Sandwich, found with female ornaments Fig 1 and 7 see Pl XVIII accompanied it In the possession of Mr Faussett, who has another specimen

Fig 5

"from the maid servant a *pocket mirror*, and having practised her features to try the power of her "charms, she adjusted her economical drapery, and repaired with great haste to the temple of Venus "to make her offerings" The same author, in satirizing the profession of [illegible], says, that the room of this [illegible] was [illegible] pin-dust, mixed with vermilion and [illegible], [illegible], what was most extraordinary, the dust of a *mirror*

Many of these funereal relics may be interpreted as ornamental decorations for apparel, such as the beads, gems or various [illegible], and when other relics occur in forms differing from personal decoration they may be considered as relics in which the owners delighted, and in some instances may apply to magical uses. Superstition may have prevented surviving kindred or friends from appropriating them, as their minds may also have been apprehensive of contamination from the possession of [illegible] and have consigned to the grave many valuable effects, which the less superstitious would have preserved. But as, in authors heretofore cited, it appears that the dead in several ages, and in different regions, as also of dissimilar persuasions, have been buried with many rich decorations, we must conclude, by a natural interpretation, that those relics which bear no affinity to the above have been buried with them for some other kind of usage. We have found several relics to have been evidently appropriated to magical ceremonies, and though a *mirror* may have been applied to the operations of dress, as well as a pot or vessel to the ordinary offices of domestic life, still, if such implements are discovered to have been used by the antients in magical rites, and as having [illegible] found several relics so applied, why scruple to consider the *speculum* as such? See Lucian in his Dialogue between Melissa and Bacchis, on love-spells and potions; he thus makes Melissa request Bacchis to bring back her lover to her. The passage is curious, so far as it relates to the magic spells of the ancients, it is therefore here translated

Melissa You will do me a far greater pleasure, were you to find me a Thessalian woman, who, by her incantations, could bring him back to me

Bacchis I know a Syrian who can do it, for she caused my Parias to return after an absence of four months, having despaired to see him again

Melissa And what was her skill?

Bacchis Some kind of necromancy according to the usual custom of these women, first, having given her [illegible] trifling present which she asked, and having drank by herself out of a cup, but you should have some keep-sake of your gallant

Melissa As what?

Bacchis [illegible]—or some such trifle

Melissa I have his sandals in my chamber

Bacchis They will suffice. She will hang them on a pin, and make suffumigations under them, she will then throw salt into the fire in pronouncing both your names. Then, drawing forth from her bosom a magic mirror, she will turn it on all sides, muttering in a low voice several words. This she did for me, and Parias, notwithstanding the remonstrance of his friends and the tears of his new mistress, returned to my arms. She also taught me the art of [illegible], by walking on the footsteps of the person, placing the right foot where he had placed his left, and the left where he had placed his right, then saying, *I overcome, and I am stronger than thee.* I have tried it, and have found it to succeed

Cælius Rhodiginus, lib VIII c XXXIII assigns a moral reason for the invention of mirrors, and say, [illegible] philosophum scribit Apuleius, speculo, quod [illegible], ad morum disciplinam esse usum. [illegible] discipulis [illegible] in speculo contemplarentur, [illegible] corporis [illegible] pollueret. A most excellent apology for self-admiration. Seneca says, cited by Rhodiginus, [illegible]. No man should therefore go without one in his pocket

[5] These tintinnabula, or campanulæ, were used by the primitive Christians in exorcism, and appear to have been buried with the dead for the expulsion of evil spirits, in like manner as it has heretofore been observed of the [illegible] and other vessels which contained the lustral water. Wecker's

Secrets,

Fig 5. Iron instrument[6] to curl the hair Found with female ornaments Chatham *tumuli*.

Fig 7 A brass handle of a clasp knife[7] in the form of a hound running after a hare; much worn. The contents of this grave were a circular fibula on the collar bone. See Fig 7 8. Pl II exactly similar on the reverse part of the silk drapery, adhering to the rust of the tongue, which evidently perforated a small fold of it, and is now compacted by the rust On the right side, an iron knife with a brass shoulder, the blade five inches long, close to Fig 7 An iron buckle, several other fragments of the same metal, and a small piece of thin fluted brass Chatham *tumuli*

Fig 10 Metal speculum[8], brass and tin The handle when found was of iron. From the Ash *tumuli*.

Fig 11. A crystal[9], with an engraved cross upon it From a barrow, with coins of the Lower Empire, on Blood-moore Hill, near Peakfield and

Secretis, lib xv c xvi fine, that *Bells* are used against the power of the devils in raising storms, and for which purpose also, lustral, or water consecrated by the priests, was placed at the doors of houses against these accidents, et adversus diaboli potestatem, opera, et quaecunque maleficia velut prerogativa quadam valere It is not uncommon in some towns of Germany and France to ring the bells of churches in a thunder storm, the custom arising from the above superstitious custom, and now continued on a philosophical principle, though perhaps not well grounded, that the reverberation of the air, occasioned by the bells, may divert the electricity of the clouds Little bells are frequently found attached to priapeid relics, grotesque figures, in form of the god of fecundity, have them oftentimes pendant to them in the most whimsical parts, multiplied frequently about lamps assuming that form, or appropriated to those rites They also occur as votive ornaments of considerable magnitude, presented to the temple of Pan, and hung up on his statues and altars Most collections of any consequence of Roman antiquities contain them These relics in all probability, being Christian, were from the Pagans handed down as amulets against evil contaminations

They may have been purchased by the Primitive Christians, and a kind of traffic carried on by the priesthood, as we are well informed is at this day practised in most of the Catholic countries it may therefore be conjectured from the discoveries of these trifles, that the sepulchres were ancient Christian

6 Perhaps the antient Calamistrum An iron instrument, when heated, to crisp and curl the hair See Servius *Calamistrum* acum majorem quae calefacta et adhibita intorquet capillos To what other use could it have been applied?

7 See a similar handle of a knife in Dr Batteley's work on the Antiquities found at Reculver It was a favourite ornament among the Romans in the latter ages

8 This mirror is frequently described on the reverse of Roman coins of the Empresses, and on bas reliefs, also gems, or engraved stones, of Venus attiring

9 This crystal has been engraved to shew its analogy with the various crystal relics found in tombs, and also to compare it with a crystal in the Liath-Meisicith of the Irish Druids, or stone of speculation See that uncommon curious speculating box of silver, Plate II Numb VII Vol IV of Vallancey's Collect de Rebus Hibernicis In the possession of I Kavenagh, Esq, of Ballyborris, in the county of Carlow

The description of this box, bearing such a reference to the relics found in these small conic barrows, may perhaps be acceptable to the reader

" The Liath Meisicith, or Druid magical stone of speculation, is a crystal enchased in a box,
" two inches deep, of brass cased with silver, which contained a number of loose sheets of vellum, on
" which are written extracts of the Gospel and Prayers for the Sick in Latin, and in the Irish cha-
" racters There are also four drawings of the Apostles, not ill executed In the center of the [illegible]
" is a large crystal, the Meisicith, it was originally set through the cover, that the light could
" pass through, on the back of it is a foil of tin, moveable At the right hand corner at the top
" is another crystal on a red foil (This crystal is exactly of the same size of fig 11) Next
" to it a bead of [illegible] transparent composition, the ornament that was enchased next to it is lost
" those of the two left hand corners have been taken out, and the socket filled with common [illegible]
" on a red foil At the right hand corner at bottom is an oblong piece of crystal on a red foil, next
" it a transparent bead, and lastly an amethyst drop of a deep purple colour, these have been
" ornaments at the two ends of the Meisicith, which are also lost." See the Amethyst beads, Pl IX of this work, similar to the one here described

and Loweftoff, in Suffolk, in May, 1758, by Mr Gardner, a great collector of thefe relics In the Author's poffeffion, who received it from Mr. White, of Newgate-Street, and with a well authenticated account of its difcovery A penfile coin of the Emperor Avitus, and an engraved onyx, were alfo found at this time See note p 8

FIG 12 AN IRON INSTRUMENT Size of the original; with female ornaments, beads, &c From Chatham *tumuli* Perhaps ufed for a fimilar purpofe to FIG. 5

The Author conceives it to have been the Druidical Liath Meifictn, or Liath Ful, in which the Druids pretended to draw down the *Logh*, the effence or fpiritual fire or prefence of Aefer (God), whenever they confulted this oracle See the analogy of the *Cryftal Ball* to the MISICITH, or fpeculating ftone *Note* to p 15.

I have prefixed this note to afcertain a poffibility of thefe fmall tumuli being early Chriftian

Col Vallancey fays, that he has been favoured with drawings of feveral of thefe boxes, fabricated fince Chriftianity, and ornamented with crucifixes

MONILIA EX AURO ET GEMMIS.

AC VELUT OFFICIIS TREPIDANTIBUS ORA PUELLÆ
SPE PROPIORE TORI MATER SOLLERTIOR ORNAT
ADVENIENTE PROCO, VESTESQUE ET CINGULA COMIT
SÆPE MANU, VIRIDIQUE ANGUSTAT JASPIDE PECTUS,
SUBSTRINGITQUE COMAM GEMMIS, ET COLLA MONILI
CIRCUIT, ET BACCIS ONERAT CANDENTIBUS AURES.

CLAUDIANI DE VI. CONS. HONOR. PAN.

PLATE XXI. N° I.

IT is difficult to ascertain whether these jewels are the decorations of women or of children. Some will be found evidently of the latter, and worn as amulets against fascination. Perhaps many of them may be considered as ornamental; but when by form, or other exterior marks, they carry an evidence of their having been used as amulets, we may justly interpret them as such.

Amulets, from *amula*, vas lustrale, ad aquam gestandam religionis expiandorum malorum gratia—amula ab amoliendis periculis—also from amoliendo—expelling all things that are noxious to the human body[1]. The same interpretation as Φυλακτηριον, antidotum contra venena, from Φυλαξ, custos, servator, conservator, hence *Philtre*. We have now the explanation of the lustral vessels found in urns, which are absurdly called lacrymatories from no reason whatever, and which any Lexicon would have pointed out. The Φυλαξ, *amula*, vas lustrale, is the ΦΙΑΛΗ, phiala, poculum, patera, or phial. This is evidently the little glass PHIAL found in urns, which contained the lustral water, and which was worn about the persons of the Romans and other Pagan nations, perhaps for the sake of purification and expiation. The Φιλος, or Φιλ[illegible], amicus, *friend*, or *conservator from harm*, and as such adopted for sepulchral purposes, to defend the manes hovering over the ashes of the dead from the visitation of evil spirits or any other contaminations.

FIG. I. A GOLD AMULET[3], one inch and an half diameter, extremely thin

[1] See Vossius.

[2] See, p. 70, a note on this subject.

[3] The interlacement on this amulet is the *knot of Hercules*, and efficacious in green wounds; the wound being tied up and swathed in that form, is also beneficial in several other respects. The ends of the swathing, or band, are not to be seen, and so intimately woven, that with difficulty they can be unloosened. See Pliny, Lib. XXVIII. c. vi. Vulnera *nodo* Herculis præligare, mirum quantum ocyor medicina est. Atque etiam quotidianum cinctus tali nodo vim quandam habere utilem dicuntur, quippe cum HERCULES eum prodiderit.

The facility of healing green wounds with such a knot may have given rise to this ludicrous folly. Certain handles of antient pitchers were called the knots of Hercules. See Cœlius Rhodiginus, lib. XIV. c. IX.

I remember taking a sketch of a Saxon capital in the Back-walk near the cloisters of the cathedral in Canterbury. The ornament, which was something similar to this knot of Hercules, and the workmanship in general, of the fashion displayed on the jewels found in these small cemeteries [illegible]

found

Found with four amethyst beads, several brass pins one inch and an half long, with round flat heads, through which were small round holes, also with *Fig.* 3 4 and 5 PL XVIII At the West end of Chartham or Swadling Down, near Mistole, in Kent, the seat of Sir William Fagg These barrows were opened by Dr Mortimer, whose account will be found in the minutes of the Society of Antiquaries. The relics that were found are now in the possession of Sir William

FIG 2 A GOLD PENDANT inlaid with a tessera of glass[a] Two were found in the same grave, and appear to have been worn as ear-rings From a range of barrows on a down called Siberts Would, near a seat of the Earl of Guildford, with other female relics, in the collection of Mr Faussett To fasten these pendants to the ears, the ancients seem to have made use of a small silver hook, which was applied to the ear and to the ornament Mr Faussett has one, and Sir William Fagg another

FIG 3 A SILVER PENDANT From Sibert's Would Anno 1772

In Mr Faussett's collection The barrow contained female relics, but I have no particular account with it

FIG 4. A GOLD PENDANT The stone, garnet on a gold foil

FIG [illegible] A GOLD PENDANT[b], set with *Lapis Lazuli* The metal quite pure

The

[a] This inlaid ornament is extremely beautiful, and very delicately executed The large concentric strips are of a light green glass, and the interior of light blue and crimson

The ancients used this Mosaic of variegated glass for the pavement of their houses Remains of it are to be found in the island of Farnese, they resemble of green glass, and about the thickness of small tiles The Abbé Winkelman (livre 1 chapitre 11) records the extreme industry and ingenuity of the ancients in their glass productions "Two small pieces of glass within a few years have " made their appearance at Rome, and which are not above an inch in length, by the third of an " inch in breadth One of these specimens, on an obscure, though coloured ground, represents a " bird of the duck kind, with a variegated and very brilliant plumage, more representing a Chinese " colouring than a natural effect The contour is sharp and determined, and the colours beautiful " and effect very soft, the artist having arranged alternately the opaque and transparent glass ac- " cording to the nature of the work The most delicate pencil of a miniature painter could not " have expressed with more neatness the [illegible] of the eye, or the apparent prominent plumage of the " neck and wings, close to which this fragment is broken But what surprises most is the reverse, " which represents the same bird in all its most minute parts Hence it may be concluded, that the " same figure of the bird is continued throughout the fragment

" This figure appears to be on both faces [illegible] and put together with applicable pieces in " the Mosaic [illegible], but it is composed in such an united like manner, [illegible] with [illegible], " the smallest articulation cannot be discovered From the first contemplation of this work, it would " be difficult to form an idea of its execution The [illegible] remained [illegible] " [illegible], if discovery had not been made at the broken part that the threads, or rods of glass of " the same colours which appear on the surface, and which pervade the diameter, were united into " each other In consequence of this discovery it may be concluded that the picture of this frag- " ment was composed of several slips of coloured glass, which were cemented by fusion Thus the " picture was cut off from a piece much longer, and, being continued through all its length, the " figure could have been as often multiplied, as the thickness in question was continued throughout " the length of the rod"

By a similar process many of the beads found in the small conic tumuli were manufactured, and particularly that bead in Camden's Britannia, which is called the [illegible] See Fig 7 N 2 PL XXI

[b] I conceive this to have been worn as a kind of *Phylactery* See Carl Rhodiginus who cites Ittu-thius, lib [illegible] c xxi Phallum [illegible] in Cule [illegible] pro [illegible] ornamentum, [illegible] *scuta quasi [illegible]* admodum This amulet is in the form of the small orbicular shields of the lower ages, and which is exactly of the form, and indeed fashion of the Scotch shield used with the broad sword, continued almost to the present era Many Scotch shields are ornamented with similar umbones to those represented in *fig* 3 Perhaps this amulet may have been worn by a female against the mischances of war

[c] There can be little doubt but this pendant was an amulet of a child, which the relics in general may perhaps in some measure confirm the smallness of the pendant and the beads, but more par-

ticularly,

The pendant was concealed with great care in a ſmall caſe, compoſed of a thin piece of braſs wire, turned into the form of a trinket, and which was apparently covered with two pieces of ſhell[7]. The pieces of ſhell much periſhed, collapſed againſt the wire, and thus encloſed the trinket in a caſe. In this grave were alſo found twenty-eight beads, a braſs ring, and a knife, thirteen beads of tranſparent glaſs, very ſmall, to imitate pearls, ten of a Naples yellow, of an opaque vitrifaction, three in form of ſmall pendants, two of which of light green-coloured glaſs and one of tranſparent purple, one ſmall opaque crimſon vitrifaction, and one of ſhell, the one of ſhell about one third of an inch in length, cut off from the lips of the large cowrie, or the cypræa. See *Fig.* 10. PL. XVIII. Mr Fauſſett has ſeveral of them Chatham. The bones ſmall.

FIG. 6. GOLD PENDANT[8], or amulet, enchaſed with a garnet on a gold foil. Found with the ſilver croſs and other relics, Fig. 1. PL. XVI.

FIG. 7. GOLD PENDANT. It is enchaſed with chequered glaſs. The Moſaic worked with uncommon care and wonderful neatneſs. The drawing conveys but a ſketch of this beautiful jewel. The dark chequer is green glaſs; and the light, light green. The chequered border of a carnation colour. It was taken from a barrow at Sibert's Would by the late Mr Fauſſett, who opened moſt of thoſe barrows anno 1773. With it were found a ſilver gilt Gauliſh coin of Clovis[9], two large gold pendants, one of which, the circular pendant with a croſs in the *vignette*, p. 67. and Fig. 2. of this plate.

FIG. 8. GOLD PENDANT. In the four compartments of the croſ, A KNOT OF HERCULES. Kingſton Burham Down. From Mr Fauſſett's collection.

FIG. 9. A CIRCULAR ENCHASED FIBULA. Silver ground.

The field a gold plate of filagree work. The firſt circle of the center hemiſphere a garnet on a gold foil; the ſecond circle alſo garnet, the ground of the hemiſphere I conjecture to be ſhell. The centre of the three other hemiſpheres, a garnet. The triangles connected to the centre hemiſphere ſet with garnets on a gold foil. The ſmall hemiſphere tangent to the triangles enchaſed with a ſmall garnet in the center. The reverſe a verticle *acus*. The drawing the exact ſize. From Mr Fauſſett's collection. Theſe jewels are of ſuch beautiful workmanſhip, that a repetition in this place I thought might be acceptable to the antiquary.

ticularly the bones, which are perhaps the moſt convincing teſtimony. Bartholine de Puerperio Veterum, p. 165, ſays, *lapis lazuli* was worn as such. Et iis inſuper amuleti ſpecies ex *lapide lazuli* continebat cryſtallo, quæ apud Pignorium in menſa Iſiaca. The bead, made from the cypræa, or the *porcellana* of the Romans, was an amulet alſo. Puerinus quæ res turpicula e collo pueris appendi. Varro, lib. vi. See note on the Ithyphallic ornaments, p. 73, of this work.

[8] I call this alſo an amulet. See Bartholine, p. 160, de Puerperio Veterum. Cui ſiſcino infanti ſuccedere grandioribus bullæ ad invidiam propellendam, *detractoribus cura* illis coriacei, figuræ cordis vel lunæ pectori appenſæ. Adverſabatur eidem faſcino Crux Dei, & proſeſſim Chriſtianis veteribus crucis ſignum. The croſs on this gold pendant ſhould indicate that it was a Chriſtian amulet.

[8] See note, p. 72, where relics found in the ſame grave are deſcribed.

[9] See plate of theſe lower tumuli coins. This coin reads on the head ſide MARS CLOVIIS, the reverſe MONETA RIOMOIO, a croſs within a circular wreath, very ſimilar to the general ſtyle of Gauliſh coins. See Le Blanc and Petavius. It has a loop at the head for a pendant, and which indicates its having been ſo uſed a conſiderable time perhaps after its circulation. I conceive this penſile coin to be of CLOVIS I. the founder of the French monarchy, who expelled the Romans, Germans, and Goths, from Gaul, and which provinces he afterwards united to the circumſcribed dominions of France. He removed the ſeat of government from Soiſſons to Paris, which he made the capital of his new kingdom. (Henault's Hiſt. of France.) He died 511. A pious Chriſtian king. Gregory of Tours has recorded an inſtance of his Chriſtian piety when he defeated the Germans. I am hence inclined to believe, that the perſon interred with this pendant coin may be deemed a Chriſtian.

N° II. PLATE XXI.

As ſome Antiquaries have collected beads under the conception of Druid amulets, I have ſelected a few ſpecimens to ſhow their real uſe, and which perhaps may diſſipate an idle veneration for theſe relics

FIG 1 A CIRCULAR AMBER BEAD [10]. Flat on the reverſe

From a barrow on Saliſbury-plain, opened by Dr Stukeley, and bought by Mr White, of Newgate-ſtreet, when his collection of antiquities were ſold at his death

FIG 2 A GLASS BEAD The exterior ground is a dark blue, the firſt convoluted line, white opaque glaſs, the ſecond ground, opaque red glaſs, the ſecond convoluted line, white, the third ground tranſparent, uncoloured, the third convoluted line white opaque, and the laſt ground next to the perforation tranſparent, uncoloured. The ends are ground hexagonally; Fig 7 being a larger bead of this kind, ſhews the ends more diſtinctly

Thoſe beads are deſcribed by Biſhop Gibſon, in his Annotations on Camden, as the *glein nadroeth*, or glaſs-adders of the Druids [11], and which he ſays are found in Scotland, and by the people called by that name, wherefore a bead of this kind has been prized of ineſtimable value, and called the Druid Anguinum See a fooliſh deſcription of this Druid-charm in Pliny, LIB. XXIX C. III.

I have three of theſe beads which came from Dr Stukeley's collection, *Fig* 7. and one conſiderably ſmaller than fig 2 Fig 2 and 7 I ſuſpect are the identical beads engraved in Biſhop Gibſon's Camden.

FIG 3. A GLASS BEAD [12] The convoluting figure is of a bright Naples yellow The ground black The whole bead opaque Perhaps uſed, from its ſize and greatneſs of perforation, in the ſame manner as *fig* 1.

From Dr Stukeley's collection, now in the Author's

FIG 4 and 5 GLASS BEADS [13] of an opaque bright verditer vitrifaction From Dr Stukeley's collection, and which were found in one of the detached and large barrows on Saliſbury-plain

Fig 9

[10] See the uſe of this bead deſcribed as a brooch to compreſs the fore parts of the drapery, from Rubenius, Fig 7 p 64 N B The Figures in Pl XV are miſprinted, which a trifling attention of the reader will ſoon ſet right

[11] Camden, p 651 Theſe beads are cut from a ſimilar rod of glaſs to that in the Britiſh Muſeum, from the collection of Sir William Hamilton, and found in Italy, I believe at Naples and [illegible] evidently demonſtrates the ſpot where was ſituated this glaſs manufactory, which by traffic was circulated among all the Northern people, who with much avidity, like the iſlanders of the South Seas, received ſuch baubles to pleaſe their fancy in dreſs or to appropriate to ſome ſuperſtitious charms which prevailed ſo much among them, and to favour which, the dexterous Romans had invented every device of this kind which could poſſibly ſerve their turn Beads exactly ſimilar are now manufactured in England for the African ſlave trade one of which, before mentioned, had been conveyed among a cluſter of beads in a grave which the Author was opening at Aſh, by a very worthy friend, who was deſirous, for the ſake of the jeſt, to ſurprize him with a diſcovery of the celebrated *Glain Neidr*.

[12] See ſome beads of this kind in Britiſh Zoology, vol III p 73 under the article SNAKE

[13] See THE VENETIAN [illegible] with ſome others, were taken out of a mummy of a large ſize The interior mould is porcelain thickly glazed with verditer vitrifaction, and exactly ſimilar to the compoſition of the beads, Fig 4 and 5 From the Author's collection

FIG 6. A JET BEAD[14] From a barrow on Blood-more Hill, near Peakefield in Suffolk, where the other relics were found

FIG 7 GLASS BEAD, ſimilar to FIG 2. From the Stukeley collection, and is conceived to be the ſame as engraved in Gibſon's Camden

FIG 8 GLASS BEAD[15]. The ground common tranſparent glaſs; the ornamented lines yellow

FIG 9 BONE[16] Evidently turned into a lathe, and uſed as a button to connect the drapery Flat on the reverſe Given to the author by Dr Burnaby of Greenwich, and found in a barrow at Baggrave in Leiceſterſhire, within the ſame range with the umbo of a ſhield and ſpear-head, *Fig* 2. and 4 PL VII

Engraved to ſhew its reſemblance to ſome of the beads and other relics called amulets

FIG 2 Alſo of a bright verditer porcelain caſt in a mould, perforated at the back, which ſhews its uſe as a pendant ornament It is an uncommon curious Egyptian relic, and the exterior ornament of a mummy, very like the Papæus of the Scythians, and the Pan of the Romans, and not unlike the Manonde of the Mogul Empire of this day Formerly in the poſſeſſion of the late Dr Green, of Greenwich, and given to Mr Latham, of Dartford, from whom the author received it

FIG 3 EGYPTIAN VERDITER OPAQUE GLASS, perforated on the reverſe to ſerve as a pendant. A kind of ſiſtrum, perhaps the ornament of a mummy

The Author has prefixed the figures in the VIGNETTE to ſhew the great analogy of this kind of vitrifaction to that found in our apparently very antient tumuli, wherefore, by this analogy, a remote period of time may be eſtabliſhed for its introduction into our iſland, ſuppoſing the beads to be of a contemporary age This argument, though apparently juſt, will ſtill require a more correct enquiry, for it is not very ſatisfactorily proved that this kind of vitrifaction is of an equal date, eſpecially as in the lower tumuli ſome of this opaque verditer vitrifaction in form of beads has been found But the author has ſeveral of this kind, which he can atteſt to have been found in ſome of our largeſt and detached tumuli

14 Pliny ſays, lib xxxvi p 589, that axes when heated, called by the Magicians, Axinomantia, and having the jet ſtone caſt upon them, will burn, if the thing wiſhed for is to happen Evidently kennel coal He enumerates many of its properties, and ſays, that its name is derived from Gagates, or Gages, a river and town in Lycia

15 Mr E Lluyd, in his Obſervations on Wales, ſays, that theſe antient beads are worn as amulets by the inhabitants of Scotland

16 See a ſimilar button, PL XV fig 7 This bone is turned out of the epiphyſis of ſome very large animal It is not in the leaſt decayed, and the texture uncommonly hard Query Is not this the property of the epiphyſis of a lion or tiger? From which bone *Fig* 9 has been conjectured to have been turned Many of the relics in theſe ſmall conic tumuli have undoubtedly been tranſported from the Eaſt, as muſt be confirmed by the diſcovery of the cypræa ſhell why not therefore this relic? The bone of an ox or horſe is more ſpongy and ſoft in its parts

BARROWS IN GREENWICH PARK

ON the 22d of January, 1784, under favour of the Surveyor General of the Royal Domains, I employed labourers to open fome barrows in Greenwich Park, to the amount of about fifty, and which the Kentifh hiftorians have affixed to the fepulchres of the Danes. By their conic ftructure and circular trench at their bafe I was inclined to clafs them with thofe which, with their contents, have been the fubject of the foregoing fheets, and I therefore began the refearch with an eye to afcertain this fact.

Lambard, in his Perambulation of Kent, fays, in the reign of Ethelred, Anno 1011, the Danifh fleet were three years anchored before Greenwich, and the encampment of their army was on Blackheath. Hence it has been conjectured, by fucceeding writers, that thefe fepulchres were raifed over the Danes, not confidering that fo fmall a number could not apply to the occafional dead of fo great an army, which hiftory reported to have been ftationed for fuch a length of time in that quarter; and if with an idea that thefe memorials had been raifed over the flain in battle, it muft then be prefumable, that only fifty men had fallen in their conflicts on the fpot. But to convey, by inferences drawn from other difcoveries already explained, more fatisfactory information, the account of a few barrows from this clufter will be here given.

N° 1. A large central barrow. The trench in which the body was laid appeared to be juft deep enough to admit of it, not more than a foot and half deep to the native gravel, beneath the furface of the circumjacent plain. Several accreted lumps of iron were found in it, and fome uncommon thick and broad-headed nails two or more inches in length, with decayed wood adhering to them. By the quantity of fine mould apparently produced by the decayed wood, I conjectured this body had been interred in a very thick coffin.

N° 2. A fimilar barrow, of middling fize, the cift at its bafe fheeted with fine mould, fmall fragments of iron, with decayed wood, and an iron fpear-head, ten inches long.

N° 3. An IRON KNIFE, converted to an [illegible], feven inches in length, near the centre of the grave, and towards one end a quantity of human hair.

N° 4. Human hair near the head.

N° 5. Hair near the head.

N° 6 Situated almoſt in the centre of the cluſter, ſeemed to have been the largeſt, part having been removed for the ſake of the ſoil In this grave, which did not exceed more than a foot and half in depth, in the native unremoved gravel was one of the largeſt Iron ſpear heads I ever found, fifteen inches long and two broad to the ſocket, which was not more than two and an half from the blade The ſpear near the head; towards the centre a knife of iron, and fragments of an umbo of a ſhield of the ſame metal No remains of bones; but on a line where the body ſeemed to have been laid, a conſiderable quantity of fine black vegetable mould; probably the decompoſed particles of ſome woodden caſe in which the corpſe had been depoſited

N° 7 As uſual, the ciſt not deep in the native ſoil, and which proves that the barrow had been raiſed from a circular excavation near the cluſter In this grave a conſiderable quantity of woollen cloth ſheeting the whole extent of it; black and chiefly decompoſed, but very obſervable from the diſtinct appearance of the warp and woof I am particular in mentioning this circumſtance, and in the enumeration of theſe burial places, as they produce very evident proofs that human hair and woollen cloth have been preſerved a conſiderable number of ages, when the reſt of the body had been totally conſumed.

N° 8 A large barrow, which contained the ſame ſingularity of hair and woollen-cloth to N° 7.

The ſucceeding day I proſecuted the reſearch, and opened twelve more, moſt of which preſented the ſame extraordinary phænomenon of the preſervation of human hair and woollen cloth. The following relic, *fig.* 1 is the beſt preſerved ſpecimen of the hair [§].

PLATE XXII.

FIG I. A BRAID OF HUMAN HAIR, of an auburn colour The barrow almoſt compreſſed to the level of the plain, and the foot path from Crombs-hill paſſing over it. About three quarters of a foot under the ſod, the ſhallow ciſt in the native gravel very diſcernible, and which with conſiderable accuracy was previouſly defined from the ſurrounding undiſturbed ſoil Towards the head the above relic was diſcovered, as alſo,

FIG 2 TWO BEADS of tranſparent dark blue-green glaſs. One of white opaque glaſs and one of brown-red opaque glaſs Which, on a critical compariſon, will be found ſimilar to others found at Chatham and other places where theſe cemeteries have been diſcovered

FIG 3 A SMALL SHRED OF WOOLLEN CLOTH, of the herring-bone wool, and which cloth was diſcoverable almoſt throughout the extent of the grave. In various places was alſo very diſcernible a finer texture of cloth, which, by trial in the fire, was proved to be linen, and ſeveral ſpecimens of which I preſerved.

[§] See note * page 56, where the relic has been ſpoken of

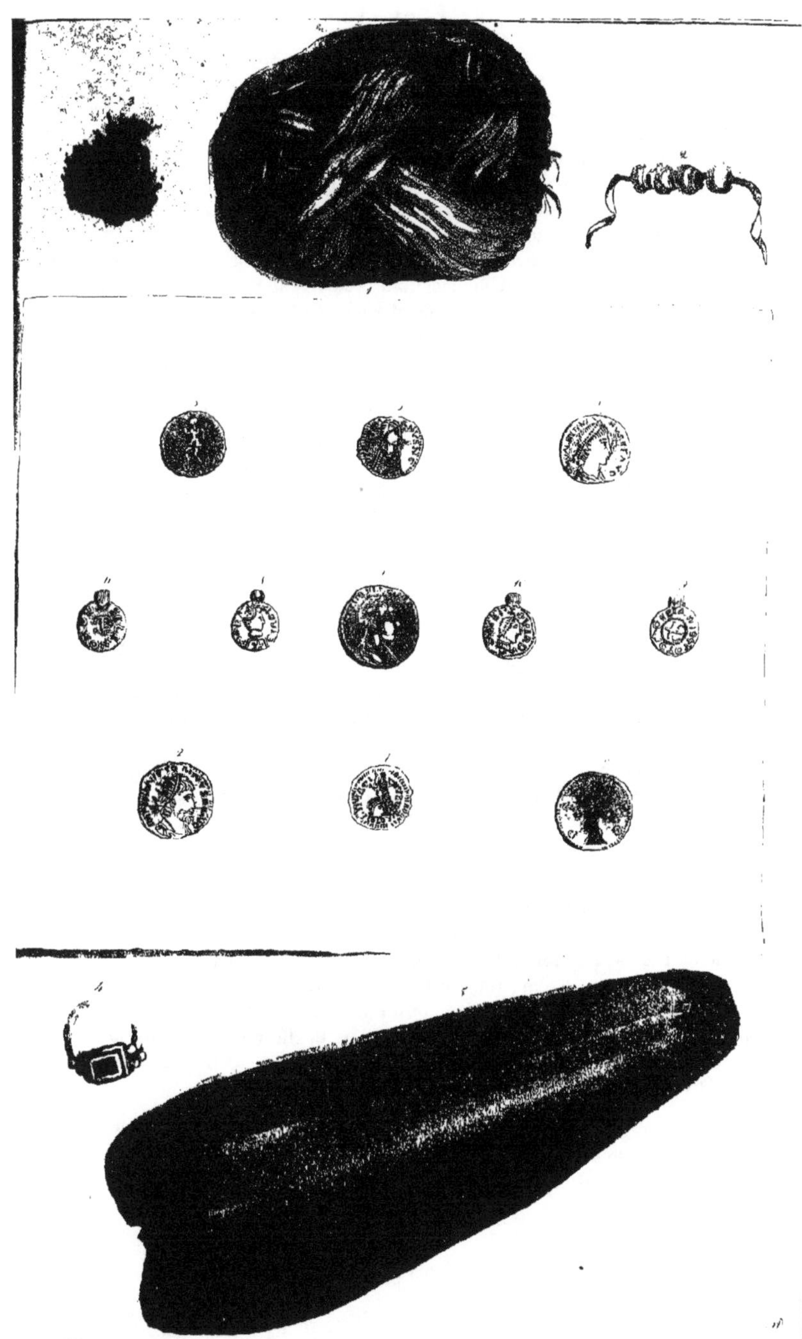

In a ſmall grave from the above, I found three BEADS of tranſparent blue-green glaſs, and one of Naples yellow opaque glaſs.

It may not be unreaſonable to conclude theſe graves to have contained female bodies; as in all probability ſome others did the ſame, eſpecially where military weapons were not found. The inference might therefore be naturally drawn, that this place of interment was peculiar to perſons who had not fallen in battle, and with no great colour of probability ſhould it ſeem to have been appropriated to the expedition of the Danes under Swein.

Lambarde ſpeaks of barrows raiſed on Black-heath over the rebels ſlain under the blackſmith Michael Joſeph and Lord Audley, in the reign of Henry the Seventh. Which fact he aſſerts; but of which I alſo entertain no ſmall doubt. The opening of the one on which the plantation has been made would ſoon ſettle the truth. Had my reſidence in that neighbourhood been longer, it was my intention to have attempted it. Should the ſpirit of enquiry lead the preſent occupier of the ground to make this reſearch, I have reaſon to think, that an earthen veſſel, or urn, with aſhes, would be found to be the only contents.

Manes temerare ſepultos. The old adage may alarm many perſons from ſuch curious reſearches, but, if cuſtom can reconcile the Antiquary to ſuch purſuits, we may ſee the modern *foſſarii* in church-yards fill the charnel houſes at this expence.

The ſoil on which theſe *tumuli* are ſituated, is gravel, and in ſome places extremely compact. The inciſion for the body about a foot and an half, or leſs, in ſome of them, below the ſurface, in the native ſoil, the barrow, or the conic mound of earth raiſed above it moſt probably collected from the trench, which encircles it, and from a ſpot of ground excavated on the Eaſt ſide of the range of *tumuli*. This excavation is annually filled up with the dead leaves collected and thrown into it.

The ground which the cluſter occupies is nearly in a circular form, and the diameter about one hundred feet. The barrows, great, medium, and ſmall, about the ſize of thoſe deſcribed in Pl. XXIV.

About ſeventy years from the date of my reſearch, a park-keeper of the name of [illegible] was known, by ſome of the old inhabitants of Greenwich, to have dug on the ſpot where the barrows are ſituated, and to have found ſeveral things of value. Having had reaſon to believe a prior opening had been made in ſome of the large barrows, by the compreſſed part of the apex, and in digging into a few of them, finding the earth had been removed, I was deſirous of directing my enquiry to obtain the above information. As the largeſt of theſe barrows had been opened by this man, it might not be improbable that he found ſome curious and perhaps very valuable relics, as were uſually interred in theſe ſmall conic ſtructures over the dead.

FIG. 4. A SILVER RING. No ſtone in the ſocket. From a barrow on Sibertſwold (a). Found with other relics, in the poſſeſſion of Mr. Fauſſett, near Canterbury. The barrow was opened Anno 1772.

(a) See the Groupe, Pl. XVIII.

FIG.

FIG. 5 STONE CELT, or Chissel [20]. From the burial place at Ash. With a circular flint stone and a Roman *fibula*. The Celt is of a grey flint, and polished with a remarkable fine surface, as also the part towards the edge where there has been a part accidentally chipped off. In the possession of Mr. Boys of Sandwich.

MISCELLANEOUS COINS,

FROM THE SMALL BARROWS.

PLATE XXII. N° I.

FIG. 1. COIN, of the Younger Gordian, inscription not perfect. Middle brass. From a barrow on Chatham lines. Bones, but no other relics.

FIG. 2. SMALL BRASS. IMP. C. PIAV. VICTORINVS. P. F. AVG. FIG. 3. Reverse, PAX. AVG. The contents of the barrow in which this coin was found is described in *note* 1. p. 79. The reverse by mistake is VIRTVS, AVG and the female genius, instead of a patera, has a sprig of laurel with a v and * on each side.

FIG. 4. Small Brass [21]. D. N. VALENTINIANVS. PF. AVG. The reverse not legible; a military figure in an offensive attitude. I conceive this coin to be of FL. PLACIDIVS VALENTINIANVS. Anno 454. Found with FIG. 2.

FIG. 6. GOLD PENDANT COIN. Perforation at the bottom of the head. D. IVSTINIANVS. Reverse, FIG. 7. VTIVHITAVH I in the exergue CONO. Figure a Victory sitting. From a barrow in the groupe at Ash, Anno 1760, and in the possession of Mr. Fauffett, whose father was present when it was found, the late Rev. Bryant Fauffett.

FIG. 8. SILVER GILT PENDANT COIN, with a loop. Head. MARS CIOVIS. FIG. 9. Reverse, TOTO MONETARIO. The cross between the words I conceive only to be an asteric, and not an X. From a grave at Sibert's Woold, or Shepherd's Well. See p. 86, note [9], further particulars. Mr. Fauffett.

FIG. 10. GOLD PENDANT COIN. Head. VIRTVS THILI.

FIG. 11. Reverse similar to the Gaulish coins, SELENO MON. From a barrow at Sibertswold, with other relics. Mr. Fauffett.

[20] Stone adges, chissels, or arrow-heads, are not unusually found in the tombs of the Northern nations, and they imply, that the inhabitants to whom they appertained were not in the use of weapons or other instruments of metal. There is in Montfaucon an account of a tomb where several stone adges were found, each skeleton having one under the skull. Most barbarous nations, in all parts of the world, seem to have shaped out of stone these kind of instruments for art as well as war, and it might hence be inferred perhaps that this barrow would apply to a very high date of antiquity; but as a coin of Justinian, see Pl. XXII. N. I. Fig. 6 and 7, was found in a neighbouring grave, and as it has been remarked a Roman *fibula*, it cannot be well placed much higher than Anno 530, the date of Justinian's reign, and especially as iron weapons, such as swords and spear heads, were found in the groupe. See note [illegible], p. 26, and fig. 1, the iron boss of a shield. It may not therefore be improbable that this stone instrument was deposited with the dead, as an amulet, and which the owner had found and preserved with a superstitious veneration. See Mr. Edward Lhuyd's Remark on these articles, p. 77, note 4.

[21] This coin is also incorrectly described in note 1, p. 79.

MIS-

COLDRED CHURCH on the Area of an INTRENCHMENT
W
N
No 1
No 3
B
C
D
2
1
5
3

MISCELLANEOUS VESSELS,

FROM THE SMALL BARROWS.

PLATE XXIII. N° I.

FIG 1 Of a light grey, almoſt approaching to white earth, ſeven inches in height, and very near as much in diameter. Chatham Tumuli The ſkeleton almoſt perfect. No other relics. The component parts of this veſſel are very extraordinary It is remarkably thin and extremely tender, ſo much ſo, that in the handling, with conſiderable delicacy, it fell to pieces, notwithſtanding it had the good fortune to be taken out of the barrow whole It has a ſalt taſte, and ſo friable, that a gentle ſqueeze with the finger and thumb will reduce it to powder.

FIG. 2. Of black earth, not unlike the Wedgewood-ware; beautifully turned in a lathe; eight inches and three quarters in height, and ſix inches and three quarters in diameter Chatham Tumuli. Thrown up promiſcuouſly from a barrow The top of this veſſel ſeems to have been broader than the ſmalleſt part of its neck

FIG 3 Of dark-grey brittle earth, nine inches in height, five inches and an half in diameter. From a barrow at the extremity at Aſh, opened May 6, 1783 Head of the ſkeleton in a South Weſt direction, near the left breaſt boſs of a ſhield, two bracers [a], one or more ſtuds. Iron ſpearhead on the ſhoulder, nine inches and a quarter in length. On the ſide an iron knife, five inches in length, and at the feet Fig. 3

FIG 4. Small veſſel, dark-brown greyiſh earth, three inches in height and three in diameter. From a barrow on Wimbledon-Common, opened September 29, 1786. No other relics, and little or no appearance of the body.

Theſe barrows on Wimbledon-Common are ſituated on the left of the high road from London to Kingſton, a ſmall diſtance from Mr Hartley's fire-houſe on the other ſide of the road, about twenty-three in number By the information of a farmer at Rochampton, of the name of Souchei, moſt of the largeſt had been opened twenty-eight years from the time I opened the remainder, by a perſon from London, and who, by his deſcription, ſeems not improbable to have been Dr. Stukeley. The ſoil on which theſe barrows are ſituated is gravel, blended with ſand, in ſome places interſperſed with a ſaponaceous marle, and ſtrongly ſaturated with the vitriolic acid, the cauſe why the bones in theſe barrows were entirely decompoſed. The largeſt do not exceed twenty-eight feet in diameter. They were evidently raiſed in their campani-form ſtructure from the circumjacent ſod ſcraped off and piled up with care and elegance over the body They have all a circular trench at their baſe, which doubtleſs received the water from the ſides of the barrow, and which perhaps was intended as well to keep the body dry, as to ſerve the purpoſes of a funeral ſuperſtition, which ſome Antiquaries may be led to ſuppoſe

[a] See Pl I fig 6

At about five furlongs from this groupe is a very large barrow of the more antient claſs; and which, from cannon having been exerciſed at a point-blank ſhot at targets raiſed in front of it, was conjectured to have been thrown up for that purpoſe. At a ſhort diſtance from the town of Wimbledon, on the Common, I was told, there is another of this ſize. This idea of theſe mounds of earth having been raiſed for the point-blank ſhot of cannon, prevails in ſeveral places. The people in the neighbourhood conceive the three barrows on Blackheath [24], mentioned in Lambarde as thrown over the rebels who fell under Lord Audley, in Henry the Seventh's reign, were raiſed by General Deſaguliers, for the above purpoſe. Two of theſe barrows have ſince been carted away for their materials; but I do not hear any human bones were diſcovered.

It was ſaid that the late Dr. Whitfield declaimed, on the remaining barrow, to his field congregation.

In many parts of England, where theſe large barrows are detached, and ſituated upon eminences, they are frequently aſſigned to the baſe of wind-mills, which, indeed, have evidently been raiſed upon them, the proprietors availing themſelves of this advantage. There is an inſtance to be met with of this nature at Walton Bridge, on the Thames, where was ſituated a range of barrows, ſeveral of which were opened, and which ſpot retains the appellation of Wind-mill Hill [25]. They are now entirely leveled to the ground.

Wimbledon-Common is divided into the right of ſeveral pariſhes, and it may not perhaps be improper to ſuggeſt the idea, that to each pariſh a cemetery might be attached, previous to the burial in church-yards, firſt introduced into Britain, anno 742, through interceſſion of Archbiſhop Cuthbert, who obtained from the Pope a diſpenſation for this purpoſe [26].

The right of common ground is of extreme early date, and may be traced much beyond the Conqueſt.

Though ſepulchres were placed by the ſides of roads, *admonere prætereuntes et ſe fuiſſe et illos eſſe mortales*, and that the dead might receive the benediction of the paſſenger, they were likewiſe conſidered as boundaries in the diviſion of property, particularly in military allotments of land. See the laws of Tiberius in the "Authores rei Agrariæ," Paris edition, 1554. *Cum agri diviſus in l.. traderetur extremus a compaginantibus agris limitibus, monumenta ſepulchrorum faciebantur*. And, *eorum igitur ſepulchrorum ſequenda eſt conſtitutis, quæ extremis finibus concurrentes fines agrorum curſu ſpectant*.

Theſe conic burial places on waſte or common grounds have been conſidered, in ſome reſpects, in the courſe of this work, as of Pagan relation, it will be perhaps neceſſary to exhibit hereafter ſome proofs in contradiction to this opinion: the reader will therefore have an opportunity of judging for himſelf, and of maintaining the argument which he eſteems moſt pertinent.

[24] Theſe barrows are almoſt at a ſimilar diſtance from the ſmall barrows in Greenwich Park as the one on Wimbledon Common is from the neighbouring groupe.

[25] When the ſtone bridge was building, the foreman of the works was in poſſeſſion of a boſs of a ſhield, ſome ſpear heads and earthen veſſels, taken from theſe barrows, which I made drawings of, and which were ſimilar to thoſe I have heretofore deſcribed in other *tumuli*.

[26] See Onuphrius Panvinius, in lib. de ritu ſepeliendi mortuos.

Fig.

CHARTHAM
Agger

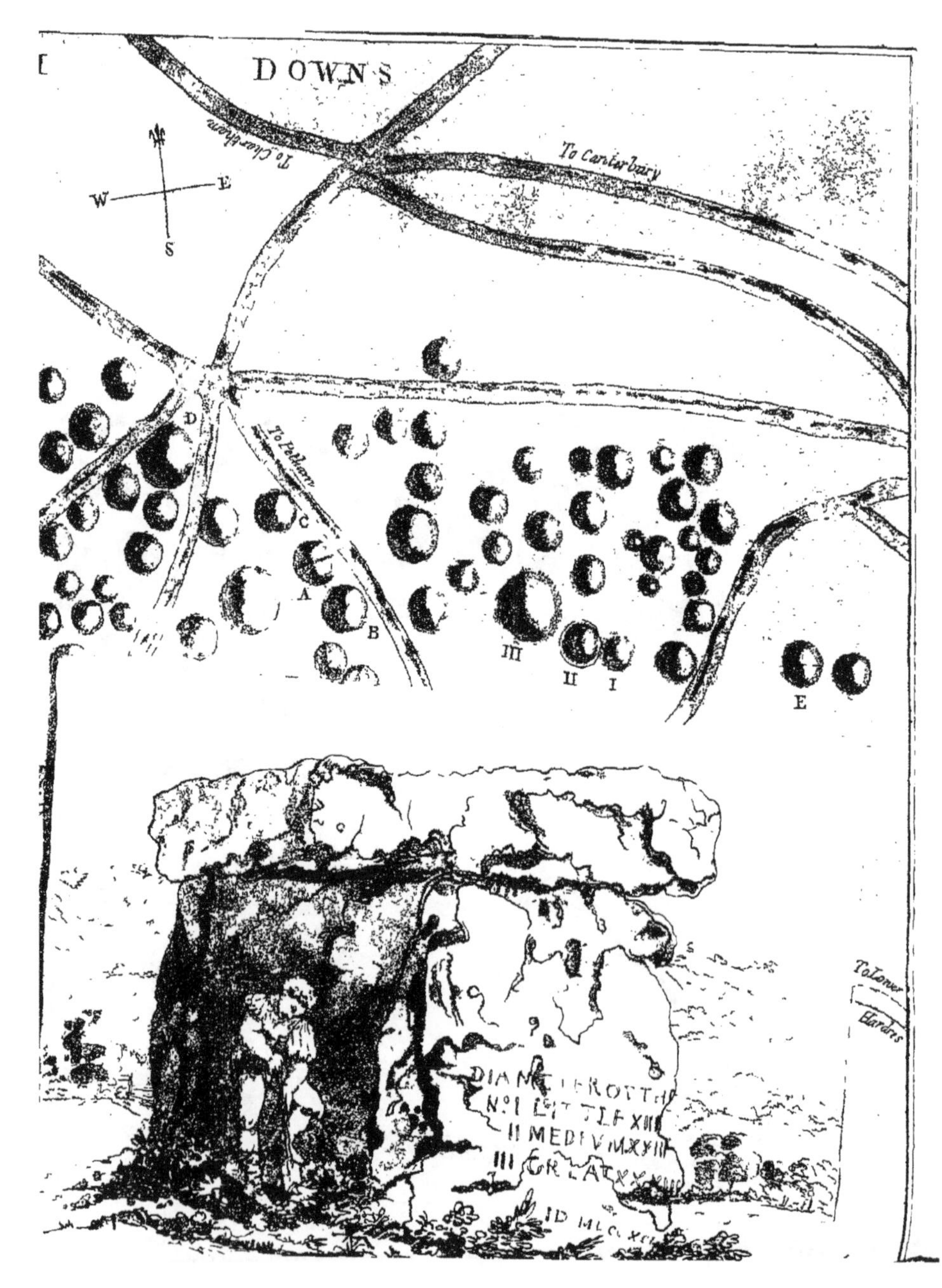
DOWNS
To Canterbury
W
E
S
D
C
A
B
III
II
I
E
DIANT
II MEDIVM
III GREAT

FIG 5 A BROWN-GREY EARTHEN VESSEL, UNBAKED three inches eight-tenths in height, and three inches fourth-tenths in diameter What renders this veſſel intereſting to the eye of an Antiquary is, that it was taken out of a barrow at the Aſh cemetery, where the coin of Juſtinian, FIG 6. PLATE XXII N° 1. was found

I have ſeveral urns, and one with aſhes of unbaked clay, from the larger barrows, and which has been the cuſtom to refer to remote antiquity, but as this coin of Juſtinian will bring the date of the Aſh cemetry as low as Anno 526, we may venture to pronounce this veſſel of nearly a contemporary date It would be therefore unreaſonable to ſuppoſe theſe people were unacquainted with the art of pottery, as their graves have produced ſeveral ſpecimens of a good kind, and as the glaſs veſſels, and other relics of ingenious workmanſhip, found in theſe barrows, warrant a belief that the people to whom they belonged were well acquainted with the full extent of that art, we may, therefore, be permitted to conclude, that ſome myſtic or religious ceremony prevailed when theſe veſſels of *unbaked clay* were depoſited with the dead

S I B E R T S W O L D D O W N BARROWS

P L A T E XXIII.

This PLAN will ſerve to explain a cluſter of the bell-faſhioned ſmall barrows on a down or waſte land, now called Shepherd's-Well, about three quarters of a mile from Waldeſhare, the Earl of Guildford's, in Kent

AAAAAA. A deep trench, confining the burial ground on two ſides

BB. Two deep trenches.

CC A wood.

The reſt of the ground in the plan all down-land.

The places to which the roads lead, and marked in the plan are BARFRESTON, EYTHORN, SIBERTSWOLD, SHEPHERDS-WELL, COLDRED, and WALDERSHARE, probably all of Saxon derivation

BARFRESTON, called Barſton or Baron, in Domeſday *Berfreſtone*

EYTHORN, perhaps, does not occur in Domeſday. Saxon heah, *Altus* Dopn, Dumus High Buſhes

SIBERTSWOLD, in Domeſday *Sibertſwalt*. Saxon Siberts Wald.

ƿald, Dominium. Siberts Demeſne, or ƿold, Locus indigus Sylvæ, Planities, a Down.

COLDRED, in Domeſday Colret Saxon COLR, ſubfrigidus. ridan, Equitare Cold Ride

The diſtances from theſe Saxon places to the cemetry are, from Waldershare one mile and an half, Eythorn, Shepherdſwell and Barfreſton, about a mile

There are two ranges of the barrows on the crown of the hill, in a broad ridge, fifteen rods broad, at a medium The direction nearly NE and SW

2 The

The other beginning at the SW extremity, and pointing towards the SW. The Southern extremity of the firſt range about three quarters of a mile from Shepherd's Well, and about South from the church. In this place the tumuli are very thick. The horſe and carriage tracks have apparently erazed thoſe in the middle, and have left them as it were in two diviſions. At the diſtance of twenty-eight rods the *tumuli* terminate at a deep ravine, apparently an old road, which traverſes the ridge. From this ſpot thirty-ſix rods more were meaſured, at which diſtance are ſituated the large *tumuli*[17], adjoining each other, as marked in the plan. This intervening ſpace, in all probability, contained barrows which might have been leveled by antient tillage, cultivation, or horſe and carriage tracts. At four rods from the large *tumuli* begins the other range of graves, which continue in a cluſter fifteen rods broad and thirty-ſix rods in extent. The ground on the declivity of the hill, on both ſides the range, in cultivation, which may have probably obliterated a great many more. In both ranges there cannot be leſs than two hundred barrows, which were all opened by the late Rev. Bryant Fauſſett, of Heppington, near Canterbury.

The pendant coin of CLOVIS, FIG. 8. PL. XXII. muſt bring this cemetery as low down as Anno 511, the date of the French king's reign; and, as the analogy of the relics found at the Aſh cemetery with thoſe of Sibertſwold and the coin of Juſtinian, will alſo produce a contemporary date, we may perhaps advance with a degree of eſtabliſhed truth on the hiſtory of theſe interments.

It may be perhaps neceſſary to remind the reader of what he may have previouſly conſidered, that theſe pendant coins do not atteſt the exact age of theſe ſepulchres; and he muſt be well aware, that their loops ſhew them to have been worn at ſubſequent dates, for purpoſes of decoration or of ſuperſtition[18]. The difficulty will therefore remain to fix their dates, and alſo to fix their owners. To diſcuſs this ſubject with perſpicuity it would be proper to conſider the ſtate of Britain from the beginning of the ſixth century, the date of the coins, to the final converſion of the iſland to Chriſtianity. By this means we may be enabled to decide, whether they may be conſidered as Pagan or Chriſtian. Anno 742 we are informed, that Chriſtian ſepulture was admitted within the walls of towns, and the iſland was then converted; it will hence appear, that theſe cemeteries exceeded that date. In the year 582 St. Auguſtin converted Ethelbert king of Kent; it is therefore probable they may have exiſted between Anno 526, the date of Juſtinian's coin, and 582; and if we can trace any relative features in the hiſtory of fifty-ſix years, the intervention of theſe dates, to apply to them, the owners may then be found at no great diſtance. Add to this, the poſſibility that theſe interments may not have taken place till the latter number of years after the date of the coin of Juſtinian, we may then, from hiſtoric agnation, reaſon with ſome certainty.

It may admit of a favourable conjecture, that theſe places of ſepulture were affixed to the neighbouring villages before cemeteries were annexed to churches; it will therefore be concluded they muſt belong to the primitive Chriſtians; with this ſuppoſition let us eſtimate the reaſons for this concluſion.

[17] It may be proper here to remark the diſcovery of the large barrows near the groups in Greenwich park, Wimbledon common, and St Margaret's on the Cliff, ſee note 4, page [illegible], which ſeem to ſhow a peculiar coincidence.

[18] See note *, page 68. See a coin of Burgred, Archaeolog. vol. IX. p. [illegible], found in a Saxon grave in Cornwall, with curious relics, in various reſpects ſimilar to the contents of theſe ſmall and uniform *tumuli*.

In

In the firft place, they are found to be near the fite of Saxon ftations, Chartham, Chatham, Burham, Sibertswold, Wimbledon, Afh, and other places that might be enumerated. They have alfo been productive of various relics, which may, with great prefumption, be given to the Chriftians, fuch as CROSSES, COINS, VESSELS OF GLASS, IRON SPEARS, RINGS, and other funeral depofits, which were adopted in early Chriftian fepulture [30].

The primitive Chriftians were fcrupuloufly obfervant of the decent and even magnificent rites of funeral; and braved the moft eminent dangers in the funeral honours of their martyrs. Though all nations concurred in rendering pious offices of careful fepulture to their deceafed relatives or friends, yet hiftory feems to adduce many proofs that the Chriftians, in the early church, were more zealous in this refpect. Dionyfius Bifhop of Alexandria applauded the Chriftians for their fedulous care in the burial of their brethren during the plague which raged in that town, he particularly fpecifies their *wafhing*, *dreffing*, and *adorning* their bodies, at the great hazard of receiving the infection, bearing them forth on their fhoulders, which many of them did receive, and perifhed

Tertullian afferts [31], that the Chriftians in his time, though they abftained from fumptuous and effeminate decorations and applications to their perfons when living, yet beftowed on their dead the moft choice and expenfive fpices, perfumes, odours, drugs, and ointments They were alfo embalmed and entombed with fkill and great magnificence .

During times of Chriftian perfecution the dead were buried without cities and towns, but when peace was reftored to the church, fepulture was permitted within the walls, and foon within the churches [33] Archbifhop Cuthbert, as before cited, eftablifhed cemeteries, Anno 742, throughout England [34].

From what has been faid the Reader will probably find fome reafon to apply thefe fmall barrows in clufters to the Chriftians of the fixth and perhaps beginning of the feventh century, and alfo to affix them to the fmall burgs or ftations within their vicinity, before cemeteries were attached to churches, or before their affemblies were held in confecrated edifices. In the neighbourhood of cities and great towns they have been obliterated by agricultural improvement.

[30] See Roma Subterranea Paulus Aringhius, p 299 Lib VI Cap xxii for the coins *Veffels of glafs* Lib III Cap xxii p 2?7 *Iron Spears*, Lib VI Cap I p 3?, Which Aringhius believes to have been the inftruments by which the martyr fuffered *Rings*, Lib VI Cap 1 *Chains*, *forceps*, *keys*, and other inftruments, with which martyrs were tormented or fuffered by, were oftentimes buried with the dead Cap xxix Lib 1 Many of the Fathers, and the early Chriftians, wore chains, in honour of Chrift's fufferings, fee Plate VIII N° 1 fig 3 where chains have been found in a grave, in the Chatham cemetery And alfo Plate X fig 5 from the Barham Downs *tumuli*

[31] Apol I 42 p 34

[32] There was a particular defcription of men for the purpofe of entombing the dead Conftantine appointed fix hundred of them They were called *Copiatæ*, from the pains they took in their employment, [illegible] Cod Theod Lib xiii Tit 1 de luftr

[33] Onuphrius Panvinius, in lib de Ritu fepeliendi mortuos

[34] In the commencement of this work, the author, in too great hafte, fubmitted his fentiments to the public on thefe clufters of fmall barrows, and which he referred to the fifth century A more careful felection of notes and arrangement of the facts will, he trufts, apologize for the overfight

N° 2 PLATE XXIII.

The Plan of COLDRED CHURCH, in the Area of an INTRENCHMENT As this church is no great diftance from the cemetery on Shepherd's-well down, it is here annexed from the peculiarity of the intrenchment, which might probably be fuppofed to have a relation to the barrows If the PLAN N° 3, be adverted to, it will naturally occur that the intrenchment was thrown up before the CHURCH was erected, and that the dimenfion of it could not apply to a military ftation of any confequence. I viewed it with fome attention, and am convinced it could not have ferved any other purpofe than that of an exploratory port of the Romans, much antecedent to the date of the barrows Perhaps thrown up by the *Comes littoris Saxonici*, in the time of Theodofius.

A. the church B a mount, but which is evidently the continuation of the vallum, now feparated from the other parts by the high road E The South fide of the work is deftroyed by the eftablifhment of a farmhoufe and its appendages, not very lately

C. the VALLUM D. the FOSSE. E. the HIGH ROAD.

CHARTHAM DOWNS BARROWS.

I SHALL here ſubjoin, for the ſatisfaction of the Antiquary, the manuſcripts of the late Dr. Mortimer, whoſe tranſmits on the diſcoveries made at this burial place were laid before the Royal and Antiquarian Societies, as alſo the one of Mr Lewis, of Margate, in Kent, on the ſame ſubject.

PLATE XXIV.

"About four miles South Weſt from Canterbury lies a large open field ſituate "in the Pariſh of Chartham, commonly known by the name of Swadling-"down, part of which is the eſtate of Charles Fagg, of Myſtole, Eſq. At the "Weſt end of theſe Downs is a riſing ground, or hill, of about a quarter of "a mile moderate aſcent every way except to the Eaſt. At about two hundred "yards from the top of the hill on the South ſide lies the road from Canter-"bury to Wye, and about the ſame diſtance from the North ſide runs the road "from Canterbury to Chilham, which is about two miles from this place, at about "half a mile's diſtance due North ſtands Chartham-church, to which is a very "gradual deſcent, and along the bottom runs a tract of meadows through "which flows the River Stour, cloſe to Chartham church-yard, and after hav-"ing paſſed the city of Canterbury, empties itſelf into the ſea a little below "Sandwich, which is about twelve miles from theſe Downs. About a year "ago, in ſtubbing a bank, in order to widen one of the roads, which runs acroſs "theſe Downs, the workmen lighted on a human ſkeleton almoſt entire, lying "in a trench cut out of the ſolid chalk, whereof the whole ſoil of this conſiſts, "covered lightly over with chalk rubbiſh, and about two feet of common mould "above it, which is alſo found to the ſame depth in all the neighbouring "ground before you come at the chalk rock: this accident raiſed in Mr Fagg "a curioſity of opening ſome Burrows or Tumuli Sepulchrales[35], which ſtand "very cloſe to one another all along the top of the hill, to the number of one "hundred, and, by the inhabitants of the country, and in the ancient deeds of "Mr Fagg's eſtate, are called The Dane's Banks. By the road ſide, where the "ſkeleton was found, ſtood three fair barrows in a row, about twenty-three "feet in diameter, but not above three feet in perpendicular height, the rain, "probably, in the courſe of ſeveral ages, having diminiſhed their height, and "ſomewhat increaſed the baſis by the mould waſhing down on all ſides. On

[35] See the Plan Pl. XXIV.

"opening

" opening the top, they found in theſe, as in all others, ſomewhat more than " a foot of common earth, then chalk rubbiſh for above two feet, which was " eaſily removed with a ſpade; but when they came to the level of the baſis, " or a little lower, they found the natural ſoil to be ſolid chalk, in which was " hewn a trench about eight feet long, two broad, and one and an half deep, " commonly running nearly Eaſt and Weſt, this ſeemed to have ſupplied the " place of a coffin to the deceaſed the bones of one perſon, ſometimes the " ſkeletons nearly whole and entire, with the head to the Weſt, lying at the " bottom of them, in ſome with large flint ſtones ranged on each ſide the body, " in order, I ſuppoſe, to keep the earth from preſſing on the corpſe, and all " the reſt was filled with chalk rubbiſh lightly flung in, ſo that even now it " could be removed by the hands; and in caſe, in the firſt opening the barrow, " they did not light on the trench, the eaſy working of the looſe chalk rubbiſh " was a certain guide to bring the workmen into the trench where the body lay

" The barrow A in the Plan, the middlemoſt of the three, was the firſt " Mr Fagg pitched on to open When they had got down to about half the " depth of the trench, they found, among the looſe rubbiſh, a beautiful Roman " Fibula [36], it conſiſts of a plate of ſilver one inch and ſeventh tenths diameter, " and one tenth of an inch thick on the foreſide round the margin it had a " circle alternately ſmooth and corded half an inch together, within this is " another, but flat circle, on which are ſome blind remains of an indented line; " round the inſide of this runs a ſmall corded wire of gold, and all the ſpace " within this cord is a plate of gold of one inch and a quarter diameter, it is " cloſely ſtudded with ſmall circles of that corded gold wire which ſome may " call roſes, but, in reality, exactly reſemble the duſt of the flower of the holy-" oak, when ſeen through a microſcope. In the center is an hemiſphere of " ivory of half an inch diameter, with a ſocket in the middle, in which pro-" bably was ſet ſome ſmall ſtone, round this is a circle of thin plates of gold, " with four rays like a ſtar, all ſet with garnets, having a triangular piece of " Lapis Lazuli at the extremity of every point, and a ſemicircular piece of the " ſame ſtone at the baſis of every ray cloſe to the ivory hemiſphere in the " middle between each ray on the golden plate ſtands a circle of gold holding " a ſmall ivory hemiſphere of a quarter of an inch diameter, in the middle of " which is a ſocket, in one whereof is ſtill remaining a round garnet, and in " another the foil which is uſed under all theſe garnets, which is a thin plate " of gold with lines acroſs it, that it ſomewhat reſembles a ſmith's file On the " back ſide was a lump of ruſty iron, which had been the ſetting on of the " tongue of the Fibula, which was uſually of iron, becauſe that metal is " the moſt ſpringy, which was a neceſſary condition, in order to make it hold " the firmer, when haſped under the hook, which is likewiſe to be ſeen on " this ſide I have ſeen one of theſe tongues and fibula entire, where the " tongue was not moveable on a hinge, as in our common buckles, but was " riveted into the plate, and then made two or three ſpiral circumvolutions, in " order to give it the ſtronger ſpring

" This is delineated in ſeveral fibulæ, in tab 28, tom III of Montfaucon's " Antiquities, and in tab 29, is repreſented a round-plated fibula, with a ſtar " upon it, ſomewhat reſembling ours

[36] Plate V No 1 Fig 1

5 " At

"At the bottom of the trench lay some remains of bones, but mostly "mouldered away, not one so whole as to know what bones they were, and they "all seemed to have been burnt. The workman struck against a glass urn, "which he broke before he was aware; but then turning over the rubbish "carefully he found, close to the first, another glass urn[37] of a yellowish "green colour, two inches and a half wide at top, three inches and a half "in the belly, and two and a half at bottom; from the brim of it began a spiral "cord in the glass, which went round it several times, descending almost im- "perceptibly to the belly, where it crosses the bottom four times, in form of a "figure of eight, and terminates in the center. The urn had at first a fragrant "smell, as if some sweet gum had been put into it. There were no bones nor "resemblance of ashes in either of them, but a white impalpable powder "clodded together, with several small *atoms or shining particles among it, not un-* "*like talc*; the inside of the urn was coated over with a thin skin reflecting all "the colours of the iris. This is usually found adhering to antient glass, "which hath laid several ages buried deep under ground, and is called by "some Antiquaries *Electrum*, by others the *Armatura*. Near to the broken "urn, or perhaps contained in it, were a small round Turquoise-stone[38], and "two pendants like those of our modern ear-rings, being garnets set in "gold[39], one of them nearly oval, only ending in a point at top, being "five eighths of an inch long and half an inch broad; the other oval, five "eighths of an inch long and half an inch broad; which stone being out of "the socket plainly discovers the foil it had under it, as before described, and "a sort of grey paste, which filled up the back of the socket. With these was "also found a piece of gold[40], six tenths of an inch diameter, consisting of "four gold corded wires forming so many circles within each other, and closed "in the middle with a cross of the same wire; on one side was fastened a shank "of gold a quarter of an inch long, with a hole through it, and a golden "pin[41] an inch long, with a small chain an inch long fastened to it. I imagine "this must be one side of a clasp to fasten some garment, and that there was "such another piece of gold with two shanks which fitted in with this; and so "the pin, going through all three of them, fastened the two sides together, "and the chain was fastened to one edge of the garment, to prevent the "pin being lost. That the bones have remained so whole, and that any of "the iron, which is a metal soon consumed by its own rust, hath remained so "long, and kept nearly its shape which it had when buried, must be attri- "buted to the chalk in which all these things were buried: chalk, we know, "absorbs all acidities, and so may here, in some measure, even retard "the progress of the rust of these pieces; for it is highly probable, had they "been laid in common earth or gravel in which any saline or vitriolic particles "were lodged, they would have been entirely consumed long since, and "which is the reason that iron weapons are seldom found among antiquities, "which are commonly of copper or brass, or some few of silver. As for gold, "it never decays or tarnishes, as may be seen in the pieces found here. I do "not remember that any blades of knives were ever found in England before;

[37] Pl. V. Nº I. Fig. 7. Antiquaries about this period gave the name of urn to all kind of sepulchral vessels without distinction.
[38] Pl. V. Nº I. Fig. 4. [39] Fig. 6. [40] Fig. 2. [41] Fig. 5. Nº I. Pl. V.

 "nor,

" nor, indeed, any ornaments compoſed of precious ſtones. After having thus " run over the ſeveral particulars which were dug up, it will not be amiſs to " offer ſome conjectures concerning the depoſiting of them here. In the firſt " place, I think there is little reaſon to doubt that the fibulæ and urns are all " Roman, that, in the barrow where the jewels and glaſs urns were found, " ſome perſon of great rank and diſtinction was buried, and that where the " earthen urns were dug up muſt likewiſe have lain perſons of ſome though " inferior note, that in the barrows where the ſingle ſkeletons lay they may " have been ſome ſoldiers, who, in memory of their ſingular valour, had ſingle " graves made for them, and the arms they fought with buried along with " them; that in the great *Tumuli** were promiſcuouſly buried the common " ſoldiers, and the horſes ſlain in the battle. the ſkull bruiſed or almoſt ſqueezed " together, and the other ſkull with the holes in it, are great proofs that a " battle was fought here. This place is almoſt exactly twelve miles from the " flat coaſt near Deal. This ſpot of ground is an eminence with a gentle deſcent " down to the Stour, which is the firſt river as one comes marching directly " from Deal. About a mile South Weſt from the Barrows lies a wood in which " are the remains of a ſquare fortreſs, encompaſſed by a double earthen ram- " part. There is another wood, called Iſſen Wood, about a mile South Eaſt " from the Barrows, in which is a camp, allowed by moſt people, as well as " the tradition of the country, to be Roman, it is ſituate by the Roman Road, " called Stone ſtreet, which leads from Romney-marſh to Canterbury. Now, " Julius Cæſar, in his "Commentaries de Bello Gallico," Lib IV. Chap 5 " ſays, that the firſt land he made in Britain was hilly, "in omnibus collibus " expoſitas hoſtium copias armatas conſpexit. Cujus loci hæc erat natura, adeo " montibus anguſtis mare continebatur, ut ex locis ſuperioribus in littus telum " adjici poſſet," which anſwers to the coaſt near Dover. He adds a little lower, " "Circiter millia paſſuum VIII ab eo loco progreſſus, aperto ac plano littore " naves conſtituit." And in the vth book he ſays, "Ipſe noctu progreſſus, " millia paſſuum circiter XII, hoſtium copias conſpicatus eſt. Illi equitatu " atque eſſedis ad flumen progreſſi, ex loco ſuperiore noſtros prohibere et præ- " lium committere cœperunt. Repulſi ab equitatu ſe in ſilvas abdiderunt, " locum nacti egregie et natura et opere munitum, quem domeſtici belli, ut " videbatur, cauſa, jam ante præparaverant: nam crebris arboribus ſucciſis omnes " introitus erant præcluſi. Ipſi ex ſilvis rari propugnabant noſtroſque intra " munitiones ingredi prohibebant." Which anſwers to the ſaid Downs near " Deal. In Lib V. Chap 4 he ſays, he landed at this ſame place, "qua " optimum eſſe egreſſum ſuperiore æſtate cognoverat." he marched twelve miles " up into the country by night, when he met with the enemy, who advanced " with their cavalry and chariots to the river, where, having the advantage " of the riſing ground, they endeavoured to ſtop the march of the Romans, and

* These *great* tumuli, ſince this paper was written, have been [illegible] opened, and no promiſcuous depoſit of bones, [illegible] human, diſcovered. The ſkull with holes in it might have been accidentally injured with the ſpade of the workman, which I am rather inclined to ſuppoſe was the caſe when I ſaw it at the late Sir W. Fagg's. The bones of horſes, or ſome other animal, were only found in the mould [illegible], where [illegible] by carting of compoſt might have thrown them.

The [illegible] and by every other obſervation made [illegible] no induction whatever can be made to favour Dr. Mortimer's opinion that a battle had been fought on or near the ſpot.

" ſo

" so began the battle, but being repulsed by the Roman horse, they retired
" into the woods, having a place there already fortified, both by nature and
" art, which had been a fortress built formerly in some of their domestic
" wars, the Romans soon dislodged them, and took possession of their fort,
" which he fortified for the encampment of his own army, next day he had
" the news of his ships being shattered in the storm, whereupon he set out
" immediately for the sea-side, drawing out of the legions all the carpenters
" and other workmen whom he thought proper to assist in repairing his fleet
" after having staid ten days, he returned again to the place where he had
" left his army, where he found the Britons got together in much larger num-
" bers than before. In the vth Cap he gives a short description of the whole
" island, with an account of the inhabitants, and their manner of fighting, and
" says, they had frequent skirmishes with parties of the enemy, especially with
" the out guard, while they were fortifying their camp. He says, " that day
" was slain Q Laberius Durus, a Tribune" Thus you see the situation of these
" Downs seems to answer to the place where Cæsar first encountered the Bri-
" tains, and the fortress S W. of the barrows must be the place whither the
" Britains retired, for as one comes up from the river that wood lies in a
" direct line behind the Downs; whereas the camp in Iffen Wood lies quite
" back again above a mile to the left, and nearer the sea and as it stands
" by the side of a Roman Road, seems to me to be a fortress made after the
" road in which a garrison was kept to guard some pass; and not that it was
" the place in the wood into which the Britains retired, as Dr Harris, in his
" History of Kent, p 316, saith, was the opinion of Dr Plot Our first
" mentioned Wood is about a mile East of Chilham, and about half way
" thither, and about a mile and an half West from the Barrows, is that fa-
" mous Tumulus called Julaber's Grave it is a bank seventy paces long and
" twenty over, and ten or twelve feet high, which is a form very different
" from any of the Tumuli Sepulcrales, which were always round The late
" Earl of Winchelsea had a trench dug across it, in which they found some
" stags' horns, but no human bones, and there was a fœtid smell, which
" much annoyed the workmen Indeed, from the situation of it on the side
" of an hill, and the ground being common earth about it, and this bank
" being a knole of chalk, I took it to be natural, the rain having washed away
" the loose earth

" There was besides found a SPHERICAL CRYSTAL BALL, one inch and a half
" diameter *, not well polished nor clear, having several flaws in it. And,
" lastly, in this grave was found part of a very thin helmet, or scull-cap, as
" I believe, only for ornament, or a defence against the weather, there was
" some of the lining remaining in it, coarse and of a dark brown colour, the
" metal seemed by its pale yellow to be a mixture of copper and brass † On
" one part of the margin was the remains of a hinge, this cap was not thicker
" than a common card, its diameter was six inches and a half, and in depth
" one inch and three quarters.

* Plate V N I Fig 3

† I am inclined to think this relic was the remains of a metal vessel, not unusually found in these small barrows Numerous discoveries have never exhibited any remains of body armour The lining, I apprehend, was only some decayed filaments of the vestment of the body

" In

“ In the barrow B was found AN URN OF RED EARTH, three inches and a quar-
“ ter wide at top, ſix inches in the belly, and three inches and three quarters
“ at bottom, and a large black urn, there were ſome burnt bones. In the
“ urns were aſhes mixed with chalk, but no arms found here

“ In the barrow C were found TWO URNS OF BLACK EARTH, one of them with
“ a round lid on, flat on one ſide, and a little rounding on the other These
“ urns were broke, and their contents ſpilt

“ In the barrow D, which was much larger than either of the former, there
“ was found only 1 BLACK URN, but ſo rotten it could not be taken up
“ whole.

“ In the barrow E was found a PIECE OF GOLD [42] one inch and a half in dia-
“ meter, with a corded wire round the edge of it, and an eye, by which it ſeems
“ to have been hung to ſomething, on the piece itſelf are chaced out ſeveral
“ odd figures, perhaps the characters belonging to ſome angel or ſpirit, and
“ that this piece of gold was worn, hanging from the neck upon the breaſt,
“ as an amulet or charm to keep away evil ſpirits, and may have been buried
“ with the dead for the ſame purpoſe Along with this were alſo found four
“ amethyſt beads and ſeveral braſs pins nine inches and a half long, with
“ round flat heads through which are ſmall round holes, then the pin is round
“ for half an inch, and after that ſpreads out a little, having a ridge along the
“ middle three quarters of an inch long, which falls off to an edge on each ſide,
“ and tapers to the point, theſe, I believe, were faſtened by a loop through
“ the eye to the edge of the garment, and were uſed to faſten the garment
“ together, by running them through it, as we do common pins, there is one
“ piece exactly like another, except that inſtead of ending in a point it ends
“ in a *croſs* [43]; and ſuch another was found in a lump of ſeveral of them ce-
“ mented together by the ruſt of ſome adjacent iron, there are two ſuch other
“ lumps of ſeveral joined together by ruſt; but in each there appears a pin,
“ which, inſtead of a croſs, hath ſomething at the end in form of a ſmall
“ battle-ax: theſe three ſomewhat reſemble a very odd ſort of fibula, repre-
“ ſented by Montfaucon in the 29th Tab Vol III. of his Antiquities, it con-
“ ſiſts of a bar with a double-ax at one end, and two half-moons ſet on the
“ bar, with two ſhanks at the other end, it was uſed like double-buttons,
“ each end being paſſed through a ſlit in the garment, but ours were
“ faſtened by the eye to one ſide of the garment, and the croſs or piece like a
“ battle-ax was paſſed through a little ſlit on the other ſide, probably there
“ was another like piece on the other ſide the bar, as in Montfaucon's the
“ two half-moons Here were likewiſe found ſeveral pieces of braſs, in form
“ of a ſmall barrel [44], three quarters of an inch long at one end, joined to a
“ flat piece of braſs two inches long, a quarter of an inch over where it
“ joined to the barrel, and three quarters of an inch wide at the other end,
“ where were the remains of hinges What these could be I cannot imagine,
“ never having heard of any ſuch thing being found any where before, nor
“ any deſcription given of them in any book I have met with.

[42] Plate XVI N° I fig 1 [43] Plate XVIII fig 3 and 5 [44] Plate XVIII fig. 4

" In the barrow F, which was one of the largeſt of all, being full thirty-
" three feet diameter at the baſis, and near ſix feet in perpendicular height,
" were found ſeveral bones, as if many bodies had been buried there, and
" among the bones ſome were the ſhin-bones of horſes, but lying in the com-
" mon mould, which in this was four or five feet deep, they were almoſt
" periſhed; at the bottom was a larger trench than uſual in the chalk, in which
" lay ſome few bones, but none entire here were found ſeveral pieces of
" rotten wood, and ſome nails clenched with the wood adhering, and two
" plates of iron, with broad-headed rivets at each end, and ſome remains of
" wood alſo adhering to them near to theſe were found the two braſs nails
" with round heads ſtanding cloſe together and rivetted through a piece of
" wood, which fell to pieces as ſoon as touched

" In all the reſt of the barrows which have been opened, to the number of
" about twenty, there were nothing particularly obſerved, they were all of
" them nearly of the ſame depth, and in each a ſingle ſkeleton pretty entire,
" lying the head towards the Weſt, and the feet towards the Eaſt in the
" cavity of the ſkull, and about moſt of the bones, was a large quantity of
" worm-caſts, [or] a ſort of earth much reſembling fuller's-earth though all was
" covered over with chalk. About the Weſt of the ſkeletons were found, in
" ſeveral barrows two, three, or four, ſilver buckles, about half an inch
" broad, and to ſome, part of the leather ſtraps are ſtill adhering Among the
" leather which was found here there is one piece about half an inch broad,
" very nicely punched in form of lozenges. The ſhanks of one of the ſmall
" ſilver buckles whereby it was faſtened on to the leather is ſet with ſmall gar-
" nets, there were alſo two or three ſilver ſtaples to paſs the end of the leather-
" ſtrap under, after it was buckled A copper buckle one inch broad, with a
" ſhank two inches long, hath a very particular contrivance of a round piece
" joined to the hinge of the tongue, by which means the tongue cannot be
" fillip'd up, but the ring part muſt be depreſſed, in order to get the leather
" through

" In another Tumulus was found a pair of ſquare braſs hinges [45], two
" inches and an half long and one inch broad In others were found rings of
" ſilver wire, of about two inches and a quarter diameter, one of them had
" a blue glaſs bead, half an inch diameter, on it [46], [ſuch as theſe are figured
" by Montfaucon, vol III tab. 32], a ſilver pin two inches long, with a rivet
" at each end, and with theſe a ſmall ſilver hook ear-ring In all the tumuli
" except thoſe where the urns were found, were ſeveral pieces of ruſty iron,
" moſt of them ſo decayed that it was impoſſible to aſcertain what they were,
" it is reaſonable to ſuppoſe they were the ſame with ſome few which
" had ſtill retained ſomewhat of their antient form, as in two barrows were
" found two heads of ſpears *(pila)* pretty entire, one of them ſix inches and
" a half long, one inch and three quarters broad in the head, the ſhank
" ſeven inches long, wherein ſome wood was ſtill remaining, the other eight
" inches long and two inches broad; the ſhank was broken off, but there was
" ſome wood likewiſe on th[…] They lay even with the heads of the ſkeletons

[45] Plate XVIII Fig 11 [46] See ſimilar beads, Pl II Fig 1c.

" on the right ſide, and, by ſome ſmall ſplinter of rotten wood, ſeem to be laid " in the right hand of the corpſe. Theſe *haſtæ* of the antients were uſually " the height of a man. Among the rubbiſh in another was found the head " of a javelin ſeven inches long, two inches broad, the ſhank ſix inches long " with wood in it, as likewiſe the head of an arrow two inches long, one " inch broad, and the ſhank (in which was ſome wood) two inches long, and " beſides theſe ſeveral pieces of ruſty iron, not ſo entire, but yet whole enough " to know they were parts of the like weapons, one of them, which ends " with a round ſharp point, was probably the bottom or ferril of a pike[47], " with which the ſoldiers uſed to ſtrike them upright into the ground, or if " the head ſhould be broken off, they could ſtill make uſe of this end, which " was very ſharp too, this ſort of pike was peculiar to the horſemen. In others " were found the blades of knives, in ſhape like our common pen-knives, " having thick backs and ſharp points with ſtrait edges, the ſmalleſt three inches " long, and half an inch broad. There was alſo found a piece of iron round at " the top, two inches and an half long and one inch and a half broad, in form " of a modern ſpatula, with two holes in it, and part of a ſmall iron handle " two inches long. In another was dug up a pair of iron ſhears[48] eleven " inches long, like thoſe our cloth-dreſſers do at this time uſe. In two others " were found lying at the head of the ſkeleton two boſſes or umbos of ſhields, " one of them is an almoſt exact hemiſphere, ſix inches diameter, with a ſpike " in the center, and the brim turned up half an inch, wherein are the remains " of four rivets, by which it was faſtened to the ſhield. Near this was found " ſeveral nails with heads, and which had been evidently riveted into wood, " whence I conclude, that the whole ſhield was wood, cloſely ſtudded with theſe " broad-headed nails, which ſtood ſo cloſe that their heads touched each other. " The other umbo is conical, with the brim turned up half an inch, wherein " were the remains of three rivets, one part of the brim being broken off. " Among the rubbiſh of ſeveral tumuli were found parts of ordinary iron fibulas " without plates, theſe conſiſt of a ſemicircle and a ſtraight tongue, joined to- " gether by an hinge at one end, and an hook at the other end of the ſemi- " circle, under which the tongue is to be hitched. There were beſides ſeveral " fragments of iron, which ſeemed to be parts of ſuch like things. *On the* " *ruſt of one was the impreſſion of the threads of ſome coarſe linen*, another was " an iron ring and eye, and one was ruſty iron incloſed in decayed wood, to " one *a ſmall cockle-ſhell was adhering*; with theſe was dug up an iron hook " reſembling the hook of a ſword as are now in uſe. And, laſtly, we found " two iron buckles, like thoſe we wear, with buff belts; one of them is one " inch and a quarter broad, and hath ſquare corners, the other is broad, and " is of an oval ſhape. In ſome of theſe graves we light on glaſs-beads, about " the ſize of peaſe, red, green, and white, and one larger made of brick, red " ſtriped with yellow. In others were ſome few pieces of blue glaſs. In ano- " ther a ſingle amethiſt bead. In moſt of them were ſeveral ſmall pieces of " charcoal. No medals were found. The ſkeletons were very entire, but the " ſmall bones would not bear removing, the heads were moſtly whole, and the " jaw full of ſound teeth, one of the ſkulls ſeemed cruſhed as if a cart-wheel

[47] See Pl. XIX. fig. 5. a ſimilar ſpecimen.
[48] Pl. V. N° II. fig. 1 and

" had

“ had run over it; another had a ſliver off of the head, by which means
“ there were four holes cut through the *os occipitis*

“ The learned Camden, in his Britannia, vol I. page 238 Lond. 1722. fol.
“ thinks that the word *Julaber* is a corruption of *Laberius*; or, as I believe the
“ country people might, by miſtake, call him Julius Laberius, becauſe he came
“ over with Julius Cæſar, but then, inſtead of this being the place of his
“ burial, I offer it to the further enquiry of the Antiquary, whether *our*
“ *barrow marked A, in the plan, is not the very ſepulchre of this Roman general*
“ *Q Laberius Durus, and that glaſs urn, jewels, and ſuch things, as were found*
“ *in that barrow would have been buried with no one of leſs conſequence than one*
“ *of his poſt*; that the other barrows were the tombs of the other ſoldiers; and
“ ſo we may conclude theſe Downs to have been the ſpot where Cæſar firſt
“ encountered the Britons, it is likewiſe probable, that many ages after the
“ Saxons and Danes, finding ſome tumuli on this ſpot, might likewiſe bury
“ here too, for I believe the amulet or chaced piece of gold is Daniſh, per-
“ haps ſome piece of ſuperſtition But I think there can be no doubt of thoſe
“ barrows, in which the urns and ſpears were found, being truly Roman
“ burying places. Some may object that after a battle people do not
“ take much care in burying the dead, and that they have not time to burn
“ the corpſe, to which I anſwer, that in this caſe here was the main body
“ of the Roman army encamped without any remarkable action for ten
“ days, and Cæſar ſtayed two or three days after, which ſurely was time ſuf-
“ ficient for them to take care of the decent burial of their fellow-ſoldiers, but
“ more particularly of one of their leaders and beſides, the raiſing theſe tumuli
“ over them was a means of handing down the memory of the action to after-
“ ages, as we find the name of Julaber's grave hath remained to the preſent
“ time; and the notion of his having been ſome great man may have been a
“ natural reaſon for the people to pitch on that great bank as the place of his
“ burial”

There requires but little penetration to obſerve in this manuſcript the great veneration which the Antiquaries of thoſe days had for every thing that was Roman; and but a ſlight reference to the body of this work to correct the inimated zeal of the Doctor, when he is pleaſed, in the fever of conjecture, to place barrow A over the aſhes of Q Laberius Durus. As to the whole of the good Phyſician's conjecture, they are really too puerile for a comment

Mr Lewis, of Margate, after deſcribing the ſite of the barrows on Chartham-Downs, and their contents, from the account of Dr. Mortimer, thus begins his conjecture “On Chartham-Downs, about three miles from
“ the city of Canterbury, are ſeveral hillocks, or heaps of earth, which the
“ inhabitants thereabouts call Dane-barrows In the year 1730 ſeveral of theſe
“ were opened, by the order of the late Charles Fagg, Eſq of Myſtole, in the
“ pariſh of Chartham, to whom this Down belonged In opening of them
“ were found the following things, thus deſcribed by C Mortimer, M D

" The umbo of a ſhield, and the nails with which the ſhield was ſtudded " One entire ſpear, another a little broken in the ſocket three pieces of ſpears " the head of a javelin the head of an arrow, with a muſcle ſhell joined to " it, thirteen knives or pieces four nails, one of which drove through a piece " of wood, and clinched a hook of the ſcabbard of a ſword. two other " hooks a tongue of a large fibula, or buckle eight pieces of claſps or " haſps two pieces of iron, ruſted, with a piece of linen, as it ſeems, adher- " ing to them. ſeven nails with wood to them ſeveral pieces of broad " buckles ſeveral long pieces of iron, with holes made through them an " iron ring and eye a piece of iron incloſed in a ſubſtance like wood

" Several pieces of iron cemented together with a piece of copper, with an " eye at one end, and a croſs at the other two pieces of iron with pieces of " copper, with an eye at one end, and the other end reſembling a battle-ax. " one piece of iron, containing two pieces of copper, which is flat and triangu- " lar at one end, in which has been a hinge, and reſembling a little barrel at " the other end two pieces of iron ſeparate, and a larger piece with a hinge, " and ruſty iron ſticking to it, four Amethiſts, *Beads*, &c *A piece of enchaſed* " *gold, as large as a broad piece*, with an eye on one ſide: thirteen copper " pins, with eyes at one end, and pointed, and four cornered, like a ſpear " at the other. a ſingle pin ſticking to ruſty iron a ſingle pin with a croſs. " All theſe were found in one barrow.

" A round ſilver fibula, or claſp, faced with gold, ſet with a croſs of gar- " nets · a pair of garnet ear-rings ſet in gold four circles, or rings of gold, " faſtened together with a croſs in the middle, and an eye at one ſide, with " a gold pin and ſmall chain a *chryſtal ball or pearl of Pliny* * one whole glaſs " urn, and another broken in pieces · one braſs cap broken, and lined with a " piece of woollen cloth Theſe were found in another barrow.

" A ſilver wire ring with *a blue glaſs bead on it* two ſmaller rings a bro- " ken ſilver ſocket a ſmall ſilver bar, with a hole at each end ſome bits of " leather, pinked diamond faſhion a flat amethiſt, and BEADS OF SEVERAL " COLOURS AND SIZES a ſmall piece of braſs rivetted to a piece of wood

" Two braſs hinges ſeveral pieces of *blue* and *green enamel* a ſmall *tur-* " *quoiſe ſtone* a ſilver S three ſilver buckles, with the pieces belonging to " them, one of which has two garnets fixed to it

" Four copper buckles one large copper buckle a ſkull, with both the " upper and lower jaw, with four holes in the hinder part, ſeeming to be oc- " caſioned by a large ſliver cut off ſeveral cinders or wood coals two broken " decayed urns, one urn perfect, and of a red colour, and another black a " ſilver pin two ſtaples of belts ſeveral decayed pieces of wood

" ſeveral other buckles, like the former a piece of iron, reſembling the " umbo of a ſhield human bones bones of horſes heads of iron javelins "

By this account of relics found in theſe *barrows*, it ſeems as if the country people are right in calling them *Dane-barrows*, and that they are the graves and monuments of ſome of the Daniſh commanders and their ladies, who were ſlain here by the Engliſh, in oppoſing their paſſage over the river Stoure juſt by, when they came hither from the ſea-coaſt, in order to march further up into the kingdom

* Whence the cuſtom of calling the *Cryſtal ball*, ſometimes found in tombs, by this name

The

The learned John George Keysler, *Antiq. Septentr. Hanov.* 1720, observed of the Gauls, that at the burning of their dead they brought to the fire every thing which they supposed was agreeable to the deceased when they were alive, that the Germans brought the arms of the deceased and to some their horses, and the Danes liberally provided for them arms, gold, and whatsoever was best, that in the barrows are found bones, ashes, money or coins, cinders, ashes, broken shells, and chalk. He adds, "Magnates nordici (p. 163, 168.) "una cum defunctis, equos, gladios, pugiones, hastas, aliaque arma-"rum genera sepeliverunt." By this, are these *barrows* in evidence, in which it is plain was buried the wearing apparel of the deceased, their armour, swords, shields, darts, javelins, and horses. That they were the *barrows* of persons of eminence and distinction seems to be plain, not only from the gold and silver ornaments, and precious stones found in them, but the leather found with them, since Keysler observes this was so rare and scarce that shoes made of it were very uncommon, and appropriate in a manner to their Gods and Princes, and that others wore shoes made of wood. It appears that here were buried bracelets, ear-rings, costly apparel, rings, here was likewise found, *one piece of silver coin*, but without any inscription.

Of what use *the crystal ball was* I do not know, but the fibula was to fasten on the breast the loose gown or garment worn uppermost.

In 1658 was published, by Thomas Brown, Doctor of Physick, at Norwich, a little tract, which he entituled "Urne-Burial, or a discourse of the Sepulchral-"Urnes lately found in Norfolk," of these four of different sizes are there described of black earth, and the biggest of them holding about a gallon, and with short necks, whosoever compares them with these will not observe much unlikeness. But the two glass urns are, I think, uncommon, though the lachrymatories or tear bottles were made of it, when the making of glass was first invented, or by whom, I do not know, but Thomas Stubbs assures us, that here in England glass windows were first introduced by Wilfred Bishop of Worcester, A D DCCXXXVI.

Perhaps some would infer, from the mention of *crosses* in this account of the things found in these barrows or burying places, that the persons buried here were Christians, but the learned Keysler has shewn, that the Gentiles also had the sign of the cross on their monuments, and that therefore it is a good proof that *non omnes cruce signatos lapides a Christianis* esse erectos. No more are the several crosses here mentioned an evidence that there were Christians to whom they belonged.

In the isle of Tenet (so called from the beacons erected in it to give notice of the invasions by the Danes to the Continent), is a gate or way into the sea, made by the fishermen, called Bartlem-gate, from a battle fought near it by the Earls Alchere and Huda, two English generals, with the Danes, A D 853. Just by it were two long banks (one larger than the other), called by the inhabitants *Hackem Down Banks*. In May, 1741, these banks were opened by Mr Thomas Reed, in whose land they were, and in it were found many sculls and bones of men, women, and children, which, by the smallness of their bones, seem to be unborn, some of these bones were found but a little below the surface, others a little lower, in the firm chalk, a deep trench seemed to have been cut in the middle, on each side of which seem to have been cut holes in an oblong form, into which the bodies were thrust, head and heels together, two of the sculls were covered with coals and ashes. There were likewise found some bones of horses and three urns of very black coarse earth, and seemed not to have been half-burnt. One of these was so large as to hold about half a bushel; these probably were bodies of the chiefs of the Danes and their Ladies, who lost their lives in this battle; and an evidence of the Danes being conquerors, as our historians assert. Asserius bishop of St David's account is this: "Eodem anno 853, *Ealhere* comes cum *Cantu-* "*ariis*, et *Huda* cum *Suthriis*, contra Paganorum exercitum in insula, quæ "dicitur in *Saxonica* lingua Tenet, *Britannico* autem sermone *Ruim* *, animose "et acriter belligeraverunt, et primitus Christiani victoriam habuerunt, pro- "longatoque diu prælio ibidem ex utraque parte plurimi ceciderunt, et in aqua "mersi suffocati sunt, et comites illi ambo ibidem occubuerunt."

* The Britons seem to have called this island by this name, as a part of the Richborough-port, which they called *Inis Ruim*, and which the English Saxons altered to *[illegible]*, *Retesburg*, and *[illegible]*.

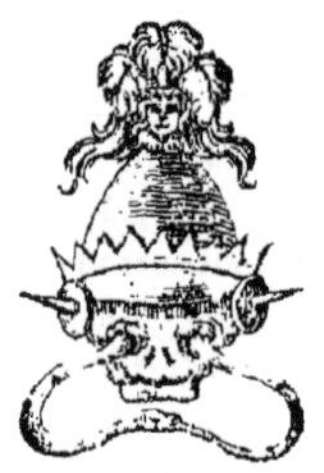

CONTENTS OF THE SMALL BARROWS.

VAIN ASHES, WHICH, IN THE OBLIVION OF NAMES, PERSONS, TIMES, AND SEXES, HAVE FOUND UNTO THEMSELVES A FRUITLESSE CONTINUATION, AND ONLY ARISE UNTO LATE POSTERITY, AS EMBLEMS OF MORTAL VANITIES. BROUNE'S HYDRIOT

A Selection has been made from the moſt ſtriking relics found in our ſmall barrows in cluſters, and exhibited as the genuine records of paſt ages. The toil, expence, and length of time, required for one man to explore, and diligently to ſeek after, the ſcattered and almoſt effaced traces of theſe only true remains of our anceſtors, through the various counties of Britain, would fill up the ſhort period of human life. I have therefore availed myſelf of occaſional diſcoveries and of tranſient opportunities to purſue them at the interval of other avocations. The chief pleaſure which I derive from the accumulation of theſe facts, with their comparative features, is from the hope that they may eſtabliſh a ground for ſucceeding enquiries concerning the antient inhabitants of this iſland, and of their proving a uſeful reference to the accurate hiſtorian in the illuſtration of his pages.

The collection I have made from theſe barrows conſiſt, of ARMS, SWORDS, SPEARS, REMAINS of BOWS and ARROWS, UMBONES of SHIELDS, GLASS and EARTHEN VESSELS, DECORATIONS OF DRESS, BEADS, BROACHES, BUCKLES, PENDANT ORNAMENTS, INSTRUMENTS OF MAGIC, COINS, and SEVERAL FRAGMENTS OF BRASS AND IRON, not eaſily applied to their original uſe.

SWORDS

The ſwords are generally of the ſame length as have been deſcribed, and of iron, excepting a fragment of one, which exhibits the ſame breadth, and only one edge The blade long, ſharp, doubly edged, not pointed with a regular ſlope to the end, but obtuſely terminated, made more for cutting than for piercing, and no guards They have a perfect reſemblance to the arms of all the Northern nations, which antient and more modern hiſtory have deſcribed. They imply, that the owners were not embodied under the diſcipline of a Roman army, but in the habit of excurſionary conteſt in ſmall bodies, when men were individually oppoſed to each other. Their pummels and handles were of wood, and not ornamented with coſtly metals From perfect ſpecimens they ſhould ſeem all to have been of the ſame ſize The various fragments of others, and from the information I have received at places where they have been diſcovered with human ſkeletons, they do not exceed thirty inches in the blade

SPEAR-HEADS,

Are of iron The conſiderable numbers which my cabinet contains, ſhow them of different forms, and ſcarcely two alike They ſeldom exceed a foot in length from the point to the ſhoulder near the ſocket of the ſhaft, and never more than a foot and a half, including blade and ſocket part a proportion which ſeems to have been regulated on the weight and length of metal to the length and ſize of the haft; their breadth from two inches and an half to one in their broadeſt part, their ſhapes vary conſiderably. Some are in their blade of a continued breadth to the ſhoulder, others ſpread to three inches from their ſhoulder, and decreaſe proportionably to the point Theſe ſpear heads do not exceed a foot in length; others ſpread from the ſhoulder to an inch and an half, and continue ſloping to the length of a foot to the point, others ſlope from the ſhoulder to an oval, and decreaſe in the ſame proportion to the point; others continue the breadth of an inch from the ſhoulder for the length of a foot, and ſuddenly ſlope obtuſely to the point I have one ſingular ſpecimen, which ſlopes from the ſocket two feet to the ſhoulder of the blade, which does not exceed three inches and a quarter in length, and a quarter of an inch in its broadeſt part The iron from the ſhoulder to the natural ſlope for the ſocket is not thicker than a common ram-rod of a fowling-piece. Some heads of pikes, about three inches in length, and not very unlike the Roman *pila*, at firſt I concluded theſe anſwered the purpoſe of pikes at the end of ſpears to fix in the ground, but, as they were found in graves where no other arms were diſcovered, they ſeem to have been applied to the uſe of miſſile weapons.

UMBONES

The umbones or central protuberances of iron from ſhields are not uncommonly found in the ſmall *tumuli* I have great numbers in fragments, and only a dozen entire. Their forms are alſo continually varied, ſome partake of conic forms, ſharp at the end, and progreſſive for four inches to their circular baſe of half a foot in diameter, others do not exceed two inches in height to their baſe, of the diameter of three quarters of half a foot. The cap of the boſs ſcarcely five inches in diameter, protruding an inch from the rim, the point armed with a circular button not an inch in diameter From this latter form they vary to the conic form throughout all its parts; their rims, which rivet them to the wood, and under which the accreted particles of this decayed ſubſtance are generally diſcovered, are ornamented ſometimes with ſilver and braſs caps to their ſtuds The metal is hammered extremely thin, and in conſequence of the hollow cavity under the boſs, which was evidently open to the ſhield to receive the gripe of the hand, a ſound would proceed from it when ſtricken upon it with the flat of the ſword Under the boſs is generally found a flat piece of iron, with dove-tails at the end, and which appears to have been riveted acroſs the hollow of the boſs for the reception of the hand, and alſo to ſecure the boſs Iron ſtuds are occaſionally ſcattered near the boſs, an indication of their ornamental uſe to the ſhield

It is here proper to remark, that on the diſcovery of theſe iron *umbones*, ignorant people have given them the name of ſkull-caps, and which name has been alſo applied to brazen veſſels found in our *ſmall conic tumuli*

FRAGMENTS OF BOWS.

I have only two ſpecimens of BRACES to ſtrengthen the back of bows. Probably the many barrows, which contained ſkeletons and no arms, may have been occaſionally buried with wooden bows, which, like the hafts of ſpears, the orbs of ſhields, and perhaps coffins, had periſhed through the ſucceſſion of ages.

ARROW-HEADS

Are alſo but few in number There is about half a dozen in my cabinet, their forms vary, ſome an inch long, others to four inches

KNIVES,

Of all ſizes, and in great numbers, from eight inches to three in length, ſome curved, ſome ſtraight in the blade, and all of them pointed, no one of them claſped Several ſpecimens of decayed particles of wood, mixed with the ruſt, which ſeem to ſhow the nature and quality of their caſes Their breadth from one to a quarter of an inch.

Vessels of Earth

Confift of light red, grey, and brown, unglazed earth. They do not partake of the form of urns, which are found with cinerітious remains Some are in the form of bottles with necks, containing from one to two quarts of liquid, others not more than half a foot in height, without necks These are ufually found at the feet of fkeletons, and oftentimes in thofe graves which contain fwords, fpears, and fhields, efpecially thofe with necks to them.

Vessels of Glass

Some are rounded at their bafe, and indicate their exprefs ufe for fepulchral purpofes No fpecimen of the kind has been found in thefe fmall barrows fimilar to the luftral veffels of the Romans, improperly called *lacrymatories*; which are in general of a thinner glafs, and differ always in fhape, and indicative of a different period of glafs workmanfhip Glafs veffels found in our fmall tumuli in groupes are generally peculiar to thofe graves which contain ornaments of the women.

Beads

The fpecimen of thefe female ornaments amount to fome hundreds They confift of Pale Rubies, Amethysts, Garnets, or Hyacinth, Amber, Crystal, Glass, and Shell.

The *Amethyfts* have evidently undergone the lapidary's tool, and fhow figns of their having been confidered as valuable decorations Several of the amethyfts are in the fhape of hearts, and in which form[1] they have been found as ornaments of pins in Italy They are of various fizes, from an inch to $\frac{1}{5}$

The *Garnet-beads* are rough, unpolifhed, perforated, confift of one entire ftring, and ferved for the ornament of a full neck, if clofely encircled They are feventy-three in number, of the fize of a large pea

Amber-beads are of various fizes and forms, from an inch in diameter to the $\frac{1}{10}$ of an inch Some are chipped to circular forms, or polifhed to the fize of the natural lump or fragment, others are turned to the form of lozenges, others fquare, flat, and circular, few are perfectly round Amber is doubtlefs a foffil gum, and in its natural ftate folid, and not gritty, yet many of thefe amber relics, whether from the lixivial falts of the body, or from what other caufe, difficult to explain, are gritty and eafily broken

Cryftal-beads appear to have ferved for the decoration of the wrift, feveral having been found in the pofition of that part of the body Their fize from an inch to half an inch Some are circular, and not perforated, and have been found in that form in the grave with other relics I have two large fpecimens

[1] See one of this form, in the poffeffion of Charles Towaly, efq.
[2] See Plate II fig 21.

of

of cryftal of a ruby tinge, and which have been confidered, by their hardnefs, to be of this fpecies of gem.

The *Glafs-beads* are tranfparent and opaque, and imitating in colour every fpecies of precious ftone, from the ruby to the pearl. The large kind exceed two inches and an half in diameter, with great perforations, tranfparent with opaque fpots of white, fome rayed with convoluted ftripes of yellow on a black opaque ground. But thefe, by their perforations, appear to have been ufed as *fibulæ* on the drefs, receiving the loops of drapery to faften the garments. Alfo feveral amber-beads of the largeft fize appear to have been fo ufed. The middling fized beads of glafs vary in all fhapes, to circular, flat, conic, barrel, oblong, fquare, round, button, two round united, virmicular, pendant *bulla*, and lozenge. The tranfparent, ornamented with difcoloured opaque variegated glafs; blue ground, with convoluted white lines and fpots; red ground, with yellow convoluted lines and yellow fpots, black, brown, blue, dark and light fea-green, verditer, dark and light blue, Orange and Naples yellow. Several imboffed on different grounds, with varied colours, and various coloured ones the fize of a large pin's head. The workmanfhip difcovers elegance and expence adapted to the rank or fituation of the wearer, a perfect intelligence in the fmelting arts and of the chemical preparations of colours to receive the fire.

The beads fafhioned from fhells[1] are generally fragments cut from teeth of the Cyprea, an Eaft Indian chonc, and which, as before remarked, has been applied by the antients as an amulet.

From this enumeration of fepulchral relics in the inftance of drefs, the antiquary will in all probability conceive thefe ornaments to have been the manufactory of regions remote from our ifland[2].

Several beads have alfo been found in thefe *tumuli* of a green verditer opaque porcelain matter; and others alfo of the form and fize defcribed by Camden as the *Glain Naidr* of the Druids, but which are evidently of a lower date to the time generally affigned to them[3].

ARMILLÆ,

Ivory, glafs, and brafs, chiefly with female apparel[4].

BRACELETS

OF GOLD WIRE WOVEN, apparently with filk or fome other thread. Brafs or copper; fome with thick wire of the former metal. Some fpecimens of black and dark blue glafs: the latter could not keep on the wrift but with the affiftance of the drapery of the arm, and too brittle to continue long entire in ufe.

[1] See Plate XVIII. fig. 10.

[2] See p. 87, note [u].

[3] See note, p. 59, note * on glafs.

[4] I believe Mr. Fauffet has one found at the Afh burial place with the pummel of a fword.

Broaches of various forms

The circular Broaches or fibulæ have been occafionally engraved in this work, and exhibit fpecimens of elegant and fingular jewel workmanfhip. Several not engraved in my cabinet are worthy of a repetition, if their forms had materially varied. They are fet with garnets on a filver ground, milled and inlaid with a different compofition on the rim with a zigzag pattern, the ground near the ftone ornamentally ftamped and ftrongly gilt, and fometimes with a milled plate of folid gold on the filver ground. Mr. Strutt favoured me with the one which he engraved in his work on Saxon drefs, and which I think he has properly placed to the time of its depofit, and perhaps to the nation which had a right claim to it.

I have a beautiful circular ornament of this nature not engraved, of metal ftrongly gilt, two inches in diameter, with an interlaced engraved chord encircling the inner part of the rim, and another an inch in diameter, fhowing evident figns of fimilar and contemporary workmanfhip: the former from the Afh, the latter from the Chatham, tumuli.

Buckles

Any antient rufty or corroded buckle has been too often honoured with the name of Roman *fibula*, but the buckles, found in thefe barrows, an antiquary will foon difcover to be different from Roman. The Roman *fibulæ* frequently occur in Montfaucon, and their forms are too fingular to admit of any mif-application[1].

The ordinary buckles or clafps found in thefe graves are clumfy, and made to receive loops faftened to the drefs over the tongue or *acus*, which evidently, by the obtufenefs and breadth of the point, was never intended to perforate. Others are like modern buckles, oval, thin of metal, and for more delicate ufes. Some of iron, from two inches to one and an half in the longeft part. The others are fcarcely worth defcribing, excepting one, which fhows the form of a necklace compofed of a row of beads; three fmall beads and an intervening large one to the number of thirty-one; not quite two inches in diameter, with an acus of iron. Some of the clafps approach the Roman in form, but not one fpecimen which has the form of the antient *fibula*, which any cabinet of the *Vetufta Monumenta* can exhibit.

Magical Instruments.

A Crystal Ball in a clafp of filver[2]. There can be no doubt of the ufe of this apparatus for the above purpofe. Brafs veffels, &c., and other fingular inftruments, which feem to apply to magical ceremonies as univerfal in the

[1] See *Vignette*, p. 37. A Roman fibula of the Lower Empire, found in the cemetery at Kingsholm, near Gloucefter.

[2] See Plate IV. fig. VIII. and the explanation of its ufe in the note.

ages to which theſe barrows have been aſſigned, are likewiſe found. There is alſo a probability that the perforated ſpoon was uſed in theſe ceremonies (ſee plate II.), and ſeveral other relics, which an unlettered people appropriated to theſe myſteries.

Amulets.

Of various kinds. Moſt of the gold pendants, with and without gems, were conſidered to have had virtues of this nature[1]. Mr Fauſſet has a bone connected to a ring, and a variety of ſingular and trifling relics, which the antients conceived to have productive virtues, have been found in theſe ſmall barrows.

Rings.

Rings to the finger ſeldom occur of any ponderous metal, like the Roman, of gold, ſilver, or bronze. Small and thin ſilver wire perforating glaſs beads[2]; ſome of a ſpiral ſilver, open plate $\frac{2}{10}$ of an inch in breadth, extending to any ſize for the wearer. Thin braſs with an ordinary ſtone.

After-diſcoveries may produce others of greater value; but I do not remember ſeeing, excepting in the poſſeſſion of one gentleman, any relic of this nature of beauty and value, which would be attributed to theſe times and nation. It is the property of Mr Godſal, banker, in the Strand, and was bought, to the beſt of my recollection, at Mr. Duane's ſale, of Mr Gerrard, the auctioneer, when I was preſent. The ornament at the top is broken from the ring, and is of gold, inlaid with garnets of the ſame workmanſhip as the large *Broach* in Plate X. fig 6. and 7, the height the ſame as its breadth, with four angular ſides ſloping to the top, the ſurface about $\frac{3}{10}$ of an inch broad, and of the ſame inlaying as the ſides.

Circular rings of braſs and iron are found in numbers in theſe barrows, from two inches and an half to one inch and leſs. Fragments of ſmall iron chains, the links of iron bars, an inch and an half long, with connecting loops, and various other lumps of accreted iron, difficult to aſcertain their uſes, hooks of iron, pins, and ſtuds, but ſeldom any nails which might aſcertain the bodies to have been encloſed in coffins.

The teeth and bones very perfect when found in chalk and clay-ſoils. The former exhibiting proofs of decay ſimilar to modern teeth. The only particularities diſcovered has been on the ſurface of the *molares*; which appear to have been much worn by the maſtication of hard ſubſtances, and which remark has more obviouſly been made on the teeth of adults.

Fragments of *ſtags' horns* were found on Chatham-Hill near the barrows. And, through time, as calcareous as the bones in the graves; they appeared from their ſize to have belonged to red-deer.

[1] See Plate V. N° I. fig. 2, and Plate XXI. N° I. [2] Plate I.

Near the ſite of the barrows were two holes of the ſhape of an inverted cone, eight feet in diameter, and twelve in depth. Appearances of ſimilar holes may be ſeen near the cluſter of barrows on Barham Downs, near Canterbury.

The looſe ſoil was carefully excavated from the native; but no indication of their having been applied to ſepulchral uſes.

No 1
No 2
April 12 1720 The Revd Mr Winne Monster of
Boughton Aloagh presented me the following piec-
-es of Antiquity wch had been discover'd
Feb 1719/20 in his Parish
Where the Skeletons of two Men are found
by one of wch a large Sword (wch I have not yett
seen) & by the other what follows viz A a
Spear head (they are all of iron B C & D sever-
-al views of somewhat I do not understand unless
they are the Umbo of a Shield. E a Fibula
they are drawn by the Scale according to their
due propor-tions —
A
B
C
D
E
Scale of Inches
1 2 3 4 5 6 7 8 9 10 11 12 13 14 15 16 17 18

PLATE XXV. Fig. 1.

Barrows near St. Margarets on the Cliff*, between Deal and Dover; the drawing will shew their perspective view, elevation, and proximity to the village. This evidence of their proximity to the village will shew their affinity to it, and produce a natural reason for concluding on their having been a sepulchral deposit antecedent to the annexing of cemeteries to churches. Their size and contents will also shew their analogy to the ranges of barrows at Sibertswold, Barham Downs, Ash near Sandwich, Chartham near Canterbury, Chatham, Wimbledon, Greenwich, and other places described in this work.

These barrows do not exceed above thirty in number; they are, respecting size, of the proportion of the barrows described in the plan of the Chartham range, Plate XXIV. and which accords with the usual dimensions of the small barrows in clusters.

The cluster extends from 548 feet to 130 feet, including all the barrows, with the admission of a certain interval, and intersected by a small unoccupied portion of ground, which I did not think of sufficient consequence to place or to set down. The N. E. range I shall therefore mark at 225 feet, and the S. W. at 240; and there being a barrow situated on the other side of the road in a ploughed field described in the drawing, at 80 feet distance from the S. W. range, the extent may be of the above number. As a road passed in this interval, it seems not improbable but several barrows have been erased, and especially the smaller ones, by the plough, in the field I have described. Their general line is in a S. W. direction, ranged parallel to the sea coast, and commanding a prospect of the channel, half a mile from the village, and occupy about an acre and a half of ground.

In December, 1782, I visited this range, having read of these barrows in Dr. Stukeley's work, and finding them not all explored, I opened about fourteen of the remainder, but my discoveries were not productive in relics, having only found an iron knife, about eight inches long, handle part included, and about half an iron boss. The bones in this grave were of a delicate texture, one containing bones of a child, which was coated with clay; several skeletons of adults, the bones large and of a strong texture. In one I found the alveoli of the jaw perfectly grown up, indicating the great age of the person, which seemed to be confirmed by the firmness of the bones.

In the year 1775, an inhabitant of St. Margarets, of the name of Tucker, opened seven or eight of these barrows. In a deep grave he found upwards of twenty glass beads; and in another the arrow-head engraved in Plate XIX. fig. 7. taken out of one of the two barrows, the largest, situated at the extremity of the N. E. range; the smaller one I opened, which contained the bones of a child.

* These barrows are mentioned by Dr. Stukeley, Itin. Curios. Iter V. p. 12.

The large barrow, rather at the extremity of the N. E. range, contained the burnt bones of a young subject, the bones had passed a very ardent fire, exhibiting fragments of a very small portion of the body, a few parts of the small fistular bones, pieces of the skull, and three teeth; their size indicating the subject not to have exceeded the age of ten or twelve years old: the bones were deposited exactly in the centre of the barrow on the surface of the native soil, without any excavation whatever[1], the mound of earth raised simply over it.

The bodies in the other graves were generally deposited in the direction of E. and W., but others indeed varied their positions, indicating, perhaps, that this cemetery was used by Pagans and Christians, or, if the objection might be made to the rejection of Christian near Pagan inhumation, it may be perhaps accounted for by the ignorance of the usual form of Christian sepulture among the first converts.

The discovery of a barrow where cremation had been used, must either imply an earlier age in sepulture, a singular variation at the time, or a distinction of honour[2], as is mentioned by the Danish writers from the laws of Frotho the Great.

I shall not pretend to decide on the peculiarity of this place of interment: all that can be expected from an author is to detail facts, and reason with an eye to facts. Innumerable conjectures may be found, and every conjecture liable to opposition, analogy may persuade; but history, well attested, or records on the spot of interment, can alone place the matter beyond a doubt.

The only remark I can feel myself justified in laying before the reader, to shew the probability of Pagan and early Christian burial being promiscuously blended, is founded on a law of Charlemagne in the ninth century. "Jubemus ut corpora Christianorum Saxonum ad cœmiteria ecclesiæ deferantur, et non ad tumulos Paganorum[3]." This law would never have been instituted unless the custom of the Pagans and Christians mutually buried together had existed. When the ecclesiastical and civil laws were incorporated, which took place about this period in Britain, as well as all over Europe, this distinction might be made, but it should seem that the first promulgators of the Christian faith would have retained their primitive humility, and on the wisest and best of principles, to support their pious undertaking, they would have assimilated with the Pagans in most of their customs, which did not materially affect the cause.

This conduct of the pastors and their flock, it is natural to suppose, would have been adopted, yielding by gentle methods to the occasional prejudices of their converts, and which has been confirmed by all the Fathers, and more especially in respect to Britain, by the venerable Bede, in the History of the Early Church.

If any regard be entertained for this observation, the disparity of the position

[1] The same I observed in a barrow which I opened near the bush a little out of the town of [illegible]

[2] Olaus Wormius, Monum. Antiquit. Dan.

[3] Baluz. T. I. p. [illegible] Conf. cap. 6.

of bodies, and feveral other peculiarities, difcovered in thefe fmall barrows in clufters, may be eafily reconciled, and their Danifh claim finally excluded

Fig. 11 is the autograph of Heneage Finch Lord Winchelfea, of Long Leate, from his common-place book in my poffeffion He was the patron or friend of Stukeley, and an antiquary with the moft infatiable paffion for every thing which bore the name of antiquity. The firft Iter of Stukeley was written to this nobleman

The fize and fhape of the fpear, the umbones of the fhield, the brafs fibulæ, are evidences to prove thefe graves to have been fimilar to thofe defcribed in the groupe of the fmall barrows Whether other graves were opened, or whether the exterior furface of the ground indicated a mound being thrown over them, is not mentioned. My conjecture is, the difcovery was a cafualty, and the fpot cultivated

On the reverfe of the leaf is the following memorandum of the Earl

"May 4, 1720 At Godmerfham, Colonel Brodnax gave me two pieces of the fword which was found with one of the fkeletons one piece of the blade is one foot four inches long; the other, three inches and half long, and fome other pieces between thefe are miffing, but I hope to retrieve them, that I may fee the whole dimenfions of the fword In the broadeft part which the ruft has left it is two inches I hope I may recover too fome pieces of the hilt of this fword, though I am told it is almoft eaten up with ruft, and I fhall be informed more particularly of every thing relating to thefe antiquities"

This fword was evidently fimilar to the one engraved in Plate I and in every refpect fimilar to the others which are found in thefe *tumuli*. Entire ones and fragments I have feveral, the blades met the handle, confequently there was no hilt, evidently demonftrating that the ufe of the fhield was fufficient to defend the body, and which, at this period, was protruded by the arm in every direction which required the warding off of the adverfary's blows The fmallnefs of the fhield indicates its ufe, and as we have found, from the pofition of the *umbones* in the graves, it could not exceed two feet in diameter at the moft, and in many inftances not more, perhaps, than one and a half

OBSERVATIONS.

SMALL BARROWS IN CLUSTERS

LIBERA FORTUNÆ MORS EST; CAPIT OMNIA TELLUS
QUÆ GENUIT: COELO TEGITUR, QUI NON HABET URNAM.
LUCAN, LIBER VII.

THESE small campaniform barrows are seldom found near towns of any importance at the period of their structure. Though agriculture may have obliterated their site, they must have existed in numbers proportioned to the inhabitants, and similar relics as have been discovered in them must have been occasionally found.

A coin of Burgred[a], found in a grave in Cornwall, with relics evidently Saxon, and in various respects similar to those of the small barrows, would apply the date as low as ann. 874; but as no barrows were discovered near

[a] Burgred was king of Mercia, and a Christian prince. See Chron. Saxon, p. 79. Burhredus, (ut in numm. antiquis BVRGRED), autem Merciorum rex, quique proceres rogabant Ætheredum, Occidentalium Saxonum regem, et Ælfredum ejus fratrem, ut sibi auxiliaretur dum contra Pictos depugnarent. The contents of this grave are uncommonly curious. The stone of silver wire, which [illegible] here attached to it was probably used as a girdle. A charmed zone consisted of high ethical [illegible] *high-bosomed women*, and frequently worn by Christian enthusiasts in ancient times. See the relics [illegible] in Archaeologia, vol. IX. p. 8. The plate [illegible] prefixed to this girdle [illegible] well known in Cornwall, of [illegible] call [illegible] Glain Neidr, [illegible] supposed to be [illegible] from the spume of snakes, the *anguinum* of Pliny. See this described in Borlase, p. 13[illegible], from [illegible] which say "they are small glass rings, commonly about half as wide as our finger rings, but much thicker, of a green colour usually, though sometimes blue, and waved with red and white." Camb. [illegible] Whoever finds these is supposed by the vulgar to prosper in all his undertakings: hence the glass ring at the end of the girdle. See more on charmed girdles, p. 2[illegible], no. [illegible], of this work.

it,

it, this grave must be considered as a casualty, and not to be classed with the campaniform barrows in clusters which, for reasons already stated, were discontinued after ann. 742, when cemeteries were connected to religious edifices

There may be thus very satisfactory inferences drawn from the discovery of these valuable and rare coins, to prove an historic coincidence, and to shew the great probability of their affinity to early Christian ceremonies The perforated coins in these tumuli appertained chiefly to Christian princes, attested by those of Anthemius, Valentinian, Justinian, and Clovis Under circumstances of this nature, when it appears that coins of the Christian emperors and princes, being perforated for pensile use, were deposited with the dead, and worn as ornaments or dress; conclusions may hence be drawn of their being types of their Christian persuasion Several, indeed, of these gold coins have been set in a loop of gold for the purpose of wearing them, as may be seen in a coin of Heraclius in Chiflet's plate of *Nummi perforati* Though doubtless, as in the instance of Childeric's grave, many Greek and Roman coins were perforated, and evidently used as ornaments of decoration, objections may be made, yet, as the presumption is great, when crosses have also been found, *Vignette*, p 67, and Plate XVI in these barrows, that the inhumed were Christians, the natural argument will follow.

Childeric was a pagan prince, and, if Chiflet's book be authentic in ascertaining the discovery of the grave at Tournay to be that of this king, the relics in question must apply to a pagan interment, but as I have offered my doubts on the subject with comparative reasons no consequent conclusion should be drawn from a work which evidently must mislead, to apply the similarity of the Tournay relics with those occasionally found in our small tumuli

When coins of a late date are found in barrows, it does not follow that the body interred existed at a contemporary date of the coin, it should rather prove a more subsequent deposit therefore, deducing the date of the lowest of these coins, it will be found reasonable to proceed to a still lower date of their deposit, and hence, if a striking analogy should be found between our barrows in England with those of Tournay, we must bring the Tournay barrow or barrows as low as the coin of Justinian, ann 5[illegible]6 and unless we admit of the truth of the discovery of Childeric's ring, we may venture to conclude that the above grave was of a lower date than Chiflet has assigned to it

As cemeteries were connected with churches, ann 742, it would be natural to conclude, supposing all the country to be converted, and the ecclesiastical incorporated with the civil law, the detached *tumuli*, situated on our moors and waste lands, would have had their disuse at this period, but the Saxon Chronicle, p. 79, proves that there existed many conflicts between the Christians and Pagans, who were doubtless the Danes, yet, as Kent was entirely converted at this period, it should seem very probable that the dead were buried in cemeteries contiguous to their churches, provided the religious edifices were united Where the Pagans had assured their conquests, their tumuli would have existed on their waste grounds at this period, and in those countries which were under their influence, the Christian inhabitants would have doubtless interred their dead on waste land, as was common with the Pagans Hence the difficulty of ascer-

 taining

taining the precise history of these graves; but I should suppose the reader can have no doubt, but the entire conversion of the kingdom to Christianity would have effaced the custom of burying on uncultivated lands, and remote from habitable places, till the general and formidable invasion of the Danes, five years after the accession of Egbert, the beginning of the ninth century.

Here it should seem, that in every respect, whether Pagan or Christian, the period of this mode of sepulture should end, but as these small barrows have been assigned to the Danes by several antiquaries, it will be proper to discuss some concurring circumstances which may lead to the conjecture, and the antiquary will thus have an opportunity of forming his own conclusions, and decide as the evidence which seems to be the most apposite and confirmed on either side.

The Danes, before their total conversion to Christianity under Canute, were perpetually, from their first principal inroads, from ann. 808, at war with the Saxons and Britons. It is for this reason we cannot admit of a belief that they were scattered over the face of the island in small bodies, occupying places of no considerable importance in history. Wherever their principal establishments were formed, and which were at no great distance from the sea-coasts, they would be consistent with the nature of their offensive operations, consequently their number formidable and numerous.

These small barrows in clusters we have described to be proportioned to a very small number of stationary inhabitants, and seldom, or, I may say, never found near great towns of known repute in history, the facts not being as yet ascertained, and they are found in most parts of the kingdom. The inhabitants were evidently in a state of peace, proved by the discovery of male and female children's bones, with ornaments of apparel peculiar to the two latter. Had they been the remains of the Danes fallen in battle, they would have been in greater numbers, and the proportion of males would greatly have exceeded that of the females and children.

The Danes, in the seventh century, adopted Runic inscriptions on their places of sepulture, and as these barrows in clusters evidently attest the inhabitants existed in a peaceable state, there would have been a great probability that some remains of Paganism, with their inscriptions, would occasionally have been discovered.

In a work, entitled, DIE GOTTESDIENSTLICHEN ALTERTHUMER DER OBOTRITEN AUS DEM TEMPEL ZU RHETRA, AM TOLLENZER SEE, published anno 1771, are described a variety of Danish deities, knives, swords, and daggers, with Runic inscriptions on them of their votive gods, attesting the use of these religious relics in the seventh and latter centuries, previous to their conversion; it is therefore presumable some of these relics would have been found occasionally in their graves in Britain.[1]

Our English antiquaries, when they quote from Wormius, Saxo, Torfæus, and other Danish writers, not discriminating between the antient and the more modern Danes, receive the old-woman-ish tales of giants and devils from the Scaldic bards without scrutiny into their distinctions of the [illegible], and

[1] The short swords, arrow heads, spurs, and knives of the Danes, were of brass. Worm. Mon. Dan. p. [illegible], 49.

th.

the Danish writers themselves have not discriminated in this respect. Among the Northern nations, in their second age, the HOIGOLD, or HOELST tid, *Tumulorum ætas*, the dead were probably buried under the conic hillocks, "Arenam et terram exaggerando usque dum injustam monticuli exsurgerent altitudinem[1]." If this custom had been adopted before the Danish conversion in the country, we should have found the body with its ornaments, as described by Wormius, with a circle of stones round it, and many concurring and typical marks of the people, which, I may venture to pledge, has never been instanced in the researches among these small barrows in clusters.

But there is a still greater argument to prove these small barrows could not be Danish. The Danes in their pagan state buried under immense large barrows. "Dum olim in memoriam regum et heroum, ex terra congesti ingentes moles, montium instar eminentes, erexisse, credibile omnino ac probabile est, atque illis in locis ut plurimum, quo sæpe homines commearent, atque iter haberent, ut in viis publicis posteritati memoriam consecrarent, et quodammodo immortalitati mandarent."

Among these small barrows in clusters no discovery has yet been made of barrows of enormous size, in which the mode of inhumation has been found very different. But it is fairly stated, that at no great distance, a barrow of a greater dimension than the smaller ones has been found, and which has contained burnt bones, as was the case at St Margaret's on the Cliff, cited in this work, and to which the smaller ones have been concentered, attesting, that a succeeding people had buried near one of a more antient date, when cremation had been used. Burning the dead, we know, the Danes had disused on their expedition into Britain, and owned by their writers as having ceased before that period as a general custom, though perhaps used in the burial of a particular hero. Their *Rojold*, or *Brende tid*, *ætas ignea*, must have preceded their *Hoigold*, *Hoelst tid*, *Tumulorum ætas*. This argument of itself should seem sufficient to prove that the barrows which contain urns and ashes are not of Danish structure.

But the æra computed by the Northern nations for burning their dead may induce the antiquary to consider these graves as Danish, if he believes Saxo and Olaus that Ungauus or Frotho were the institutors of the law, that princes and their commanders should be burned; and it may appear, from the Northern writers, that the fact is established, so far as applied to a more early period than their incursions in Britain in the Saxon times. Starkatterus, if such a person ever existed beyond the lines of the bard, was burnt; and Ringo caused the same funeral honour to be performed on the body of Harold, when, at the same period, the common people were interred in an entire state.

The curious reader will observe from these remarks, that every precaution has been taken not to adopt a conclusion without investigation, and no fact asserted to preclude him from his own conjectures. It is the duty of an author to state all inferences, and to oppose every argument where the least pretence for doubt can enter. Truth can only be accomplished by these means; *aut facere scribenda, aut scribere legenda.*

[1] Olai Wormii, Monument. Danic. lib. [illegible]
[2] See [illegible] The barrow of [illegible] Hill.

The

The ſmall barrows in cluſters at Sibertſwold, Barham Downs, Chartham, Chatham, Aſh, and other places in Kent, as well as in various other parts of England, from every appoſite relation, ſhew their owners to have exiſted under a peaceable eſtabliſhment. When the Danes had conquered the iſland, they almoſt inſtantly embraced Chriſtianity and as, conſiderably previous to their converſion, the Saxons, from the time of St. Cuthbert, anno 742, actually had their cemeteries near their churches; the ſmall barrows or cluſters ſeem to have exiſted before that period All the Chriſtian part of Europe appear to have adopted this cuſtom in the time of Charlemagne[1], "UT CORPORA DEFUNCTORUM IN COEMETERIIS ECCLESIÆ SEPELIANTUR Jubemus ut corpora Chriſtianorum Saxonum ad cœmiteria eccleſiæ deferantur, et non ad tumulos paganorum[2]."

St Chryſoſtom, when biſhop of Conſtantinople, in his Sermon concerning Faith, anno 403, ſays, "there was no Chriſtian city, town, or village, in the world, which had not a cemetery connected with them But theſe cemeteries were at this period without the walls[3]."

The fathers often ſpeak of cemeteries as ſet apart and honourable: and this reaſon would incline the Antiquary to conclude on theſe ſmall concentered barrows being Chriſtian ſepulchres. The Pontifical ſays the ſame ceremonies were uſed at the conſecration of cemeteries as of religious edifices; St Denys, the Areopagite[4], in his Hierarchy, Tertullian, in the 51ſt chapter on the Soul, Optatus Milevitanus[5], St. Cyprian[6], St Ambroſe[7], and St Auſtin[8], ſpeak of their ſacredneſs from theſe reaſons we may be induced to believe many of them to be early Chriſtian, eſpecially thoſe with the typical marks of Chriſtianity; and more ſtrenuouſly ſo, as we find them ſituated at no great diſtance from villages, which, by their names, infer a very antient period of eſtabliſhment; and where the firſt propagators of Chriſtianity appear to have founded religious edifices or convenient places of aſſembly, to convert the rural or agricultural inhabitants

Near ſome of theſe antient cemeteries there is an evident mark of the remains of an agger[9], the antient boundary of theſe ſacred depoſits of the dead Many other reaſons may be alſo adduced to ſupport this argument, and which the well-informed antiquary will readily perceive have a tendency to prove their Chriſtian claim

Had they been Daniſh, not only circques of ſtone would be found near them, but their ſizes, for reaſons hereafter mentioned, would occaſionally have been larger Hubba was buried under a very large barrow, and occaſionally, in the courſe of exploring theſe ſepulchres, ſome large ones would be found among them Thoſe who had ſignalized themſelves in war would have been

[1] Capitul tio Caroli M de partibus Saxoniæ, cap 22

[2] Ap Paluz T I p 254, cont capit 6 See 1 Cor xv. v 35 and John xii v [illegible] on which theſe laws were founded A proof from this interdiction, that Chriſtian and Pagan inhumation was indiſcriminately uſed

[3] St Jerom, ſpeaking of the cemetery of the firſt Chriſtians at Antioch, ſays it was out of the gate of Daphne

[4] [illegible] [5] Lib 6 [6] l p 68. [7] [illegible] [8] l p [illegible]

[9] See the plan of Sibertſwold tumuli, Plate XXIII. Chatham Plate XXIV

buried with men of leſſer note, but this is not the caſe; they are always found of a moderate ſize, ſeldom exceeding 40 feet in diameter. Hubba was ſlain anno 487 "Dani vero cadaver Hubbæ inter occiſos invenientes, illud cum clamore maximo ſepelierunt, cumulum apponentes quem Hubbelow vocaverunt, unde ſic uſque hodiernum diem locus ille appellatus eſt, et eſt in comitatu Devoniæ [1]" I have cited this paſſage to ſhew that the latter age of burial among the Danes was interment of the body under a mound of earth or ſtones, and which already has been proved was of a large ſize in honour of the chieftain, and, conſequently, whenever urns are found under barrows which contain the aſhes of the dead, theſe barrows muſt apply either to an earlier date of ſepulture, or to a diſtinct people from the Danes, for it appears from hiſtory, that the Danes, on their piratical inroads into this kingdom about the period of the eighth century, had diſuſed their firſt age of burning their dead, and it is therefore a conſequent proof that our barrows which contain urns and aſhes are not Daniſh

It may now be expected that the author of this work ſhould not remain ſatisfied with a bare relation of facts, but that he ſhould aſſimilate thoſe facts, and arrange them for the neareſt approach poſſible to the true hiſtory of theſe ſmall barrows

The Antiquary is at liberty to entertain his own private opinion, but if leiſure and opportunity can have any claim to a literary combination, and to render opinion reſpectable from reaſonable inferences, no preſumption can be laid to the charge of the writer who even attempts to convey a glimmering of light on thoſe ages, which hiſtory at beſt has been ſo imperfect to tranſmit to modern times

The Roman claim to theſe ſepulchres, notwithſtanding their coins have been found, muſt be totally out of the queſtion Their peculiarity, the nature of their relics, without recurring to hiſtorical fact, muſt diſmiſs all concluſion of this nature [2]. A very brief remark will ſuffice for a proof The uſurper Conſtantine, contemporary with Honorius, defeated at Arles, tranſported all the legions from Britain [3], and in the year 429 the Saxons arrived The kingdom ſoon after this period was deprived of all aid from the Roman provinces, who were themſelves a prey to the Northern arms Our moſt authentic writers agree that the Saxon Heptarchy was eſtabliſhed A D 582, and all Roman interference in the iſland was then finally cloſed The coins of Anthemius, Clovis, and Juſtinian, found in the barrows, will, without further diſcuſſion, prove them to have exiſted after the departure of the Romans, and on the conſideration of their being Chriſtian ſepulchres, they may naturally be placed at the period of St Auguſtin's arrival in England, anno 582, to the period of

[1] Brompton's Collectane [illegible]

[2] See the diſtinct character of the Roman cuſtom of burial in this work under its particular head

[3] The revolt of Britain from the Roman government may be dated about anno 41[illegible] See Procop[illegible] de B B, Vandal, lib 1 c[illegible], where the election of Conſtantine by the Britons is mentioned and his defeat This author, in the ſame part of his hiſtory, has alſo decidedly fixed the ſeparation of Britain from the Roman power [illegible] Procop[illegible] [illegible] Bed Eccl Hiſt Gent [illegible] lib 1 c 11 ſays the Romans left Britain in the reign of Honorius, but which appears to date [illegible] [illegible] 7 Cambridge Edit 1644, fol

 admiſſion

admission of cemeteries within the walls and near to churches anno 742. We shall thus acquire the period with no material distance of 160 years, when they were actually existing under discriminating forms, to the larger barrows discovered in various places of this kingdom, and which their numbers, conformable to their situation, will be found to have a natural relation. This period of 160 years must be then placed to the Saxon æra when Christianity was embraced, and when the nature of the arms, the most convincing proof of a parity of custom, found in the barrows, affix them to their Saxon owners, the truth will be discovered at no great distance[1].

The shield was small and orbicular, with a boss in the center[2]; they could not exceed more than a foot and a half in diameter from their position in the grave, the correspondent proportion agreeing with the one of the Saxon soldier in the manuscript of Prudentius. The swords are also similar[3]; several of which are in my cabinet. Spears, knives, and axes, which I have in great numbers, answer to the Saxon arms by an internal evidence scarcely disputable. The swords are found with their blades introduced into a handle of wood, the scabbard of the same materials: the decayed parts adhering prove the fact.

There is no ornament of brass or other costly workmanship, excepting the magnificent one in the reputed grave of Childerick, which distinguishes a leader or a particular personage, to prove them the arms of a people for whom peace and affluence had provided the decoration of art or ingenuity, and which would have been evidently the case if these interments had existed after the Saxons had become the entire possessors of the kingdom, when the arts had acquired some dawning among them. At this period the Christian sepulture had varied among them, and when they buried in their cemeteries near their churches, this custom of depositing their arms had probably ceased. The Saxons, on their first entry into Britain, were naturally armed in a rude manner, similar to their barbarous neighbours, than at their completion of conquest, and these discoveries prove the inference. Generally speaking, the arms of the Saxons would be thus found[4], and though it were possible that an occasional polish of art might be discovered among them, the general prevalency would not be adopted till they had accomplished the subduction of the country. 'Tis true, many of their leaders made excursions in the Roman provinces, and even prior to this æra doubtless a great intercourse might have prevailed with the Roman provinces, from the continued inroads of all the Northern hoards of people, as well as there having been many detachments incorporated into the legions. Hengistus was trained to arms under Valentinian[5], and much

[1] See a Saxon foot soldier's dress in an illuminated manuscript, marked Cleopatra, in the Cottonian library, by Aurelius Prudentius, in Latin, with Saxon annotations and illustrations.

[2] Plate VII. fig. 3 and 4.

[3] Plate I. fig. 10.

[4] On the opening of these barrows, it was not in the proportion of one in twenty which produced arms of any kind, and, though the bones by their texture might be discriminated in some degree from those of the women, there appears to have been numbers of men buried without them: a circumstance which should prove that the graves which contained no arms were those of the peasantry, or of the [illegible] who were not under military enrolment.

[5] It was the custom among the Northern nations to send their young princes and the sons of eminent men for military distinction into foreign armies of renown. See Olaus Magnus, lib. v. c. xxi. where Harald is reported to have been at Constantinople. The pious archbishop of Upsal tells a few old womanish stories, but they are [illegible] with curious facts.

antecedent

antecedent to his time the Romans had abundantly recruited their armies from the ſtock of the barbarous nations. But it is obvious, from the want of a ſimilar refinement and permanent eſtabliſhment to the Romans, their arms and armour could not be of any comparative excellence.

It has been conjectured in the courſe of this work, that the relics diſcovered in theſe barrows have a great ſimilitude to the decorations of Eaſtern apparel; it may therefore be proper in this place to aſſign ſome reaſons for this ſtriking ſimilarity, reaſons which may perhaps eſtabliſh the fact of their Saxon claim, and of their Chriſtian affinity.

The illiterate Saxons, who were Pagans[1], on their firſt deſcent into Britain, had not the art of producing works of ſuch ingenuity as are obviouſly defined on the *fibulæ*, gems, and other coſtly trinkets, found in theſe graves; and their burial places would in all probability be in different ſituations, and under different deſcriptions. In all probability they burned their dead, which will, in the courſe of this work, meet with ſome illuſtration; but their cuſtoms will be found to have greatly varied from their firſt advent to the time of Egburt.

Plates II IV V. VI VIII IX X. XI XII XIV XV XVI XVII XVIII XX XXI XXII exhibit relics which apply, with every minute affinity, to Eaſtern cuſtoms. They might have been, it may be alledged, introduced among the Saxons by traffic; the Northern troops returning home from the ſpoils of thoſe regions, others paſſing from thoſe expeditions into the Saxon ſervice; various other hiſtoric proofs might be evinced to ſhow this commixture. But hiſtory is clear in one particular, and ſupports the Antiquary in his conjecture. A colony of Greek Chriſtians, A D 668, followed by Theodorus, Greek archbiſhop of Canterbury[2], who was diſpatched to Britain for the inſtruction of the Saxon youth. Venerable Bede, St. John de Beverlaco, Tobias biſhop of Rocheſter, and Albinus abbot of St Auguſtin's, Canterbury, were reputed to be of this ſeminary. The two former, his ſcholars, and the two latter are ſaid to have underſtood the Greek as well as their mother tongue[3].

If

[1] The Anglo Saxons were not converted till A D 570

[2] Godwinus de Præſulibus Ang. in vita Theodori

[3] Matth Parker de Antiq. [illegible] Eccl. Brit. in vita Theod. It will not fail to ſtrike the Antiquary, when he compares the relics in our [illegible] barrows to the decorations of other people, how great a ſimilarity will be found. The better ſort of the Morlach women[4] adorn their caps with *ſtrings of ſilver coins*, among which are frequently ſeen very ancient and valuable ones, [illegible], and *ſmall ſilver chains*, with the figures of half-moons faſtened to the end of them. The poorer ſort [illegible] themſelves with plain caps, or if they uſe ornaments, they only conſiſt of *[illegible] ſhells*[5], round glaſs beads, or bits of tin, [illegible] to attach admiration by their dreſs, and hence the greateſt [illegible] of ſplendid trumpery [illegible] half-moons of ſilver or tin, little chains and beads, [illegible] ſtones and ſhells. Both old and young women wear about their necks *long ſtrings of [illegible] beads of [illegible]*, and *many rings of [illegible], or ſilver on their fingers*[6]. The cuſtoms of the nations bordering on the Eaſt ſeldom vary, the Eaſtern never, [illegible] has in modern times pervaded the Weſtern region, to the excluſion of all ancient cuſtom, and though it may be found that the ancients underwent certain mutations, the total annihilation of their former cuſtoms did not take place. In the Morlach women we have evident proofs of their continuance of the ancient Greek dreſs, the ſoles of their ſhoes are of undreſſed ox hide, the upper part of ſheep ſkin thongs

[4] See the Abbé Fortis's Travels into Dalmatia

[5] See the Cypræ [illegible] XVIII [illegible]

[6] See [illegible] in other plates of this work

knotted

If any connection can be thus applied from the discoveries in these graves to this colony of Greek Christians, the difficulty to assign the relics in question to their right owners will be cleared up, and the most perfect and consistent analogy produced.

This suggestion will be found as singular as it is curious, and the historic relation will assign a satisfactory reason why these *small tumuli* in clusters have been found more generally in Kent than in any other parts of the kingdom.

The circular *fibulæ*, of such singular and superior beauty to other discoveries of this nature, the glass Mosaic pendant ornaments in Plate XXI; the East India shells, beads of singular workmanship, Gothic art in the fashion of the fibulæ, Plate II and XV, glass vessels similar to those described by *Paulus Aringhius, in his Roma Subterranea*, Lib III c XXII p 297, and which in our barrows may have served for similar purposes; and every other sepulchral relic descriptive of the same mode of inhumation among the primitive Christians in the Greek and Roman empires, prove the relics to be of Eastern origin[1]. The affinity of the ornaments of the Moslich women in the Grecian islands to these relics, which modern travellers have proved, by the insular situation of the inhabitants, to have been preserved, without much variation, from the Byzantine period to the present day, will be also a strong voucher for this conclusion[2].

The custom of magical and superstitious ceremonies, so uncommonly prevalent in the Greek islands, will also apply in the most satisfactory manner to the undoubted discoveries of similar relics in the small conic tumuli, and which ceremonies, history has produced every decisive reason for concluding, were

knotted, which they call *aputc*, a barbarous derivative from the Greek [illegible], and these they fasten above the ankles like the ancient *cothurnus*

Stabis furas evincta cothurno.

The girls keep their hair tressed under their caps, but when married they let it fall dishevelled on the breast; sometimes they tie it under their chin, and the rays have *medals, beads*, or bored coins, twisted among it.

It is evident the relics found in these sepulchres are not of British manufactory. This the reader will have made up his mind to believe, and he will doubtless have reason, from the nature of the gems, the circular fibulæ, &c to believe them the workmanship of the East.

The Abbé Fortis has engraved a noble young lady of Coconcl, and a young lady of the Kotar. They both exhibited brooches similar to those engraved from the small tumuli. The lady of Kotar has on her breast a circular one, very similar to fig 1 N° II Plate VIII and of the proportion of the size of fig 6 Plate X. Both have double and treble rows of beads.

The similarity of these relics cannot be happier traced than from the treasures in the renowned grave of king Childeric, seen in Chifflet, discussed p 53 of this work. I examined the relics in question in the king of France's cabinet with minute attention; and they appeared to be of Byzantine workmanship, in the latter ages. The *crystal ball, sword*, [illegible], *coins*, and *fibulæ*, evince a perfect similarity with the relics of the British small conic tumuli in clusters.

We should not, therefore, hesitate to pronounce these graves, which contain relics of the opposite kindred, to a people of some national affinity, that a mixture may have occasionally blended itself with the inhabitants there can be no doubt, but that the people in question, who buried under these sequestered grassy tombs, were distinct from the indigenous inhabitants of the country, or who had, by mixing with them, introduced their fashions, must be obvious.

When the Heptarchy was established, and the entire conversion of the kingdom completed, cemeteries were then annexed to churches, and the sequestered propagation of Christianity no longer current in the country. The period of the conversion may be placed about 800, when the Saxon states were united, and the government assumed a kingly form under Egbert.

[1] Plates IV and V.

[2] See note [3], in the preceding page.

introduced

introduced among the rites of the primitive Chriſtians. Impoſing arts of ſuch influence among an unlettered and ignorant people would readily find their value in faſcinating their minds, and rendering them the more open to the Chriſtian converſion.

The magical uſe of the CRYSTAL BALL[1], frequently found in theſe tumuli, were evidently brought from the Eaſt, whence Paracelſus and Dr Dee, in the time of Charles the Firſt, were ſuppoſed to have introduced them, but proved, in the courſe of this work, to have exiſted in this country ages before this period.

The coin of Clovis, found in a barrow of the cluſter of Sibertſwold[2], will introduce a chain of facts to eſtabliſh a ſimilar coincidence of cuſtoms with the French nation at this period of his enquiry, and to atteſt their Saxon claim. This coin will alſo eſtabliſh a ſimilar analogy of ſepulchral relics between thoſe diſcovered at Tournay, ſo often mentioned in this work, and thoſe which are found in this country. Ethelbert, the firſt Saxon Chriſtian king, a deſcendant of Hengiſt, 150 years after his arrival in Britain, married the Lady Bertha, daughter of Clothaire the firſt king of France, a pious Chriſtian princeſs, whom the king permitted before his converſion to adhere to her perſuaſion, and to entertain biſhop Luidhard in her ſuite, which were all compoſed of Chriſtians. Clovis, a Chriſtian prince, the firſt founder of the French monarchy, died anno 511, ſeventy-one years before king Ethelbred's converſion, which appears to have followed ſoon after his marriage with queen Bertha. This pendant coin, of ſingular rarity, adorned with a loop, therefore evinces its having been worn by a Chriſtian at this period, and ſupports the argument in favour of a Saxon and French intercourſe.

From the valuable diſcovery of theſe curious coins, a period could be thus aſſigned to theſe ſmall barrows in cluſters, a proof eſtabliſhed of their Chriſtian claim, and a ſure ground diſcovered on which the Antiquary can raiſe other arguments to found a hiſtory of our more ancient barrows.

The period of their uſe may thus reciprocate from A. D. 582, of Ethelbert the firſt Saxon king's converſion to A. D. 742, the period when cemeteries were connected to religious edifices, hence 160 years will be the longeſt period of their exiſtence, and which will be found to accord with the hiſtory of the riſe of our early Chriſtian eſtabliſhment[3].

[1] See p. 15, where the diſcuſſion of theſe curious magic ceremonies has been treated of.

[2] Plate XX.

[3] If the Antiquary will compare the contents of the fifty urns found at Walſingham, in Norfolk, which furniſhed a ſubject for Doctor Browne's Treatiſe on Urn Burial, with the relics of the ſmall barrows, he will readily pronounce the ſpot to have been a burial place of the uncon[illegible] Saxons, and which ſeems to [illegible] their cuſtom of burning the body on their firſt entry into Britain. The [illegible] town of the name of Burnham ſeems to adduce ſome teſtimony, and the nature of the urns, relics, and ſituation of the ſpot, which is five miles from Brancaſter, alſo prove the burial place not Roman. Coins, plate like boxes faſtened with iron pins, and [illegible] like the necks of [illegible] of muſical inſtruments, braſs nippers, &c. [illegible] to the contents of the ſmall barrows, and the [illegible] ſmallneſs of the bones and teeth of children found in theſe urns, prove the people to have been [illegible] in a time of peace. Dr. Stukeley opened a barrow on Salisbury Plain, which was [illegible] Saxon, but which the [illegible] of his fancy [illegible] British [illegible] Stonehenge, the barrow which [illegible] found. Though the urn [illegible] by which [illegible] the dead, it was no evidence of its British antiquity; for it has already been proved, that [illegible] have been [illegible] when [illegible] of pottery was well known.

SEPULCHRAL REMAINS OF THE ROMANS.

'TIS TIME TO OBSERVE OCCURRENCES, AND LET NOTHING REMARKABLE ESCAPE US; THE SUPINITY OF ELDER DAYS HATH LEFT SO MUCH IN SILENCE, OR TIME HATH SO MARTYRED THE RECORDS, THAT THE MOST INDUSTRIOUS HEADS DO FINDE NO EASIE WORK TO ERECT A NEW BRITANNIA. D. BROWNE'S EPIST. DED. HYDRIOTAPHIA.

THE uncertainty of applying the ſepulchral relics found in this kingdom to their true owners has chiefly ariſen from the neglect of careful diſcrimination. Caſual diſcoveries of this nature ſeldom fall into the hands of literary men who have attended the actual ſpot where the diſcovery was made, and who have at the ſame time been in the poſſeſſion of leiſure and other requirements to exemplify their hiſtory.

The ſpade and pick-axe, unceremonious deſpoilers of the enſhrined dead, conſign to a freſh oblivion the name and virtues of the hero, as well as the vices of the baſe and infamous. Confuſion lies under the ſtroke, and little correct information can be ſelected by the Antiquary when the ignorant labourer is made the voucher for the veracity of paſt ages.

The fallacy of reports, the uncertainty of ignorant authors, received opinions of learned men, prejudice in the purſuits of the curious, and the little patience beſtowed on the inveſtigation of antiquity, have c[illegible]ed the moderns, and routed all reſpect and confidence in the poliſhed reader.

The Briton, the Roman, Saxon, and Dane, may have occaſionally buried their dead on or near the ſame ground. Diſcoveries have proved this fact. The difficulty will, in this inſtance, ariſe from the diſcrimination of [illegible]. Sir

Chriſtopher

Christopher Wren attempted this discrimination[1] when he viewed the North side of the foundation of St Paul's, but his conclusions were not founded. Long and patient enquiry into the customs of the antients must be the only security of antiquarian studies Modern writers can seldom be trusted when they speculate from hearsay, and quote from antient authors only for the gratification of pomp

PLATE XXVI

Exhibits several sepulchral relics found at a place called King's-Holm[2], near Gloucester The spot is situated within about fifty yards of the Ermin Street; and it is recorded that a palace of the kings of Mercia was situated in the field where these relics were discovered. Stone coffins were also found near the spot, and a leaden coffin[3] within about five or six feet distant from the relics in this plate Some foundations of this palace are now said to be extant but the inference cannot apply to the sepulchres A monastic edifice may have risen on its ruins, and the coffins may then apply to later times

At all events, the conclusion from the evidence of facts will attest a succession of interments on the same spot

Fig 1. The BLADE OF A SWORD, nineteen inches and a half to the handle, which appears, from the bend of the part which entered the handle, to have been broken off for the purpose of sepulture The iron has not lost its magnetic quality, and is very thin throughout its dimensions, six inches from the point was in increase in breadth from the middle, and which indicates, by the peculiarity of the shape and size, the property of the Roman legionary *Gladius*. The drawing is the exact size, and broken off to admit of a fac-simile representation in the plate

Fig 2 and 3 FIBULÆ of brass, the workmanship evidently Roman; found near the SWORD

Fig 4 BRASS GILT The appendages to the ring have rivets on their reverse, which shew them to have been connected with leather straps, and which apparently may have served for the use of the sword, two of the appendages serving to encircle the waist, and the third to support the sword

[1] Parenthesis Ivory and wooden pins are no discriminating types of British graves, nor are urns always Roman marks of sepulchre

[2] Glebum colonia, legio vii Aug Claudio Iter X Richard of Cirencester

The *legio Claudia* stationed at Gloucester was the vii Aug This legion came over into Britain with Julius Cæsar, he calls it *decima legio* It was named Claudia from the emperor, and called *pia fidelis* by the Roman senate, hence Gloucester was called *Claudio Cestria* from its residence here, and that it resided here we learn from our author, who says he has it from writers of the most ancient Roman times It remained here in Carausius's time Richard of Cirencester

Richard again, in his Itinerary, says, Glevum or Glebum, Gloucester, was a Roman colony, constituted by Claudius, "ut scriptores de illis temporibus affirmant"

The multiplicity of the coins of Claudius found there is a great voucher for the truth They certainly, in a great proportion, exceed the number of any other Roman emperor

[3] See this coffin, published in the Archæologia, vol VII p 379, from a short and hasty letter to Lieutenant General Melville, on the subject of fig 1 in the plate

The

The uncertainty of the account which accompanied these relics will not admit of a critical assertion as to the position in which they were discovered

PLATE XXVII.

N° 1 fig 1. A pendant BRASS IMPRESS The parts of the metal to which it hangs collapse, and, receiving a pin, indicate its being connected with a leather strap, the relic used perhaps as a private stamp Found in the same place with the sword

Fig 2 and 3 BRASS FIBULA, of cast metal, signs of the mould upon them With the sword

Fig 4 BRASS RING [1]. The surface shews no signs of its having been worn as an ornament of dress, or of its utility in this particular The metal is cast, and appears to be similar to that of the brass instruments, called celts, found in various parts of this country. With the sword

N° 2 fig 1. VESSEL of reddish brown earth; the form and decoration attest its Roman application the drawing of the exact size With the sword.

Fig 2 and 3 COIN of the middle bronze ANTONIA AVGVSTA, reverse, TI CLAVDIVS CAESAR AVG P M TR P IMP. S. C *Figura stolata stans, dextra simpullum tenens* The wife of Drusus This coin is a gem in beautiful execution, and of equal workmanship to any of her husband's, which indicate a die though in less relief as fine as the Greek

Fig 4 and 5 COIN OF MIDDLE BRONZE. TI CLAVDIVS CAESAR AVG P M TR P IMP P P, reverse, S C *Pallas gradiens, dextra hastum, sinistra clypeum ferens*

Fig 6 and 7 COIN of the smallest brass, and of the lowest emperors, the head something similar to the coins of *Arcadius*, reverse, SPES ROMANORVM *Templum Jani.*

Great numbers of Roman and Saxon coins have been found at King's-holm at different times, the Roman coins chiefly of Tiberius, Antonia, Claudius, Nero, Tetricus, and the lower emperors; some of the higher emperors have also been occasionally found Those I received, through courtesy of a very obliging person on the spot, consist of Antonia, Claudius, a Nero, various lower

[1] As this ring was found with the coins of Claudius, fancy might lead to the hazard of a conjecture of the possibility of its being a specimen of old British money Caesar, lib v speaking of the British money, says, "Utuntur aut aere, aut annulis ferreis ad certum pondus examinatis, pro nummo" See comparative reasons in the note on the coins of this plate, N 2 fig 2, 3 and 6 The ring preserved is a relic, and which evidence may be noted in the Celt found in the Anglo Saxon barrows at A[illegible], Plate XXII fig [illegible], which Celt had been preserved as an amulet

From points of reason and concurrence of fact, there is a strong colour of curious proof to [illegible] the coins of the High Empire were buried at the same period with the coins of the Lower Empire In the Author's collection of sepulchral remains near Canterbury, a Claudius Caesar of the [illegible] size and reverse was found in one of the smaller barrows in groups with a coin of Carausius of the third size See [illegible] grave, Plate XXVII fig 2 and 3 of Nero and M[illegible] See a small barrow, where [illegible] Roman coins were found, Plate XXII fig 2 and 3 of Victorinus and Valentinianus See Morant's Hist of Essex, vol I B III p 182 A urn with two brass coins, Antoninus Pius and Alexander Severus These facts will admit of the question, whether the [illegible] had

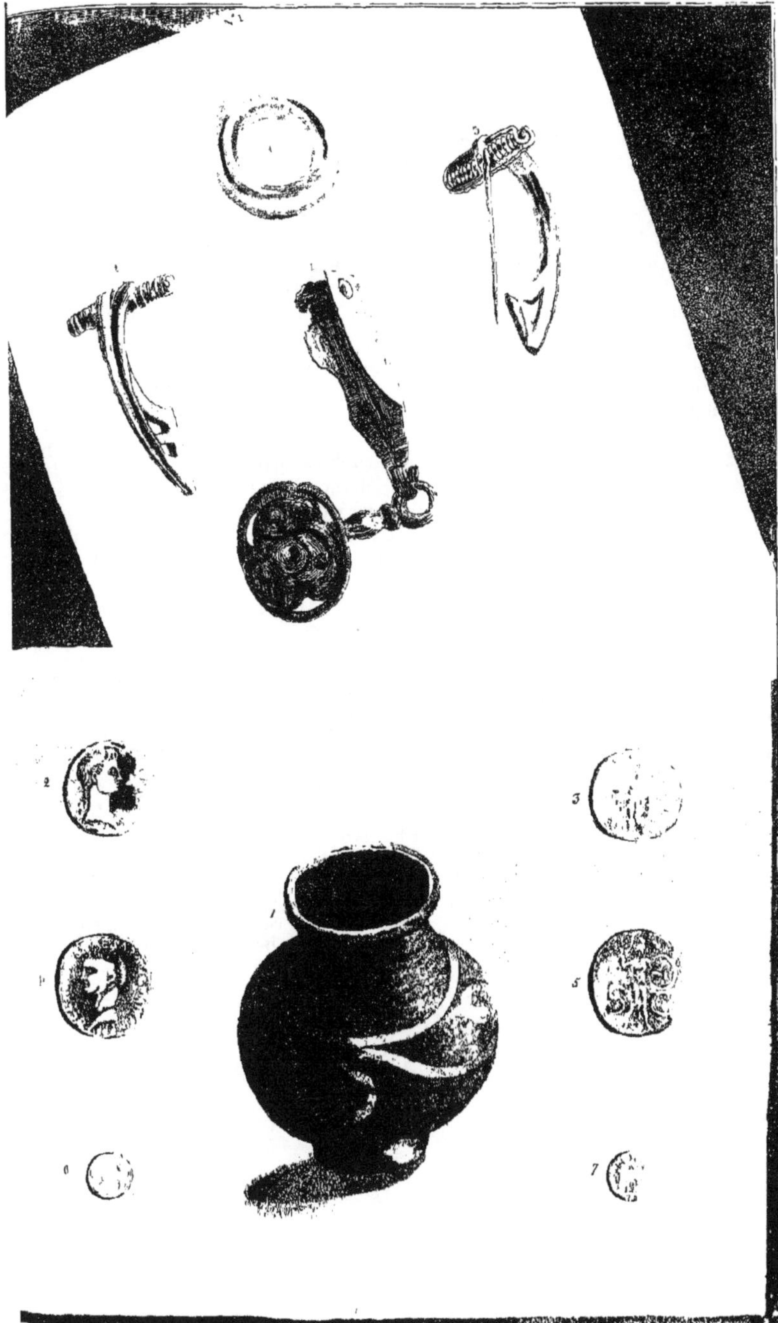

[illegible] emperors, the lowest I conceive to be the one engraved fig. [illegible] 7. Of [illegible] and Claudius to the amount of sixteen, twelve of Claudius, and four of Antonia. Half a peck of Saxon coins, my [illegible], was found in a heap between some stones, [illegible] deposit, but which [illegible] no relation to the coins found in the burial-place.

Other discoveries on the spot, and which were sent to a person in London, consisted of an iron AXE, in the form of a [illegible], with a [illegible] at one end, and a broad curvated chipping edge on the reverse. Two specimens of iron SPEARS, one near a foot and a half in length. A SPEAR-HEAD OF IRON, fibulæ, fragments of metal very thin, apparently the remains of a vessel. A vessel of earth large at the belly, with a neck and two handles, about a foot in length, and some few Roman coins. Various other vessels were also found, but no ashes in them.

These [illegible] the [illegible] reader will probably apply to a Roman Christian interment, and which he will conclude from the relics to have existed in a lower period; especially from the coins of the later empire.

If the sword, Plate XXVI. fig. 1. be Roman, it must evidently, from the coins, apply to a later date, and indeed the dimensions, as conceived by Lieutenant-General Melville, do not correspond with the early Roman legionary G[illegible]

[illegible] one of this great distance of time [illegible] reign, [illegible] by the lowest coin the [illegible] Many Romans were [illegible] probably incorporated in the [illegible] Anglo Saxon times in this kingdom, and their funeral obsequies thus distinguished [illegible] are [illegible] of [illegible] never be [illegible] The [illegible] of date [illegible] coins of Antonia to Arcadius, or [illegible] of the lower emperors, [illegible] near 400 [illegible] Claudius to Carausius 232, from Nero to Magnentius, [illegible] from [illegible] to Valentinian, [illegible] from Antoninus Pius [illegible] Severus, [illegible]

[illegible] the [illegible] concerning the brass ring, the additional evidence of the [illegible] Antonia, [illegible] period after [illegible] visit to Britain, should [illegible] Many of the [illegible] must have existed at this period, and [illegible] not [illegible] buried [illegible] of such [illegible]

[illegible] with [illegible] will not therefore be right [illegible] found in the [illegible] the multiplicity of early Roman coins [illegible] Roman [illegible] continued to after [illegible]

[illegible] of cremation, they rather infer a Christian burial place. [illegible] spot where [illegible] the first Christian king was buried. [illegible] undoubtedly established, induce the early Roman converts to establish their [illegible]

 S E P U L-

SEPULCHRAL REMAINS OF THE ROMANS.

MANY authors have written on this ſubject, and they have not been deficient in materials to complete their work. Roman authors have produced paſſages to convey great ſtore of information, and their authority has been validated by ſepulchral inſcriptions, the only certain teſtimony of truth. The Greek and Latin poets have been alſo cited to aſſiſt the arguments of learned men; but, unhappily, the poetical grace of deſcription has been but too often applied to cuſtoms and times, remote from the periods of the cuſtoms which the poet has deſcribed, and which a ſubſequent change of government and laws have entirely obliterated.

The Romans, who copied their laws from thoſe of Solon, reſtrained the decoration and magnitude of their ſepulchres. The XII Tables decreed that no expence of perfumes, jewels, inſcriptions, or [illegible], ſhould be carried to exceſs, that no ſepulchre ſhould exceed the workmanſhip of ten men in three days, or ſepulchral ſtones of one man in three days.[1]

Servius, on a celebrated paſſage, often cited by authors, *fuit ingens monte ſub alto*, aſcribes it with great juſtneſs to the early Romans. The paſſage in queſtion, "Apud majores nobiles aut ſub montibus altis," &c. is ſufficient to prove that the Roman ſepulchres had formerly exceeded in magnitude thoſe of his day.[2]

Had not a reſtriction taken place, the increaſe of the city of Rome, and the other large towns in the empire, would have cauſed the circumjacent country to be covered with *tombs*, and which in a ſhort time would have become inimical to agriculture. The law of Solon which forbids the erection of the [illegible], on account of the great portion of ground which in time they would

[1] [illegible] was declared infamous for exceeding theſe bounds. Antiquit. [illegible] De Relig. et Sumpt. Funer. &c.

[2] [illegible]

[3] [illegible] not becauſe Mercury had the charge of highways, but becauſe the [illegible] of the ſtones [illegible] conſecrated to this god.

 occupy,

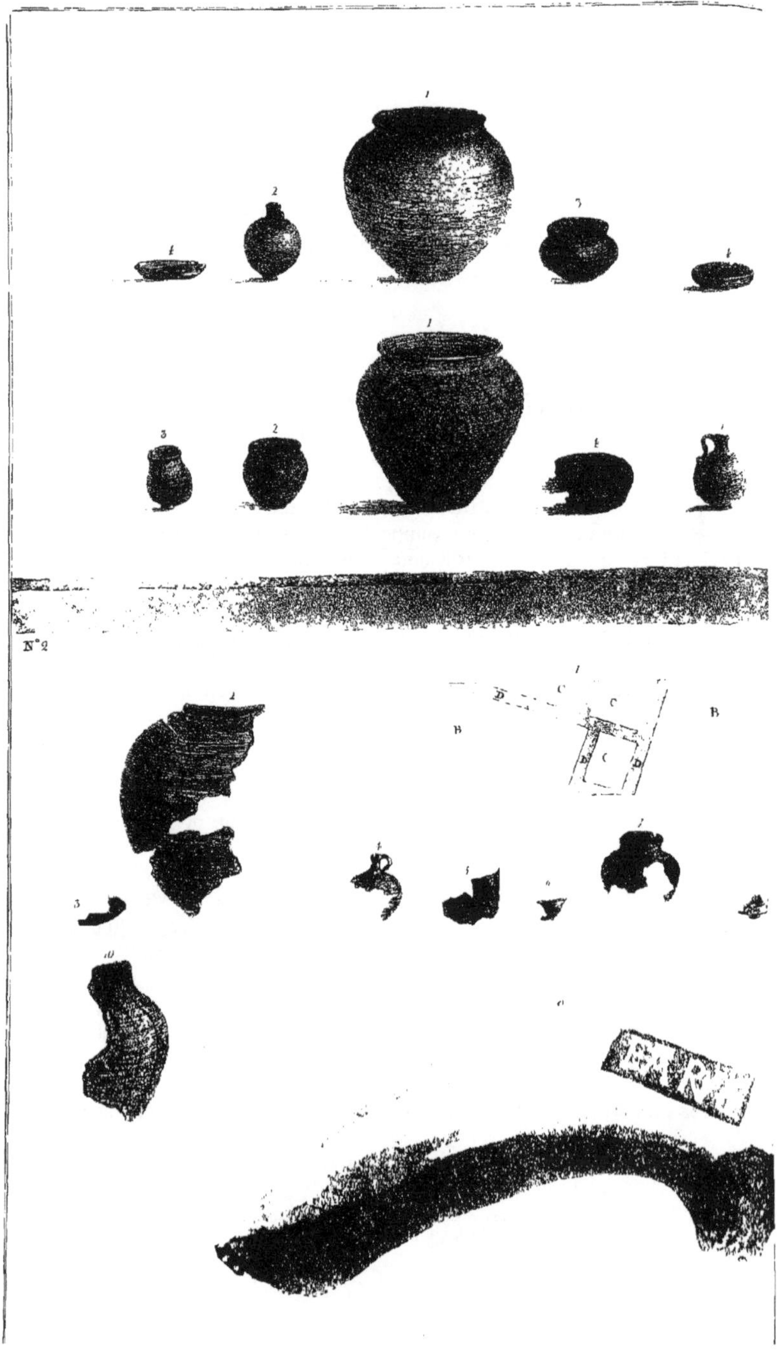
N°2

[illegible], was adopted by the Romans before the time of Cicero. The highways were thus principally adorned, excepting the sepulchres near their villas, which has been also exposed, and we should hence be inclined to infer that the generality of Roman burial-places would be found under [illegible] or, if a *tumulus* of earth should be erected over them on a particular occasion remote from their towns or camps, such *tumuli* would not exceed a moderate size. This reason, united with the fact of a Roman road cut through one of our large *barrows*, may probably admit of a conclusion, that many of the very large barrows on our downs or waste lands have preceded the time of the early Romans in this kingdom, whose sepulchres this enquiry will attempt to prove, have been for the most part discovered near their stations and encampments.

The generality of our writers on the discoveries of Roman *tumuli* have been so much confused in their conjectures, statement of facts, and local applications in this respect, that an attempt to decide on more certain grounds will perhaps be well accepted by the Historian and Antiquary.

"[illegible]," says Mr. Battely, "Examine the [illegible]," there cannot possibly be any other method of deciding on the fact; and here it is necessary to observe the precaution proper to be taken before any facts can be established. The Antiquary must be acquainted with the customs of the ancients, and have judgement to discriminate their relics and their peculiar modes of interment. A coin found in an antient grave will not always attest the owner, unless other descriptive forms of sepulture have a striking similarity with the people to whom the coin is attributed. But not to expand on a subject, the uncertainty of which is so well attested, a palpable discrimination of Roman interment is here offered to the Antiquary. "Plus scire velle, quam sit satis, intemperantiæ genus est." There is no end to diffuse references.

PLATE XXVIII.

The drawings in this plate exhibit specimens of undoubted Roman vessels found in graves.

CAMBORICUM COLONIA. CHESTERFORD.

No. 1. fig. 1. Contained ashes, of brown earth, 13 inches by one foot; found with

Fig. 2. and three others of the same kind, and with *pateræ* of the red polished Roman ware, in the possession of Mr. Shepherd, of Ickleton, a place which takes its name apparently from the Icening-Street, and situated on the other side of the river Cam.

Fig. 3. Found at Chesterford, containing the bones of a cock, and close to a large urn with human ashes; of darkish brown earth.

Fig. 4. 5. Pateræ of red polished earth.

[1] Stukeley's Abury.

[2] Urb. Rutupiæ.

DUROVERNUM STIPENDIARIA, CANTERBURY, CANTIOPOLIS

Fig. 1. From the eminence opposite the Dane John-hill, near the Watling-Street*, containing ashes, of a light brown earth, to the best of my recollection, one foot by 9 inches; in the possession of Mr. Boyce, of Sandwich.

Fig. 2. near to fig. 1. which contained the bones of a cock, about 8 inches in height, of a dark brown earth, in my possession.

Fig. 3. Of dark brown earth, empty; near the urn.

Fig. 4. Of dark coloured earth, 6 inches and a half wide, two in height, near the urn.

Fig. 5. Of light brown earth. Fig. 3, 4, 5, in Mr. Boyce's possession.

Nº 2. DUROLEVUM, DUROPROVIS, ROCHESTER, STIPENDIARIA, DUROBROVIS, CHATHAM HILL, ROMAN BURIAL PLACE.

Exploratory post of Durobrovis.

Fig. 1. A *Redoubt*, B Foss; C C C subterraneous apartments, which contained a great quantity of fragments of urns and other funeral vessels. D D D the walls.

Fig. 2. Of dark brown earth, mingled with grit.

Fig. 3. Red Samian ware.

Fig. 4. Dark brown fine earth.

Fig. 5. Samian ware.

Fig. 6. Samian ware.

Fig. 7. Light brown fine earth.

Fig. 8. Samian ware.

I also found [illegible] DIVI FILIUS IMP. CAES. VESPASIAN. AUG. P. M. TR. P. P. P. COS. III. CEN. IVDAEA CAPTA. Figura muliebris [illegible] sedens ad trophaeum. This coin had evident signs of having past the fire; it was mutilated, and too common to be worth engraving. I picked up also a defaced coin of the middle bronze.

Fig. 9. Handle of a large vessel.

Fig. 10. Fragment of a coarse urn from the circumjacent ground, about 20 yards from the subterraneous building, and which I do not consider to be Roman.

Having consulted most of our county writers, from Camden to this period, and occasional observations in others respecting Roman sepulchres, but finding none satisfactory and sufficiently accurate to depend upon, I was therefore determined to explore those stations to which I had convenient access.

[illegible] afforded me some information: on the South west side of the station, without the walls, on a level ground, to the left of the London-road, where some earthen vessels and urns with ashes had been discovered, and which I concluded to have been the burial-place. I employed workmen to open, but the trench was not productive; I found no regular interment; a few fragments of Roman pottery, which had been torn up by agriculture, and only sufficient to ascertain

* This station is perpetuated by Stukeley, in his Iter Curiosum, p. 7[illegible], and which he calls CAM[illegible]. Mr. Shepherd, who lives [illegible], has found urns, other vessels, and coins, which were found on this station.

that

that the ſpot had been appropriated for burial purpoſes. Some time after this reſearch, in paſſing through to Cambridge, I undertook a more correct one, and which turned out as I expected: the principal part of the Roman burial-place is ſituated near the turnpike behind ſome houſes, where coins, fragments of pots, Roman fibulæ, and leaden coffins, were diſcovered; the latter apparently belonging to the ancient cemetery of the church, and which had been ſituated on the ſite of the Roman; having entered the foundation of a houſe which was then excavating, I diſcovered a variety of graves which contained ſkeletons, but which I concluded were Chriſtian; however, to put the matter beyond a doubt, in ſearching at their baſe, I found many fragments of Roman urns, which, from ſimilar ſpecimens, led me to believe they had contained aſhes [1]. There was a probability alſo that ſome of theſe graves were Roman, as I found fragments of earthen veſſels near them.

At Rocheſter, the ancient Durobrovis, I made frequent ſearches, and was always unſucceſsful in the diſcovery of a perfect Roman grave; a circumſtance not to be wondered at, from the various changes and buildings near and upon the ſtation, which have obliterated their remains.

This ſtation evidently embraced the ſpot where the preſent caſtle is ſituated, and ſeems to have been raiſed on the principle of the *caſtra*, built on the Saxon ſhore for the *Comes*, to defend them againſt the invaſions of piracy, ſo frequent in the lower ages of the Empire, of the form and ſize of Richborough, Reculver, and the other ports in Kent. The ſite is very diſcernible at the baſe of the ancient walls, where I repeatedly found numberleſs ſpecimens of Roman fragments of pottery. To eſtabliſh the fact of the ſite, I opened the entire *arena* of Gundulf's tower, called the Keep, which the labourers excavated to the depth of 12 or 14 feet. At about five feet from the level I diſcovered human bones, which had evidently been interred for ages; but they were in no order, and ſeemed to have been thrown in with occaſional exuviæ. Below this depth, a great quantity of Roman red ware was found [2], and other fragments of the ſame pottery, known to have belonged to the Romans. The burial-place to this ſtation I conjecture to have been near Boley-hill, where coins have been found.

On Chatham hill, probably an exploratory poſt of the Romans, I was fortunate in the diſcovery of a real Roman ſepulchre.

When the redoubt on the apex of the hill was raiſing, 1779, on the excavation of the ditch the ſoldiers threw up a coin of FAVSTINA, of the large bronze, preſented to His Majeſty by Lieutenant Colonel Debbieg, the chief engineer. On the ſide towards the gorge of the lines, a few feet from the ſurface, diſcovery was made of a ſubterraneous vault [3], which, being cleared on the progreſſion of the work, exhibited manifeſt proofs of its having been a ſepulchral remain. Having attended the courſe of the workmen, and with Lord Amherſt's permiſſion to purſue the diſcovery, it was traced with ſome attention; and, as far as the line of the work would permit, without much intruſion on

[1] See Plate XXVIII.

[2] See Plate XXIX.

[3] Camden, in his Britannia, mentions a ſubterraneous building at Coggeſhall in Eſſex, which he calls a hypogeum, in which were found urns (it was the faſhion in thoſe days to call all Roman veſſels *urns*) and diſhes of the red coralline ware.

the

the plan, I found sufficient remains to convince me of its history. The parts excavated exhibited a wall composed of rubble and hard mortar [1] 30 feet in length, intersected by three apartments with their walls, the two on the side of the redoubt, as not explored, were not definable, one was 10 feet in breadth, the other towards the exterior side, towards the counterscarp of the ditch, was complete, and was 9 feet three inches by 7 feet 3. The walls on the inside were covered with fine white plaster, on which were painted stripes of black and red, some an inch broad, and some in lines. These apartments contained a great quantity of fragments of Roman vessels, indicating their having been discovered at a prior period, mutilated and thrown into the spot again with the incumbent earth and other rubbish. Among the fragments, I took up a small silver denarius already described, also a middle brass of the Higher Empire, which, by its colour, had evidently passed the fire; there was no possibility of decyphering the head, or of assigning it to any particular emperor.

The fragments of vessels were of all shapes and sizes, some of coarse brown earth, near an inch thick, their sections shewing the largest to have been at least one foot and a half diameter, others of the finest earth, particularly the red coraline Samian pottery, consisting of the ornamented and plain, the former exhibiting soldiers with spears, lamps, and stars, which seemed, by their segments and bulging forms, to have been similar to fig. 1 and 2, in Plate XXX. Fragments of platters, and small vessels of this quality, were in great numbers, necks of bottles and arms of large amphoræ were also discovered; on one of the latter, in my possession, these letters, LARVS, are very perfectly stamped. Fragments of glass, and a carved cylindric piece of ivory an inch long.

Round the spot, and very contiguous to it, in the process of the ditch, I discovered several obvious signs of urn burial, urns, with ashes compressed together by the incumbent soil, and of thin and thick burnt earth, but near them no smaller vessels to ascertain the identity of their being Roman, or indeed sufficient reason, from the fragments of the urns, to class them with the contents of the Roman interment above described. Whether prior or posterior to it, I shall not determine.

About two hundred yards on the slope of the hill, which faces the town of Rochester, were situated several hundred of the small barrows in clusters, the chief part described in this work.

In the year 1783, I received information from Canterbury that part of an eminence, on which was situated an orchard, to the South-east of the Don John, or Dane John hill, near the Riding-gate, through which the Watling-street went in a straight line to Dover, had fallen down by the frost; when discovery was made of antient earthen ware [2], which contained burnt bones. Considering this spot to have been the burial-place of the Romans so often sought for by Antiquaries, I visited it, in the year following, in May, and evidently discerned the impression of the urn and one of the vessels situated on a stratum of wood ashes, about a foot above the native soil, over which was thrown the

[1] See Plate XXVIII. No. 2. fig. 1.
[2] See Plate XXVIII. described.
[3] See Plate XXVIII.

bank of dark factitious ſoil, blended with Roman potſherds, fragments of Roman brick, oiſter-ſhells, and animal bones

Having procured a labourer, I found, cloſe to the other veſſels, another about 7 inches in height, of a conic form, of ordinary brown earth, and which contained the bones of a cock, diſcernible by the bone of the leg, and the one which entered the horn of the ſpur [1]

The ſepulchral veſſels, I ſhould hope, would ſpeak beyond conjecture in favour of the people to whom they are attributed The ſpot where they were found is near the principal highway of the Roman city, and every criterion in reſpect to the veſſels themſelves equal the beſt demonſtration

The Roman ſtations which I have viſited have uniformly produced ſpecimens of the pottery which *Plate* XXVIII has deſcribed, and which, in my opinion, leaves no doubt of the authenticity of their Roman claim. Subſequent buildings, the repeated changes and conſtant moving of the neighbouring ſoil, and which has been occupied in ſucceeding times, appear to have obliterated, in a great meaſure, the remains of Roman interment Caſual diſcoveries are doubtleſs often made, but as no memorial ſimilar to the elevated barrows found on moſt of our waſte-lands has left traces of theſe depoſits, it is only chance, or great labour in the purſuit, which can afford a critical diſcovery of them

Quidquid ſub terra eſt in apricum proferet ætas is a difficult taſk for the Antiquary, but it is only through theſe means that conjecture can be removed, and this kind of ſtudy rendered reſpectable and ſecure

[1] Socrates, when dying, turned to Crito, ſaying, " We owe a cock to Æſculapius, diſcharge that vow for me, and pray do not forget it " Quare Socrates, ut apud Platonem extat, jam moriturus, teſtamento gallum Æſculapio legat, vir ſapientiſſimus innuens, de lucis uſuram, cujus eſt gallus nuncius hoc eſt vitam civilem bonitati omnium morborum curatrici, quam Æſculapius deſignat quæque divinæ providentiæ, ab Apolline ſuapte umbratæ eſt proles, reſtituere, aqua et mutuato acceperit Vincentius Chartarius, tranſlated by Antonio Verderius Im. Deor a curious and ſcarce book, p 59 Kirchman ſays the Romans buried cocks, p 628

SUPPLE ET AVITA USU, SI POTES ASSEQUERE

I SHALL here aſſemble a few facts, which the Antiquary will not fail to apply to the funeral cuſtoms of the Romans. To eſtabliſh truth by obvious analogy, I have alſo introduced ſome of the moſt curious ſpecimens of ſimilar relics found on one of their provincial ſtations on the Continent. Their burial-places in this kingdom are very rarely diſcovered from an obſervation already made, owing to their cuſtom of interring the dead at no great diſtance from their ſtations by the ſide of the public-road, and in ſuch ſituations as have been occupied by a ſucceeding people to modern times. Their principal towns and cities are the actual reſidence of the preſent generation, hence, through the various changes of different people and different cuſtoms, their traces have been long deſtroyed, and it is now only to accident we are indebted for the few remains which this country has preſerved.

I have more particularly been inclined to introduce a few ſpecimens of the Roman graves found on the Continent, to demonſtrate the undoubted proof of coincidence, they will always ſerve as unerring guides to point out the criterion of theſe antient remains, and, as ſeveral of the urns have on them Roman inſcriptions, their forms and peculiarities will always produce an indubitable authority.

PLATE XXIX.

N° 1 Is a copy from a bad engraving of Petavius[1], it exhibits a Roman interment of the body, accompanied with the ſame ceremonies as are uſually found with the urn which contained the aſhes, and a ſtriking proof that the ſame veſſels which accompanied cremation were depoſited with the body buried entire. The author ſays,

"Alia itidemque pergrandia olla cum lapide [illegible] [illegible] [illegible] et Brachialis [illegible] [illegible] obruta in Johannis Amalrici [illegible] [illegible]

[1] Pauli Petavii. In Francicae curiae consiliarii [illegible] [illegible] [illegible], MDC[illegible]

conditoris

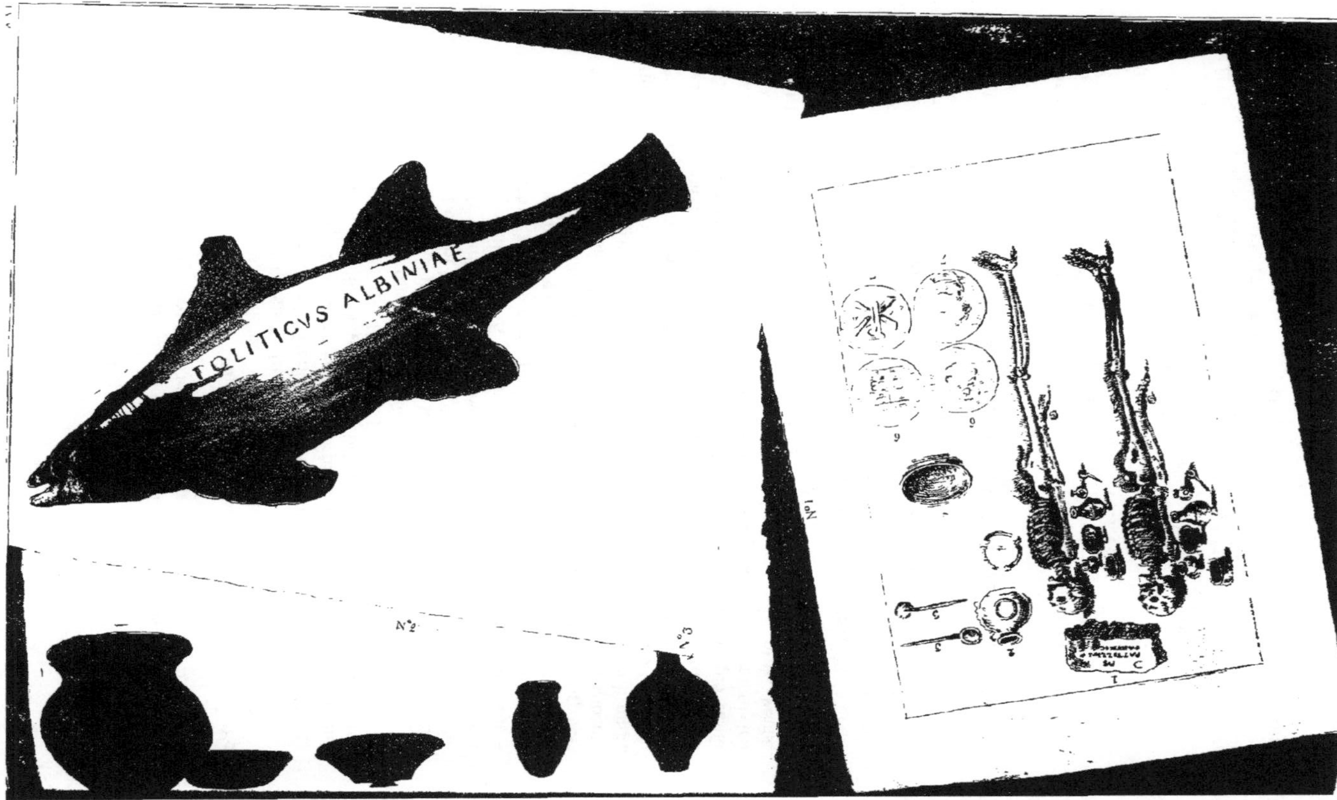

TOLITICVS ALBINIAE
N°1
N°2
N°3

cenſitoris ædibus, quæ pars veteris domus Andegavenſium comitum fuere, quaſque ille Pariſius in vico Textrinario a fundamentis reparabat Anno hoc DNI MDCXII reperta ſunt."

Fig. 1. A ſtone at the head. One foot long, and half a foot broad, the D. M. M. Dis manibus, memoriæ, and the inſcription ſhow its Roman claim.

Fig. 2. A glaſs veſſel, called a lacrymal urn by Petavius.

Fig. 3. The interior and exterior ſide of a ſpoon, "Minutum cochlear corneum, quo exceptæ lachrymæ in ampullam mittebantur." It is from this deſcription that theſe veſſels have been probably conſidered as depoſitaries for the tears. The ſize of the ſpoons he has not mentioned, but their being of horn is not probable: this ſubſtance ſoon periſhes in the earth, they might have been of ivory. Spoons are not uncommonly found in Roman graves, and a very ſmall one of braſs has been found in a barrow at Sibertſwold, in the poſſeſſion of Mr. Fauſſett, but too low down to be Roman. Their lacrymal uſes are very doubtful. "In ignem poſita eſt fletur[1]" has determined Antiquaries to contrive veſſels for this purpoſe, and ſpoons to catch the tears. The Romans were whimſical enough to adopt this cuſtom, but I ſtill contend there is no authority for it in any writer to apply theſe veſſels to ſuch purpoſes. Many ſepulchral veſſels I conceive to have contained milk, which the antients conſidered as congenial to the nutriment of the manes, as ſuch, with milk, the ſpoons may have been of ſervice. "Ideo lactis et ſanguinis mentio facta eſt, quia affirmantur animæ lacte et ſanguine delectari," alſo, "Bene animam lacte et ſanguine dicit elicitam ad tumulum. Lacte namque nutritur corpus poſt animæ conjunctionem, et anima ſine ſanguine nuſquam eſt, quo effuſo recedit[2]." When the ſacrifices to the *inferiæ* were in a great meaſure interdicted or reſtrained, the cuſtom of depoſiting with the dead unguents, milk, beans, and lettuce, moſt probably ſupplied the place.

Fig. 4. A braſs *armilla*, on the great bone of the arm.

Fig. 5. A Samian red veſſel[3], with this inſcription of the maker, SECANDI W.

Fig. 6. Braſs coins near the right hand, NERO CAESAR AVG GERM IMP reverſe, PACE PR. VBIQ. PARTA IANVM CLVSIT; fig. 7. D N MAGNENTIVS P F AVG, reverſe, SALVS DD NN. AVG ET CAES. The monogram of Chriſt. X. P.

The other veſſels, being of common earth, are not deſcribed.

N° 2. From the common-place-book of Lord Winchelſea. The veſſels are by a ſcale marked in the drawing.

[1] Ovidius 1 de Ponto 1 eleg. 10.

[2] Servius. Debita ſpargens lacrymâ favillam
Vatis amici. Hor. Od. 6. lib. ii.
Miſſa bibunt molles lacrymas unguenta favillæ. Ovid. 3 Faſt.
—— —— Felix bibat ultima liquores
Et lacrymas. Statius, l. iii.
Theſe paſſages ſimply imply tears ſhed on the aſhes.

[3] Theſe veſſels appear to have been the peculiar workmanſhip of the Romans, and, from their neatneſs and beauty, moſt probably made in the Roman empire, and imported with the troops by occaſional ſupplies. See Archæologia, p. [illegible], a paper of Mr. Jacob, on the red Roman earthen ware, from the Pan-pudding rock, where a Roman veſſel, which contained this ware, had foundered. Several of theſe pateræ I have in my poſſeſſion from the ſpot.

This

This burial-place was discovered at a place called Grove, in the parish of Boxley, near Maidstone and Chatham, in Kent, July 18, 1721, about four miles from the latter. The hill of Boxley commands a great portion of the country near the coast, and from its bold and high situation would be well adapted to a speculatorium.

They were found about four feet from the surface, and in the position represented in the drawing.

There were two deposits of these vessels, almost similar in number and size; one of the largest contained a small glass phial, both the large vessels contained human bones, which had passed the fire.

Fig. A Contained ashes, and on one side was deposited

Fig F. which the Antiquaries of those days fancied into lacrymal bottles; and which the Earl says *was stopped with a cork very sound and fresh, with some signs of oil, or the like, which had become dry, and of the colour of an oak wainscot.*

Fig B. A red polished patera, empty; maker's name, ACRIMINI

Fig C Of the same earth.

Fig D Contained an unctuous or bituminous matter, and conceived, probably through fancy, to have had an aromatic smell

Fig E Contained earth, but no ashes A red patera

With these vessels were also found fig. 2. Plate XXX. which, by Lord Winchelsea's drawing, the position of the fragments, and other vessels of a similar nature, may produce a tolerably correct specimen Many other fragments of vessels were also found, and from repeated discoveries of Roman pottery casually thrown up, with coins of Hadrian, the spot evidently appears to have been a burial-place of the Romans

N° 3. An urn[1] from a *tumulus* near the castle of Betho, at no great distance from *Tongres*[2], in the Bishoprick of Liege. The *tumulus* was one of the largest kind;

[1] Among the antient Christians the fish was frequently admitted into their sepulchral symbols The earthen lamps and other utensils found in Christian cemeteries evidence the fact. See Paulus Aringhius Roma Subterranea, p 332 This author cites several passages from the antient fathers to prove the frequent use of the symbol, and has engraved a sepulchral lamp with two fish upon it, and the X P the monogram of our Saviour, the fish much in the form of the urn They were the signs of the faithful, in allusion to the passage in the 13th chapter of St Matthew They were also baptismal signs "Illi pisces intelligendi sunt, qui conferunt de fonte baptismi migrant ad Dominum" Bede, lib 1. in Joh c 12, and the same on Luke "Piscis est fides invisibilium vel propter aquam baptismi, vel quia de invisibilibus locis capitur"

[2] Cæsar chose this spot for a fortification in his wars against the Eburones, or people of Liege. The town takes its name from an antient castle "Id castelli nomen est, hoc fere est in medius Eburonum finibus" Lib vi Atuatuca Tungrorum The Tungri were the first people who passed the Rhine, and the bravest among the German nations The Roman army abundantly recruited from them; and they served in most of the territories of the Empire Several inscriptions have been found in Britain commemorating the Tungrian cohorts

Pliny mentions this town as famous for its chalybeate waters he says it is purgative, a cure for tertian agues and the stone "Tungri civitas Galliæ fontem habet—purgat hic corpora, tertianas febres discubit calculorumque vitia Lib xxxi cap 11 I must here beg to make a short digression in favour of this antient town, in the support of old Pliny's assertion, that the waters of this place are of a renowned medical quality Father Harduin, Pliny's commentator, and indeed the most eccentric commentator on all the antients, says that Pliny's Tungri is a pure Spadense, the waters of Spa This assertion will not require much trouble to confute, as well as many other assertions of reputed authors The medical quality of the Tungrian waters are highly extolled by the younger Pliny in his 31st book, where he

says

kind, and what renders the circumstance extraordinary is, that in the neighbourhood the burial-places of the Romans are numerous, and have been often explored, exhibiting incidental relics, which greatly differ. If an urn, there are generally other vessels found near it; and if the body is inhumated, it is generally surrounded with similar vessels. The inscription is on both sides

POLITICVS ALBINIAE,

KARISSIMAE SVAE.

and doubtless Roman.

This drawing was sent me in the course of my correspondence with the Abbé Van Muyssen, of Tongres, in September, 1783; of whose repeated favours I am happy to acknowledge a grateful sense.

In the year 1773, passing through this country from Maestrich, on a long excursion into the heart of Germany, I was often amused with many antient vestigia, barrows, and Roman roads, on which I frequently stopped to make observations. Approaching Tongres, casting my eye on many fragments of Roman pottery in a valley through which the road passed, at no great distance from the town, I was determined to enquire, on my arrival, if any person in the town had a taste for collecting similar relics; and in a short time I was conducted to the house of the Abbé. His cabinet consists of a fine collection of coins, and a great variety of the Roman supellex.

After the enumeration of the specimens of Roman pottery found in sepulchres, and which will admit of a just inference to similar remains in this

says the sick and wounded, Romans and Gauls, made use of them, for their wounds and their baths, as well as to drink them, being highly salutary in many diseases. Ludovico Guicciardino has written copiously on the subject, but equally unsatisfactory. Now the fact is, that, from the ruins of the old town, the source of the antient springs being closed up and lost, a fresh discharge was made at some distance; and the same property as described by these antient venerable writers has been elaborately attested by skilful physicians.

An old poet, probably of the town, has written these lines on its medicinal properties, and his panegyric is found not to be exaggerated.

Quem ferrugineum fert Plinius esse saporis,
Fons hic saxifragus febrifugusque fuit.
Renibus et stomacho, splenis jecorisque molestum
Pellere scorbutum natus ab ore malum.
Tot vulneribus medicina est optima fons
Potioque interior certa medela simul.
Contra pallentes tuta est medicina colores,
Et suppressa locis menstrua solvit aquis.
Quin illi et obstructos ventos et pellit humores
Hippocondriacos sic juvat ille viros, &c.

Through respect to this old town, and not to admit of the imposition of authors, who may in all probability have had their views in decrying the veracity of Pliny, on the salubrity of its waters, the better to uphold the celebrity of those of Spa, I will briefly allege, that thirty-one physicians actually assembled at Tongres, on the 24th of August, 170[illegible] to analyze the spring, and to enquire into the assertion of Pliny, and their attestations, with several others, have been recorded. Dr Bresmal has described their medicinal qualities in an accurate and comprehensive light. M. Philip Gerinx, chief physician and chemist to Prince Ernest of Bavaria, Bishop of Liege, has also written a book on the same subject. In short, the efficacy of this chalybeate is considered of a higher degree of excellence to that of Spa, much more agreeable to the palate; and the situation of the town, though not so diversified with picturesque scenery, is more open and salubrious, as being less subject to humid exhalations. Were Tongres to be frequented by a few English who travel for the actual purpose of restoration of health, and not for the dissipation of play and the other amusements of Spa, it would in a short time increase in popularity, and the superior excellence of its mineral springs be more known to the world.

country, a brief deſcription of his diſcoveries may probably be well accepted by the antiquarian reader.

PLATE XXX.

Fig. 1. A Roman veſſel[1] of a fine poliſhed red earth; the ornaments in relief. From Offulkin, a little village at a ſmall diſtance from Tongres, which has produced great numbers of ſepulchral veſſels of various kinds; the ſhape, ſize, and workmanſhip perfectly ſimilar to many veſſels and fragments of pottery diſcovered on the Roman ſtations in our iſland.

The various enquiries which I have made, and the peruſal of almoſt all our writers on antiquity, not proving ſatisfactory, I thought it might be poſſible to authenticate, with a greater degree of certainty, the Roman burial-places, and at the ſame time to draw an unerring line between our Roman and Britiſh barrows, to reſort to ſimilar diſcoveries on the Continent. My correſpondence with the Abbé Van Muyſſen, of Tongres, being ſufficiently ſatisfactory, I have therefore ſelected the beſt ſpecimens which he has tranſmitted me.

That part of the correſpondence which will explain where the Roman burial-places are ſituated, as alſo produce a fair analogy with thoſe in this kingdom, I ſhall here tranſcribe.

Having remarked to him, that in the courſe of having opened many of our largeſt barrows, which produced but few urns, and unlike the Roman, and which inclined me to ſuppoſe they were leſs productive than the ſmaller, he thus corroborated my opinion: "Your remarks are juſt on theſe *tumuli*; the large ones, which are detached, contain few or no urns; that which is ſituated near the caſtle of Betho only produced the one in the form of a fiſh[2]. The great quantity of urns and other veſſels are found on our hills or grounds little elevated above the plain, and without circular mounds of earth over them, in conſequence of our lands having been cultivated and levelled from the remoteſt period, and proved by that of Yſerenborn, or the ſteely ſpring applauded by Pliny, Coningheym, or the royal-palace, Savelberg, or Sandy-hill, all which have doubtleſs been uſed as antient cemeteries. I alſo confeſs, that diſcoveries of this nature have been made on plains, but not often; among ſimilar reſearches, ſepulchres of a different kind have been found on the declivity of hills, but not on the heights; thoſe of the men conſiſt of fourteen great and long red tiles, in the following diſpoſition: four are perpendicularly placed on each ſide of the ſkeleton; four horizontally, which ſupport the former; the thirteenth at the feet; and the fourteenth at the head, in which poſition is generally found a veſſel, in the ſhape of one uſed for drinking, about a palm in height. I am inclined to think this kind of ſepulture ſhould be affixed to the antient Gauls. If the body was ſmall, the number of tiles diminiſhed in proportion."

[1] The ornament of a bird on this veſſel appears to be that of a crow. If ſacrificial, the veſſel may have been ſacred to Apollo.

[2] Plate XXIX. No. [illegible]

On

N° 2
2
1
4
3
6
5

On the receipt of another letter he was ſo obliging to add, " Concerning the places where urns have been found, the hill, called Yſenborn, has been the moſt productive. Urns, veſſels, and other funeral inſtruments, have been, from time to time, diſcovered there in great numbers. Coninxheym, near the antient walls of Tongres, the hill near St Antony, without the gate of Maſtricht, where it joins the field of the convent of St Agnes; at Offulken, a little village at a ſhort diſtance from Tongres, where the ſepulchral urns are frequently found, though not ſo numerous, yet more beautiful, and in general decorated with a variety of ornaments, ſome with figures of men combating beaſts, others with gladiators and idols; others adorned with foliage; ſome plain, ſome ſtriated, but moſtly all of the beautifully poliſhed red earth.

Fig. 2. Fragment of the decorated red Samian veſſels of the Romans, which I diſcovered at Mancheſter[1], near the Caſtle-field, the Roman Mancunium in the purſuit of the burial-place, and which appears to have been of the ſame nature as fig. 1. and 5. This fragment is extremely curious, as it exhibits the offering of a Roman to Apollo, the dreſs appears to be that of an emperor, or a perſon above the rank of a common ſoldier. This ſubject, compared with a variety of other ſpecimens, inclines me to believe that theſe veſſels were ſacred to ſacrificial and funeral purpoſes, and not fabricated for the uſes of domeſtic life. With theſe fragments an immenſe quantity of other fragments of pottery were diſcovered, and other relics, teſſellated pavement, and iron inſtruments, coins alſo have been found, one of large bronze of Hadrian, which a labourer had procured from the ſpot which I occaſionally viſited.

Fig. 3. Another fragment of ſimilar pottery, an Etruſcan vaſe, evidently of the high workmanſhip and ſacrificial, with the hind part of a horſe in relief, from the ſame ſpot.

Fig. 4. Similar fragment from the ſame ſpot, the figure of Pan.

Fig. 5. The laciniated veſſel deſcribed in the Earl of Winchelſea's manuſcript; from the ſtag and hounds emboſſed upon it. This veſſel may be conſidered as ſacred to Diana, and to whom the Romans ſacrificed at funerals.

PLATE XXXI.

IN this plate are indiſcriminately ſelected the ſepulchral veſſels of the Romans found in the neighbourhood of Tongres, they are applied as near as poſſible to the order in which they are uſually diſcovered. They are drawn by a ſcale of inches at the bottom of the Plate.

No. 1. Fig. 1. Red veſſel of coarſe earth.

Fig. 2. Small ampulla, uſually found in urns; and by ſome writers ſuppoſed to contain lachrymal offerings.

[1] See the Hiſtory of Mr Whitaker.

[2] There is no Roman ſtation in Britain, or in any part of Europe, but exhibits ſpecimens of theſe veſſels, and, wherever found, they may be naturally deemed a criterion of the people.

Fig 3 A ſmall Capeduncula; of a light reddiſh brown earth.

Fig 4 A veſſel, by the Romans called Obba; of dark brown earth.

Fig 5 Lamp of light grey earth.

Fig 6. Veſſel of light blue-grey earth, with the initials S. C. I.

N° 2 fig 1 Urn [1], of light blue-grey earth.

Fig. 2. Glaſs phial.

Fig 3 Fine coraline red earth.

Fig 4. Purple, red, or dirty lake-coloured earth.

Fig 5. Reddiſh brown earth.

Fig. 6. Light brown earth.

PLATE XXXII.

N° 1 fig 1 Dark brown earth.

Fig 2 Red earth, the head [2] drawn with white.

Fig 3. Dark brown earth, with three animals.

Fig 4 Reddiſh brown earth [3].

Fig 5 Light red-brown earth.

Fig 6 Very dark brown earth, letters and ornament yellowiſh brown, and relieved with a lighter tint

Fig 7 Fine red coraline ware; foliage of the ſame.

[1] The Romans generally appear to have had a peculiar form for their veſſels adapted for their funeral ceremonies Many of their urns are ſo extremely narrow at their baſe as to prevent their ſtanding unſupported, an apparent evidence they were deſigned for laying in the ground The ſmall glaſs and phials found in urns indicate the ſame purpoſe

[2] The head of Pan, the moſt celebrated of the Mythic deities; the great archetype of nature "Hæc ejus in currendo velocitas, celerrimum mundi motum innuit, nam hic Deus rerum univerſitatem significat, ΠΑΝ enim omne ſonat" Chartarius Imag Deor p 91 In the Hymns of Orpheus, under the term δικέρωτα, or two horned, Pan is called the ſoul of the world. Horns are the earlieſt emblems of power, the Sacred Hiſtory has frequent alluſions to this emblem 'the horn of might, of ſalvation, of defence' Human beings, from the earlieſt ages of the world, ſeemed to have uſed them in battle They were probably put on by captains and leaders of armies, to appear more tremendous and impoſing to the enemy "And Zedekiah, the ſon of Chenaanah, made him horns of iron: and he ſaid, thus ſaith the Lord, with theſe ſhalt thou puſh the Syrians, until thou have conſumed them" 1 Kings, c xxii v 11. David, in his trouble, invoking the Lord, alludes to warriors armed in this manner "Many oxen are come about me, fat bulls of Baſan cloſe me in on every ſide." Pſ xxii v 12 Bacchus, the great Scythian leader, was typified under this emblem. The rays of light emanating from the head of Moſes have been tranſlated, by Rabbi Kimchi, into horns R Salomon explains קרביתהוד cornu magnificentiæ Alexander, who ſtyled himſelf the ſon of Jupiter Ammon, had horns on his coins. See alſo the coins of Lyſimacus.

——— nemoriſque regna
Corrigeri Jovis. Silius Italicus, lib 3

And again,

Exin Cornigeri veneratus numinis aras
Captivis onerat donis

I have curſorily thrown theſe ſelections together only to ſhew in what manner the Romans have tranſferred this ſublime deity, in the antient Mythology, into the moſt abſurd and ridiculous worſhip

[3] Tintinnabulum, or little bell, a votive relic to repel evil ſpirits See an iron bell, Plate XX fig 4 found in a barrow

Fig 8

Fig 8 Light yellow earth

Fig 9 Light red, relieved with white lines

N° 2 fig 1 Dark brown earth

Fig 2 Dark blue earth

Fig 3. Bright and full red earth, with black lines.

Fig 4 Light brown earth

STAMPS ON THE VESSELS

These stamps are supposed to be the potters names, they are always found on those of the fine red earth on the Continent, as well as in this country. Those in the neighbourhood of Tongres, which have been sent me, are the following MAI PIAC ODVP C M GVMVZ SILVI OF OPVL PORTIS LVCAIZ AM'O F CAVLAS FISTVSIO CLAMISSA AM INIIACVS. These are stamped on the bottom of the vessels and platters

Other vessels of the Romans doubtless are often stamped, but this is chiefly on those of a larger kind, on the arms and handles, and with a much larger kind of letter, this earth is also peculiar in its nature, of a light dirty yellow, and which appears to have been produced from Italy.

Among other relics, apparently from tombs, in the Abbé Van Muyssen's collection, are handles of swords, one with a lion's head upon it, bracelets of gold and bronze, two of gold enamelled, enriched with pearls, and enchased with engraved stones, heads of lances and spears, enamelled clasps: gold, silver, and bronze rings buckles and *fibulæ*, of bronze, variety of bronze keys, and one the nuptial ring key, not uncommon, stiles, in ivory, bronze, and in various shapes, enamelled buttons, one of gold, another of silver, others of ivory and bronze, pins of silver and bronze, needles and thimbles of bronze; handles of knives of various shapes, one of ivory in the form of a stag's foot, *Spoons* of bronze, and one of a singular shape of silver; and one of ivory, which the Abbé believes to have been used by the preficæ at funerals to introduce the tears into the phials

Many instruments and attributes of Roman deities the thyrsus of Bacchus, silver sickle, sacred to Ceres, serpent, hatchet, scales; votive small sceptre and various similar relics, many engraved stones, and some of good workmanship, which the Abbé sent me impressions of

Among a variety of discoveries of *penates* and emblematic relics, the Abbé sent me a singular drawing of a bronze in relief, which he considers of great curiosity, and which he believes to be the head and dress of an archdruid.

PLATE

PLATE XXXIII.

SPEARS OF BRASS AND ARROW-HEADS OF FLINT FROM TUMULI

SEVERAL ſpecimens of arms have been ſelected in this plate to connect thoſe that are demonſtratively applied to a barbarous people with thoſe which have been found in our detached and large barrows From the known fact, that ſimilar arrow-heads as are found in our antient ſepulchres are uſed at this day by the barbarous natives of the globe, it is a natural and reaſonable inference that they were uſed by a barbarous people who were, at a certain period, the inhabitants of this iſland

Admitting this argument, which common ſenſe muſt aſſent to, the reader may expand his thoughts on the period in which theſe barrows were raiſed If he ſhould be inclined to ſuppoſe theſe arms were Celtic, they may have exceeded the period of the arrival of the Belgæ, who paſſed into the South of Britain about 300 years before Chriſt [1], and who are ſuppoſed to have driven the Celtæ, or other barbarous clans, to the remote and diſtant parts of the iſland, to the Weſt and to the North.

The braſs arms in this plate, found in a large detached barrow in Dorſetſhire, will probably connect the ſimilar ſpecimens, frequently found in this iſland and in Ireland, to a kindred people. Their workmanſhip in ſome reſpects, are not greatly differing from the arrow and ſpear heads of flint or ſtone, particularly the part connected to the ſhaft, and the fact of their being found in ſimilar large barrows to thoſe in which the arrow-heads of flint were diſcovered, evince a period of time at no great diſtance; and it will therefore remain for diſcuſſion, whether they are to be aſſigned to the progreſs of art among a barbarous people, or to a foreign people their ſucceſſors by conqueſt.

Fig. 3 Exhibits a unique relic found with braſs arms in a barrow; the ornamental marks upon it are evidences that they muſt have been produced by a ſtamp or milling inſtrument, and this period could not have followed the immediate progreſſion of art from the arrow-head of flint to the ſpear head of braſs depoſited with this relic, the natural implication muſt then follow, that a more powerful people, advanced in arts and warlike ſcience, had followed the barbarous inhabitants; and, with the concurrence of hiſtory, we may be induced to repreſent the Belgæ as the real claimants of theſe ſepulchral relics

The application of the braſs arms, found in our barrows, to any particular inhabitants of this country, has been conſidered of ſome importance to aſcertain its antient colonization, and although the fact may not be aſcertained to a deciſion, we may approach it ſufficiently near to leave conjecture at ſome diſtance, Cæſar may be cited with effect, and his authority received without any evaſion The braſs which the Britons uſe, he ſays, is imported; and the iron found on the ſea-coaſt "in maritimus ferrum; ſed ejus exigua eſt copia, ære utuntur importato [2]." Iron, he obſerves, though in ſmall quantity, was uſed at this period by the Britons, it might therefore be a natural concluſion to believe the miſſile arms were chiefly braſs; and ſuch in all probability were the arms of

[1] Gough p 187.

[2] De Bello Gallico, lib. v.

5 the

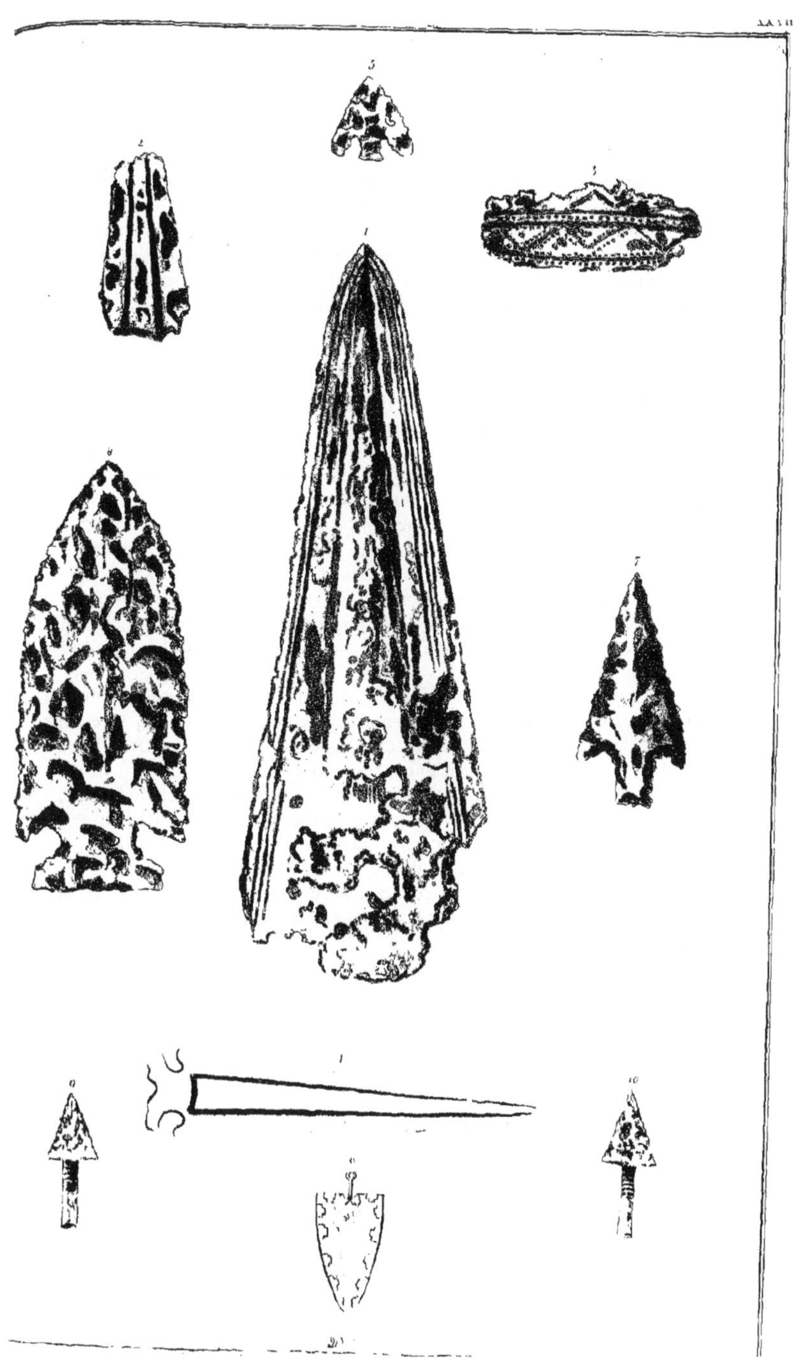

the Gauls. But the four thouſand chariots, uſed by Caſſivellaunus againſt Cæſar, ſeem to atteſt the uſe of iron; and it would be ridiculous to ſuppoſe that this uſeful and powerful metal was not adapted to this purpoſe. But it remains to ſhew whether braſs arms, ſuch as ſpears and ſwords, were peculiar to the Gauls and Britons. It ſeems a truth, that the Belgæ incorporated themſelves with the Celts in Gaul; and, if we can ſhew that the Belgæ or Scythæ were, at an early period, in the habit of uſing braſs arms, it will follow, that the large barrows which have produced them muſt apply to a period before the final ſubduction of the iſland by the Romans.[1]

The preface of M. Gerhard Schøning, at the head of his ſecond volume of the Hiſtory of the Kings of Norway, by Snorro, aſſerts, that in 1776, by the order of Prince Frederic, of Denmark, the very antient tombs near Jegerſpris were opened, in which were found ſwords, hatchets, and hammers of a very hard ſtone, with their handles worked out of the ſame block, ſimilar to thoſe diſcovered in the Tchouder mines near Schlangenberg; with theſe laſt were found inſtruments of braſs, and no relics of iron; a natural concluſion was made that theſe tombs preceded the times when iron was in uſe. M. D'Hancarville, vol. I. p. 119, in his work on the Origin of the Arts of Greece, ſays, that at the time he reſided at Naples, there were diſcovered in a part of Lucania, formerly inhabited by the Oenotrian Pelaſgians, which hiſtory proves to have been a Scythian colony, tombs, in which were depoſited the heads of arrows with a ſword of ſtone. Theſe relics are now preſerved in the Britiſh Muſeum among the antiquities purchaſed of Sir William Hamilton, and which are memorials of thoſe antient people, from whom the Greeks, and all the Northern nations, received their funeral cuſtoms: the ſhape of their ſepulchres was taken from theſe people, with the ceremonies of encloſing thoſe things uſeful in this life, in the hope of their proving equally ſo in the other world. As the nature of theſe arms, found in the Oenotrian Pelaſgian tombs, precede the time of the Dactyli Idæi[2], who, according to the Arundelian marble, introduced iron into Greece, ſo theſe inſtruments in the mines and tombs of the antient people of the North of Aſia and Europe, demonſtrate that the colonies, detached from the latter to the former, preceded, by a time of very remote antiquity, thoſe ages which hiſtory has tranſmitted.

The proof that the antient Scythians uſed entirely braſs arms is obvious from Herodotus[3]; and, admitting the Belgæ to be of the ſame parental ſtock, the braſs

[1] See proofs of the large barrows being erected antecedent to this period. *Argument and Hiſtorical Relation.*

[2] So called from Mount Ida, where they lived. See Diodorus Siculus, lib. v. Primi ergo, quorum ſit memoria apud nos, Cretæ Incolæ, Idæi Dactyli, *[illegible]*, circa montem Idam habitantes.

[3] Lib. iv. Melpomene. I have lately publiſhed in my ſecond Diſſertation on the Celts, and other [illegible] found in this iſland. I ſhall once more tranſcribe it for preſent elucidation. "Between the rivers Boriſthenes and Hypanis there is a place called Exampæus, in which place there is a copper veſſel, ſix times larger than a ſimilar veſſel at the mouth of the Euxine ſea, which was conſecrated by Pauſanias, ſon of *Cleombrotus*; it contained about ſix thouſand ſix hundred gallons, and ſix inches in thickneſs. The inhabitants of theſe parts ſay, that it was made from the Heads of Arrows or Spears of the Scythians; that Ariantas, king of the Scythians, deſirous of knowing the number of his ſubjects, demanded that every Scythian ſhould, on pain of death, bring him the Point of an Arrow [illegible]." This is ſufficient to prove that the Scythians were in the uſe of braſs arms.

arms will then be found among the Belgic Gauls of Britain. The facility of casting these weapons, for they all appear to be so fabricated, would, in the most expeditious manner, arm an immense body of men; and, unless the necessary conveniences of forges and other operose arts to complete missile weapons of iron were at hand, it is very natural to suppose, notwithstanding the preference of iron, that brass arms would become of general use, till such conveniencies had taken place. As to a belief that these arms were Roman, it will be necessary to advance some remarks to combat the opinion, which an Antiquary, perhaps, will not stand in need of.

When Hesiod[1], Homer[2], or Virgil[3], are cited to prove that brass arms were used by the antients, poetical imagination must not be admitted into history; they only mean to inform us, that the antient Greeks and early Romans used such arms: their assertions do not apply to the Greeks in Solon's time, or to the Romans in the days of Virgil, in proof of which we have Greek and Roman history. There is no passage in Pliny which attests the use of brass arms by the antient Romans, and which would not have escaped him had this been a general use. On the contrary, there is a striking passage that particularizes the interdiction of iron[4] after the expulsion of the kings, in the articles of peace of King Porsena to the people of Rome, setting forth, that iron should be only used in the tillage of ground, and which evinces its general use. He also says, that brass was held sacred by some nations, and probably therefore preferred to iron.

The fact, however, will, in all probability, be found in the following remark. When Homer mentions brass arms, he means to infer an early period of time; and, as to the use of iron by the Greeks, we may safely state it to be much antecedent to the time of Solon, 559 years before Christ, when the Greeks were sufficiently refined to adopt the general use of iron[5].

The fiction evidently portrayed in the Iliad must lead every natural commentator to conceive that Homer was not portraying the customs of his own æra; and the exquisite structure and language of the poem proves the age in which he flourished, which, by the most probable conjecture, was 907 years before Christ, to have been equally refined in the arts, as well as in all other polite attainments. It is a natural conclusion, therefore, to suppose iron was in general use at this period, which will also agree with many passages in Sacred Testimony, among a polished people, and hence be handed down to the Romans. Therefore, when the Romans entered Britain, there can be no doubt but they were armed with iron.

The Scythians peopled Germany, Scandinavia, and a great part of Gaul, about 500 years before Christ, and the Belgæ of the same stock entered Britain and

[1] [illegible] Ἔργα καὶ Ἡμέραι.
This passage only proves that brass was used before iron.

[2] [illegible] ΧΑΛΚΕΟΝ [illegible] ΙΛ. Η.

[3] [illegible] Æn. viii. v. 743.

[4] Lib. 34. cap. [illegible]

[5] See the Abbé Winkelman, Histoire de l'Art de l'Antiquité, who proves that the art of sculpture was at its acme in Solon's time.

4 Ireland

Ireland about 300. This coincidence with history, and the suggestions of the classic poets, will date our large sepulchral structures of earth, in which the brass arms are usually found, at least to two centuries before the Christian æra.

Though Wormius[1] asserts that the Danes made their swords, spurs, and arrow-points, of brass, such authority will not apply to the brass arms found in places where the Danes never came, and the only inference which can be drawn from this assertion is, that the Danes used brass arms as well as other nations.

It has been already suggested that the Danes, from the nature of their inroads into Britain, and from their sudden conversion to Christianity on their conquest of the island, would not have adopted such a general custom of interment on our waste lands, as we find the remains of at this day, and where the brass arms have been occasionally discovered; it will be therefore more reasonable to refer these arms to the early inhabitants, and of course decidedly ascribe the barrows to the same people; the Roman claim having been already proved to be totally out of the question, no intermediate argument can be admitted.

PLATE XXXIII.

Fig. 1. The HEAD OF A SPEAR or lance of brass. It was in the possession of the late Colonel Drax, and found in a barrow on the Downs of Dorsetshire, with an entire skeleton, under his inspection. The end, when perfect, was incased into wood, and, from other similar specimens, appears to have been fastened with rivets, and with thongs to the shaft. On comparing this weapon with the Irish *skean* daggers, or knives, found in the bogs in Ireland, there seems to be a great similarity; the end may have been riveted to a handle, which would have answered this purpose; and as the brass spear-heads differ so much in form, being obviously defined as such with sockets, I rather incline to the latter belief.

Fig. 2. A fragment of a smaller spear-head of brass, found in the same barrow with fig. 1. There is a groove, departing from the point in an angle, and extending to the shoulder, in both these specimens, and which proves a striking similarity with others found in various parts of Britain and Ireland.

Fig. 3. Fragments of an ornament of very thin copper or brass gilt, found in the barrow with fig. 1 and 2. Although the arms indicate a high period of antiquity, and which are generally received as such, the ornamental marks on this relic, compared with others evidently of a period as low as the sixth and seventh centuries, evince a posterior date than is usually understood when such arms are found in our barrows; and the concurring fact of the interment of the body unburnt should seem to be an addition of argument against the

[1] Mon. Dan. p. 48, 49. There is a good specimen of Danish [illegible] weapons to be found in Wagen's Alterthümer [illegible] Obotriten. They have all Runic characters of a date of the seventh century upon them, and differ in shape in the most striking manner from those the subject of the discussion. There are nine specimens. The author calls the spear [illegible].

On a critical investigation, the [illegible] will be found to apply to a period not higher than the eighth or ninth century.

very remote antiquity of the ſepulchre, yet on comparing theſe ſpear-heads with others of ſtone and flint, of ſimilar ſhape and diſcriminating peculiarities, their earlier date ſeems to be atteſted.

Fig 4 A SPEAR-HEAD OF BRASS[1], ſelected from ſeveral ſpecimens of the ſame kind, found in the bogs and other places in Ireland, the channel in the weapon is ſimilar to *fig* 1 and 2 and appears to have been faſtened to the ſhaft in the ſame manner as *fig* 1 The analogy is ſtriking, and will lead to inferences deduced from ſimilar diſcoveries in our barrows.

Fig 5 ARROW-HEAD of flint found in a barrow[2], in the poſſeſſion of Sir Joſeph Banks

Fig 6 ARROW-HEAD OF FLINT, ſize of the original, found in Ireland[3] The peaſants call them elf-arrows, and frequently ſet them in ſilver, like the figure, and wear them on their necks as amulets againſt the AITHADH, or elf-ſhot This is engraved to ſhew the analogy with FIG 5

Fig 7 THE HEAD OF A JAVELIN, or dart, of a hard black ſtone, in the College Muſeum at Dublin, found in Ireland.

Fig 8 SPEAR HEAD OF FLINT, found in North America in the earth, in the poſſeſſion of Sir Joſeph Banks.

Fig 9 ARROW HEAD, delicately chipped from a fragment of white tranſparent glaſs of the ſhip's company by the natives of Terra del Fuego, when Sir Joſeph Banks viſited thoſe parts

Fig 10 ARROW-HEAD OF FLINT, from Terra del Fuego, in the poſſeſſion of Sir Joſeph Banks

[1] This ſpecimen is engraved from Plate XI Collect de Reb Hibernicis, N° XIII. vol IV where the modern Iriſh name of theſe arms is compared with the Chaldee *Lanneach-catha* לנך lanek, a ſpear Romane, the Iriſh for a ſpear thrown at the enemy, from the Phœnician *rima*, to caſt, whence רמח rimahh, a lance, Greek, ῥομφαία, Arab rumh With the concurrence of the diſcovery of theſe braſs weapons and the etymon, their Eaſtern claim may poſſibly be eſtabliſhed, and whether *the affectation of common ſenſe* may apply them to the Celts or Belgic Gauls, inſtead of the Phœnician colony, this Eaſtern claim, without much labour of argument, could ſtill be proved

[2] See Mr Pennant's Tour, 1769, p 139, 140 Arrow heads found in a barrow, which contained a coffin or bags, in which were three urns, and near two circles of ſtones This barrow contained alſo a ſtone coffin made of ſlabs, which encloſed a perfect human ſkeleton and a deer's horn See arrow heads of flint uſed as amulets, and of Druid origin, in note [4], p 77 Herodotus, lib vii ſays, the Ethiopians under Xerxes, on his incurſion into Greece, had their arrows pointed with ſtone The ſame people had clubs alſo armed with iron, and the ſhafts of their ſpears pointed with horn It ſhould be remarked, that theſe barbarians, being incorporated with the army of Xerxes, will account for their iron weapons, their [illegible] of ſtone or horn were the characteriſtic marks of their recent barbariſm

[3] Collect de Rebus Hibernicis Plate XI fig 2 See the *deſcription of the elf-arrow, note* [4], p 77 Mr Lhuyd's obſervation on Wales, where he ſays they were certainly handed down from parents to children from the time of the Druids, who uſed them Iron or braſs could not be always at hand for military uſes Ammianus Marcellinus, lib xxxi ſays, the Huns, for want of metal, pointed their darts with bones, "quod procul miſſilibus telis, *acutis oſſibus* pro ſpiculorum acumine arte mira coagmentatis, ſunt diſtinctis." This may be ſaid of any barbarous nation at this day The ſame of the [illegible] Pelloutier's [illegible] i p 37, or of the Germans and Gauls mentioned in Tacitus They are evidences of a people not in the uſe of malleable metal, and it therefore implies, that, wherever theſe arms are found in barrows, they are inconteſtibly the relics of a primitive barbarous people, and preceding the æra of thoſe barrows in which braſs or iron arms are found

GREAT

GREAT BARROWS.

FOR WHO TO DUMB FORGETFULNESS A PREY
THIS PLEASING ANXIOUS BEING E'ER RESIGN'D,
LEFT THE WARM PRECINCTS OF THE CHEARFUL DAY,
NOR CAST ONE LONGING, LING'RING LOOK BEHIND?
GRAY.

THE large barrows, situated on the moors and waste lands of this country, have engaged the attention of the curious and the learned, and some pains have been occasionally bestowed to affix a discriminative character to them. This discrimination has been considered of historic importance to treat of the early inhabitants of Britain, the Greek and Roman writers having transmitted to modern times very imperfect relations of the remote ages of British colonization, and those relations having been variously interpreted and received, it only remains for an enquiry into these ancient memorials, the relics of the people in question, to supply materials for more satisfactory argument.

The discussion of the small barrows in clusters will afford a palpable discrimination to the period of the seventh century; the striking characteristic marks of the Roman sepulchres, already treated of in this work, will in all probability sufficiently demonstrate a striking dissimilitude to the contents of the large barrows in question; and thus, by a succession of facts, the way may be cleared for a nearer approach to truth.

It is allowed by all writers, that the Northern nations[1], from the most remote period

[1] [illegible] Wormii Monumenta Danica, Jornandes [illegible], which occasionally treat on the burial of the Northern nations. Their descriptions concur with the related evidence of human sepulchres, but [illegible] will shew the little authority beyond the tradition of their bards which could be depended on [illegible] and how often they confound the barrows which apply to [illegible] to subsequent period. Olaus Rudbeck counted twelve thousand three hundred [illegible] in the environs of [illegible] Upsal. Rud. tom. I. cap. vi. [illegible]

period

period of antiquity, adopted the ſame mode of interment; and, as their ſucceſſive eruptions into Britain muſt have blended their ſepulchral remains, great difficulty will doubtleſs occur to thoſe who attempt their hiſtory; yet, in all probability,

There are many Swediſh and German Theſes on the diſcovery of Northern ſepulchres, and many Latin tracts publiſhed in the Northern parts of Europe, but they chiefly contain claſſical commentaries, or caſual diſcoveries of ſepulchral relics, and the application of Greek and Roman authors to many facts, on which the Northern hiſtory is more immediately concerned in the inveſtigation. Chriſtian Nettelſtadt, Theſes de variis Mortuos ſepeliendi modis apud Suiones et de Urnis Sepulchralibus, Roſtock, 1727, cum fig. Eliæ Nibelii Upſal, 1733. Ritus Græcorum Sepulchrales. Adam Henr. Lachmanni de variis Exequiarum Ritibus apud utriuſque Ducatus Cimbrici Nobiles Commentatis, Kronii, 1748. Joh. Chriſtoph. Olearii, Mauſoleum in Muſeo, ſive Urnæ Sepulchrales Jenæ, 1701, cum fig. Chriſtiani Frederici Reuſel de Tum. et Urnis Sepulchralibus in Pruſſia, Tractatus, cum fig. Joach. Hartwig Muller's Treatiſe on the Ancient Urns of the Scandinavians, Altona, 1756. And. O. Ryzelii de Sepultura Suio Gothorum Tractatus, Upſal, 1707, cum fig. 5. Chriſtiani Schiſii de Urnis Lignicenſibus et Pilgramdorſenſibus Epiſtola, Wratiſlaviæ, 1704, cum fig. Th. Bartholine Antiq. Dan. 1689, cum fig. Jodoc. Herm. Nunningii Sepulchretum Weſtphalia Mimigardus gentile ſive de Urnis et Lapidibus Sepulchralibus. I have thought proper to note theſe authors for the uſe of Antiquaries who would wiſh to conſult further on this ſubject.

The diſcovery of bodies interred, and urns which contain aſhes, in the ſame ranges, and oftentimes in the ſame barrow, is doubtleſs a difficult ſingularity to explain. When Dr. Stukeley opened ſome barrows on Stonehenge, an urn was found to contain aſhes and female ornaments, and cloſe to which, a larger barrow, which contained a ſkeleton entire. This is alſo atteſted, I believe, in Hutchins's Dorſetſhire, and I have alſo repeated the ſame obſervation in the opening of theſe large barrows. It may probably infer the adoption of both cuſtoms at the ſame area. But this is conjecture only, and I am perſuaded, as the authorities of ſome of our writers on the burials of the Britons, Stukeley and Whitaker, who founds his argument on the former, are, and ſhould be, received as doubtful, as they exhibit no proofs for aſſuming a diſcrimination. If we can apply the cuſtoms of the old Danes deſcribed by Wormius, their period of burial and burning the dead, it may probably afford ſome little parallel with the Britons, but we muſt in this caſe conclude that a ſimilarity of cuſtoms exiſted among the Northern nations. Hence, as a natural poſition, ſanctioned by the oldeſt teſtimony of ſacred and prophane hiſtory, we may prove the moſt antient mode of burial was the interment of the body, and we may hence believe our firſt colonizers would have adopted this cuſtom, and which preceded the Daniſh hiſtory of burning, a ſucceeding rite introduced perhaps on their expedition from the Eaſt, while the Britiſh expedition, being diſtinct from the more Northern, exceeded thoſe times, and which ſome writers have ingenuouſly advanced. Probably the old Celtic or Scythic cuſtoms, both which are very ſimilar, may have adopted burial, and, on the introduction of the Druid religion, the old patriarchal rite might be changed to burning. Cæſar and Tacitus atteſt, that the Gauls burnt their dead, and we are here inclined to think the Britons did the ſame in thoſe days, but this does not afford the diſcrimination. The Druids were evidently ſubſequent to the diviſion of the antient Celts or Scythians into Germans, Teutones, and Spaniards, and the cuſtom of burning may be deduced from their time, which will agree with Cæſar, and the Northern writers may then have adopted it. After the Druid expulſion in the latter ages, burial may have been reſumed again. The barrows which contain urn and body burial, may have received theſe ceremonies at different periods, as I am well perſuaded was the caſe of the two diſtinct barrows opened by Stukeley. On ſearches made into theſe large barrows, I have evidently perceived the earth to have been diſturbed for the admiſſion of a ſubſequent depoſit, and the fragments of urns have proved a prior ſepulchral rite, a natural approximation to a ſpot of ground for the interment of the dead and rendered inviolate by the ſolemn denunciations of the moſt remote periods. There can be no deduction, therefore, made in this reſpect, but what muſt be the reſult of combination, and various other ſituations of burial, and as no inſcriptions or coins have yet been our guide in the enquiry, it muſt be the reſult of other inferences whereby we can approach the truth. The account of Roman coins diſcovered in a ſtone barrow in Cornwall, mentioned by Borlaſe, has but ſlender authority, and even the diſcovery itſelf will not decide, unleſs Roman veſſels, or other marks of Roman ſepulture, can be identified. I muſt not diſmiſs this note without a remark of ſome conſequence to the curious enquirer after theſe remains. It has been advanced, that the Welſh memorial verſes, on the *Graves of the Warriors of Britain*, point out to whom many of theſe monument belong. Camden, in his account of Merionethſhire, deſcribes the remains of a warrior found in a grave near [illegible], whole [illegible], by theſe verſes, is Gwrthmwl Wledig, a perſon often mentioned in old fragments of the Welſh hiſtory. By carefully examining theſe verſes, it is ſuppoſed many more of the graves of the Britiſh Princes would be aſcertained, the original name of the places mentioned on them being moſtly retained, particularly in Wales. Theſe facts, if aſcertained as ſuch, do not apply to a period before the ſeventh century, and ſince theſe graves may, on their opening, produce a diſcrimination between the lower and old Britiſh: if the body be found entire, it will corroborate the identity, and, in all probability, prove they were Chriſtian. If urns and aſhes are found, they may apply to an earlier period, and deſtroy the evidence of the bards

b,

as some distinctive and relative features may be occasionally traced in their interments, the most antient may be selected, and the curious enquiries of the historian more amply gratified.

As to the general description of British barrows, little more can be said than is found in Borlase, Stukeley's Works, and most of our county histories. Many quotations, from the most early writers, have been made, which only prove the universal adoption of raising artificial mounds of earth over the dead, to perpetuate their funeral honours. "Suæ sunt metis metæ." They were considered of a more lasting nature than other kinds of memorials. The obelisk or the pyramid may be rased to the ground, but the more humble structures of earth might withstand the despoiler's labour, and retain their identities to the period of the worlds destruction.

On comparing the contents of the large barrows, explored in various parts of England, Scotland, Ireland, and the adjacent isles, the greatest analogy will be found. Whether the rough-stone sarcophagus, the urn of unbaked or baked clay, the cist in the native soil which contains the bones of the body burnt, the body interred with or without earthen vessels, urns, or other relics, the similarity will in these countries be very apparent.

The many barrows of large magnitude which I have occasionally explored, containing urns with ashes, the body interred with and without earthen vessels, have afforded no decisive criterion to decide palpably on the owners; nor have I been successful in the discovery of any coins in them. From an information that coins were found in a large barrow levelled for the race-course at Newmarket, when the late Lord Bolingbroke was steward, I visited that place in March, 1791, with a view to open several of them on the Downs, in hopes of finding coins, the great desideratum of exploring the large barrows; but my labour was fruitless. Those near the Kings Chair contained urns and burnt bones of undoubted higher antiquity than the Danish inroads; one near the Bush, which had been carted away for the mould to level the exercise-ground, afforded an easy labour, having discovered in the native chalk, at a little depth, burnt bones with no vessel. The other barrows, which I dug into, were two of the groupe in the bottom, half a mile on the left hand of the Bury-road, leaving Newmarket in that direction: they were of considerable size; but, though several labourers were employed, and the excavation made upwards of 12 feet in diameter to the native soil, no relics whatever were found.

The barrow opened on Needham Plains was 30 feet in diameter, and 8 feet deep. In the centre on the level of the native soil were three vessels of brown earth, and the body interred; over the barrow some stones were laid; in short, the barrows on the plains[*] afforded similar specimens of urns to those found in all directions of Britain, and which are indiscriminately ascribed to the Britons, Saxons, or Danes. See VIGNETTE, fig. 2.

[*] The Rev. Mr. Ashby, of Barrow, in Suffolk, who is curious in all kind of antiquarian and natural history research, and who has amassed a considerable collection in both these pursuits, shewed me some specimens of urns and fragments from barrows in his neighbourhood, but no one with any typical marks of Roman workmanship, which convinces me of their claim to other nations.

In

In Kent, one of the large detached barrows was opened, which contained a large brown-coloured urn of unbaked clay, 10 inches high, and ſeven and a half in diameter, with a few burnt bones, the fragments ſo few in number, that they did not correſpond but to a ſmall proportion of the human body[1]; a circumſtance very common in urn-burial, and which, corroborating with antient authors, prove, by the pains taken to conſume the bones, and to reduce them into a ſmall compaſs, the greater the honour to have been ſhewn the remains of the dead[1] This urn is in my poſſeſſion, and engraved in the VIGNETTE to the *Great Barrows*, fig 1 A good ſpecimen to diſcriminate between the Roman and thoſe uſually called Britiſh.

Fig 2 VIGNETTE, is an urn of elegant form in my poſſeſſion, and, as I am informed, found in Hertfordſhire near St Albans, a circumſtance which I very much doubt The ſhape and ornaments upon it are of Etruſcan workmanſhip, but as the compoſition proves it to be of unbaked clay, or clay baked in the ſun, I have engraved it as a relic of extraordinary curioſity, as well from its appearance of the higheſt antiquity, as from the ſingular decoration of animals upon it, which decoration in intaglio was tooled out of the veſſel after it had been turned in the lathe, and which, in all probability, had been filled up with an artificial compoſition, periſhed by time But whether Etruſcan, or whether in reality found in this country, it is worthy of being preſerved as a ſpecimen of fine ſhape, and as being of a compoſition ſo very ſimilar to the veſſels found in the large barrows It is not entire, and the beſt ſide is repreſented in the engraving

The late Colonel Drax, of Dorſetſhire, ſhewed me, at his town-houſe in Portman-Square, ſeveral ſpecimens of relics found in barrows which he opened on the Downs in this county The contents of one barrow produced a ſkeleton, and near to which a conſiderable number of the Belemnites, evidently ſea-petrefactions, found frequently in chalk and other ſoils[3] Their ſize and form ſeem

[1] Snorro Sturleſon ſays, "the body of Odin was burnt in the moſt honourable manner, ſurrounded with the moſt elevated flames, and it was the belief in thoſe times, that, in proportion as the flames aſcended, the greater honour the dead received in the other world" From the ardent nature of ſuch fire, it is natural to conclude that moſt of the bones of the body would be conſumed Snorro's authority for Odin's Sepulchre, and his own comment grafted on it from the Greek and Latin poets, in relation to the funeral honours beſtowed on the dead

[illegible]
[illegible] Ἀχιλλεὺς,
[illegible]
[illegible] Il. Ψ.

[2] The urns attributed to the Northern nations diſcover the greateſt analogy See fig , N° 1 Plate XXIII where a ſmall urn of unbaked clay was found in a Saxon barrow, which proves that the cuſtom of depoſiting urns of unbaked clay with the dead was continued to the ſeventh century If any doubt ſhould ariſe of theſe veſſels not having paſſed the fire, their decompoſition in water will prove the fact The water being evaporated, will produce no ſalt, whereas the contrary will be found with thoſe that have paſſed the fire

[3] The Latins, from the Greek [illegible], called theſe foſſil *Belemnites*, from their reſemblance to the heads of arrows or darts, they were alſo called *Cerauniae*, *C[illegible]*, [illegible] *lapis*, and according to Dioſcorides, Theophraſtes, and Pliny, *lapis lyncurius*, from the Greek [illegible], quod [illegible] one [illegible] of their ſingularity, and of the abſurdity of antient conjecture Pliny [illegible], ſays the [illegible] ſet much ſtore by this ſtone, which he calls Ceraunia, and that it is only found where

5

seem to be well adapted for the p[illegible] [illegible] for which purpose [illegible] have been [illegible] of [illegible] [illegible] some of [illegible] letters or [illegible] and [illegible] people [illegible] [illegible] these [illegible] is engraved.

The most [illegible] of Greece [illegible] fig. 2, 3, 4, 5 [illegible] the [illegible] commonly [illegible] obelisk, from [illegible] figure [illegible], which puts [illegible]

wh[illegible] [illegible]

[illegible]

cleareſt light. Before the uſe of braſs or iron[1] the antient Greeks were [illegible] fairly armed in this rude manner, and, if we follow the evidence of [illegible], we may date this æra 1288 years before Chriſt.

The moſt convincing proofs of this ſtone's being conſidered under the double ſignification of the Belemnite, the dart-ſtone or the ceraunia, the thunder-ſtone, may be found on ſeveral early Grecian coins[2], and hence a [illegible] proof of their early adoption among the Greeks as darts or heads of [illegible], and an atteſtation of a ſtriking coincidence of the diſcovery of the [illegible] darts, or heads of arrows, in a Britiſh ſepulchre.

In December, 1782, I opened a large barrow on the eſtate of Sir Nar[illegible] D'Aeth, on Singleton-down, in [illegible] pariſh, in Kent, the depth and ſingularity of the excavation have induced me to mention it. The excavation in the [illegible]

[1] Hyginus *fab.* cclxxiv. Cadmus Agenoris filius *æs* [illegible] primus inventum [illegible]. The Arundelian [illegible] places the diſcovery of iron at the year 87 before the arrival of Cadmus in [illegible]. [illegible] Sext. Pomp. Feſtum, calls the arms of this nature *Sparos*, [illegible] flint or ſtone.

[2] Recherches ſur l'Origine et les Progrès des Arts de la Grèce, Lib. I. cap. [illegible] vols. quarto. See the Vignette to the firſt chapter of this work, where the coins of Apollonia illuſtrate the ſubject in the moſt happy manner poſſible, and which furniſh the reader with an introductory key to antient Mythology at the expence of little trouble.

Founded on analogy or the general compact of communities, metaphyſics, the Author [illegible] the mind with beings eaſily explained by words, but impoſſible to be repreſented by forms, and [illegible] offſpring of imagination, the configuration cannot be determined by natural repreſentation. Hence to inviſible [illegible] those of invention have been ſubſtituted, which were to ſupply the repreſentation [illegible] organs of ſight what words were to diſcourſe. This is exactly the ſource of all hieroglyphic writing, and in ſome reſpects letters themſelves. It is the key to Egyptian hieroglyphics, and evidently [illegible] briefly proved, the key to Grecian mythology. Theſe belemnites, or marine petrifactions, being found in the earth, were by the common people conſidered as the produce of thunder, hence they received the name of *Ceraunites*, or thunder ſtones: the firſt expreſſing the uſe of the *belemnites*, the ſecond marking the idea entertained of their origin. The common people, who in all countries prefer the marvellous to truth, have preſerved this very antient opinion, and artiſts availing themſelves of the name of theſe ſtones, and the idea entertained of their origin, adopted the belemnite as the repreſentation of thunder-bolt. Thus, to repreſent the diſcharge of thunder, artiſts have adopted the form of [illegible] ſtones, antiently uſed as darts, or arrow-heads, and, by oppoſing two together, the [illegible] known things, they could indicate the action of lightning in all directions. See Vignette [illegible]. The eye, confeſſing the things preſented before it, brought to the mind the analogy of the [illegible] to the ſubject which it was deſirous of recalling to the conception, thus the figure of the [illegible] the ſubject appears to expreſs the nature and the effect. By giving the thunder-bolt a [illegible] the whirlwind was indicated through which the bolt was darted, and as the lightning [illegible] the clouds, formed by the circumambient waters, the figure was ſurrounded by the leaves of an [illegible] plant. See Vignette, fig. 4. Theſe leaves, which ſurround the ſymbol of the thunder-bolt, [illegible] of Linnæus, more generally known by the name of *Typha*. To indicate the lightning which [illegible] the thunder, darts of ejected fire, in all directions, were alſo prefixed to the bolt, and [illegible], to expreſs the prodigious velocity of this formidable meteor, the terror which it inſpires, and its irreſiſtible power, the wings of the eagle were alſo introduced to it. See Vignette, fig. 3. The [illegible] conſidered the eagle as, of all other birds, the moſt rapid in flight, and the ſovereign, was for this reaſon armed with the thunder-bolt in its talons. See Vignette, fig. 3. [illegible] Rech. ſur l'Orig. et les Prog. des Arts de la Grèce, and the Vignette, fig. [illegible], where the eagle is placed on the medal extracted from the above work.

Accuſtomed by the poets to hear the rays of the ſun compared to darts, "Sagittarum nomine non [illegible] radiorum ictus oſtenditur," Macrobius lib. I. the artiſts repreſented the ſun under the figure of Apollo, and he was thus armed with bow and arrow; but long before this period, the darts then uſed were the belemnites, and hence the [illegible] became the ſymbol of the ſun. See Pliny, lib. xxxvi. c. viii. "Obeliſcos vocantes ſolis numini ſacratos. Radiorum ejus argumentum in effigie eſt, et ita ſignificatur nomine Ægyptio," and thus [illegible] to the expreſſion of the poets, "[illegible] [illegible], longe jaculans, jaculum ſpiculi, petens jaculum." See Vignette, fig. [illegible] medal of Apollonia where the belemnites form the glory round the head of Apollo, and from which ſymbol the antient artiſts derived this prefiguration, which has been retained to modern times.

chalk,

chalk over which [illegible] as [illegible] deep, the barrow on the superfices [illegible] feet [illegible] in [illegible], [illegible] feet [illegible] [illegible] [illegible] [illegible] excavation, [illegible] proved [illegible] ferred. The form [illegible] of an inverted cone, at the bottom [illegible] square hole in the [illegible] two [illegible] [illegible] [illegible] depth, which appeared to [illegible] contained the [illegible] urns, or the [illegible] without [illegible], are [illegible] very shallow in the native soil [illegible] sometimes [illegible] ground, and oftentimes in the mound itself[1].

The [illegible] hill at Silbury, generally considered as a barrow, was [illegible] under the direction of the late Duke of Northumberland [illegible], under the impression of its being a place of sepulture. Miners from [illegible] were employed, and great labour bestowed on it. The [illegible] the bottom, and which Colonel Drax shewed me, [illegible] by burning the end of it [illegible] was [illegible]. We proved [illegible], which had been so reported. The smell of vegetable [illegible] vinced the Colonel of his mistake. He had a [illegible] over a Druid oak, and he thought the remains of it [illegible] the excavation. There was, however, no reason for concluding [illegible] place of sepulture by the digging into it. [illegible] Stukeley, and his assertion of a monarch being buried there, [illegible] line of conception to recommend it. It is not likely the monarch would have been buried near its surface, when such an immense mound of earth [illegible] raised for the purpose, and the time in raising of it would not [illegible] nature of a funeral obsequy, which must require a greater degree of [illegible].

In looking over my notes, I find no barrows which I have opened [illegible] cular forms, or of sufficient importance, to distinguish from those [illegible] Stukeley, Borlase, Plot, Dugdale, Hutchins, and several others of our [illegible] historians. My great object was to discover coins, inscriptions, or [illegible] to establish a descriptive relation, and to serve as undoubted principles for [illegible] application.

I discovered a singular barrow in the centre of the Watling-Street road, on the crest of the hill ascending from Rochester to Canterbury, this barrow [illegible] compressed, and is on the right hand of the Canterbury road, which runs into the Watling Street, a little above the spot. After breaking [illegible] the road which consisted of moderate-sized boulder-stones I dug to the depth of four feet, and found a skeleton, which appeared, by the mould and dust round it, to have

[1] These [illegible] hills I have often [illegible] considered as temples to the [illegible] people [illegible] of the Scythian [illegible] religious rites [illegible] similar to those of the [illegible] Holy Wain. They are frequently found [illegible] and sometimes within [illegible] Castles. See Canterbury, Cambridge, Windsor, and many others. [illegible] the Donjon hill, evidently preceded the Roman station, [illegible] the site. In Somersetshire there is one of these [illegible] hills, called [illegible] Plate XLIV. Stukeley's Iter VI. Belvoir, the seat of the Duke of Rutland, [illegible] one of these hills. [illegible] hills were used, [illegible] remote period, to [illegible] fortified towns. [illegible] 2 [illegible] "And he shall make a fort [illegible] Calais, [illegible] on a tower of the Swift, called one of [illegible]

been

was interred in a coffin, and kept uncommonly dry from the superincumbent pressed with stones. Near the body was an iron knife, which, by comparing with the knives found in the small barrows, appear to be very similar. I have been hence inclined to consider this as a Saxon grave, and which seems to be of a low period, from the Roman road having been then apparently disused[1]. To discover the breadth and boundary of the road, I had the soil pierced with an iron crow in all directions, and by which means I had the most unequivocal proofs, as well from the known tract of the Watling Street, as from the nature of the soil being chalk, to ascertain the fact.

In the parish of [illegible], near Godalming, in Surrey, close to the division of the county of Sussex, on the 8th of November, 1790, I opened a very large barrow, at a place called Gostead[2], and traditionally preserved by the country people under the name of Golden-hoard, from a conception, by its size and structure, of its containing a treasure: the only treasures found were the remains of a skeleton, and brown vessel of unbaked clay, usually placed in our large barrows. The vessel, from the fragments of the rim and the application of the fragments, might measure about 9 inches in height, and 1 foot in diameter at the mouth. It fell to pieces on taking out: there was no appearance of burnt bones near it, and it is hence reasonable to suppose it was not intended for that purpose. Near the skeleton were some trifling fragments of corroded brass, probably the remains of a clasp or buckle.

The base of the barrow was about 30 feet to the level of the soil, and its elevation about four. The ground on which it is situated commands an extensive prospect towards the North-east, and is the highest of any in the neighbourhood. Before the field had been tilled, it had been considerably elevated above the surface of the earth, and, within the memory of man, it has been considerably depressed by successive plowings over its summit.

The labourers broke into the centre, with a trench 6 feet by 10, to admit of room for a circuitous research; less than two feet from the summit the mound gave evident signs of its having been disturbed from the base of the monument, by the wood ashes blended with it, and the irregular appearance of the soil. At the depth of four feet, the base of the barrow, there was a circular hearth of the iron stone of the neighbourhood pitched in boulders, the size of a man's fist, the diameter of which extended about 10 feet; this had probably served for the hearth of a funeral fire, perhaps for sacrifice, the body not being burnt, by the stratum of wood ashes that covered it, and by the blackness of the superficies of the stones.

[1] See a memoir on the Roman road, *Ad Portum* ... Plate XC. p. 99.

[2] In the parish register, 1590, it is written Gosthoard. If this name may be considered as a corruption of Goldhead, which is not very likely, the large barrow may probably have been the burial place of a single family of the spot, which, from its very retired and woody neighbourhood, could not have been much peopled. Imagination may therefore [illegible] to etymon, and try the name of the spot compounded with the British Cawr, or Gawr, giant, or powerful man, and the Saxon stede, a dwelling. Hence the Saxon prefix to the British Cor, the dwelling-place of the powerful man, and a proof of the barrow being more early than the Saxon era, which, waving conjecture, it doubtless must be from the nature of the contents. The Saxons, it is already proved, p. 5, note, burned their dead on their arrival before their conversion to Christianity, and, after their conversion, their barrows were not of this magnitude, and their vessels very different. See the Plate to Dr. Brown's Hydriot.

To

To enumerate other barrows of this description would only be a repetition of similar remains of sepulture, and the discrimination being sufficiently explained, I shall here select some of the best specimens, which, having many curious particularities connected with them, will probably be deemed of some importance to this kind of research, and for which the reader will doubtless feel himself much indebted to the accuracy of Mr H Rooke, of Woodhouse-Place, near Mansfield, in Nottinghamshire. This gentleman, with much diligence and well-informed enquiry in these pursuits, has already proved himself a great acquisition to the Society of Antiquaries, and it would only be considered as a redundancy of panegyric, to attempt a further addition to that esteem which is now universally bestowed on his labours.

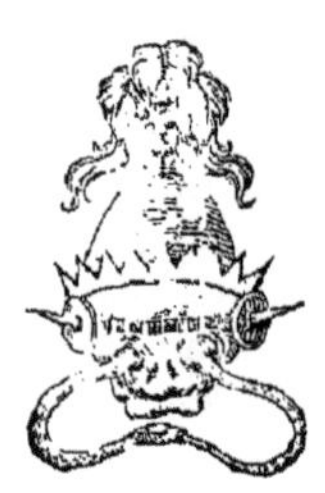

PLATE XXXIV.

NUMBER 1. PLAN of the CIRQUES[1] and BARROWS on STANTON-MOOR, in the PEAK of DERBYSHIRE. The description which here follows is Mr. H. Rooke's. "Towards the North-east end of Stanton-Moor is a small Druid circle, inclosed with a vallum of earth and stones, not raised above two

[1] These circular monuments have been discussed by various writers, but by none so elaborately as by Borlase. See his Cornwall, chap. VII. He has shewn their affinity to the patriarchal customs, and this idea, with the Scythic and Belgic history, may establish the remote period of their erection. Rowland conjectures, in his *Mona Antiqua*, that the expulsion of the Pagan Britons, under Druid influence, by Christian pursuit, more efficacious than the Roman sword, caused the ancient inhabitants to fly to Norway and Denmark; hence the circular erections of stones, *Cromlechs*, and other similar remains, found in Britain, had their rise; hence similar relics also in Ireland, which he did not recollect had been peopled from Norway, and where the Scaldry had been so long preserved. Their preceding date to the Danish invasion is evidenced by the elliptical erection of stones near Castel Gyt[illegible], in Carnarvonshire, forty-two in number, between two mountains, a spot where the Danes never visited, and which Rowland thinks is likely to have been raised by these people, as the pillars of Tadmor, or the pyramids of Egypt. To support this argument there is another proof, which will finally exclude the Danish claim: the Danes, at the period of their invasion, used Runic letters on their sepulchral erections, and which doubtless would be occasionally discovered on these cirques in Cornwall, Britain, Scotland, and Ireland. Woden's law has this injunction for sepulchral perpetuity: "Ut super Regum et principum sepulcra, *magnos terræ tumulos* in æternam memoriam congererent, atque ut alio[illegible] *literis Runicis* inscriptos erigerent lapides super eorum sepulcra, qui rem [illegible]." Many of the names of places in the Isle of Anglesey agree with the distinct order of the Druids described by Strabo, Cæsar, and Tacitus, and in which places are formed the cirques and other remains of the ancient Britons peculiar to their religious and sepulchral customs. The circular ranges of erected stones in the Western Isles of Scotland are to this day called *Drum Cranny*, the Druids circle (see Martin), and believed by tradition to have been their temples. Nor can this tradition be accounted incredible, when it is well known that the Druid religion prevailed in Europe many years after the introduction of Christianity. See Concil. Nant. Labb., tom. IX. p. 4[illegible]. Hence, if these cirques of stones contiguous to sepulchres be not Danish, it is evident the sepulchres are also not Danish. And this will then be established by [illegible] others under similar circumstances, and every reasonable inference deduced to place the large barrows, generally discovered on moors and plains, to a period prior to the Roman conquest of Britain.

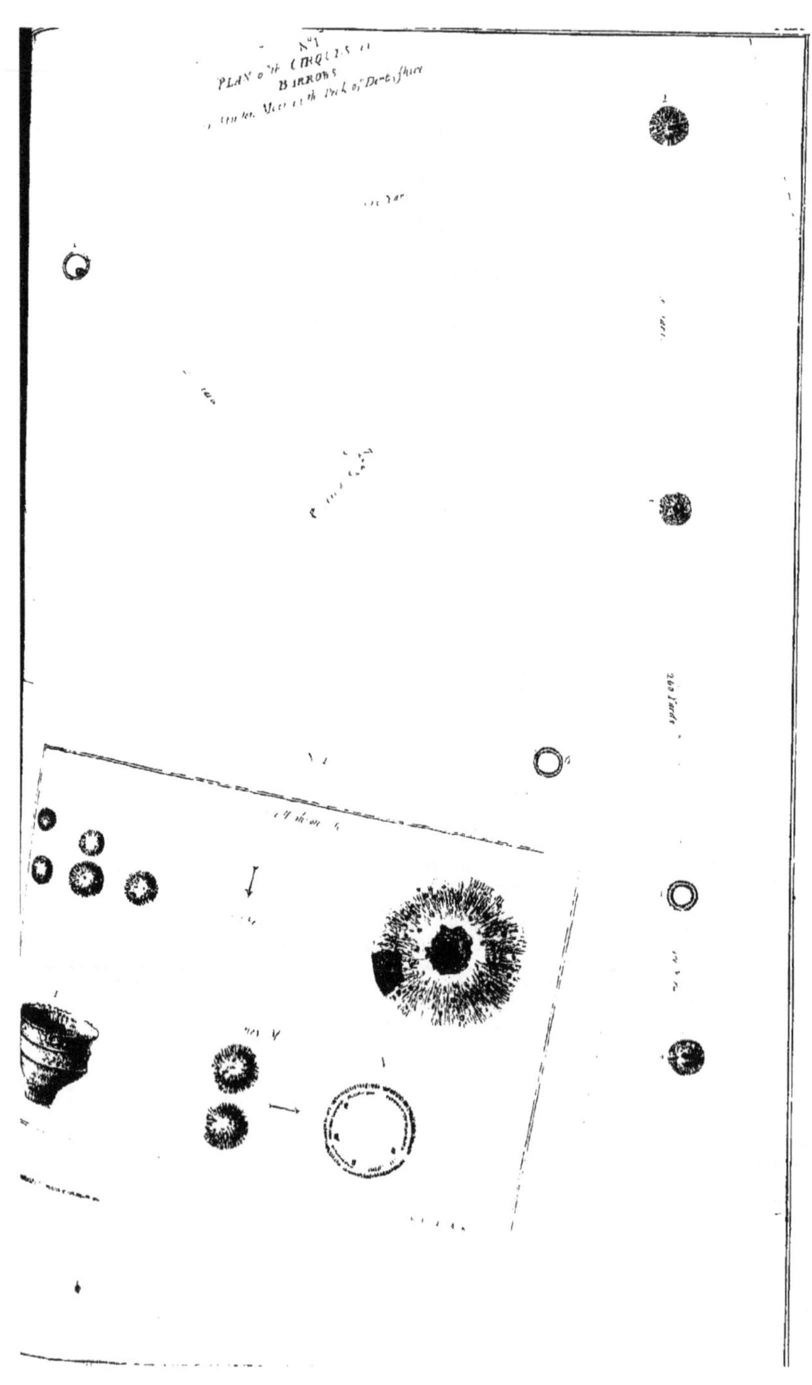
PLAN
BARROWS
260 Yards

two feet, within this at the West end, was a little barrow, about [illegible] feet [illegible]meter, very little higher than the natural soil. Upon opening it, I found three large urns of coarse clay, placed in a row, about 8 inches from each other; they rested upon stones, but had none on their sides or tops; they stood but little below the native soil, and within 12 or 14 inches of the top of the barrow; being so near the surface, the hard stones and the roots of fern and gorse, which had penetrated the urns, made it difficult to move them without their falling to pieces, however, I contrived to preserve sufficient of one to make a drawing of it, which I have sent you. In taking out the ashes and bones in this urn, I found towards the bottom a small urn full of burnt bones, and covered with a round piece of clay; this I have quite perfect, of which likewise you have a drawing. See these URNS, fig. 3. and 4. VIGNETTE to p. 155. which have been engraved as good specimens of our very antient sepulchral vessels, and as facts which may be relied on.

The very singular manner in which these Druid circles and barrows are placed is worthy of notice; you will observe, by the plan I have sent you, that the three barrows and Druid circle, N° 4, lie in a direct line, and N° 2, 3, and 4, are at equal distance; the circles, N° 1 and 6, are in a straight line with the single stone, called The King, 34 yards from the Druid temple of the Nine Ladies (which I mentioned in the sixth volume of the Archaeologia), and are at equal distance, as you will see by the plan.

The placing the circles and barrows in so regular a manner, was probably for some mysterious purpose, which we are ignorant of, therefore, can only form conjectures. May not the circles, N° 1. and 6, enclose the sepulchres of the principal Druids of this district, and placed near the temple, where they presided as priests or chief magistrates? for circles of erect stones were used for

That circular erections of stones were intended by the Northern nations for sepulchral purposes seems evident from Olaus Magnus, c. xv. The whole passage is curious, as evincing the high antiquity of these monuments in the North; and as this passage in Olaus has not been quoted by any of our Antiquaries to elucidate this research, I shall transcribe it at full length. "Among the Ostrogoths, Vestrogoths [illegible], and also in vast deserts which have been at remote periods desolated by plague, famine, and war, [illegible] high stone obelisks, [illegible]. These stones are skilfully and wonderfully raised in many places, from ten to 15 and 30 feet in length, [illegible] or 6 feet in breadth; characters are inscribed upon them, [illegible] distinguished order for certain purposes of their erection. By [illegible] they [illegible], by a *square* [illegible] troops of warriors, by a *round order*, the burial of families [illegible] *wedge-like* order, that [illegible] the spot where armies of foot or horse had been victorious. The writing is [illegible] the top [illegible] to the bottom. The letters have the thickness and length of the middle finger of a man. [illegible] of them, by weather and [illegible], are defaced, particularly those at the bottom of the stones, yet the following interpretations [illegible]: '[illegible] for my country, having killed thirty two armed men, was at last slain by the champion [illegible] and with my sword put about me, rest in this spot.' 'I [illegible] other men seek by war, deserve memorial [illegible].'

[illegible] Monte [illegible] Alexander [illegible]

civil as well as religious purposes The small urn might possibly contain the ashes of a favourite child, these barrows and circles, being contiguous to the many Druidical remains in this neighbourhood, favour this conjecture The rocking stones on Rowtor, Bradley, and Cratcliff rocks, are all within half a mile of these barrows Another reason for the above suggestion is, that wherever I have met with barrows on the Derbyshire Moors, I have always found the remains of Druid temples (or circles of erect stones) near them It is natural to imagine, that the Druids, and those that belonged to that order, would be desirous of having their ashes deposited near their sacred groves and temples

I must observe to you, that I only paced the distances marked in the plan; the weather was so very bad the whole time I was out, that I could use no other method of measuring, however, I believe they are pretty exact"

Measurements of the CIRQUES and BARROWS on Stanton Moor, in the Peak of Derbyshire, according to the annexed plan

N° 1. CIRQUE, nine yards one foot diameter, surrounded with a vallum of earth and stones, within the circle was a small barrow, in which were three large urns, and one was a small urn. See VIGNETTE, fig 4

N° 2 A barrow chiefly of stone, 60 yards in circumference; it had been opened at one end and in the middle.

N° 3 A stone barrow, 55 yards in circumference, had been opened in the middle

N° 4 CIRQUE, 11 yards diameter, with a vallum of earth and stones

N° 5. A stone barrow, 53 yards in circumference, had been opened in the middle

N° 6 CIRQUE, 16 yards diameter; with a vallum of earth and stones.

N° 7 Nine stones, 11 yards diameter, called the Nine Ladies

N° 8 A single stone, 34 yards West of the Nine Stones, called The King These circles and barrows run in a straight line.

N° 2, 3, 4, 5. are in a line, N° 1 and 6. are in a line with the single stone N° 8. and are at equal distances

[1] Archæologia, vol VI p 114
[2] Ibid p 112
[3] Ibid

HIGHLOW-

HIGHLOW MOOR

N° 2

ON HIGHLOW MOOR, in Derbyshire, about two miles from Hatherfage in the Peak, are several lowes or tumuli of earth and stone, the largest is 189 feet in circumference, near it are five small ones, which are now very flat at the top. See Plan, N° 2.

ABNEY MOOR

At the east end of Abney Moor, adjoining Highlow Moor, is a small circle of stones, 93 feet diameter, enclosed with a vallum of earth and stones, within it are four upright large stones. In the year 1755 there were nine large stones standing at equal distances; near it are two small lowes. See PLAN, N° 3. On these and Offerton moors are many lowes of various sizes, and several have been destroyed for roads and walls.

It has been observed, that where there are any very large lowes, small ones have been scattered near them; in the large lowes urns have been found, sometimes single, and sometimes four in a lowe, also beads and rings.

In a paper I lately sent to our Society, giving an account of some Druidical remains [illegible], I mentioned the above lowes, but sent no drawings of them.

The Peak of Derbyshire is not without Roman monuments; upon a hill, called [illegible], belonging to the West end of [illegible] Park, are traces of a Roman work, of an oblong shape, which takes in almost the whole hill, but the exact dimensions are now very difficult to make out. On the South end of this work is a tumulus, which I opened, and found near the bottom a small urn, [illegible], it was placed between two stones set edgeways, and one on the top; it is made of very coarse clay, and not ornamented, [illegible], the height four inches three quarters, diameter at the top, to the outside edge, five inches three quarters. See Fig. 1.

PLATE XXXV.

N° 1.

KARN on Stack-houſe Scar, about two miles and a half from Settle, in Craven, Yorkſhire, on very high, rocky, and barren land; it is formed entirely of looſe ſtones, 73 yards in circumference, and there are the remains of a Cromlech in the centre of it. See the drawing: two of the upright ſtones, A and B were ſtanding in the year 1778. A five feet high, and three feet eight inches broad, B four feet in height, C a ſtone fallen down, three feet in height, and ſeven feet in length, D appears to have been the tranſverſe ſtone on the top when the Cromlech was entire. This ſtone is ſix feet nine inches by five. FIG. 3. PENY-GENT-HILL.[*]

At about 32 yards Eaſt of this Karn is an aſſemblage of rocks (ſee DRAWING, N° 2), in the ſtone (A) is a rock baſon, with a lip to carry off the water when at a certain height, near the bottom of the ſame ſtone is a ſpout cut in the ſide, which ſeems as if intended to convey water from another rock (B) now tumbled down, and which probably was part of the ſtone (b), which has a ſpout at the top. FIG. 3. PENYGENT-HILL. I could not diſcover any more Druidical remains in this tract.

MINING LOWE.

N° 2.

Letter of Mr. ROOKE.

"WHEN I had laſt the pleaſure of communicating to you a little account of the tumuli in Derbyſhire, I had not then ſeen Mining Lowe, laſt ſummer I viſited that very magnificent ſepulchral monument, where on the top appeared five kiſtvaens; theſe were diſcovered ſome years ago in removing the earth and ſtones from the top, for making the walls which now incloſe the plantation round the tumulus; the kiſtvaens had been all opened, and I was told that an iron ſword, with the handle of one entire piece, was found in that marked (2) in the PLAN. They vary in their poſitions, ſome ſtand nearly Eaſt and Weſt, others North and South.

[*] Probably a religious erection to the ſun.

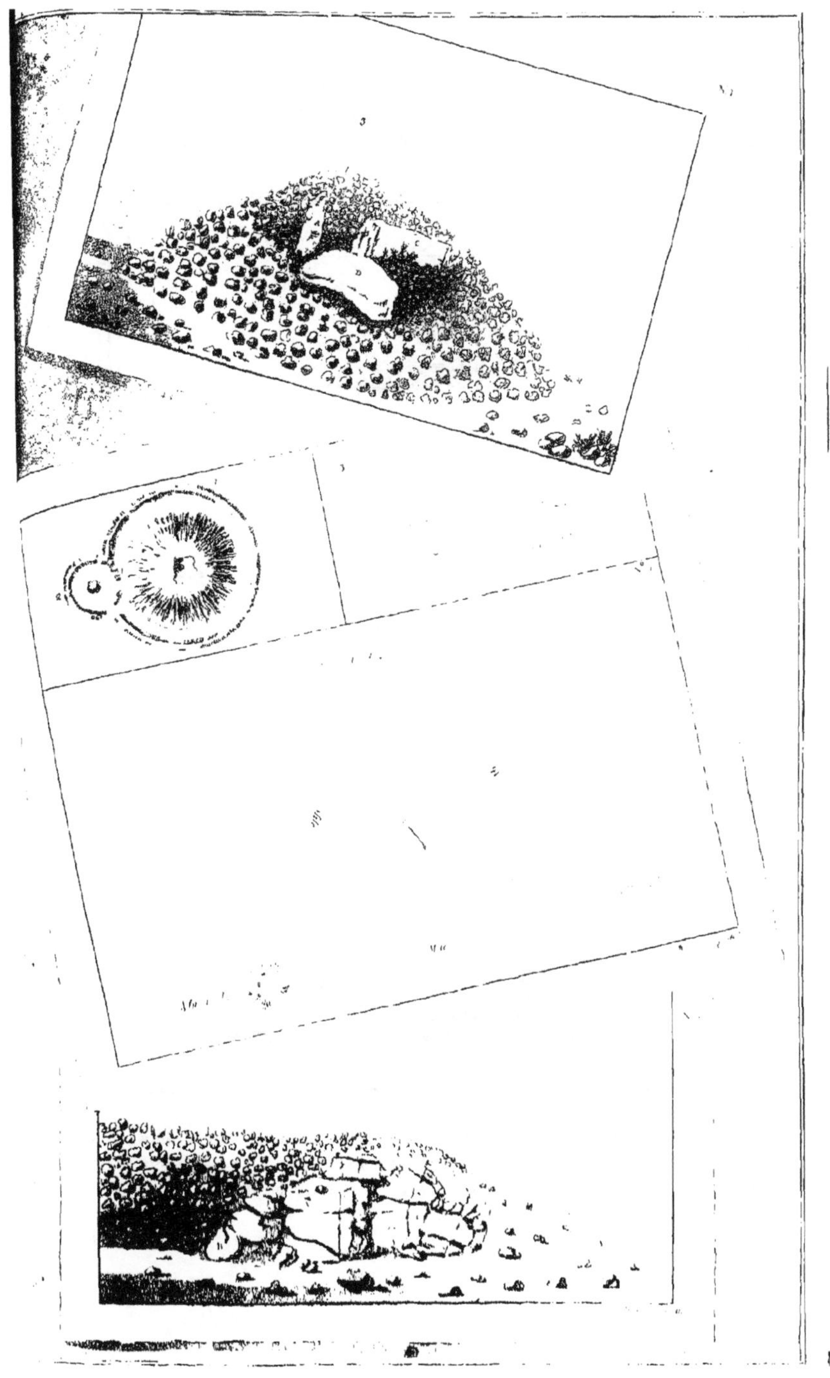

N° 2. A plan of the top of Mining Lowe, 81 feet diameter, with the situations of five kistvaens, (2) (3) (4) (5) (6), (A) in N° 1 is a perspective view of the kistvaen marked (2) in the plan, which stands nearly East and West; the top stone is nine feet by six, (B) is a ground plan of the same, length eight feet,

width three feet six inches, depth five feet eight inches; four unhewn stones form the sides, and two the ends; (C) the inside view of the kistvaen marked (5) in the plan. The circumference of this lowe at the base is 1348 feet. This plan was taken in May, 1786.

"The

"The diameter of the present top of the tumulus (for I look upon it to have been originally one third higher) 81 feet, the circumference at the base 1348 feet; this is by far the largest lowe in Derbyshire, and may be looked upon as the second in England, exceeded only by Silbury-hill, near Marlborough, which is [illegible] feet in circumference.

"Hence, I think, every one [illegible] to suppose that Minning Lowe was a family burying place of some very considerable person[1]. We [illegible] the ancients increased the size of their tumuli according to the rank of the person deposited; this, therefore, must have been intended for a person of consequence, probably a British king, who had distinguished himself in the service of his country. It [illegible] on the highest part of the Moors about four miles [illegible], and one from the Lowe with a Kistvaen in Ballington Moor, which I mentioned to you in a former letter.

"*Woodhouse, Dec.* 30, 1786."

"In the last letter I had the pleasure of receiving from you, I think you expressed a wish to have a perspective view of MINNING LOWE; engagements in Lincolnshire and Cheshire have been the occasion of my not complying with your request sooner. On my return, I again examined that Lowe, and find I must have made a mistake in the account I sent you of the measurement of its circumference, which might be owing to the difficulty I had in getting round a very thick plantation. I now find the circumference on the outside of the wall to be about 300 yards. At forty two yards from the East side is a small lowe, 39 yards in circumference.

"At about a mile South east of Minning Lowe is Colledge Lowe, 60 yards in circumference, not on so elevated a situation, but commanding an extensive view; it appears to have had a vallum of earth round it. On the East side, about three yards from the base, is a circular vallum of earth, 27 yards in circumference, inclosing a small lowe, 12 yards in circumference. See PLATE XXXV. in the PLAN, N° 1 and 2.

"I find most of these great lowes have small ones annexed to them, and there is something singular in the position: Minning, Colledge, and Stone Lowe (of which I formerly sent you an account), form an equilateral triangle, whose sides are about one mile in length. See the PLAN, N° 3 PLATE XXXV. It evidently appears, in many places, that the ancient Britons paid great attention to the placing their lowes, undoubtedly for some mysterious purpose. Those on Stanton Moor and those above mentioned have fallen under my observation.

"*Woodhouse, Oct.* 7, 1787."

[1] Probably the mound of earth was raised before the stone coffins, and [illegible] for a succeeding interment.

PLATE

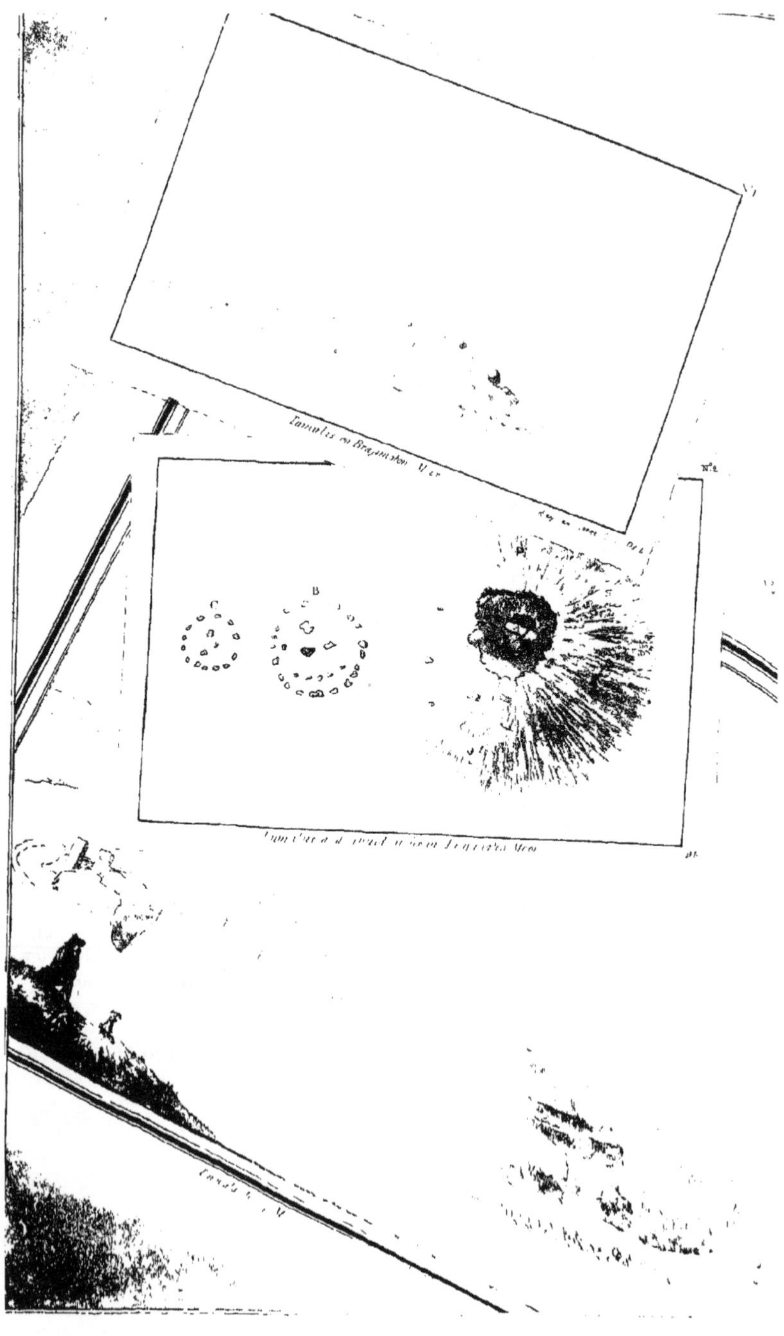

PLATE XXXVI.

On Braſſington Moor, in the Peak of Derbyſhire, two miles South of the village of Elton, is a large tumulus of earth and ſtone, 360 feet in circumference (ſee N° 1. and 2 of PERSPECTIVE VIEW and PLAN), great part of the top has been taken down for the repair of walls, but there are ſtill the remains of a kiſtvaen The large ſtone (A) in the plan is ſix feet in length, and ſeems to have been placed at the top, under it is a hollow place, about three or four feet deep, probably the ſeat of the kiſtvaen, an oblong ſtone lies near it, which might have been one of the ſides, the reſt have been taken away for the purpoſes above-mentioned On the Eaſt ſide of the tumulus is a circle of ſtones not exceeding two feet in height, the diameter of the circle 39 feet At about fifteen feet from this is a leſſer one, 22 feet diameter. See (B) and (C) in the PLAN

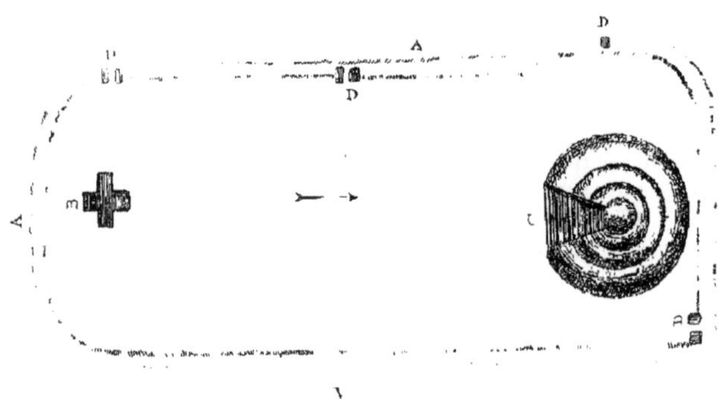

THE TINEWALD.

N° 3.

AN artificial mount in the Isle of Man, on which the kings of the island were formerly inaugurated [1], the tradition of which custom is preserved to this day, and confirmed by the present custom of promulgating all new laws from it for the government of the island, which are called the acts of Tinewald [2]. This antient place of inauguration is surrounded with a ditch, see A, A, A, A, A, within which, at the end facing the steps, is a small church, B, where, previous to the publication of any new laws, the chief magistrates attend divine service. The entrance into this area is through some upright stone columns with transverse imposts, D, somewhat like those of Stone-

[1] The late Captain Grose favoured the author with this drawing, which he took for him at his request several years before [illegible] the [illegible] of it in a lecture on Stonehenge, [illegible] which he considered [illegible] key to that [illegible], which has so often excited the curiosity and abilities of many learned men.

[2] The word Tin, or Dinn, in british, sharp, terrible, severe [illegible] Greek, Δ[illegible]. This word [illegible] [illegible], [illegible], fabulous genius. In the Islandic, Tin is an assembly of the people, [illegible] a field [illegible] Worm. Mon. Dan. p. 53. Dinc publicum, Ding-stad [illegible] Sedes tribunalis, or [illegible] Keller, [illegible] [illegible], [illegible] Ejus eum etiam Ajebn hus appellatum in [illegible] [illegible] quod idem est ac locus judicii subsequentis [illegible] various other sorts of election under the oak groves, or other trees, which were called Tings. In Mythol. xiv. "Eddæ Dii quotidie sub [illegible] judicia exercuisse perhibentur." There is an election at this day of the mayor of Rochester under [illegible] tree [illegible] of this city. This coincidence of etymon and custom should appear sufficiently convincing to establish the nature of the Tinwald.

henge,

[illegible], and the ascent of steps formed in the [illegible]. Most of these [illegible] are now down. The TINEWALD is about three miles [illegible] in [illegible] from thence to Douglas. There is no [illegible] its erection, [illegible] considered of [illegible].

This engraving [illegible] made to [illegible] [illegible] upright [illegible] [illegible] probably [illegible] acceptable [illegible] to the [illegible] his enquiries into the [illegible] monument on Salisbury Plain, notwithstanding [illegible] learned and ingenious men, [illegible] doubted [illegible] investigation [illegible] is [illegible] from the [illegible] henge? The [illegible] of the piece, [illegible] of these erections [illegible]

[illegible]

* [illegible] magnificent [illegible] [illegible]

[illegible]

Northern writers, customs and names of places derived from the old British word *Ting* in this country, seem to point at their remote antiquity, and when analogy, the strong concurrence is produced, when the indubitable record is wanting, it should seem surprizing that the human mind will not rest satisfied with such an arbitration.

By comparing the trilithons of the Tinwald to those of Stonehenge, their magnitude and shape should seem to prove a contemporary date, or a similarity of custom, preserved perhaps by a similar people in posterior times.

If the Isle of Man may be considered as a resort of the Britons, under the conduct of their chief leaders or Druids, on their expulsion by the Romans [*], and if, by combining the known antiquity of the *ting* with the nature of this event, and with the natural supposition of this sequestered island, so well

Northern regions had received the rough stone erections at periods much subsequent to those when the Cirques, Kistvaens, Cromlechs, and Logan stones were erected in Britain.

Olaus Magnus, lib. i. c. xviii. says, [illegible] in Sweden stones of great height are raised and wonderfully joined together like [illegible], and which he describes exactly like the trilithons at Stonehenge, [illegible] they are raised by the strength of giants, with upright and great stones over them. [illegible] of Scania, [illegible] of these stones are seen, [illegible] with [illegible] on them, which have been considered as Runic inscriptions. He attributes them to the Goths and Northern nations.

The builders of Stonehenge, from their skill in architecture, so fully proved, must also have been well informed in the property of the lever, inclined plane, and pulley to raise such stones, and the wonder of bringing the stones from a rock or quarry, eleven miles distant, must vanish when many hands and the multiplicity of cattle to draught be considered, and which a gregarious people, like the antient Britons, were so equal to. The Northern writers have described the transport of immense stones to decorate the sepulchres of their chiefs, and when we compare the raising of the enormous Agglestone on a barrow near Poole [illegible] in the Isle of Purbeck, computed 400 tons in weight, [illegible] evidently raised by human art by a similar people to the erectors of Stonehenge, [illegible] Holmen in Constantine parish, Cornwall, the work also of a similar people, the wonder of raising the stones at Stonehenge, and their transport must vanish before the most cursory investigation of human effort. The immense stone which serves for the base of the equestrian statue of the Czar Peter at St. Petersburg, far exceeding in weight any of the stones here discussed, was transported from the plains of Moscow by the simple construction of the lever and roller, and a simple contrivance of framework. [illegible] were the only requisites to accomplish the business, and, on the consideration of an army, or body of people, inactive and subsisting on personal produce in great numbers, and having [illegible] leisure to raise this structure, it seems surprizing the human mind will still rather adopt [illegible] founded on the indisputable proof of experiment, and an experiment [illegible] in a remote and modern period. See Pliny, Hist. Nat. lib. xxxvi. c. ix. on the [illegible] obelisks from the quarry, and transporting them from Egypt to Rome, and the raising [illegible] It is a vain conceit of the moderns to suppose an early people had no ingenuity to accomplish such a work of [illegible].

In all probability the [illegible] at Stonehenge, an open country, well adapted for their purpose. [illegible] to this British monument seems to prove their acquaintance [illegible] which is well known they practised in all their dwellings in this country. The [illegible] Saxon word from [illegible], or D[illegible], and [illegible] the [illegible] Saxon [illegible], as also of the Seven [illegible], or Seven brothers, [illegible] on Matlock Moor in Derbyshire. [illegible] be admitted, the [illegible] on the subject, [illegible] Cambrensis, Ranulph, and Geffrey of Monmouth, may be accounted for, and [illegible] The stones of the monument were certainly [illegible] from the adjacent parts of the plain, [illegible] have been formed. It is also [illegible] to be found on chalk downs. [illegible] was the spot, eleven miles from Stonehenge, [illegible] component parts of the [illegible] are [illegible], similar to the blocks of stone of the external circle of the antient piles, and the name of the spot [illegible], should seem to account sufficiently for the tradition of their being brought from Ireland, and the marvelous tales of the monk on the subject [illegible] fully and superstitious [illegible] delighted.

[*] The assertion of Strabo, that the Roman [illegible] to extirpate the Druids, without success [illegible] is curiously confirmed by the [illegible] of the Druid religion [illegible] in Ireland and Scotland. See [illegible] p. 5[illegible], and [illegible] Vallancey's Collect. de Reb. Hib.

adapted for the preſervation of ſuch antient remains, it will be a probable inference for comparing it to the venerable ſtructure of Stonehenge. We may thus be enabled to clear the way, through groundleſs conjecture and ſpeculation, for the admiſſion of a natural interpretation, and approach the fact by identities that are generally acknowledged.

That both religious and judicial ceremonies may have been uſed at these places ſeems poſſible from the antient church within the area of the Tinwald, conſecrated in all probability, on the Pagan ſpot, to Chriſtian worſhip. See Plan, which compare with a Britiſh incloſure, called *Tan Ben y Cefn*[1]. Mona Antiqua, Plate III.

[1] It is not improbable but the Tinwald may have been originally a large tumulus, and ſelected for the purpoſe of inauguration by a ſucceeding people. Mounts were alſo uſed for military orations, a natural convenience for diſtinguiſhing a particular character to the ſurrounding crowd. Dion Caſſius ſays, that Queen Boadicea delivered her military harangue from a heap of *turf*, a proof that the Romans had this cuſtom, and which was applied to the Britons; but this is confirmed by Plutarch, who ſays, "when news was brought to Pompey of the death of Mithridates, he was placed on pack-ſaddles, there being no *military mount* near the army."

ARGUMENT.

——— EHEU,
QUAM TEMERE IN NOSMET LEGEM SANCIMUS INIQUAM!
NAM VITIIS NEMO SINE NASCITUR: OPTIMUS ILLE EST
QUI MINIMIS URGETUR
——— ——— ——— ———
——— ET MIHI DULCES
IGNOSCENT, SI QUID PECCAVERO STULTUS, AMICI;
INQUE VICEM ILLORUM PATIAR DELICTA, LIBENTER.

HOR. LIB. I. SAT. III.

ON the occaſional diſcovery of the ſmall barrows in cluſters, they have been variouſly applied by hiſtorians and antiquaries, and there can be no doubt but many errors and miſtaken concluſions, from the want of ſatisfactory materials, muſt appear in their writings. An aſſertion or miſrepreſentation of the contents of a barrow has laid the foundation for a ſyſtem, and ſucceeding antiquaries have followed each other on the ſame miſtaken principles; hence the contents of the grave at Chatteris, in the Iſle of Ely, have been pronounced three thouſand years old, the meaſurement of the ſword, ſpear-head, and umbo of the ſhield correſponding with the Druid or Oriental cubit, the glaſs veſſel aſſerted to be the workmanſhip of the antient Britons, and the diſſertation continued to prove it was brought from the Phœnician coaſt.[1] From this diſcovery at Chatteris, Stukeley has conſidered the ſmall barrows on Barham Downs, in Kent, as old Britiſh. Theſe having been accidentally opened, diſcovered beads, and a ſword and ſpear near them; he therefore pronounces them Britiſh, becauſe beads are ſeen round the necks of the Britiſh kings on their coins, ſee *note*, p. [illegible], where the contents of theſe graves are proved to have belonged to men and women, and not higher than the fifth century of our era, and may have been continued to the eighth. The learned publiſher of the new edition of Camden's Britannia, from ſome incorrect information, has alſo confounded the contents of the burial-place at Aſh one with another, [illegible], that beads have been found round the necks of ſkeletons in the

[1] See Dr. Stukeley's letter in the Gent. Mag. of March, [illegible]66, and *note*, p. [illegible]

ſame grave with arms, whereas an inſtance of the kind has never been known in the courſe of the numerous barrows of this nature which have been explored with much curious attention.

Beads found in a barrow opened near Stonehenge by Dr. Stukeley (ſee his STONEHENGE, p. 45), have been conſidered as Britiſh by Dr. Whitaker, in his Hiſtory of Mancheſter. See cap. ix. ſect. ii. Some of theſe beads are in my poſſeſſion, and the contents of the urn and nature of the barrow prove them to have been the relics of an unconverted Saxon female, as low down as the fifth century. The beads anſwer the deſcription of a multiplicity which I have taken out of the ſmall barrows, many ſpecimens of which are engraved in this work. They were in all probability introduced into this country by barter from Marſeilles, or ſome place on the Italian coaſt of the Mediterranean. As the amber is generally very diſſimilar to the workmanſhip of the other relics, being chipped from native lumps, and the forms very inartificially worked, I conjecture it to be the produce of the Baltic, where it is well known the Romans traded for it, and preſerved by the Northern people for the decoration of dreſs. Had it been in the hands of the artificers of the beads, it would have been ſhaped with more elegance.

Pucke's map of the country round Canterbury conſiders the ſmall barrows on Barham Downs as Roman, and Goſtlings Canterbury calls them the burial-places of the ſame people. Dr. Mortimer, in his Manuſcript, has aſſerted the group of ſmall barrows at Chartham to be Roman, and aſſigned one of them to Q. Laberius Durus. Mr. Lewis believes them to be Daniſh, and every aſſertion, furniſhing matter for conjecture, is occaſionally woven into hiſtory.

The diſcovery of coins, the workmanſhip of the relics, arms and nature of the burial places, either conſidered externally or internally, ſhew them to belong to a ſimilar people, to a people in a ſtate of peace, and in general poſſeſſion of the country. Their ſituation near villages of Saxon names, their numbers proportioned to a ſmall clan of people exiſting at a peculiar æra, afford the critical evidence of their owners. They are ſcattered all over Britain in places which the Saxons occupied, and are not diſcovered in the parts of Wales which they had not ſubdued. The relics compared with thoſe diſcovered in the urns found at Walſingham, in Norfolk, the ſubject of the beautiful old treatiſe on urn-burial by Dr. Browne, ſhew the identity of people, and evince the funereal cuſtoms of the Saxons on their viſiting this country, to be that of burning as well as interring the dead, which certainly was more general. From their being ſcattered in ſuch ſituations near places of Saxon names, at a convenient diſtance for ſepulture, and no remains of Britiſh ſepulchres near them, inferences may be deduced that the Saxons had totally extirpated the Britons from the parts which they then occupied.

The ſtructure of the conic mound of earth thrown over the body proves this cuſtom to have been of barbaric or Pagan origin, and the various contents of the graves alſo prove Chriſtians to have been interred in the ſame manner.

The

The Franks, in the days of Pharamond, buried under hillocks. The king himſelf, anno 428, was buried in this manner[1]. Forty eight years after his period, the Saxons entered Britain, and on comparing the barrows of this deſcription with the ſmall ones in cluſters, it may be preſumed the Saxons adopted the ſame cuſtom, and perhaps, in ſome inſtances, burnt their bodies, urns having been found at the Chartham burial-place in Kent, and alſo at Wiſingham; but this circumſtance is extremely rare, and will certainly be found ſo when future diſcoveries are made of theſe ſmall barrows in cluſters.

The name of Daniſh prefixed to them may be naturally accounted for, when we conſider that theſe dreadful invaders, ſpirited on by reſentment, with horrid cruelty and devaſtation, intimidated the inhabitants to that degree, that moſt of our antiquities have been aſcribed to them by tradition; but diſcoveries in theſe barrows, and the concluſions already drawn, are ſufficient to exclude the Danes from the claim. This kind of tradition muſt be therefore diſputable, and fully condemned.

As the relics will alſo in many inſtances ſhew their affinity to the Roman, an intermixture can be thus aſcertained, and which hiſtory has ſufficiently warranted[2]. The magical ceremonies will alſo prove this aſſertion, juſtify the aſſertion of a commixture of cuſtom, of their being continued to a conſiderable period after the introduction of Chriſtianity, and perhaps in ſome reſpects blended with its rights. But at the period when theſe barrows ſeem firſt to have been erected, which may perhaps date about the middle of the fifth century, the Saxons and Gauls were apparently the hoſtile invaders againſt the Britons, and acting as confederates[3]. The Saxons were evidently a mixed people, and ſeem occaſionally to have been engaged in continental wars before their expedition into Britain. Their ſkill and bravery in the Britiſh expedition ſhew their knowledge in war, and prove the abilities of their leaders. Sidonius Apollinaris, a writer in the year 486, ſays, the bodies of the Pagan Gauls were burned[4], and the bodies of the Chriſtians interred. Theſe contrarieties of hiſtoric evidences may be explained by the actual diſcoveries of places of ſepulture, which prove a mixture of theſe ceremonies, and which ſeem to atteſt the poſſibility of Pagan and Chriſtian rites exiſting at the ſame period.

Roman burial-places have perhaps been accurately defined in this work, at leaſt ſufficiently ſo to provide the antiquary with ſufficient caution in his enquiries. Moſt of our county hiſtorians have not ſcrupled, on the diſcovery of an intrenchment on a hill, whether the area be the ſize of a cock-pit or a bowling-green, to pronounce the ſame Roman, and the voucher for it has ſometimes been a barrow within the camp, a circumſtance by no means probable, and which, on the moſt correct enquiry, muſt indicate a more ſubſequent erection to the vallum or to the original defence of the poſt, as alſo a proof that the

[1] See [illegible] p. [illegible]

[2] Paulus Diaconus, lib. [illegible] 3, ſays, the force of the Gothic and Northern powers ſerved in the war [illegible], and who were not permitted to [illegible] with their [illegible], and their [illegible] [illegible] attached.

[3] See [illegible] p. 15, where this [illegible] has been deſcribed.

[4] [illegible] p. [illegible]

tradition

trifling rather [illegible] [illegible] barrow [illegible]

The size of our large [illegible] the distinction between the Romans and the Saxons, and the contents which have been [illegible] criterion to [illegible] [illegible] known [illegible] the Romans [illegible] [illegible] of [illegible] over the [illegible] will [illegible] the [illegible] [illegible] with [illegible] that [illegible] [illegible] [illegible] [illegible] [illegible] the [illegible] [illegible] the [illegible]

[illegible] in his [illegible], [illegible] the [illegible] hill, [illegible] [illegible] the [illegible] obtained [illegible] the [illegible] [illegible] of the old [illegible] [illegible] the Saxon [illegible] [illegible] celebrated [illegible] [illegible] written [illegible] [illegible] much [illegible] [illegible] but [illegible]

Po[illegible] [illegible] the long-contested battle, before [illegible] [illegible] [illegible] their [illegible] in one [illegible] "De[illegible] [illegible] die utrique [illegible] [illegible] [illegible] interfec[illegible] [illegible] [illegible], neque [illegible] [illegible] [illegible] [illegible] either [illegible] [illegible] [illegible] coffins, [illegible] bodies, were [illegible] one of the [illegible] [illegible], it will be natural to conclude [illegible] not [illegible] by Canute. The name of the spot [illegible] hill, [illegible]low, [illegible], or [illegible]low, from the Saxon [illegible] [illegible] hlæp, tumulus [illegible], hill. Canute [illegible] after this battle, [illegible] church to the memory of the [illegible] [illegible] battle of [illegible] [illegible] it was "[illegible] Assun[illegible], et [illegible] [illegible] [illegible] [illegible] [illegible] hominum [illegible] [illegible] [illegible] [illegible] verted at the [illegible] [illegible] it is not likely he would [illegible] the [illegible] hills, which [illegible] employed an [illegible] [illegible] time, [illegible] more [illegible] [illegible] [illegible] much of a Pagan rite or burial, [illegible] the Christian rites [illegible] [illegible] spot where the battle [illegible] doubtful, it will be natural to conclude that the erection of these [illegible] [illegible], therefore, [illegible] have made use of [illegible]

[illegible] Stukeley's [illegible]
[illegible] See Morant's [illegible]
[illegible] Chronicon Saxonicum, p. [illegible]
[illegible] [illegible] [illegible] [illegible] [illegible] [illegible] [illegible] [illegible]

Danish customs in Canute's days, such authorities must not be received, and every deduction rejected as an uncertainty

Mr Wise, in his Vale of White Horse, is desirous of assigning a *Cromlech*, called *Wayland Smith*, as the burial-place of Bagsey, a Danish king, and at the distance of a mile, the *Seven Barrows* to the counts who fell under him in the battle of King Ethelred and Alfred If this suggestion of a respectable writer be admitted, it will bring these erections of unhewn stones and the large barrows to anno 901 But, in opposition to this argument, we must place the *Cromlechs* in the Isle of Anglesey [1], in the island of Minorca [2], the writings of Borlase and Stukeley, where these monuments are given to the antient British [3] The only authority for this opinion must be the result of the names of places and the British names prefixed to the monuments The corresponding similarity of the monuments to those where the lower Druid ceremonies were continued in Ireland, is doubtless a strong argument in favour of their remote antiquity The story of Tigernmas, king of Ireland, asserted by the Irish historians, will also admit of a very rational conclusion This king, by Irish testimony, was first author of idolatry, and died *anno mundi* 3034, in the plains of Magh Sleachd, the field of worship, with a great number of his subjects, whilst they were sacrificing to *Crom Cruach* [4]. This king must have flourished contemporary with Elias the prophet, however, whether it be proper or not to regard the precision of Irish chronology in this instance, it is certain these stones of rude unshapen forms have no Runic inscriptions upon them; and being found in these regions, where the dawn of history afforded sufficient twilight to trace the Celtic colony, for so it should be called, notwithstanding the Scythian confusion on the subject, they may safely be pronounced to have pre existed the invasion of the Danes

Similar remains in Britain may be probably Danish, and which may have been introduced among them by the *Celto Scythæ*, or a branch of the antient colony, by the British priests on their expulsion by the Romans, or by a kindred commixture, which history has left no traces of

There is doubtless a great coincidence between the *Cromlech*, called Wayland Smith, in Berkshire, near which Alfred encountered the Danes, and the *Cromlech*, called Kitz Coty's-House [5], near Boxley, in Kent, near which place Edmund Ironside

[1] Rowland's Mona Ant Restaur p 111

[2] Armstrong's History of the Island

[3] The probability arises from their names and situations *Cromlech*, from a bending portion, *Crom*, the bend, and *lech*, the stone, hence the stone of adoration Rowland, who attributes these Celtic words to the dispersion at Babel, derives the name of this stone from the Hebrew חרם לוח *Caram-luch* Gorsed'dau Cunedda Lolmen Logan, Leck Laver, British names, which have all a meaning to the superstitious religious uses attributed to stones which are so called See Borlase's History of Cornwall

[4] Mr Borlase, p 213, *note*, says, the *Crom cruach*, a heap of crooked unwrought stones, is the most famous idol in all Ireland, it stands in the middle of a circle of twelve obelisks, on a hill in Bresin, in the county of Cavan, and, by the Irish writers, is said to have been covered with gold and silver Vol Hist Dublin, p 103

[5] *Kitz Coty's House* is situated to the right of the road from London to Maidstone over Boxley hill, on rising ground In the valley there are the remains of another *Cromlech*, which, I was informed, had been thrown down by a farmer for material to mend the road The fragments are now obvious; the man found them too large for his purpose, and the expence of breaking them up and then transport will probably suffer them to remain in their present state The *Cromlech* standing, is mentioned by Camden

Ironside fought the drawn battle with Canute. At this monument I employed a labourer to open the ground within the area (see Plate XXIV.), but I could discover no appearance of a sepulchre. The spot had been, by the appearance of the soil, previously explored. The stones are evidently taken from the adjacent land, many of which may be seen in large quantities in the native soil peeping out of the margin of the road. They are of a reddish brown grit, and in their natural gibbous state.

The Cromlech in the Carnedde on Stack-house Scar (see Plate XXXV. No. 1.), also exhibits a great affinity with the description of Wormius (see note [3], p. 180); but this affinity may apply to a more remote period than the Danish invasion for reasons already stated.[1]

Their numbers being so small, as also the barrows, which are evidently raised over the dead, in comparison to the immense multitude of human beings which war, and the natural course of mortality, must sweep away, it should hence follow that the persons buried under them, or to whom they were consecrated, must have been persons distinguished from the ordinary mass; an evidence too strong, I apprehend, for confutation.

Carneddes, or heaps of stone, barrows of large dimensions, kistvaens or cromlechs, and stone erections of various kinds, are found scattered in such directions over Europe, as must entirely preclude the Danes, on their invasion to their conquest of the kingdom under Canute, from being their general owners; and when their writers mention them as applicable to peculiar customs of the Northern people, these relations must be admitted with the same precaution as we read the writers of our nation on similar monuments in Britain.

A great part of Saxo's work, by his own account, was compiled from the Islandic Ballads. Arn Jonas, quoted by Stephanius, in his Prolig. p. 37, says, he was not honest in his authorities, not having made use of them with that fairness as he ought. Saxo has declined this, his history being framed from the rhymes of the Scalds, he was much taken with the tales and traditions of old people. From Saxo and Sueno, published by Stephanius, most

den, and it has been the opinion of some antiquaries that the [illegible] is the vulgar [illegible] the tombs of Canute and Horf, [illegible] the spot [illegible] Canute's [illegible] Horf. Whether [illegible] be accounted [illegible] the true concoction of learning, I [illegible] not pretend to determine; but it is certain [illegible] were raised over the dead, their never having been explored, and bones found [illegible]. The following quotation from Wormius, Mon. D[illegible] p. 7. will [illegible] have been considered as [illegible] by Rowland and other writers. "Arbitrum [illegible] Mixtura ex parte [illegible] constat tumulo, [illegible] *tria ingentia [illegible] [illegible] [illegible] sustinent, ut instar mensæ [illegible]* [illegible] in quibusdam variis [illegible] dibus repleta, [illegible] deputata credebatur." There is no difficulty in perceiving that Wormius has conjectured the Cromlech to have been [illegible] without any authority, and the same may be said of every other Northern writer who have written on these remains. If sacrifices were made to the dead [illegible] would [illegible] be performed on stones which would soon be [illegible] into [illegible]ments by the [illegible] to believe the cirques of stones near [illegible] which were adapted to such [illegible] kind of religious ceremonies. See the circles in Plate XXXV. No. 3. and Plate XXXVI. No. 12.

[1] The kistvaen, or cromlech, on the stone barrow, may have been a stone enclosure for the body. When the cromlech is found on a plain soil, and no bones found under it, there may be some reason for supposing it an honorary sepulchre raised by relatives to the memory of the dead, the body not being found among the [illegible] heap [illegible] Burial of the [illegible] Edda Sæmundi Oda [illegible] Bartholin, Caus. contempt. [illegible] Danis mort. p. 121.

of the antiquities of the North are taken, and the affairs of Denmark and Britain have been interwoven in Huitfield, Pontanus, Meursius, and all other later historians of that kingdom.

Bishop Nicolson says, that Olaus Wormius and Bartholine would be our best guides, if the old Cimbrian monuments, which they treat of, could be applied to our British. The Literatura Runica would also be our infallible criterion; but as the monuments which invite the research of the British Antiquary do not produce this unquestionable index, we must tread with caution on this line of Danish testimony.

HISTORIC

HISTORIC RELATION

AND

GENERAL CONCLUSION.

> IN PRIMISQUE HOMINIS EST PROPRIA VERI INQUISITIO ATQUE INVESTIGATIO. ITAQUE CUM SUMUS NECESSARIIS NEGOTIIS CURISQUE VACUI, TUM AVEMUS ALIQUID VIDERE, AUDIRE, ADDISCERE; COGNITIONEMQUE RERUM AUT OCCULTARUM AUT ADMIRABILIUM AD BEATE VIVENDUM, NECESSARIAM DUCIMUS.
>
> CICERO, OFFIC. I.

N the course of this work we have ascended from a chain of facts, from the small barows in clusters to the Roman sepulchres, and to the large barrows detached on our moors and waste lands. The peculiarities of these monuments have been, to all appearance, sufficiently authentic to infer a claim of high antiquity. The stone monuments near them seem to be connected with their history, whether temple or sepulchral, they will naturally excite a curious investigation, and, as some distinguishing features have been apparently traced, the historic relation may in all probability be deduced from them.

To enter critically on the hiſtory of the antient inhabitants of Britain is not the view of this work, it has only to recommend itſelf by exhibiting memorials which have an undoubted relation to its old inhabitants, and ſeveral of which have been preſented with features ſufficiently expreſſive to admit of inveſtigation. To this deſirable purpoſe of Britiſh colonization a different arrangement muſt be made, and diſcuſſions entered into, which will greatly exceed the limits of its original plan; ſuch apparent facts as may therefore induce an application to certain periods, on which the probability of hiſtory may be founded, are only placed before the reader for his contemplation, and no deciſion arrogated where there is the ſlighteſt ground for conjecture.

It has been already proved, by the confeſſion of Saxo, that his hiſtory of the Northern Nations has been formed chiefly from the tradition of the bards. Torfæus, who is the moſt learned of their writers and the deepeſt read in Icelandic monuments, aſſerts, that the antient Scandinavian hiſtory is full of allegory, ſo much ſo that it is difficult if not impoſſible, to diſtinguiſh truth from falſehood, and it is generally believed, that Icelandic record of Scandinavian hiſtory does not exceed the eleventh century. This truth, any reader of moderate penetration may perceive, when he looks into Saxo Grammaticus, Olaus Wormius, Olaus Magnus, and Snorro, where he will frequently find the cuſtoms of the twelfth century involved with thoſe of an antecedent period. Their ſepulchral monuments and ſtone erections are recorded by their bards, and the fiction of their tales muſt be too manifeſt for any writer of integrity and common ſenſe to incorporate in his argument. But to adopt the fairy tale of Saxo, on the conqueſt of Britain and Ireland by Frotho the third contemporary with our Saviour, and to adduce from this account the erection of our ſtone monuments by the Northern people on this fabulous expedition, would be the height of blind credulity.

The manifeſt reſemblance of theſe remains, diſcovered in all the Northern and Weſtern regions of Europe, to thoſe in Aſia, Paleſtine, Syria, and Egypt, will naturally attract the Antiquary to aſcertain the cauſe of this analogy, and he will doubtleſs conſider whether the ſame deſcription of people may lay claim to them, or whether the natural coincidence of cuſtoms of a rude and early people may not equally apply to theſe remains in every known quarter of the globe. Hence he has recourſe to Sacred Hiſtory for his firſt luminary, and he there traces the affinity of Jacob's Bethel[1] with the rough unhewn pillar in Britain, the ſtone teſtimony of Joſhua[2], the Gentile ſtone Maſſeba, or image of adoration[3], variouſly conſidered as ſtones of memorial or adoption in our iſland. Hence the huge iſolated unhewn ſtone has been abſurdly found ſacred to the Druid, and the name of Gorſeddau[4] given to it, not conſidering that the name is a latter prefix. Profane hiſtorians are afterwards conſulted. Semiramis is found to have erected an obeliſk[5], the pyramids of Egypt, ſacred to

[1] Geneſis xxviii v 18
[2] xxiv v 14 26 27
[3] Geneſis xxviii v 18
[4] From the Britiſh word *Gorſedd*, ſeat of judgement
[5] Diodorus Siculus, l b ii c 1

the ſun, Venus alſo, worſhiped under this form, and many other quotations from antient writers, which have been repeatedly enumerated¹.

The Antiquary, on this ſtriking diſcovery of durable monuments, with ſimilar cuſtoms in other regions of the globe, enters into a profound and critical inveſtigation of the early peopling of our iſland; he attempts to diſcriminate the race of men from the general mixture, and he thus finds theſe monuments to be more certain guides than hiſtory itſelf. His compariſons have proved them to have exiſted before the doubtful records of profane hiſtory, and his authorities are rendered preſumptive by the teſtimonies of Holy Writ. They are thus rendered the unerring witneſſes of the truth of the Sacred Text, and the ground tenable on which the hiſtorian moves for the hiſtory of all antient colonization.

The exiſtence of theſe remains in all the Northern and Weſtern regions of Europe, will ſhew their erection is peculiar to a people who once held a ſimilarity of cuſtom. Hiſtory has preſerved their undoubted affinity to the Gentile worſhip; and the moſt unqueſtionable authority of the Roman writers has diſcriminated between the worſhip of theſe remote people and their own peculiar myſteries of religion. The time thus drawn between fable and atteſted hiſtory, the Antiquary may inſure a ſafe path for his extended reſearches; but to form a ſyſtem of antient colonization from the confuſed veſtiges of [illegible] will exceed the brighteſt labours of our beſt mythologiſts and accompliſhed hiſtorians. Whether it has been peopled by Scythians, Celts, Gauls, Trojans, or Phœnicians, may perhaps be deemed of little importance in theſe days; but the mind is not ſatisfied with this kind of cold indifference, nor will it always regard the poet's advice:

> "Nil admirari prope res eſt una, Numici,
> "Solaque, quæ poſſit facere et ſervare beatum."

[illegible] to the enquiry into the diſtinct races of men, is, that [illegible] from rudeneſs to civility, will be found to have [illegible] the ſame occupations, and the ſame cuſtoms and [illegible] and [illegible] granted; but the variation of climate, the different conceptions of art, inflexions of language, and, indeed, the phyſical difference of the various races of human beings, corporeal as well as mental, will give a diſcriminating peculiarity to their cuſtoms and manners, eſpecially after their eſtabliſhment in a country for a length of ages; and when monuments are found in diſtant regions of the globe of a ſtriking ſimilarity, exceeding the reminiſcence of the eſtabliſhment in their oldeſt records, they may perhaps be aſſigned, with great colouring of truth, to a ſimilar people. A Gothic edifice at Paraguay, Otaheite, or Japan, muſt ſilence all cavil againſt the poſſibility of a diſtant coincidence of architecture, and the Chriſtian miſſionary will be pronounced as the founder. Is not the hiſtory of all other monumental memorials to be traced with the ſame mind, and infallible analogy? and when religion, the cuſtom, and the furniture, or relics of names of a long-forgotten people are produced as evidence, the claim of the hiſtorian will be honourably grounded.

¹ See Rowland, Stukeley, Borlaſe, Toland, and other writers on the Druids.

The unity of the Godhead by the patriarchs was worshiped under no visible form. We are also assured that the Brachman Brouma took the bull for the representation of the Deity, and that this old Scythian mythology was perverted by the Greeks in confounding their Bacchus with the Brouma[1], and receiving a different symbol. From these monuments actually existing, and Greek medals, obvious to any eye, the customs of a people may be critically defined, and the identic separation produced beyond the possibility of contradiction.

Sacred and profane testimony has proved the existence of similar monuments to those discovered in Sweden, Germany, Britain, and in Asia[2], and modern travellers have ascertained their existence in the remotest Eastern countries at this day. Near *Chang Cheu* in China, on a mountain in the province of *Chang-Cheufû* and Tokein, are stones of enormous size, so ranged that the wind may agitate them[3]. Mr. Bryant[4] mentions a similar erection of stones at Amoy, in China: the rocking stone, which he describes to have been about 40 feet in length, could be perceived to vibrate with a touch of his cane. "In the vicinity of this were several other stones of an enormous size, and, at the same time, as round and smooth as any pebbles in the highway, three of these, which were remarkably large, lay in contact with one another, and on the top of these was a fourth. One would not think it possible for any human force to have placed the uppermost in this position." Compare the former with the *Logan* stones in our island, the latter with our *Cromlechs*, and the most satisfactory analogy must be ascertained. Compare them with the Drenthen, Bulck, Helmstad, Albersdorf stones in Westphalia and Holsatia[5], the same analogy will be perfect. Similar methods, and similar religious motives, must therefore have prevailed for the erection of these stones. Strabo[6] describes several heaps of stones on the mountain of Cape St Vincent, to which the Greeks gave the name of Sacred Promontory[7]. From the testimony of Strabo, in like manner as the stone of Jacob was called the House of God, so this promontory was held sacred to the Divinity. These stones, he says, according to an ancient custom of the ancestors of these people, were turned, and they were pretended to have been transported. Through the veil thrown over this ceremony it might be perceived that they were considered as self-moving stones, and that they had been transported by the Deity. Artemidorus asserts as a fact the rocking of these stones, of which he was himself witness, and Strabo, citing this, adds, the probability of the thing, and that it should be credited."

[1] Recherches sur l'Orig. et les Prog. des Arts de la Grèce, lib. i. c. 2. Diod. Siculus, lib. ii. p. 151.
[2] [illegible] xxx. v. 20, and Bul in the son of Reuben, Joshua xv. v. 6. Ilus the son of Dardanus, Il. xi. v. 317, Xenophon, lib. vii., Strabo, lib. iii.
[3] Kircher [illegible] p. 270.
[4] A new system of Analysis, vol. III. p. 536.
[5] Keysler, antiq. Sept.
[6] [illegible]
[7] Strabo, lib. iii. The inhabitants of this place, the most enlightened of them, in the time of Strabo, pretended to have a written history mounting to the date of 6000 years. Whatever may be thought of this pretended history, their religious monuments in the country must refer to a very remote period of antiquity.

These

Theſe well atteſted paſſages of antient authors prove the nature and exiſtence of rocking ſtones at a very remote period, and alſo their ignation with ſtones of this nature in various parts of Europe "Norden, an ocular witneſs, as well as Artemidorus and others, who mention ſimilar ſtones, ſays, that a touch of the finger will move the Pendre ſtone [1], notwithſtanding the reunited force of many men would be required to diſplace it Ptolemeus Epheſtion has remarked, that no human force whatever could remove a ſtone of this nature, but which might be put in motion by the aſphodel [2], a flower well known to have been ſacred to the deity who preſided over life, death, and ſepulchral rites Hence this ſtone could be only moved in the name of the deity to whom this plant and this monument were conſecrated In the Iſle of Tenos, where the deity, preſiding over *life*, *death*, and the *waters*, was worſhiped under the emblem of the ſerpent, repreſented on their medals [3], there was an elevation of earth, on which were two ſtones, "one of theſe, to the great aſtoniſhment of the ſpectator, was put in motion by the wind [4]" A ſimilar ſtone to this is to be ſeen near Penzance, in Cornwal, mentioned by Norden [5], twelve feet in length, by ſix in breadth, and five in thickneſs he ſays, a child may move it with its finger, hence a blaſt of wind might put it in motion, it is called *Main Amber* This name was given to the ſerpentine temple of Ambſbury, or Abury [6], and epithets of the chief or *main* deity prefixed to it by the people who entertained this worſhip Feſtivals of this nature were celebrated in Ionia [7], and at Rome they were called ambroſial, or feaſts of the amber, hence libations to this ſtone were called ambroſial The *main amber* will hence appear to have been the principal ſacred emblem of the god, conductor, or patron deity, of the countries where ſtones ſo called are found

Rocking ſtones, like the main amber, and found in various parts of this iſland, are evident teſtimonies of the antient inhabitants. They are the ſame as thoſe which Nonnus calls ambroſial [8]

> Ἀςαθεες πλωουσαι αλημονες ειναλι πετραι,
> Ας φυσις Ἀμβροσιας επεφημισεν
>
> Inſtabiles, navigantibus vagæ in mari Petræ,
> Quas natura ambroſias celebravit.

[1] Norden's Cornwall, p 79 This ſtone is on the ſummit of a rock on the height of Buſton, in Cornwall

[2] Ptolem Epheſt cit apud Phot p 475 De Iidipe Gigonio juxta Oceanum Και [illegible] Quoque ſolo Aſphodelo movetur, cum vi nulla cetera aut movere queat

[3] This medal of Tenos is engraved in the Rech ſur l'Orig & les Prog des Arts de la Grece Plat XXII N 11

[4] Apollon Rhod [illegible] lib I v 1303,

[illegible]

Poſtremo duo [illegible] ppos

Quorum alter, non ſine magno ſpectantium ſtupore,

Spirante flatibus aquilonis moveri ſolet

[5] See his Cornwall, p 48

[6] Stukeley's Abury and Stonehenge, where the words are explained

[7] [illegible] ambroſio, vel quia Dionyſio feſtum celebrabant quod dicitur *Ambroſia*, ſed Romanis [illegible] noviſimus

[8] Dionyſ, lib IX v 1 [illegible]

They are preserved on the medals of Tyre [1], they are seen on a medal of this town, where Hercules is in the act of offering a libation on an altar before the ambrosials [2], this medal explains the nature of this worship in Britain, Portugal, China, and in every other region where similar stones have been found. These monuments are attestations of those forms which the Phœnicians gave to these stones, at a period undoubtedly anterior to the foundation of Tyre, which preceded the capture of Troy [3], for they are supposed to have existed before the building of the former

The intimate relation of these very antient prototypes of the Deity, with the egg, the symbol of Chaos, is very interesting. There is a medal of Tyre, in M D'Hancarville's curious work, where the serpent is coiling round, and stricken at the same period, when the ambrosials were also represented with a serpent on a tree near them Each part of this *egg* on the medal was the model of the form given to these stones, it is so divided on a medal of Cos encircled by a serpent; the coil of the reptile indicating the action of the Deity, vivifying the germe contained in the Chaotic *egg* Much interesting matter, rising to the most natural and sublime interpretation, follow these remarks and every allusion, justified by medals and monuments, concur to prove the most striking affinity of a once all-subduing and powerful people with the British remains, the subject of this enquiry

The enormous size of these stones indicate the immense power and comprehensive attributes of the Deity, and from whence the Colossal statues were originated; they were often, as may be noted in Cornwall and other places, erected near waters, because the plastic power of the serpent was supposed to have operated in that element, on which floated the *egg* of Chaos Their situations on eminencies, their peculiar characteristics of receiving the sacred water, may now be ascertained, and the reason why they are discovered in those regions where every corroborating proof is to be found of serpentine worship

The serpent being the symbol of life, and of the Creator who had imparted his vivifying spirit to animated nature, the *ambrosial stones*, applied as a substitute for this symbol, were the same as the *betyles*, called by Sanchoniathon *animated* or *living* stones [4]

From what has been said, it may be perhaps inferred, that religious monuments of stone, very different to those which actually exist of Egyptian, Grecian and Roman, are at this day discovered at the extremity of China, or of Asia, and the same which have existed on the confines of Portugal and Europe. These extreme antient monuments are also presumptively similar to those found in some of the Greek islands, in Phœnicia and in Syria, and most of our British topographical writers have mentioned them as now existing in this island The emblems of the ox and the serpent, which are now discoverable in the East, re forgotten in those countries where they were once the object of a wide, an [illegible]

[1] Plate XXIV No 2 Rech sur l'Orig et les Prog des Arts de la Grece
[2] Plate XXIV No , of the above ingenious work
[3] Justin, lib xviii
[4] Sanch Fragm ap Euseb [illegible] Urani Baetylia [illegible] Isidore from the report of Damascius, declares that he [illegible] these stones on Mount Libanus, [illegible] Phot p 104

perhaps universally adopted worship These immense *moveable or rocking stones* are emblems much more durable, they have resisted the consuming power of time through incomputable periods, and appear, being coeval with the *three and four stone erections*, called Cromlechs, Kistvaens, and other monuments of this nature, to be the most antient memorials now existing in the world

It has been shewn, that from the most remote ages, the period of the erections of these immense piles of stone has been forgotten, or they have been explained by fables The Druids have been storied as their owners The Danes and the Saxons have also had their claim. That they preceded the Saxon æra, the names given to them by these people manifest, indicating a fanciful appellation, where the real intention was unknown Sepulchral erections near them also prove their claims to divine worship, but the memory of the cause of their erection being effaced, and no traces remaining of it, we are well persuaded that immensity of time has proved less inimical to their original structure than the oblivion to which they have been consigned. We are well assured that the religion of the Britons and Gauls, whom Cæsar, Dio, and one or two more Roman writers have handed down to us, had a very distant relation to the worship peculiar to these monuments of unhewn stones, perverted perhaps by the first Druid rites, and continued to their lower barbarous ceremonies, they have challenged their superstitious reverence, yet, certain it is, the Britons, in Cæsar's time, were ignorant of their history, which their religion, slight, as it has been handed to us, will fully evince

But where is that period to be discovered, which indicates a marked communication between the ideas and the customs of the people who formerly inhabited China, England, and Portugal? The Boitians date their history 6000 years before our æra, what a prodigious antiquity must therefore be given to the Scythic nation, who from their origin appear to have known the emblem of the serpent, representing, under this symbol, the parent from whom they sprang! However remote this period may have been, the erection of the *rocking stone*, stones erected in the number three or four were doubtless more antient than the people of Europe, the custom must have been certainly transported from Asia, where the Europeans never fixed their residence The obeliscal stones of the antient Scandinavians, those of the Egyptians, the idols which Joshua reproaches the ancestors of the Jews for worshiping before the time of Abraham, may be perhaps accounted of inferior antiquity, when compared to the monuments here treated of [1].

If our stone monuments and barrows near them concur to prove that the inhabitants of this kingdom had a very early origin, we are naturally inclined to enquire who these extreme old inhabitants were Were they Celts? were they Scythians? Are the Celts and Scythians synonymous terms for the old inhabitants of Europe? Or is one an older branch of the same race of people than the other? Cæsar seems to have defined a distinct set of inhabitants in Gaul "Gallia est omnis divisa in partes tres, quarum unam incolunt Belgæ, aliam Aquitani, tertiam, qui ipsorum lingua Celtæ, nostra Galli, appellantur Hi

[1] D'Hancarville, Rech. sur l'Orig. des Arts de la Grece

omnes

omnes linguæ, institutis, legibus inter se differunt." This division of Gaul agrees with most of the other antient writers, and we find the Celts are discriminated from the Belgæ, whom Cæsar has declared to have been the inhabitants of Britain on his arrival. But he has taken care to distinguish the old inhabitants from the Belgæ, whom he expressly brings from the continent[2], and seems to place on the sea coast. The inland people he has described as Galactophagi, and as distinct from the dwellers on the sea coast, whom he pronounces as civilized, as the Gauls. Whom of the Gauls did he mean? the Belgæ or the Aquitani? Did he mean the Celtic savages?—"pellibusque sunt vestiti." These then we are to understand were the old inhabitants, they were cloathed with skin, and lived on milk and flesh, a pastoral people like the old Scythians. The people who attacked Cæsar were the Belgæ, who were in possession of the South East of Britain, and being thus in possession, and deemed inhabitants, had consequently the appellation of Britons in common with the first possessors. The Belgæ we are therefore to consider as the nation who vanquished the old inhabitants.

The Σκυθαι και Κελτοσκυθαι of Strabo[3] is the passage which seems to have confused our Celtic and Scythic controvertists. Language is produced to shew the dissimilitude between the Scythian and the Celtic people, and their customs may prove this difference. Strabo says, the most antient Greek authors gave the name of Scythians and Celto-Scythians to all the people that dwelt in the Northern countries. These are his words, and how are the moderns to distrust this great authority? The Celts, we can also prove, were mixed with the Scythians, whether Cæsar and other writers confine them to the West, it is certain the antients have considered them as involved with the Scythians, and formerly inhabiting their country. The Celts were therefore a more primitive people; and, as the Belgæ may be proved to have been of the Scythic stock, the Britons who fought Cæsar must have been Scythians, and the Celts the pastoral inhabitants driven by these people into the interior parts of the kingdom.

Cæsar says the Gauls adored Mercury, "Deum maxime Mercurium colunt[4]." Did the Celts adore Mercury?—"qui ipsorum lingua Celtæ, nostra Galli, appellantur." The Mercury Teutat, Livy says, was a German deity[5], and some writers think that *Teu* is the Celtic for people, and *Tat*, father, he might hence be proved to be a Celtic Deity. But Mr Pinkerton, in his Dissertation on the Scythians[6], says, "of the Celtic mythology we know nothing." I should perfectly agree with him, had he remarked they were an extreme early race of people; and, when the Greek and Roman authors began to write, were almost extirpated, but they seem to have been, at a remote period, a people who had over-run the whole continent of Europe and Asia, and to these very early people the monuments, which have been here discussed may with great reason be attributed. The

De Bell. Gall. lib. i.

[2] "Britanniæ pars interior ab iis incolitur [illegible] ... maritima pars ab iis qui [illegible] ex Belgis transierant." Lib. v.

[3] Geog. lib. i.

[4] Lib. vi.

[5] [illegible] c. 41.

[6] P. [illegible]

Druids, whom Cæsar esteems the second in influence among the Gauls, were not of Phœnician extract, as may have been suggested from the Gaulish intercourse with Britain, where the Druid religion was learnt. Men are not cajoled to implicit confidence in a new priesthood, the most savage tribes are known to have their priests It would be hard to deny the Celtic Britons theirs also If the Gauls worshiped Mercury, and derived their religion from Britain, the Britons must have had this deity in their worship If Belgæ on the sea coasts were the people here meant, the inland inhabitants, who were the Celts, could not have been comprehended Their mythology was therefore different. Cæsar has described the gods which they worshiped, Apollo, Mars, Jupiter, and Minerva This must therefore be the polytheism of the Druids The monuments of rough unhewn stone in various parts of Britain, if erected for adoration or religious mysteries, were consequently not sacred to these deities, and therefore, as heretofore considered, should not be accounted druidical What can be said to all this? The facts speak for themselves, and, if admitted as such, we may place a date much anterior to these inhabitants of Britain, described by Cæsar, to the monuments in question

Cæsar says, the Gauls burnt their dead[1]; the Belgæ were these Gauls: the Belgæ of Britain therefore burnt their dead. The barrows in Britain prove the fact The large isolated barrows on waste lands contain urns and burnt bones; they also contain the bones in their natural state, the body buried without burning the former perhaps were the Belgic Gauls, the latter the Celtic Britons, a more primitive people who adopted the most early rites of burial. These barrows have been proved to have exceeded the Roman times by the nature of their contents; this inference may therefore be permitted

If the Cimmerii or Cimbri were Celts[2], the Celts were the antient inhabitants of the Cimbric Kersonesus, the monuments in that part of the world may therefore have a relation to these very early people, whose name in both Scythic and Celtic languages means a warrior These were the people whom Plutarch says[3] invaded Italy in astonishing multitudes, like swarms of locusts, and, taking a fortress on the other side of the Athesis, and finding the garrison had behaved in a manner suitable to the known bravery of the Romans, they dismissed them on certain conditions, having first made them swear to them upon a brazen bull In the battle that followed, this bull was taken among the spoils, and carried to the house of Catullus, as the first fruits of victory This is evidently the bull of the very old Scythic worship, and probably the clue which unravels the history of the Celts The Cimri being conclusively a branch of the old Celts, the Celts must have retained this worship in all the countries they visited, hence the rocking stones and other stone erections already discussed, being peculiar to this old Scythic worship of Bacchus or

[1] Lib vi

[2] Appian lib De Bello Civ p 625 from Pinkerton Ομοι Αποτ[illegible] [illegible] [illegible] εξω εν τη νυν [illegible] Ρομαιων καλουμενη γαλατια Κιμβροι, γενος Κελτων, και [illegible]

[3] See the Life of Marius, p. 18

Brouma [1], are found in all thofe regions where this univerfal and very antient conqueft extended The old Celtic mythology was therefore Scythic, and the Celts a branch of thefe people, from whom all the European and other polifhed nations arofe Whatever may be faid of Celtic and Gothic language, whatever may be faid of human folly, ignorance, or want of deep and learned penetration, thefe apparent facts rife feemingly to a demonftration With this clue the Northern nations may be traced, the facts may be difcerned from the fable, and the opinion of many writers rendered lefs defpicable than modern criticifm has announced

This fketch is only offered for the inveftigation of the hiftorian, who will doubtlefs perceive a vaft field of enquiry before him. Sacred and profane hiftory may be cited to prove a concurrence in the interefting refearch, and what the latter is deficient of, when the queftion relates to the higher periods of hiftory, the former will inconteftably fupply, to the fatisfaction of the wifeft and moft learned.

[1] See *the fecond Differtation on the brafs inftruments, called Celts, and other arms of the antients, found in this ifland*, by the author of this work, where this religion of the old Scythians has been exemplified by antient monuments and medals

INDEX

INDEX OF RELICS

FOUND IN

BRITISH SEPULCHRES,

AND

THINGS MEMORABLE CONNECTED WITH THEIR HISTORY.

A

Adges ſtone, page 92
Agger, encircling places of ſepulture, 126
Amber, 9 64
Ambroſial ſtones, 187
Amethyſts, 49
Amulets, 13 73 84 85
——— gold 84
——— in the form of a ſhield, 85.
——— of a child, 85
——— of glaſs, 122
Ampulla, Roman, 147
Anthemius, ſilver coin perforated of, 8
Archbiſhop, Greek, of Canterbury, 129
Archery, 30
ARGUMENT, 177
Armilla of glaſs, 59
——— ivory, 6 64
——— braſs, 6
——— braſs, Roman, 113.
Armilla, 62
Arms in graves, 57
Arrow heads, iron, 77
Aſh, 26 48 7
Aſhby, Rev Mr 157
Autograph of Heneage Finch, Earl of Winchelſea, 121
Axe head, iron, 49 50 135
Axinomantia magic, 88

B

Bacchus, the worſhip of, 191
Banks, ſir Joſeph, 76
Bards, Northern, 155
Barham Downs, 98
——— tumuli on, 39 64
Barrows on Saliſbury Plain, 23 156 177.
——— in Greenwich Park, 89
Barrows on Blackheath, 91
——— Wimbledon Common, 93
——— near Walton Bridge, 94
——— large, 96.
——— on Barham Downs, 177.
——— on Chartham Downs, 99 177
——— St Margaret's on the Cliff, 119.
——— SMALL IN CLUSTERS, 122 126
——— Walſingham, 131
——— King's-holm, 133
——— Dorſetſhire, 150 158
——— GREAT, 155
——— on moors and waſte lands, 155
——— Britiſh, 157
——— Newmarket Downs, 157
——— Needham Plains, 157
——— Kent, 158
——— Singledon Down, 160
——— on the Watling Street, 161
——— Chidingfold, Surrey, 162
——— Stanton Moor, 164
——— of ſtone, 166
——— HIGH LOW MOOR, 167
——— Abney Moor, ib
——— Stackhouſe Scar, 168
——— Bridlington Moor, 170
BARROWS, SMALL, argument on, 176.
——— Chriſtians, 176
Barlow hills, 173
Beads found in barrows, 9 13 23 34 35 60 64 65 76 79 87 88 90 177
——— of a mummy, 87
——— of cryſtal, 9 23
——— amber, 9 13 23 36 64 65 79 87
——— Britiſh, 11
——— of earth, 14
——— amethyſt, 45
Belemnites found in a barrow 15

Belgæ,

Belgæ, 150
——— or Britain, 190.
Bell, 81
Bethel, Jacob's, 184.
Betyles, or animated stones, 188.
Blagden, Dr. 56.
Bones, 2 11 64
—— ornament of, 28 88
Body in a copera, mine, 24
—— soon dissolved in the earth, 58.
Bottians, their history, 189
Boss of a shield, 94.
Bottle of red earth, 4.
Bow, brace of iron, 29 30
Box, brass, 71 74
Box ey, Roman remains at, 144
Boys, William, esq, 26 56.
Bracelets, the antiquity of, 59.
——— use of among the antients, 61.
——— one with iron and glass ring, 61.
——— set in a barrow, 80
Brass arms, 150.
Britain, revolt of, from the Roman government, 127.
British money, 135
Britons, 27
——— their brass arms, 150
——— the arms of, 27.
Broach, silver gilt, 14. 64. 76.
——— of filagree, 41.
Buckle of brass, 4. 8. 54. 79.
——— of iron, 5. 11. 79
——— tin and brass, 79.
Bull, the Celtic and Scythic worship of, 191.
Burgred, the coin of, 122
Burial at the Gauls, 40
—— place of Walton, 50
—— of ornaments with the dead, 40.
—— Pagan, 42

C

Cabalists, 9.
Camboritum, 137.
Campaniform barrows, 123.
Calimistrum, 82
Caw, or Gaur, British word, explained, 162
Capeduncula, 148
Carneddts, 181
Castra, 139
Cæsar, Julius, his post, 38
Celt of stone, 92
Celtic mythology, 190
Celto Scythæ, 180.
Celts, 156
—— the history of, 189
—— mixed with the Scythians, 190
Cemeteries, when annexed to churches, 126 130.
Ceraunites, 158
Chain of iron, 40
Chains, 97
Chaos, symbol of, 188.
Chartham Downs barrows, 99.
Chiflettius, 53 123
Childeric's grave, 51 53. 123
——— ring, a forgery, 55
Christian exorcism, 40
——— antient burial, 42 63. 97.
Christians sumptuously entombed, 63
Christians, primitive, 97
Cimri, what people, 191.
Circular erections of stone among the Northern nations, 165
Cirques near barrows, and remarks on, 164. 166.
——— their mystic quality, 165
Clasps, 64
——— of gilt copper, 5. 6
——— circular, plated with gold, 6.
Cloth, preservation of, 14 56

COINS IN BARROWS

Coin, silver, perforated, 8 19
—— of brass, 19 53 80
—— of Anthemius, 8.
—— of Faustina, 51 139.
—— of Valentinianus 8 17 92
—— of Victorinus and Valerianus, 79.
—— of Ant Pius and Alex] Severus, 80.
—— of Mars Clovis, 86 92 131
—— of Gordian, 92
—— of Victorinus, 92.
—— of Justinianus, 92
—— gold pendant, 92
—— Gaulish, 92
—— of Burgred, 96 122.
—— perforated, 123,
—— which adorn the Morlach women, 129.
—— of Claudius, 133 134
—— of Antonia, 134
—— Roman, small brass, 134.
—— of Nero, 134 143
—— of Magnentius, 134. 143.
—— of Alexander Severus, 134.
—— of Arcadius, 135
—— of Avitus, 8.
—— of Appolonia, 159.
—— of Constantius, 16
Coins, silver and gold, 55
Comb, ivory, 73 76
Common ground, 94
Conic burial places, 94
CONTENTS OF THE SMALL BARROWS, 111.
Copiatæ, 97
Coraline ware, 148
Coticula, 51
Coury, large Indian, 73.
Cromlech, 168 180
Cross of silver, 68
—— from a barrow on Barham Downs, 68.
—— for an amulet, 68
Cross on a gold pendant, 86
Crotalum, antient, 62
Crystal, with engraved cross, 62
Crystal ball, 14 21 123 131
——— found in tombs, 1[illegible]
——— magical, 16
——— of Paracelsus, Dee, Lilly, and Kelly, 16 131
Cup of glass, 14.
Cyprea shell, 88.

D

Dagger, iron, 76.
Danes, 52 89
——— total conversion of the, to Christianity, 125
Danes,

Danes, the Graves, Swords and Deities of the, 124
—— [illegible] not to be [illegible] on, 125
—— [illegible] of burial and burning the dead, 125
Derbyshire barrow, 153
[illegible], 158
[illegible] 180
[illegible] 40
[illegible] 71
—— [illegible], 8
Duck [illegible], 83
Durobrivæ [illegible] monuments, 155
[illegible]
Durovernum 158

E

Echinus Entocrinus defined, 65
[There is a mistake in this passage, which arose from the following passage in Pliny, lib. xxxii [illegible] admodum pisciculus, [illegible] appellatum in [illegible] [illegible] [illegible] cogit pariter [illegible]" The [illegible] is [illegible] confounded with the [illegible], the [illegible] being a [illegible] shell-fish with spines [illegible] the latter sucker fish with [illegible] of [illegible] [illegible] to the proportion of its body whereby it fastens itself to the keels of vessels, and it has hence acquired the name of [illegible], or stay ship, by the [illegible]ts
Egg [illegible], 1[illegible]
Egg, Chinese, [illegible] of, 188
Enchantments magical, 40
Etruscan vase, 14

F

Fable and [illegible] [illegible] line drawn between, 185
[illegible] 102
[illegible] 56 51 [illegible] 86
—— [illegible]
[illegible]
[illegible]
[illegible] of silver and gold, 20 23 48
[illegible]
—— [illegible]
—— [illegible] gold 56
—— [illegible] barrow in Derbyshire, 36 —Roman [illegible]
—— [illegible]
Funeral [illegible], 18[illegible]

G

[illegible] 41
[illegible] 189
[illegible]
[illegible]
[illegible]
—— [illegible]
—— [illegible]
—— [illegible]
Glass, [illegible] antiquity of the manufacture [illegible]
—— [illegible] anciently [illegible], 6[illegible]
—— [illegible] by the Britons, 61
—— windows introduced into Britain, 61
—— fragment of [illegible] barrow, 64
Gloucester, the Roman station of, 133
Gorhead, [illegible] of, 100
[illegible], 184

H

Hatchet found in barrows, 159
Hieroglyphics Egyptian, the source of, 160.
HISTORIC RELATION AND GENERAL CONCLUSION, 163
Hinges, iron, on a box, 44.
—— —— of brass 73
Holy Writ, testimony of 165
Horn of deer 77
Horns the earliest emblems of power, 148
Hubba his barrow, 126
Hair, human singular preservation of, in graves, 56, 57 89 90
—— braid of, 90

I

Jacob, M 48 49 [illegible],
[illegible]-bone, 34
Impress, Roman, 131
Instruments to [illegible] ears, 72
—— for teeth, [illegible]
—— of iron, with a ring at the end, 80
—— of iron to curl the hair, 82
—— of iron, 8
Interment [illegible], 66
—— Roman, 143
In[illegible] 08
In[illegible] [illegible], 17
Iron [illegible] 34 36 44
[illegible]
[illegible] grave, [illegible]7

K

[illegible] Stackhouse Seat, 108
King's holm burial place, 153
Kits [illegible] 171
Kits cots house, 18[illegible]
Knife iron, 4 9 11 9 24 36 56 7[illegible] 89 90
—— of brass, in shape of a dog running after a hare 8[illegible]
Knot of Hercules, 84

L

[illegible] vessels, 44 54 [illegible]
—— [illegible] application, 70.
[illegible] stone called, 6[illegible]
[illegible] sepulchral, 114
[illegible] of Christianity on burial, 120
Lead, circular piece of, perforated, 64
Leather preserved, [illegible]
Lewis [illegible] 67
[illegible] of the [illegible],
[illegible], 44
[illegible] 168
—— [illegible], 7[illegible].
[illegible] Derbyshire, 168
Lucius, first Christian King, where buried, 135
[illegible] 30
[illegible] vessels, 8[illegible]

M

Macpherson, Mr remarks on, 15 184
Magic, 46
Magical experiment, 18 45
——— ceremonies, 130
——— vessels, 46
Main amber stone, and the explanation of, 186
Minenanium, 147
Match [illegible], 15 64
Mussin, Abbe Van, his cabinet, 145
Miscellanea Antiqua, 67
Miscellaneous coins, 92
——— vessels, 93
MONILIA EX AURO ET GEMMIS, 84
Monuments of stone, similar of, in Europe and in Asia, 186
Mortimer, Dr his manuscript, 70
Mosaic of variegated glass, 8,
Mounts for military orations, 175
Mummy, bead and ornament of, 86
Mythology, key to antient, 160

N

Nadroetl or Druid charm, 71 85 87 123
Naula Charontis, 80
Needle brass, 73
Northern writers, 155
——— nations [illegible], 192
Nummi perforati, 123

O

Obeliscal stones, 189.
Oboli, whence derived, 159
OBSERVATIONS, 122
Ornaments, circular, 46
Ossian, 27 29
Ox and serpent, emblems of, 188
Oxenden, sir H 39

P

Pan, figure of, on a fragment of Roman pottery, 147
Pan pudding rock, 142
[On the coast of Kent, where a Roman vessel, containing pottery, was supposed to have been wrecked, and from whence fine specimens are frequently dragged up by fishermen See Pliny, Nat Hist lib xxxv c xii "[illegible] quoque per maria terrasque ultro citroque portantur, insignibus [illegible] officinis [illegible]" Most of these vessels are of red earth, many decorated with figures in relief, and finely turned with the lathe.]
Patera, 47
——— of [illegible], 52
——— of [illegible], 137 141
Patella of glass, 52
Pendants, gold enchased 21 85 96
——— with [illegible] of [illegible], [illegible]
——— [illegible]
——— with lapis lazuli, 55
——— with a [illegible] 16
——— chequered [illegible], 50
Pendle from Cornwall, [illegible]
P[illegible] ornament of gold, 21 [illegible] 30
Petavius Paulus on a Roman [illegible], 80 112
Phallus, 85
Phial, 84
——— found in urns, 148
Pin of metal, 14 74
——— gold, 21
——— with a garnet, 72
Pottery, Etruscan, 44

R

Radius and ulna of the arm preserved by the rust of metal, 58
Richborough, Roman station of, 26
Ring of silver, 14 64 91
——— iron, 32, 34 61 64
——— mixed metal, 62
——— of brass, 64 134
Rocking stones, 166 186 180
——— sacred to the worship of Bacchus, 191
Roman coins, 134
Romans, departure of, from Britain, 127
Rooke, H esq, 36 68 165
Runic inscriptions, 124

S

Sacred and profane history, concurrence of, 192
Sacrifices, human, 50
Samian vessels, 143
["Samia etiamnum in esculentis laudantur" Lib xxxv c xii]
Saxon capital, 84
——— stations, 97
——— shield, 128
——— swords 128
——— coins, 127 134
——— youth serving in the armies of foreign princes, 126
Scales, remains of, 51
——— and weights, 51
Scythians, 156
Scythic nation, antiquity of, 189
Section of a tumulus, 3
SEPULCHRAL REMAINS OF THE ROMANS, 132 137
Sepulchral rites, 44
——— [illegible] Christians, 61
——— erections, 189
——— law of the XII Tables, 147 137
——— vessels of the Romans, 117
Sands and pebbles, 9 31
Sheers, 21
Sibert's would, 63
Sibert's would Down barrows, 95
Silbury Hill 161
Silver fragment, 2,
Silver, piece of, clipped found in a barrow, 64
Skeletons, position of, 6,
Small coins [illegible], [illegible]
Spear head of iron, [illegible] 69 77 89 90 93 121 [illegible]
——— of brass and flint, [illegible]
Speculum, [illegible]
——— [illegible], 51
——— of [illegible], 62
Spoon of silver gilt, [illegible]
——— Roman, [illegible]
Stamps on Roman vessels, [illegible]

St[illegible]nge, the m[illegible]or of 73
[illegible]o[illegible]s, erect in [illegible]al places, 166 174
Stuke[illegible], Dr [illegible] 6[illegible] 75 95 119 131 156
Subterranean [illegible]g, 139
S[illegible]on[illegible] of iron, [illegible]
—— [illegible] [illegible]

T

Ta[illegible], or [illegible]us, [illegible] on Greek coins, 160
[illegible], [illegible] [illegible]on of, 172
[illegible]
T[illegible], [illegible] by the primitive Christians in ex[illegible], [illegible] in tombs, 51
T[illegible] m[illegible], Roman, 14[illegible]
Tomb, [illegible]
Tongue[illegible], [illegible], 144
—— [illegible] [illegible]
Tou[illegible]
Touto[illegible]
T[illegible]
T[illegible] 7
Tumuli on Chatham Hill, [illegible] 12 13 20 23 25 [illegible] 63 66 73
—— Chartham Downs, 20 99
—— St Margaret's on the Cliff, 20 [illegible]19
—— [illegible], 29 [illegible] 177
—— P[illegible] Downs [illegible]8 64 177
—— Dinton, 69
—— C[illegible]
—— S[illegible]bury Plain, 57
—— Dorsetshire
—— De[illegible]
—— Winstor, 68
—— [illegible] W[illegible], 72 95
—— W[illegible], 76
—— St Margaret's on the Cliff, 78
—— [illegible]
—— Godm[illegible]
—— Ro[illegible], [illegible], 13[illegible]
—— D[illegible], 16[illegible]
T[illegible], R[illegible]
—— Chesterf[illegible], 13[illegible]
—— C[illegible], 136
—— Ro[illegible], 1[illegible]
—— Bosley, 1[illegible]
—— Bet[illegible] Tong[illegible], 144
Tweezer, [illegible]7

V

Valentinianus, silver coin of, perforated, 8 17
Vallancey, colonel 83
Van hattem, [illegible] letter from, on sepulchral relics, 69
Vessel of glass, 21 [illegible]9 52 59 60 7[illegible] [illegible] 97
—— brass gilded, 44 47
—— brass, 2[illegible] 49
—— Earth, 36 47 93
—— magical, 45
—— consecrated, 49
—— sepulchral, 39
—— of wood, in the shape of a pail, 51
—— of unbaked earth, 93
Vessels, Roman, 134 137 138 140 143 144 146 147 148 149
—— containing bones of a [illegible], 108 140
—— lacrimated, 14[illegible]
Vignette, 53
Vitrified ornaments on the covering of mummies, 60
Volucella, 57
Vo[illegible], his perversion and ignorance of antiquity, 21 60
Vota ven[illegible], 8[illegible]

U

Umbo of a shield, 4 11 26 121.
Urim and Thummim, 15
Urn of unbaked clay, 93 157 158
—— Roman, 137 1[illegible] 146 147 148
—— in the shape of a fish, 144
—— of singular make, 156
—— from a barrow in Derbyshire, 16[illegible]
—— Abney Moor, 167
Urns, [illegible]4
—— British, Saxon, and Danish 57
—— proof of their being baked, or not baked, 158

W

White, esq, 50
Whitaker, Dr 60 70
Wire gold, in a barrow, 61
Woollen cloth, 90
W[illegible]fingham burial place, 131
Winchelsea, earl of, 143
—— his Roman vessels, 144
Writers on the history of Northern sepulchres, 156

Z

Zone, charmed, 123

FINIS.

Lightning Source UK Ltd.
Milton Keynes UK
UKHW021915020323
417959UK00005B/53